D1616319

La Salle, the Mississippi, and the Gulf

Edited by Robert S. Weddle

Three Primary Documents

La Salle, the Mississippi, and the Gulf

Mary Christine Morkovsky and
Patricia Galloway
Associate Editors

Ann Linda Bell and Robert S. Weddle
Translators

Texas A&M University Press
College Station

The paper used in this book
meets the minimum requirements of
the American National Standard
for Permanence of Paper
for Printed Library Materials,
Z39, 48-1984.
Binding materials
have been chosen for durability. ∞™

Library of Congress Cataloging-in-Publication Data

La Salle, the Mississippi, and the Gulf.

Bibliography: p.
Includes index.
  1. Mississippi River Valley—Discovery and
exploration—Sources. 2. Mississippi River
Valley—History—To 1803—Sources. 3. La Salle,
Robert Cavelier, sieur de, 1643–1687. I. Weddle,
Robert S. II. Morkovsky, Mary Christine.
III. Galloway, Patricia Kay.
F352.L344 1987   977'.01   86-30075
ISBN 0-89096-310-X

Contents

List of Plates / vi
List of Tables / vii
Acknowledgments / ix
Introduction / 1

PART I
**Exploration of
the Mississippi**

The Minet Relation: Journey by River / 17
PATRICIA GALLOWAY
Voyage Made from Canada Inland Going
Southward during the Year 1682 / 29
Translated by ANN LINDA BELL

PART II
**The Voyage
to the Gulf**

Minet's Journal: The Cruise of the *Joly* / 71
PATRICIA GALLOWAY
Journal of Our Voyage to the Gulf of
Mexico / 83
Translated by ANN LINDA BELL

PART III
**The Spanish
Search**

The Enríquez Barroto Diary: Voyage of the
Piraguas / 129
ROBERT S. WEDDLE
The Enríquez Barroto Diary / 149
Translated by ROBERT S. WEDDLE

PART IV
The French   The Talon Interrogations: A Rare
Survivors   Perspective / 209
     ROBERT S. WEDDLE
     Voyage to the Mississippi through the Gulf of
     Mexico / 225
     Translated by ANN LINDA BELL

Commentaries   Ethnological Data / 259
on the   MARDITH K. SCHUETZ
Interrogations   Natural History / 274
     DEL WENIGER
     Karankawa Linguistic Data / 288
     RUDOLPH C. TROIKE

     Bibliography / 303
     Contributors / 315
     Index / 317

Plates

1. Rouillard's Map of America, 1692, 9
2. Title Page of Minet Relation, 30
3. Minet's Map of Fort Frontenac Area, 36–37
4. Minet's Drawing of a Calumet, 48
5. Minet's "Mouths of the Mississippi," 66
6. Minet's Drawing of a Native Warrior, 67
7. "Plan de la Coste de la Floride la plus occidentale," by Minet, 101
8. Minet's "Plan de l'entrée du lac," 107

9. Seno Mexicano, 143

10. "Plano del Lago de Sn. Bernardo" (after Enríquez Barroto), 144

11. The Talons' Indian Vocabularies, from the Interrogations, 292

12. The Talons' List of Indian Tribes, 293

Tables

1. Karankawa (Clamcoëh) Vocabulary in the Talon Manuscript, with Forms from Other Sources, 294–95
2. Shared Forms in Talon, Béranger, and Oliver, 297
3. Evidence for Relative Placement of the Talon, Béranger, and Oliver Data Sources, 299
4. Caddo (Cenis and Ayenny) Words in the Talon Manuscript, Compared with Other Sources, 300

Acknowledgments

A large part of this work was made possible through the assistance of a research grant from the National Endowment for the Humanities. This support of Robert S. Weddle in his study of discovery and exploration in the Gulf of Mexico led to the finding of the Enríquez Barroto Diary and the Minet Journal. The latter was pursued from the time we first learned that it was being offered for sale by a private collector.

The text of the original Minet Journal was obtained through the courtesy and cooperation of the Public Archives of Canada. We are indebted to Robert S. Gordon, director of the Manuscript Division of the archives in Ottawa, and to Victorin Chabot, chief of French archives in the Manuscript Division, for granting permission to translate and publish the document and the accompanying drawings and for providing information concerning it. We are grateful also to George Shriever of New York and Dan Kilgore of Corpus Christi, Texas, for assistance in tracing the manuscript.

Our Lady of the Lake University, San Antonio, Texas, has contributed to the project in vital ways. From its archival collection it supplied the microfilm copy of the Talon Interrogations, then provided the services of Sister Ann Linda Bell to translate both the Talon document and the two-part Minet Journal. Sister Mary Christine Morkovsky, then a faculty member at Our Lady of the Lake, was granted the university's support during the planning phase of the undertaking, while the project was being organized and given its final direction.

The Talon Interrogations were discovered by Sister Morkovsky in Paris while she alternated a search for historical material with post-doctoral research in her special field of philosophy. We wish to express our appreciation to Marie-Antoinette Menier, director of the Outre-Mer section of the Archives Nationales, for permission to publish the English translation.

For permission to copy the Enríquez Barroto diary, we wish to thank the Biblioteca del Real Palacio in Madrid. David Block, who, as

Weddle's research associate, worked in the Royal Palace Library and located the document, deserves special thanks.

Rudolph C. Troike acknowledges Paul Gaeng and Herbert De Ley of the Department of French, University of Illinois, for their advice on seventeenth-century French pronunciation and paleography. He is also grateful to Thomas N. Campbell of the Department of Anthropology, the University of Texas at Austin, for his critique of Troike's essay and for sharing information on Indian-group names used in the literature, and to Dee Ann Story, director of the Texas Archeological Research Laboratory at the University of Texas, for her comments.

Additionally, Peter H. Wood of Duke University is due special acknowledgment for his groundbreaking assessment of La Salle as a "lost explorer" in the article cited in our bibliography. We are gratified to be able to present, in the Minet relation, evidence to support his case.

Finally, the contributors to this volume wish to thank each other. It has been a team effort, with each participant sharing with the others his or her own special knowledge and experience. It is the hope of each of us that in the process we have created a tool that will prove valuable to other scholars in the never-ending struggle to advance knowledge.

La Salle, the Mississippi, and the Gulf

Introduction

In the story of René-Robert Cavelier, Sieur de La Salle, and his landmark explorations are found all the elements of a suspense thriller: ro-
mance, pathos, adventure, and intrigue. Whatever assessment one may
make of this strange and little-understood man—magnificent hero or
blatant fool—at least one fact seems obvious: he influenced the geography and the history of North America as few have. Efforts should continue, therefore, to enhance the meager understanding we have of the
man and his accomplishments.

The translators and editors present herein translations of three primary accounts not published in their entirety, in any language, prior to
1985.[1] Each deals with a different aspect of the venture. The two-part
Minet Journal, acquired from private hands by the Public Archives of
Canada, Ottawa, recounts, first, La Salle's exploration preliminary to his
1682 journey down the Mississippi River and the journey itself; and, second, Minet's own voyage with La Salle from La Rochelle to the Gulf of
Mexico and his return to France with Captain Beaujeu on the ship *Joly*.

Juan Enríquez Barroto's diary, from the Royal Palace Library in
Madrid, details the Spaniards' 1686–87 circumnavigation of the Gulf in
search of La Salle's colony, including the most thorough examination of
the northern Gulf shore up to that time.

The Talon Interrogations, conducted in France almost a decade
after Fort Saint-Louis of Texas came to its tragic end, bring forth the

---

1 With this volume in the final revision stage, a copy of a recently published
translation of the Talon Interrogations came to my attention: R. T. Huntington, trans., "The Interrogation of the Talon Brothers, 1698," *Iowa Review*
15, no. 2 (Spring–Summer, 1985): 99–131. Two philosophies are reflected in
the techniques of the two translators, Ann Linda Bell's translation, presented
herein, being the more literal. Wayne Franklin's "Afterword" to the Huntington translation summarizes events pertaining to the Talons and other survivors of La Salle's venture from the document itself and from Robert S.
Weddle, *Wilderness Manhunt: The Spanish Search for La Salle*, but there is no
annotation or other elucidation of the text.

story of a Canadian family who suffered the colony's vicissitudes, specifically, of the two young brothers who lived first among the Texas Indians, then the Spaniards, and finally returned to France just as a new attempt to settle in the Gulf was being planned. In this piece is found the only eyewitness account of the Fort Saint-Louis massacre. The original Talon document is in the Outre-Mer section of the French National Archives on Rue Oudinot, Paris. The microfilm copy from which the translation was made is in the Old Spanish Missions Research Library, Our Lady of the Lake University, San Antonio, Texas.

If one perceives an imbalance in the treatment given the three accounts, there is a reason. The pieces themselves are diverse in subject matter as well as approach. Although Minet, as will be seen in Patricia Galloway's introductions, has parallels in other sources, the three writers whose works are translated here do not parallel each other. Although the French engineer, like Enríquez Barroto, chronicles a sea voyage, the similarity of the two ends there. Enríquez's diary, as an exploration piece, is singular. But the story told by the Talon brothers in their responses to an official interrogation approaches uniqueness. Not even Cabeza de Vaca, in his epic sojourn among the Texas coastal Indians a century and a half earlier, was able to view the Karankawas from the Talons' vantage point. Although the vaunted sixteenth-century Spanish explorer lived among the Indians, the Talons *were* Indians. They saw the natives among whom they lived as no other European ever did.

Additionally, they manifest an awareness of natural phenomena that seems to distinguish French exploration accounts generally from those of their Spanish counterparts. Just as the French approach to New World exploration contrasts with the Spanish—as the canoe stands apart from the horse—so do French descriptions of the land. The French, while often remiss in detailing other matters—including identification of themselves by first name—were by far the better naturalists, although notable exceptions do come to mind. Henri Joutel's monumental relation of the La Salle expedition to the Gulf is rich with descriptive passages of the same country discussed by the Talons. He was a competent observer, but he did not live among the Indians, eat their food, or participate in their hunts and raids, as did the brothers.

The Talons, furthermore, contributed the earliest linguistic data—scant though they may be—on both the Hasinai, or Cenis, of Caddoan affiliation, and the Karankawas, who have no known linguistic relatives. The first Spanish effort to understand the native languages of eastern Texas began with Pierre Talon's assistance.

For such reasons the editors have adjudged the Talon Interrogations worthy of consideration by scholars representing disciplines other than history; their commentaries follow the translation.

The importance of each account is discussed further in its own introduction. Suffice it to say here that each one fills gaps in knowledge of La Salle's exploits. Surely everyone who has ever tried to write comprehensively of the first French colony on the Gulf of Mexico, including the Spanish search for it, has struggled to fill the voids that existed without these accounts—and has been compelled to compromise with regard to the missing links. This is not to say that all the old doubts are here put to rest or that all questions are answered. Yet the documents translated in this volume offer palpable supplements by which to measure the "old reliable" sources. In some cases they lend new understanding of the previously known material in ways that bring forth new insights or strengthen previous conclusions.

La Salle, born of a wealthy family in Rouen, France, in 1643, was educated by the Jesuits but found the monastic life alien to his restive nature. By 1666 he was in Canada. He acquired a substantial interest in the fur trade at Montreal, but it was the unexplored territory beyond La Chine rapids that drew him. In 1669 he sold his interests at Montreal and undertook his first major exploration. From the Iroquois he heard of a great river system, which he thought must flow into the Gulf of California, providing the passage to China. He proceeded to discover the Ohio River, but his followers' desertion forced him to turn back short of the Mississippi, leaving that discovery to the Jolliet-Marquette expedition of 1673, which reached the mouth of the Arkansas. On trips to France in 1674 and 1677, La Salle received first a patent of nobility and a seigneurial grant, then a trading concession to the country "through which a way might be found to Mexico."[2] Then began in earnest his explorations toward the Mississippi, which culminated in his epic voyage to its mouth, reached on April 7, 1682—an achievement that altered the history of North America.

Again in France the following year, La Salle won Crown approval for approaching the Mississippi by sea. He proposed to plant a French colony at a secure distance up the river from which to penetrate Mexico

2 Isaac Joslin Cox, ed., *The Journeys of Réné Robert Cavelier, Sieur de La Salle,* Introduction, I, xvi. Other general works that give background on La Salle include John Gilmary Shea's introductory "History of the Discovery of the Mississippi River," in *Discovery and Exploration of the Mississippi Valley;* Frederic Austin Ogg, *The Opening of the Mississippi: A Struggle for Supremacy in the American Interior;* Francis Parkman, *La Salle and the Discovery of the Great West;* and Paul Chesnel, *History of Cavelier de La Salle, 1643–1687.*

and prey on Gulf shipping in time of war. Armed conflict between France and Spain was indeed a frequent occurrence.

The seventeenth century was marked by a general scramble of the French, the English, and the Dutch to avail themselves of the Caribbean islands that Spain had failed to occupy. France came into possession of Martinique, Guadeloupe, and Tortuga, then spread onto the larger island of Hispaniola, Spain's oldest colony in America. The English acquired Nevis, Barbuda, Antigua, and Montserrat; the Dutch, St. Eustatius, Tobago, and Curaçao. These Spanish possessions by right of discovery became rapidly expanding centers of lawlessness—the havens of pirates who preyed on Spanish commerce and plundered Spanish coastal settlements.

Anglo-Hispanic relations had somewhat stabilized in 1670 with a formal treaty by which the English right to Jamaica—seized fifteen years previously—was recognized. England agreed to respect Spain's territorial claims in the future while assisting in extermination of the pirates. Louis XIV of France, however, encouraged French incursion into the Spanish possessions whenever the opportunity arose, in Europe or America.

The tension mounted in October, 1683, when Spain, moved by Louis's aggressive policy in Flanders, declared war on France. Word reached the court that the renegade Spanish schemer Diego de Peñalosa again was importuning Louis XIV to undertake the conquest of New Spain's northern provinces. La Salle doubtless was emboldened by the erstwhile Spanish count's daring scheme, but there is evidence that he formed his own plan of Mexican conquest before he ever heard of him.[3]

The Franco-Spanish conflict, though ended with the truce of Ratisbon on August 15, 1684, did nothing to ease Spain's apprehension. La Salle's plan for establishing a base inside the Gulf of Mexico from which to strike New Spain already had been set in motion; he was two weeks at sea on his voyage to the Gulf. Despite his stopover in French Saint-Domingue, Minet reveals, the news that peace had been made failed to overtake him.

Departing from Rochefort on August 1, 1684—after a false start from La Rochelle two weeks previously—the voyage of four vessels and 280 persons was constantly stalked by disaster. It was marked by dissension between La Salle and the naval commander, Tanguy Le Gallois de Beaujeu; the loss of one of the ships to Spanish privateers off His-

3 Pierre Margry, ed., *Découvertes et établissements des français dans l'ouest et dans le sud de l'Amérique septentrionale (1614–1754)*, II, 293.

paniola; defection (or relinquishment) of some of the company to the pirate fleet; and, finally, La Salle's failure to find the Mississippi where he had supposed it to be. He landed instead at an unknown Texas bay, where the storeship was lost in the shoaly entrance.[4]

When Captain Beaujeu returned to France with his ship *Joly,* the engineer Minet, the crew of the lost ship *Aimable,* and several disenchanted colonists went with him. By the time a temporary fort was built in the spring of 1685, a series of other misfortunes had reduced La Salle's company to 180. The loss of the last ship, *Belle,* in a squall eliminated all possibility of escape by sea. In January, 1687, when La Salle left the colony on his final journey, to seek the French post on the Illinois River (also called Fort Saint-Louis), hardly more than 40 persons remained. There followed La Salle's murder at the hands of one of his followers and the Indian massacre at Fort Saint-Louis of Texas that spared only the children. Such were the fruits of La Salle's dream of empire.

La Salle was by no means the first European to view the mouth of the Mississippi or to travel on the river. In 1519 Alonso Alvarez de Pineda, in Spanish service, either viewed one of the river's multiple mouths from afar or perceived it by its mighty discharge. He named it, for the Festival of the Holy Spirit (Whitsunday or Pentecost), Río del Espíritu Santo. As luck would have it, Hernando Cortés that same year landed in Mexico and sent home to Spain specimens of Aztec gold. The spotlight, therefore, fell on Mexico's riches. The forbidding Río del Espíritu Santo still lay in obscurity, mentioned only in doubtful notations on crude maps, more speculative than truly representative.

Hernando de Soto's survivors, defeated and demoralized by the wilderness so vastly different from any they had imagined, used the great river as an escape route in 1543. In the bitterness of their failure they inspired no new effort to explore and conquer the continent's most vital waterway. Indeed, in the Spaniards' view there was little about this silt-laden torrent, spilling over its natural levees into an unfathomable maze of bayous and endless marshes, to provide inspiration of any kind.

Throughout the rest of the sixteenth century and most of the seventeenth, the Spaniards gave little concern to the northern Gulf shore. The name Río del Espíritu Santo surfaced occasionally, as in Fray Alonso de Benavides's 1630 memorial, the letters and reports of a Flor-

---

4 Henri Joutel ("Relation de Henri Joutel," in ibid., III, 92) gives the number of persons and goes on to narrate the entire episode. The 1715 English translation (*Joutel's Journal of La Salle's Last Voyage*) is much abridged and often hard to reconcile with the account in Margry.

ida governor, and a grand proposal by an erstwhile St. Augustine pilot who withdrew his offer of exploration at the critical moment.[5] In Mexico the mode of the century was, in a sense, to bring order out of the chaos left by the Conquest. Interest waned in extending discovery and exploration around the Gulf, except as dictated by the exigencies of defense. While Spain held to this defensive posture, its enemies—foreign pirates and privateers—prowled the Gulf's recesses and acquired a familiarity equal or superior to that of Spain's own navigators. But then, in September, 1685, came word of a threat before which all others paled. From captured pirates—deserters from La Salle's company—the Spaniards learned of the Frenchman's journey down the Mississippi and that, having entered the Gulf to establish a colony, La Salle was violating the sanctity of the traditional Spanish sea.

For the Spaniards such news underscored their long-standing neglect of the northern Gulf shore. With countless Caribbean islands already fallen to their European rivals, it also emphasized Spain's impotency in guarding the entire Gulf perimeter against a plethora of multinational poachers. Significantly, La Salle's intrusion brought about a rebirth of Spanish exploration in the Gulf of Mexico and attempts to secure Spain's territorial claims by occupying eastern Texas and Pensacola Bay.

In this sudden burst of activity, however, lay a lack of foresight, which, while understandable, would vitally affect Spain's remaining tenure in North America, not to mention the fortunes of the future United States of America. Even the Spaniards' daring and unprecedented explorations around the Mississippi Delta during their search for La Salle's colony would not reveal the great river's natural strategic importance. Although a settlement at Pensacola was vital for guarding the

---

5 Alonso de Benavides (*Benavides' Memorial of 1630*, pp. 63–64) advocated opening a Gulf port to serve the native provinces of Quivira and Aixaos, noting that "there is indicated on the sea charts a bay called Espíritu Santo," in 29° latitude, between Apalache Cape and Tampico. The document was not given serious consideration by the Crown until 1678, when word of Peñalosa's schemes reached Spain. On November 10, 1678, the Florida governor, Pablo de Hita Salazar, responded to a royal *cédula* of November 5, 1677, by advocating to the king a plan for securing the northern Gulf shore by extending the Florida settlements to join those of Mexico, embracing the Bahía del Espíritu Santo (Archivo General de Indios [hereafter AGI], Santo Domingo 839). In August, 1685, Martín de Echagaray, late the pilot-major at St. Augustine, offered to explore Espíritu Santo Bay, but his interest died before news of the La Salle intrusion finally brought his plan under consideration (Charles II to Viceroy Conde de Paredes, August 2, 1685, University of Texas [UT] archives, transcript, AGI, Mexico 616).

northern shore, the Mississippi was needed also. Indecision and limited resources kept Spain from getting it while the opportunity existed. In failing to avail itself of this keystone to the continent, Spain provided the means ultimately seized by France for driving a wedge between the Spanish possessions of Florida and Texas.

For France, La Salle's bold venture bore vastly different implications. In descending the Mississippi to the Gulf and claiming the river's watershed for his king, La Salle propelled his nation in a direction it had not necessarily intended to go. Minister Jean-Baptiste Colbert, viewing the French American colony around the St. Lawrence River as an economic transfusion, had opposed the kind of overexpansion that would commit his nation beyond its abilities. Yet, failing to foresee the far-reaching consequences of La Salle's proposed venture, "he unwittingly aided the process by granting . . . La Salle the right to establish trading posts in the Mississippi Valley to further the exploration of this river to its mouth." Once the vast region from Hudson Bay to the Gulf had been claimed for the French Crown, it could not be surrendered short of defeat in war. "France now had to be prepared to expend its blood and treasure to maintain its hold on half the continent without regard for the economic balance sheet."[6] To support this claim, the Crown backed La Salle in still a further venture: a voyage into the Spanish-owned Gulf to ascend the Mississippi and establish a fortified colony at a strategic point sixty leagues upstream. He overshot the Mississippi and landed instead at Texas's Matagorda Bay in February, 1685.

Historians still bog down over the reasons for La Salle's misplaced landing, ascribing it to either navigational error or his "secret" design for striking Mexico. Actually, neither reason applies. The confusion arises from assigning to the seventeenth-century explorer a geographical understanding that came only in a later period. Minet's comments here and there enlarge upon the long-known but little-heeded "Chucagoa fragment," which is the focus of a study by Peter H. Wood.[7] These sources, joined to La Salle's letters cited by Minet, render inescapable the conclusion that La Salle mislocated the mouth of the Mississippi on the maps he had; he judged it to be not the Río del Espíritu Santo discovered by Alvarez de Pineda and descended by Soto's men, as it actually was, but another, called Río Escondido. This "hidden river," which began appearing on European maps about 1550, was shown entering the Gulf in the Texas coastal bend. It is identifiable with the Nueces, dis-

6 W. J. Eccles, *France in America*, pp. 86–89.
7 Peter H. Wood, "La Salle: Discovery of a Lost Explorer," *American Historical Review* 89, no. 2 (April, 1984): 294–323.

charging into Corpus Christi Bay, the precise point to which La Salle sailed. Failing to recognize his Rivière Colbert, he made a temporary camp at the mouth of Matagorda Bay and set out to find it among the neighboring bays and lagoons. Consider, then, that La Salle was lost not only when he overshot the Mississippi in 1685 but also three years previously when he descended that river from Canada.

Minet discloses some largely unrecognized reasons for the confusion of La Salle's geographical reflections revealed in the Chucagoa fragment: with a broken compass and an "unsuitable" astrolabe, he lacked the means for determining with accuracy either latitude or direction. The latitude he observed at the mouth of the Mississippi, 28°20′, was almost a degree farther south than it was shown to be on most maps of the period. The large bay appearing on all the maps at the mouth of the river failed to appear; instead, the river flowed almost east as it approached the Gulf of Mexico. La Salle, descending the eastern passes to the Gulf, formed no concept of the extenuated delta and therefore concluded that the coast at this point ran north-south. All these factors suggested that he was on a different river from the one Soto's men had descended in 1543. "Unless all the maps are worthless," he wrote, "the Mississippi surely is the Escondido."[8] His voyage to the Gulf, therefore, was based on a wild geographical conjecture, the error in which was not perceived even by the most erudite geographers of France.

Even after La Salle's colony had failed, the French did not readily yield his claim to the Texas coastal region. It mattered not that a Spanish navigator named Guido de Lavazares (or Las Bazares) had taken formal possession at La Salle's very bay in 1558. On the basis of La Salle's pretensions, the United States later sought to include Spanish Texas with the Louisiana Purchase. Failure of this ploy was not accepted gracefully; American interlopers in Spanish territory became legion. In broad terms, they helped to turn Texas into a battleground.

For 120 years La Salle cast a long shadow over Franco-Spanish relations, then over the dealings of Spain and the United States. The man, whatever his personal attributes or shortcomings, lies at the root of a significant portion of American history, from Canada to the Gulf.

La Salle's life ended at age forty-three in abject failure—failure not only as an explorer and colonizer but also as a leader. The reasons for this multifaceted miscarriage of his aims have been much debated. As scholars argue adamantly the various alternatives, inflexibility collides with intransigence; neither side concedes a middle ground.

Of all the puzzles surrounding this man of mystery, the most in-

8 Margry, *Découvertes,* II, 198.

PLATE 1. Rouillard's map of America, 1692, based on "the best-known memorials," exemplifies La Salle's concept of the Mississippi as entering the Gulf of Mexico at its western end, with the mythical Espíritu Santo Bay "to the northeast."
(From Le Clercq, *Premier établissement de la foi*)

triguing concerns his personality and character. He is alternately condemned and praised by those who served him as well as by those who
view him in retrospect. Minet, in the series of accusatory questions appended to his journal, delivers the most stinging indictment. He pic-
tures the leader as a dark, brooding, suspicious, and secretive man,
given to paranoia and malicious diatribe against all who opposed him,
headstrong to the point that no advice was worthy, no opinion valid but
his own.

Minet, embittered by his stint in prison and by other fruits of his
dealings with La Salle, probably was less than objective in his assessment of the explorer. La Salle did inspire loyalty among many of his
followers. Where Minet is wont to villify him, Joutel, although praising
his great talent, courage, and extraordinary knowledge, is said to have
noted that his haughty behavior and rigidness made him insupportable
and occasioned his death.[9] Father Anastase Douay eulogizes him as
having been "constant in adversity, intrepid, generous, engaging, dex-
terous, skillful, capable of everything."[10]

Representative of the historian genre, Francis Parkman usually is regarded as La Salle's defender. "The staple of La Salle's character, as his
life will attest," he says, "was an invincible determination of purpose,
which set at naught all risks and all sufferings." Yet Parkman tells of numerous defections from the explorer's company in the north woods; of
a soldier who raised his gun to shoot him in the back; and of another
who placed poison in the cooking pot, from which act La Salle was
saved by a hastily administered antidote.[11] Hubert Howe Bancroft, on
the other hand, nods agreement to the assessment of John Gilmary
Shea: "La Salle aided the destruction of his party (in Texas) by his utter
unfitness for colonization. It is not easy to conceive how intelligent
writers have exalted a man of such utter incapacity into a hero."[12]

Mystery surrounds not only La Salle's character but also his exploits, not only the reasons for his misplaced landing in Texas but also
his explorations afterward. Accounts of each of these endeavors diverge
sharply, and interpreters have had difficulty reconciling them. Although
the material offered here may fall short of filling all the blanks, it adds
to, and in some cases clarifies, that which was available previously. In

9 Joutel, *Journal*, p. 103. This passage is not found in the "Relation."
10 Cox, *Journeys*, p. 244.
11 Parkman, *La Salle* (1963), pp. 44, 137, 145.
12 Hubert Howe Bancroft, *History of the North Mexican States and Texas*, I, 396n.
   For other assessments, see Carl A. Brasseaux, "The Image of La Salle in
   North American Historiography," in Patricia K. Galloway, ed., *La Salle and
   His Legacy: Frenchmen and Indians in the Lower Mississippi Valley*, pp. 3–10.

Minet's chronicle of the journey down the Mississippi, we have another account with which to balance those of La Salle, Père Zénobe Membré, Henri de Tonti, and Nicolas de La Salle.[13] His journal of the voyage to the Gulf of Mexico supplements Joutel's account of the voyage, as the Talon Interrogations augment accounts of the life of the colony.

Arguments also go forth concerning the extent and direction of La Salle's exploration from Fort Saint-Louis, on the right bank of Garcitas Creek in present-day Victoria County, Texas. At issue especially are the journeys of the fall and winter of 1685–86. Various accounts claim that he spent those months exploring the Matagorda Bay vicinity. Yet the evidence is strong that the expeditionists reached the Rio Grande and at least some of them ascended that river as far as the Cíbolo Indian village near present-day Langtry, Texas. None of the accounts translated here clarifies these points; yet a study of Spanish as well as French sources discloses events supporting such a westward march.[14]

Add to these points of disagreement and conjecture a more recent thesis that La Salle's landing place itself is not precisely known; that it was not Matagorda Bay but some other, farther west. The multitude of reports by Spanish explorers who located the fort, mapped the area, and built a Spanish presidio on the very site of Fort Saint-Louis clearly refutes such a hypothesis. The location is precisely where Bolton concluded that it was, more than sixty years ago.[15] Yet, if further support of the location is needed, the Enríquez Barroto diary, which identifies many of the coastal landmarks with precise latitudes, should serve the purpose.

We are able to commemorate La Salle on the tricentennial of his death with publication of "new" material to further understanding of both his personality and his exploits. These reports have provided challenges for the translators, with interesting glimpses into the writers' per-

---

13 See Patricia Galloway, "Sources for the La Salle Expedition of 1682," in Galloway, *La Salle,* p. 11–40, for a discussion of these sources.

14 Documents pertaining to this matter are printed in Spanish and English in Charles Wilson Hackett, ed., *Historical Documents Relating to New Mexico, Nueva Vizcaya, and Approaches Thereto, to 1773,* II, esp. 231–78. A synthesized account is in Weddle, *Wilderness Manhunt,* pp. 160–73. The Cíbolos, so named because they were bison hunters, lived in close association with the Jumanos.

15 H. Dickson Hoese ("On the Correct Landfall of La Salle in Texas, 1685," *Louisiana History* 19, no. 1 [Winter, 1978]: 5–32) offers Aransas Bay instead of Matagorda. Herbert Eugene Bolton ("The Location of La Salle's Colony on the Gulf of Mexico," *Southwestern Historical Quarterly* 27, no. 3 [January, 1924]: 171–89) is correct on the location.

sonalities. Minet's journal was written at the time of the occurrences he relates or from conversations with eyewitnesses. The Talons, on the other hand, supply answers to questions asked by an official interrogator, recorded by an official scribe, a decade after Fort Saint-Louis's tragic end.

Minet often mixes singular with plural and nominative with accusative and exhibits numerous inconsistencies. Orthographic discrepancies in names and titles are given in the translation as written. Similarly, numerical expressions retain the form used in the original manuscript. Sometimes the writer uses *qui* instead of *qu'il* of *qu'ils*. Besides having to decide whether *qui* means "who," "what," or "that," the translator must remember that in one document he is reporting what others have told him and in many instances *qui* represents "and." His use of the indefinite pronoun *on* ("we" or "they") is confusing also, especially when he is relating events in which he was not involved. Whereas the third person would seem the logical choice for the translator, Minet renders this impossible with an occasional *nous* ("we" or "us"). In Minet's syntactical impreciseness, verb tenses are of little help in determining whether first or third person is intended. The matter becomes most confusing in Part I, where the voyage down the Mississippi begins. At that point we have chosen to employ first person, as though Minet is quoting directly from his informants, Nicolas de La Salle and the Sieur Barbier, as may have been his intention.

In both Minet's writings and Enríquez Barroto's, the ship's course often is expressed in terms such as "northwest a quarter north." In each case this has been rendered "northwest by north," as it is expressed in English of the present day.

The Talon report has a remarkably cool and objective tone—reflecting the official nature of the interrogations. Minet, on the other hand, alternates in his second document between detached reporting and subjective opinions accompanied by emotional outbursts. Neither, unfortunately, makes any mention of the other. Enríquez Barroto presents an official log of the Spanish voyage in a dispassionate and objective manner. The only document of the three of which no significant part has been published previously, it stands out as an account of maritime exploration in the Gulf of Mexico—a rarity.

It should be noted that both Minet's manuscripts contain frequent marginal notes to elucidate the text. For ease of typesetting and space conservation, these notes have been inserted in the text at the appropriate place in double brackets [[———]]. The questions put to the Talon brothers also appear in the margin of the original; these have been inserted in the text as subheads. Marginal notes of a different nature are double-bracketed as in the Minet account. The editors' intention in every case has been to deal with stylistic concerns without intruding upon the information contained in the documents.

The La Salle colonization attempt is significant as the first real European penetration of the Texas-Louisiana Gulf shores since Narváez and Soto and as the very first settlement attempt between Mobile Bay and the Río Pánuco. Its impact on Spanish efforts to explore and colonize the region was immediate, and its influence on history has endured these three hundred years.

I. Exploration of the Mississippi

The Minet Relation: Journey by River

PATRICIA GALLOWAY

The Minet relation of the 1682 La Salle expedition apparently was un-known to the archival world until it surfaced in a purchase by the Public Archives of Canada in 1981.[1] As an entirely new source for the history of this expedition, it forces the reevaluation of the several other sources. It claims to be made up of facts gathered from two of the participants in the expedition, Nicolas de La Salle and Gabriel Minime, Sieur Barbier, and to have been limited to these two oral sources. Minet explicitly states that the more contradictory stories told by René-Robert Cavelier, Sieur de La Salle, and Father Zénobe Membré have not been used. But this claim may be misleading, as will be seen.

There are eight other complete or partial accounts of the 1682 expe-dition, only six of which can be ascribed with certainty to their authors. They range in immediacy from the *procès verbal* accounts—set down by the expedition's notary when the two land claims were made, at the Arkansas River and at the mouth of the Mississippi—to the two brief letters by Henry Tonti and Father Membré, which gave the outside world the first news of the journey's achievements; to Tonti's account of 1684 and Nicolas de La Salle's of 1685;[2] to Tonti's memoir of 1691, which briefly describes the expedition from the perspective of his entire service in the New World.[3] In evaluating the Minet relation, we are lucky to have the Nicolas de La Salle account with which to compare it, and that must be the starting point for any appraisal. Yet the provenience of the Nicolas account is rather obscure, so perhaps Nicolas's value as an infor-mant should be examined at the outset.

1 Victorin Chabot ("Journal inédit relatant les expeditions de Cavelier de La Salle," *The Archivist* 8 [1981]: 8–9) announced the character of this new acquisition.
2 The authorship and provenience of this document will be discussed further in the following pages.
3 See Patricia Galloway, "Sources for the La Salle Expedition of 1682," in Patricia Galloway, *La Salle and His Legacy; Frenchmen and Indians in the Lower Mississippi Valley*, p. 21.

The identity of Nicolas de La Salle is not in doubt. A career navy man about twenty years of age at the time of the expedition, he probably had family connections in high places, since it seems to have been his own interest that led to his assignment to the 1682 and 1684 expeditions and to his later settlement in the Louisiana colony as its first naval commissary.[4] With Tonti and many others, he joined La Salle's company in 1678, when the exploration of the Mississippi, although still four years in the future, was viewed as part of a master plan. Although a roster of the 1682 expedition simply lists Nicolas among the other members of the company,[5] he was one of the few to sign the official *procès verbal* accounts as witnesses. Later, he was trusted by La Salle as an oral witness when the explorer returned to France to gather support for the Gulf of Mexico expedition.

Therefore, Nicolas's role in the descent of the Mississippi must certainly have been more than that of just an able body. A careful reading of the account attributed to him alone shows that he was frequently at the side of Tonti or Father Membré, certainly La Salle's most important companions, and sometimes with La Salle himself.[6] Because of this proximity to the leaders, he had an opportunity to observe a great deal more than if he had been placed entirely in one of the boats manned exclusively by *voyageurs* or Indians. This circumstantial evidence, with the way the text of his relation is laid out, suggests a likelihood that he did, as he claimed, keep a journal of the voyage as it progressed, and that the version of this journal that comes to us through Margry probably is reasonably close to the original.[7]

4 Nicolas de La Salle, "Rapport du Sr de la Salle Escrivain de Vau de ce qui'il scait sur la decouverte de la partye septentrionale de l'Amerique" (Archives Nationales [hereafter AN], Marine, Dépot des Cartes et Plans, vol. 67, no. 15), is a synopsis of Nicolas's observations on Louisiana, sent to the minister of marine and colonies in hopes of securing a position with Iberville's new colony. See also Jay Higginbotham, *Old Mobile: Fort Louis de la Louisiane, 1702–1711*, p. 35. The chronology of Nicolas's life is not precisely as Higginbotham portrays it, however. After traveling to France with La Salle in 1683, he apparently did not return to the Americas until the 1685 expedition, and at that point he was no longer part of La Salle's company but was assigned to Beaujeu's ship's company instead. According to his own testimony, he then served for some fourteen years "on the vessels" before being assigned as a clerk in Toulon (Nicolas de La Salle to minister, July 22, 1700, AN, Colonies, Series C13B, 1, no. 4, fol. 2).

5 Henri de Tonti, 1684 memoir, in Pierre Margry, *Découvertes et établissements des Français dans l'ouest et dans le sud de l'Amerique septentrionale*, I, 594.

6 See Galloway, "Sources," p. 36.

7 See Nicolas de La Salle, 1685 account, in Margry, *Découvertes*, I, 547–70.

But this journal probably was not the only reason that La Salle took him back to France in 1683; doubtless, it is no coincidence that one of Nicolas's relatives was sufficiently important to be appointed commissioner general of the galleys only four years later. The evidence of Nicolas's account shows him to have been at the time an ingenuous young man, one who did not question either the decisions made by his superiors or their motives. The undoubted note of candor and sincerity that marked his observations of the journey—on which Minet remarks as part of Nicolas's character—would also have recommended him as a convincing witness.

The existence of a journal kept by Nicolas has never seemed to be in doubt, though the only evidence for it is the version printed by Margry.[8] Even Jean Delanglez's contempt for Margry's intellectual integrity never led the Jesuit scholar to question this source. Yet the original manuscript has never been seen except by Margry, who credits it to a collection of travel narratives in a manuscript from a bookseller's aggregation, now presumably lost.[9] As we have it, Nicolas's narrative refers to Nicolas himself in the third person as "little La Salle" and has a certain "as told to" ring about it, although it is made up in the main of the rather disjointed daily entries characteristic of an actual journal. Until the discovery of the Minet journal, there was little more reason to accept it as a firsthand account of the 1682 La Salle journey than to take Garcilaso de la Vega's narrative as such for Hernando de Soto's exploration—even though it is in basic agreement with the timetables described in the authenticated versions and with their circumstantial detail.[10] There is no reason to doubt Minet's assertion that Nicolas *had* kept a journal and that Minet had seen it during the voyage to and from the Gulf of Mexico; the timetable in the Minet relation is in nearly complete agreement with that of Nicolas, and many passages follow word for word the text printed by Margry.

The only other of Nicolas's writings referring descriptively to the 1682 journey, this one preserved in the French archives, is a synopsis of that event, emphasizing the potential value of the lands traversed. It was sent in 1698 by Nicolas, then a naval clerk at Toulon, to officials in

8 Ibid.
9 Margry, *Découvertes,* III, 655. Margry's description of the manuscript he saw, as one of several bound in three folio volumes owned by Léon Techener and copied by Margry in 1844, completely invalidates any speculation that it and the Minet manuscript were one and the same. The Minet manuscript is a small notebook of about quarto size.
10 Galloway, "Sources," figs. 1–3.

Paris,[11] doubtless in support of his application to join Iberville's coloniz-
ing venture, which he did in 1702 as the colony's first commissary. In this
capacity he later waxed far more loquacious in the official colonial
records, but never in later writings does he yield any further information about La Salle's exploration of the Mississippi.

Gabriel Minime or Barbier, whom Minet credits with having contributed substantially to the account of the 1682 journey, seems to have
been one of Tonti's men, also involved in the La Salle–Tonti enterprise
well before this exploration took place, but we know little else about
him. In fact, his origin and background are rather a mystery. Although
he is portrayed as merely an experienced *voyageur* with the 1682 company, he was commissioned a lieutenant for the 1684 venture; his final
role is as commandant of the little garrison left on the Texas coast upon
La Salle's final departure, fated for extermination by the Karankawa Indians. After arriving in Texas, he married one of the young women in
the colony. Joutel refers to him as Sieur Barbier.[12]

Yet there is no doubt that the *voyageur* and the commandant are the
same man, since Barbier, like Nicolas, was taken back to France as a witness to the 1682 exploration and since Minet states that both had been
parpticipants. In addition, the activities performed by Barbier on the
Texas coast, which included navigation in small boats and bartering
with the local Indians, proclaim the *voyageur* quite clearly.[13] The identity
is definitely established by the presence in the Minet relation of a brief
description, found nowhere else, of the way Barbier had captured
the two Chickasaws encountered on the southward journey in 1682, a
feat attested by independent accounts, which he carried out single-
handedly, making him the only witness.

One of the most certain arguments in favor of Barbier's identity,
however, lies in the fact that he was entrusted with the safekeeping of
the Texas beachhead. La Salle had justifiably developed the habit of
counting on a few loyal men, and, as he departed to meet Tonti farther

11 Nicolas de La Salle, "Rapport," AN, Marine, Dépot des Cartes et Plans, vol.
    67, no. 15.
12 Henri Joutel, *Joutel's Journal of La Salle's Last Voyage*, Henry R. Stiles, ed., pas-
    sim. Pierre Le Moyne, Sieur d'Iberville, writing to La Salle's brother the
    Abbé Cavelier in 1704, refers to "Gabriel Minime or Barbier, whom I knew"
    (Margry, *Découvertes*, III, 622). Barbier, like Iberville, was a Canadian. Marc
    de Villiers (*L'Expédition de Cavelier de La Salle dans le Golfe du Mexique,
    1684–1687*, p. 217) refers to Barbier as a lieutenant. He was, in fact, commis-
    sioned to that rank by royal order of April 15, 1684 (Margry, *Découvertes*,
    II, 387).
13 Joutel, *Journal*, pp. 79, 84, 108, 109, 114, 129.

up the Mississippi River, he would have left in charge only a man of proven loyalty. In fact, he left two such men, Barbier as commandant and Father Membré as chaplain to the little garrison.[14] Probably it was intended that at some point Barbier would head one of the string of trading posts La Salle planned to extend throughout his commercial empire.

Barbier's loyalty had been proved, no doubt, not only by his adherence to the La Salle–Tonti enterprise during the phase of establishing posts along the Great Lakes, but also by his supporting testimony in France as to the truth of La Salle's discoveries. In taking Barbier and Nicolas with him, La Salle chose witnesses of varied background— Canadian *voyageur* and junior officer. As we shall see in attempting to establish the kind of testimony given by each as witnessed by the Minet relation, both gave accounts that agree substantially while emphasizing different aspects of the exploration.

Minet may have had several reasons for choosing to talk with Barbier, not the least of which was the details that only he had observed. If Minet was, as he appears to have been, a practiced geographer, then he knew how to evaluate exploration accounts, perhaps especially those by men skilled in woodcraft, who were unlikely to deliver written narratives. There is another aspect to be considered, however, and that is that Minet and Barbier seem to have struck up a friendship prior to the departure for the Gulf of Mexico. During the waiting and false start at the French port, Minet became ill, and Barbier went ashore to care for him. The treatment involved bloodletting, done "with a broken stone like the savages."[15] An interesting sidelight may be introduced here: at one point in Joutel's relation of the Texas colony, Barbier is referred to as *le Barbier,* possibly implying that his *dit* name (sobriquet) was "the barber"; if this was the case, he may have possessed at least some simple medical skills, which would have made him doubly valuable to all of La Salle's enterprises and might explain Joutel's referring to him as though he were an officer.

Possibly it was while being offered treatment for his illness that Minet learned of the camaraderie that Barbier and Nicolas had established during their time together in La Salle's company. One can even imagine that they had been encouraged to put their heads together on the way back to France in 1683, to arrive at a harmonious account of the

---

14 Ibid., p. 116. Concerning Father Membré, see Marion A. Habig, *The Franciscan Père Marquette: A Critical Biography of Father Zénobe Membré, O.F.M., La Salle's Chaplain and Missionary Companion.*

15 See p. 85, infra.

journey down the Mississippi, and that, as a result, their stories formed the coherent whole on which Minet remarks. The other witnesses with whom Minet spoke during the voyage to the Gulf, Membré and La Salle himself, were on a different ship after leaving Haiti. Additionally, Membré had been separated from Nicolas and Barbier during part of the 1682 journey, as well as afterward.

A detailed collation of the Minet narrative of the Mississippi exploration with that ascribed to Nicolas yields some interesting information. It becomes clear that Nicolas's testimony does account for the bulk of Minet's relation. Yet there are some points that must have come from oral testimony by Nicolas that the latter had not put into his own journal, from Barbier's oral testimony, from which several incidents are quite clearly derived, and from other sources. Minet doubtless had access to the Membré and Tonti letters of 1683,[16] and probably to Tonti's 1684 account, all of which still reside among the collected papers of Bernou, one of La Salle's devoted supporters. All of these undoubtedly would have been made available to the second expedition's cartographer. It is also quite possible that Minet was able to see fragmentary materials dealing with geography collected by the royal cartographer Claude Delisle from the oral accounts of the exploration party.[17] Although the Minet relation takes up precisely where Nicolas joined La Salle's company in 1678, this may have been for the sake of the artistic unity of the whole. Certainly the opening portion owes much more to Tonti's 1684 account than it does to Nicolas, at least as far as can be told by comparing it with Nicolas's own.

The man who brought the material together to create the narrative here translated is a more shadowy figure than either of his identified informants. We know him only as Minet—his given name is not to be found in his writings. From his own testimony and that of others, including Joutel and Beaujeu, it is known that he was sent with the 1685 expedition to serve as both engineer and cartographer. What his prior training and experience were, or where he had acquired them, are so far unknown, but he must have been well qualified to be sent on such an important mission. Indeed, it is quite possible that he had been briefed by the king's geographer, Delisle, to serve as the latter's eyes in a land

16 Membré to Le Roux, June 3, 1682, Bibliothèque Nationale (hereafter BN, MSS Clairambault 1016, folios 163–165v; Tonti to ———, July 23, 1682, ibid., folios 165v–168v.

17 The Delisle papers, a collection of materials for the compilation of maps gathered by the Delisle firm, father and sons, now reside in the AN, Service Hydrographique, group 115.

Delisle himself would never have the opportunity to visit; Minet was under royal orders, for the disobedience of which he was imprisoned upon his return.[18] At least it seems that he was not handpicked by La Salle or his protector, Renaudot, since he relates that La Salle accused Minet of spying for his enemies. From that conclusion it is not far to the assumption that the royal command had been issued on the advice of Minister Seignelay, which is indeed implied in Minet's journal. In any case, the fact that he was assigned after his return to work on French fortifications under the acknowledged master of the theory and practice of this engineering science, Sébastian le Prestre, Marquis de Vauban,[19] argues for his competency as an engineer. Such qualifications, one should note, involved not only designing and building but also the skills of surveyor and cartographer.

Whether he was politically motivated, as La Salle alleged, Minet's relationship with the explorer seems to have been edgy from the start. The cause need not be sought in some complex web of conspiracy imagined by La Salle; it would have been quite natural for La Salle—staking his reputation and, as it turned out, his life on the geographical observations he had made three years previously—to feel uncomfortable with a qualified engineer looking over his shoulder as he felt his way along an unfamiliar coast. Indeed, La Salle avoided such a state of affairs by leaving Minet on Beaujeu's ship *Joly* when he himself changed to the more cumbersome *Aimable* upon sailing from Petit Goâve (Haiti). Minet does not seem to have fraternized to any remarkable degree with Beaujeu. His suggestions that so greatly angered La Salle do not seem to have contained anything of a particularly offensive nature. Yet, when Beaujeu's ship departed for France, Minet was ordered aboard. Upon his return to France he was imprisoned for more than a month for having deserted La Salle's company and for disobedience of the king's express orders.[20]

If little is known of the protagonists who figure in the creation of the Minet relation, one is free, on the other hand, to come to any conclusions that seem warranted from the document itself. It is a small volume of 140 pages. The first part contains the history of the 1682 expedition, with four years of background; the seond part is Minet's own diary of the 1685 expedition. If it began life as we see it today, a small bound book, it is hard to imagine how Minet decided where to commence his own diary, assuming that he worked on both concurrently. The main

18 See p. 122, infra.
19 Ibid., p. 126.
20 Ibid., pp. 122, 126.

narrative of the first expedition ends on page 56 and is followed by a few odd notes on page 57, a map of the mouths of the Mississippi on page 59, and a drawing of an Indian on page 61. The second part, Minet's own journal, begins with a new pagination, which runs from 1 to 77, and then, after a blank page 78, includes a seventy-ninth page bearing a note on the date of his release from prison. Hence, aside from a little leeway at the end of both relations, the two parts fit together rather tightly with very little wasted space. If in fact the volume is made up of quarto gatherings, then the 140 pages are completely accounted for as eighteen quarto signatures providing 144 pages. The break at 62/1 [63], though it would not fit with such an assumption, would do so if it is further assumed that the real break comes between pages 56 and 57, at the end of seven quartos. This conclusion would then imply that the miscellaneous notes, which can be seen actually to apply to the map that follows them on page 59, could have been made after the story of the 1682 voyage was set down, as could the map and the drawing of the Indian that follow.

I pursue this question because it is relevant to an attempt to discover when Minet actually wrote the two parts of the volume. If the parts are separable, as they can be, then it is quite possible that Minet was working on both concurrently and that only later were they joined to form a single bound manuscript. It is not illogical to assume that Minet might have left four pages blank preceding his own account, particularly if he intended to embellish it later with a title page and dedication. His prodigal use of space at the end of his own diary suggests that he had at least a few pages to spare—which ought to have been four besides the two blank pages and the note on his release from prison.

The two relations were clearly not intended for publication as they stand, if at all. Both of them include deletions, insertions above the line, marginal notes, and portions of text in a smaller version of Minet's hand squeezed in at the bottom or top of pages. They are quite obviously by the same hand, and a rather illegible one it is at times, as might be expected of someone who tried to write while aboard a small ship on a rough sea. The unpolished—indeed unfinished—appearance of the manuscript is a strong argument for its having been, as Minet says, written down when he could snatch time from his own work and was able to interview Nicolas and Barbier. Yet it is difficult to pin down the precise time at which the 1682 account was recorded, since Minet had access to one of his informants, Nicolas, on the return voyage as well as the outward one. If he began to write it during the crossing from France, it is likely that the main narrative was completed before the party's arrival on the Texas shore. Although Nicolas was assigned to Beaujeu's complement, Minet himself had no way of knowing in advance that he would quarrel with La Salle and would himself be returning on Beaujeu's ship; he would have thought that his opportunity to record Nicolas's story would end with the outbound voyage from France. Then, too, it must be remembered that Barbier could not have contributed to the manuscript after the departure of the *Joly*, since he stayed with the infant colony.

These considerations lead to the conclusion that the narrative of the 1682 exploration was in the main written before the expedition reached Texas, although many of the changes in it might have been made on the way back to France. The majority of the marginal notes, for example, generally serve as a gloss on the text, connected with Indian customs and unfamiliar flora, material that Minet could have obtained from Nicolas as he went back over the manuscript.[21] Most of the account, from page 19 to page 53, may safely be attributed to Nicolas except for several incidents not in his own relation, which seem likely to have come from Barbier. The capture of the Chickasaws and the discovery of smoked human flesh in an abandoned Indian pirogue serve as examples,[22] as does the passage describing the Quinipissa Indian attack on the party on the way back upriver (pages 43–44 of the original), which on internal evidence probably was taken from the Tonti memoir of 1684. This same source may be credited with the opening section, which details the activities along the Great Lakes that preceded the actual discovery journey.

A comparison of the styles of the two parts shows that they do not differ substantially in vocabulary, grammar, or spelling peculiarities. This fact confirms Minet's assertion that he was taking down oral accounts and explains his warning against requiring unduly close word-for-word correspondence between Nicolas's relation and Minet's version of what Nicolas and Barbier had to say. That is not to say that Nicolas did not have in his possession his original journal or a copy of it, to which he could turn to confirm dates or names of tribes, but simply that Minet may be taken at his word. The evidence suggests that, for those parts of the relation that depend on Nicolas exclusively, Minet did not merely edit a version of Nicolas's account.

There are four sketches included with the 1682 relation and repro-

---

21 If the manuscript were a clean copy, it would probably have provided more marginal space for such notes or would have made space for them by means of indentations. As such is not the case, we may safely assume that the notes were added to the preliminary draft after its completion.

22 The latter incident is told less fully in the so-called Membré relation, in John G. Shea, ed., *Discovery and Exploration of the Mississippi Valley*, p. 68.

duced in this volume. Only one of them, the drawing of the calumet, appears interlineated in the text (manuscript page 29); the rest, the map of Lake Ontario (Frontenac) at the source of the St. Lawrence River, the map of the birdfoot delta at the mouth of the Mississippi, and the drawing of a naked Indian, are presented on separate pages of the original (pages 9, 59, and 61, respectively).

The maps are of interest because of Minet's qualifications as an engineer, which extended to his mapmaking. The Lake Ontario map presumably owes its outline to an attempt to render a bird's-eye view, but the buildings shown on the map are drawn in perspective, as though the viewer were seeing them from a vantage point at the entrance to the lake from the St. Lawrence—a vista likely to be memorable. Minet's professional interest in fortifications shows up quite clearly in his rendering of Fort Frontenac as a classic four-bastioned star in the Vauban mold. The birdfoot delta map is of much greater interest, in that Minet could not possibly have seen the area it portrays (even though he was still under the impression that it was near the Texas landfall) and would have drawn from an oral account of the river's windings and the Indian tribes living along it. For all that, it is a rather accurate rendering, and one is tempted to believe that it was this map or one like it that made Iberville so angry when he could not find the branch marked "A," the existence of which Minet says was attested by Barbier and which can be taken for either the Atchafalaya River or Lafourche Bayou.

The other two drawings are of a different nature, since they portray objects or people that Minet could actually have seen. The drawing of the calumet is especially valuable, since it is one of the earliest—if not the earliest—representations of the classic "pipe of peace." Since Minet doubtless drew it under the watchful eyes of Nicolas and Barbier, who had seen them in use among the Arkansas Indians, it corresponds in almost every particular with the artifact described in the other narratives of the expedition. Finally, we have the uncompromisingly naked Indian, portrayed leaning on his longbow with a club in his hand, beads around his neck, and feather decoration in his hair. It is hard to know just how accurate this is, for we do not know how much we ourselves have censored explorers' testimonials that the Indians were in fact naked. (It seems to me that the assumption made is that this term really means partly naked or naked to the waist; if Minet is any guide, it means no such thing.) However, although the drawing is crude, it does render both the stance and the musculature of the classical male nude of the art of that day, implying that it is conventionalized to some extent. Certainly, the club in the picture is a far cry from the smaller light ones used essentially as coup sticks by the Indians of the lower Mississippi Valley.

I have discussed elsewhere why the best all-around account of the 1682 exploration of the Mississippi is the one represented as coming from Nicolas's diary.[23] Similar arguments would apply to this account by Minet, with the additional recommendation that Minet incorporates the comments, and probably the criticisms, of Barbier. It is frankly a compilation but without the fanciful or self-serving additions characteristic of other edited accounts or compilations. Since it has been shown that Minet draws also from other sources—all of them reliable witnesses—history may finally judge that his version is the best source for this journey. Yet the reader should remember that it does not record the whole story, however more complete it may be. Its apparent reliability does prompt us to use its evidence to authenticate other narratives or parts of narratives, and until there is better evidence available to the contrary, such use should be made of it after it has been examined as a primary source for the exploration; hence the value of the translation given here.

23 Galloway, "Sources."

Voyage Made from Canada Inland Going Southward during the Year 1682

By Order of Monsieur Colbert
Minister of State

MINET

[Translated by ANN LINDA
BELL and annotated by
PATRICIA GALLOWAY]

Seeing the little agreement that there was between what Mons. de la Salle was saying and what Father Zénobe [Membré],[1] Récollet, and the Sieurs Barbier and [Nicolas] de La Salle (the latter is a young boy who is not related to Mons. de La Salle) were saying on their side about the exploration of this River Colbert,[2] and not having much to do in the ship, I wrote every day what one and the other told me. As I saw that Sieur Barbier and the young de La Salle agreed enough in all they said, joined to their youth and their air of frankness, I took them aside and [they] dictated the following to me.

[Signed] Minet

Voyages in North America

Monsieur de La Salle believed, according to the testimony of the Iroquois, that he had found a passage to go to China. They told him that from their home south of Lake Frontenac [Ontario] there was a river

---

1 Father Zénobe Membré, Franciscan Recollect who served as expedition chaplain in 1682, returned to France, then rejoined La Salle for the 1685 expedition. He was one of the small garrison left at Fort Saint-Louis of Texas when La Salle last departed in 1687, and was killed in the final massacre. See Marion A. Habig, *The Franciscan Père Marquette: A Critical Biography of Father Zénobe Membré, O.F.M., La Salle's Chaplain and Missionary Companion*, for his life and his role in La Salle's expeditions.
2 So named, before La Salle's discovery, for the French minister of finance, Jean-Baptiste Colbert.

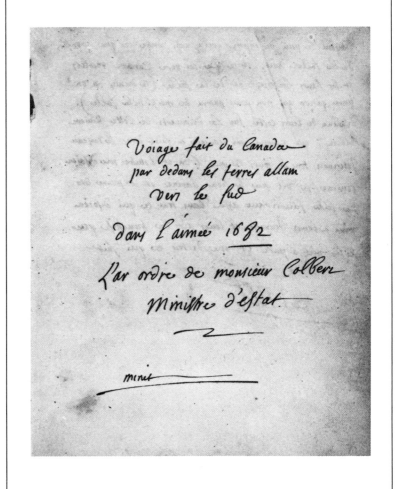

PLATE 2. Title page of Minet's relation of La Salle's 1682 Mississippi River exploration.
(Courtesy of the Public Archives of Canada)

called Ouabache [Ohio]. He descended this river, which flows west and makes its way into another large river by which they [the Iroquois] went to war against some savages who lived near a nation with customs exactly like ours. He formed a company to go there.[3] When they were among the Iroquois interrogating the elders, they told them that this river flowed west and that afterward the river to which it made its way went southeast and that [by it] they went through the lands to the east to make war against the nations who lived near another nation made just like us. He [La Salle] knew by the description that it was the Spaniards of Florida.

Sometime afterward, having satisfied himself and M. le Comte de Frontenac with Fort Frontenac, situated on a lake that bears the same name, [La Salle] came to France to ask permission to trade in furs in the direction of his fort and to go and make a settlement on the Ilinois [River], even though he had never yet been there, knowing only that it was a good country by the report of the Canadians who go there to trade and of one named M. Joliet [[and two Jesuits]] who first discovered it.[4] Monsieur Colbert granted it to him and asked him if he might not find the mouth of the rivers that are in that direction and which seem to flow south. He offered to find them and left for that purpose from Paris on the 16th of June of the year 1677 [1678], accompanied by Messieurs de Tonty, Le Page, Timbalier, [Nicolas] de La Salle, de La Motte, Mousignac, and six other volunteers and hired men with four women.[5] They embarked at La Rochelle August 6 of the same year on the ship named *St. Honoré,* accompanied by thirty-two other vessels, all for the islands of Newfoundland and Canada. They arrived at the St. Lawrence River at Quebec on September 7. They stayed eight days in

3 Reference is to the Dollier-Gallinée expedition of 1669, from which La Salle separated to explore the Allegheny and Ohio rivers as far as present-day Louisville, Kentucky.

4 Louis Jolliet and Father Jacques Marquette are generally credited with the French rediscovery of the Mississippi in 1673. The second Jesuit mentioned here may be Father Claude Allouez, who is credited by John Gilmary Shea (*Discovery and Exploration of the Mississippi Valley,* p. xxv) with reaching the headwaters in 1670. The Marquette-Jolliet exploration had established that the Mississippi flowed south and emptied into the Gulf of Mexico but had not ventured beyond the Arkansas River.

5 La Salle had gone to France in 1677 to obtain a patent to undertake the full exploration of the Mississippi. According to the Tonti account of 1684, which includes a list of those actually on the Mississippi expedition (Pierre Margry, ed., *Découvertes et établissements des français dans l'ouest et dans le sud de l'Amérique septentrionale,* I, 594–95), Tonti himself and Nicolas were the only ones named here who participated in the trip.

Quebec, where Monsieur de La Salle had a quarrel with a man named Monsieur de St. Michel [[This St. Michel [two words illegible] lieutenant on the king's ship]] over some bundles of merchandise. Monsieur de Tonty separated them.

He sent his people ahead to Monreal [*sic*] in a boat, and he remained some time longer there [at Quebec]. Monreal is an island in the St. Lawrence River 60 leagues above Quebec, which is well populated. From there they embarked in small canoes made of birch bark for Fort Frontenac, which is 60 leagues from this island. The St. Lawrence River from Monreal to his fort has five waterfalls, which are called portages because to arrive at these places one must carry the canoes on one's back to go past the falls on ascending, but descending it is not the same [because] one does not make any portages; they adroitly guide their canoes across the falls, which have a 15- to 16-foot slope over 30 fathoms' length. At the end of the last portage they met a boat that Sieur de La Forest was sending to M. de La Salle. [[It was he who commanded Fort Frontenac as major.]] It was at a place called La Galette, which is a cul-de-sac. All the canoes were filled with flour, which they were sending to his fort.[6]

He arrived fifteen days afterward, at the beginning of the month of November of the year 1677 [1678] with the merchandise, which was cauldrons, guns, axes, knives, and other hardware, as well as gunpowder and lead. As soon as he was at his fort he sent a man named Perrer to Quinté[7] with some of the merchandise to spend the winter so that with the arrival of the thaw he could go to the Ataouais [Ottawas] to trade for furs.

Spring having arrived, Mons. de La Salle left to go to Niagara, a waterfall from the outlet of Lake Erie that falls from a height of 500 fathoms and has a width of a quarter of a league, and which one hears from 30 leagues away, as well as a vapor that one sees. [[This vapor is the great movement of air that this fall causes and takes with it the lightest parts of the water.]] At this place he built a fort of posts to enclose the

6 La Galette appears on Hugues Randin's "Carte de l'Amérique septentrionale depuis l'embouchure de la Rivière St. Laurens jusques an Sein Mexique, 1674–1681" (dated prior to 1681) halfway between the confluence of the Ottawa and St. Lawrence rivers and Lake Ontario. Fort Frontenac was built in 1672 on the north side of Lake Ontario and was granted La Salle to serve as an anchor post for his Indian trade.

7 Quinté apparently refers to a bay on the northern shore of Lake Ontario, west of Fort Frontenac, labeled Kenté on the Delisle maps of 1703 and 1718. A Sulpician mission station had been established there in 1668 (Justin Winsor, *Cartier to Frontenac*, p. 214).

warehouse he had built there for the purpose of trade, with a boat that he bought to navigate on Lake Erie and the lakes of the Hurons and the Ilinois so as to trade with the Hurons, the Ataouais, the Sauteurs, the Poutouatami, the Miami, and the Ilinois, who live along these lakes.[8] It took a year [[1678]] to build this fort, its warehouse, and the boat.

During that time he had sent for trade on all sides, and Sieur La Forest sent all his furs to Monreal as soon as they arrived. [La Salle's] older brother, a priest of the Seminary of St. Sulpice, was in Monreal at that time. Either he owed him some money or they had made a deal together. As principal creditor, he seized all the furs, sold them, received the sum of 15 to 20 thousand pounds, and returned to France.[9]

As for [La Salle], as soon as the boat was ready, he embarked in it and went to the Michelimaquina villages of the Ataouais and the Hurons, where the Jesuits are established.[10] From there he went to the Poutouatami, where he made an alliance with them, danced the calumet [[I will explain in another place what it means to dance the calumet]],

8   The location of the tribes mentioned had by this date already been disturbed by the effects of European colonization and the Iroquois wars. The Hurons, an Algonkin tribe located south of Lake Huron before their dispersal by the Iroquois in the late 1640s, were found only in scattered remnants by 1678. The Algonkin Ottawas lived north and west of the Hurons and on Manitoulin Island in Georgian Bay (Frederick Webb Hodge, *Handbook of American Indians North of Mexico*, II, 169). Sauteurs ("jumpers") is the French name for the Chippewas, an Algonkin group allied with the Ottawas and Potowatomis and settled around Sault Ste. Marie and Lake Superior. The Potowatomis were an Illinois tribe located around Green Bay. The Miamis, another Illinois tribe, were in two locations, with the Potowatomis around Green Bay, Chicago, and the southern end of Lake Michigan. The Algonkin-speaking Illinois proper, composed of the Cahokias, Kaskaskias, Michigameas, Moingwenas, Peorias, and Tamaroas, had been driven west of the Mississippi by mid-century, but by 1700 they had returned to control the Illinois country proper, bounded by the Mississippi and the Wabash/Ohio. See Wayne C. Temple, *Indian Villages of the Illinois Country,* part 2, passim.
9   La Salle's older brother, the Abbé Jean Cavelier, had preceded him in Canada by a year. He served as curate in Montreal, handled some of La Salle's business affairs, and advanced him capital. On leaving for France in 1679, the abbé went to court to collect what his brother owed him—more than the value of all the peltries that La Salle had shipped to Montreal. For full details, see Jean Delanglez, *The Journal of Jean Cavelier: The Account of a Survivor of La Salle's Texas Expedition,* pp. 27–31.
10 According to contemporary maps (e.g., the Jesuit map of 1671, BN, Ge DD 2987-8695), the Jesuit mission Saint-Ignace was founded by Father Marquette in 1671 for refugee Hurons on the north side of the Straits of Mackinack, linking Lakes Huron and Michigan. Marquette was buried there in 1677. The mission name is recalled today in the town of St. Ignace, Michigan.

and gave them a quantity of furs as presents. The boat being loaded with beaver, otter, and other valuable pelts, he sent it back to Niagara and went to the Miamis. He wanted to make another settlement in that region and build a boat, but that did not succeed.

From there he went to the Ilinois. He negotiated peace with them. He built there a sort of fort with some posts and palisades and had a boat started, left Monsieur Tonty to command the said fort, and three Récollet priests—of whom he sent Father Louis [Hennepin] to the Siou, where an inhabitant of Canada named Mons. du Lud [du Lhut] had been previously[11]—and returned across country to his fort at Niagara. He learned there that the boat he had sent was lost on the way, along with all the merchandise, and said out loud that it was his enemies the Jesuits who had caused him the loss.[12] And to avenge this he proposed to two Canadians named Barbier and Andrenon that they go to Michelimaquina to trade furs with the savages, and, when they had them, ask the fathers to stow away their merchandise and give them to their people when they would go to Quebec. [He said] that he would return to Monreal at the time that the fathers would send them and that he would surprise them, making it evident how these fathers traded illicitly. But this did not succeed.

He left there in a canoe and went to Fort Frontenac. He had the land cleared and sowed and repaired his fort, which is a square of 50 fathoms per side, three-quarters made of masonry, three feet thick and 12 to 16 feet high, and the rest of posts. Inside there is a very handsome warehouse 20 by 25 fathoms in length, a guardhouse, a blacksmith shop, a house for the officers, a well, and another enclosed part that serves as a barnyard. There is a moat 20 feet wide all around. There is a Récollet monastery adjoining, a dwelling for five French families, and a village of Iroquois.

In early spring he had news that some ten of the people he had left at the Ilinois with Monsieur Tonty had deserted and had passed through Niagara, broken into the warehouse, and stolen the contents.

---

11 In early spring, 1860, La Salle sent Michel Accau, Antoine Angel *dit* Picard du Gay, and Hennepin to explore southward along the Illinois River. Reaching the mouth and turning up the Mississippi, they met a party of Sioux, who took them prisoner. Several months later they were rescued by the explorer Daniel Greysolon du Lhut and taken to Michilimackinac on Mackinack Island at the straits. Concerning Hennepin's writings on this journey, see Armand Louant, *Le cas du pére Louis Hennepin, récollet.*

12 The enmity often and openly expressed by La Salle toward the Jesuits probably was due in part to the fact that the Jesuit missions in Canada siphoned off much of the Indian trade. See Paul Chrisler Phillips, *The Fur Trade,* I, 107.

He left with people from his fort for the place where one must necessarily pass. He found them in the canoes as they were descending. He went to seize them, but when he saw that they took up their arms and were making ready to defend themselves, he was obliged to retreat. Night having come, he sent his men above and below where they had to pass. They kept watch from the trees, which leaned over the river. They did not fail to pass, and he shot at them. Two were killed, one named Bois d'Ardenne, whom he had brought from France as secretary; the other was a carpenter. They took two others whom he kept four months as prisoners in his fort.

While he was at Fort Frontenac many things happened at the Ilinois.[13] M. de Tonty, as we said, had stayed among them with the two priests, Gabriel [de La Ribourde] and Zénobe [Membré], in this fort, which the savages had wanted us to make at a place named Pimiteouy.[14] The Iroquois came to make war on this nation. Since they have guns, and they call themselves real men, they are enemies of almost all the nations and go as far as six hundred leagues to fight. To begin with, the Ilinois, who knew that they were near, sent their women, children, and aged in canoes down the river; yet, while they were retreating, they upbraided M. de Tonty, saying that it was he who had made them come. Meanwhile, the Iroquois approached and fired several gunshots while making the *saçacoye,* which is their war cry, and the Ilinois shot their arrows. Realizing that they were in earnest, Sieur de Tonty went right through the gunfire to talk to them and try to dissuade them from making war. But, not recognizing him or not wanting to recognize him as French, they fired many gunshots at him, which luckily did not strike him. And he went to them and, when he met them, a warrior took his knife and sank it into his [Tonty's] breast. The chiefs, recognizing him as a Frenchman, embraced him and covered him, telling him to excuse them, that it was the young men who had taken him for an Ilinois, that they would close the wound. At the same time they dressed it and made him a present of beavers, which he rejected, saying that if they wanted to make war with the Ilinois, who were their allies, he had nothing to do with their presents. He returned to find the Ilinois, whom he embraced. They started the combat again, always shooting from far away. During

13 The following account of Tonti's activities, which emphasizes his heroism, is almost certainly taken from his 1684 eyewitness account of these events, which it follows point for point (in Margry, *Découvertes,* I, 573–615).

14 Lake Pimiteouy or Peoria on the Illinois River, where the Peoria Indians (Ilinois) were living in 1679, when La Salle built Fort Crèvecoeur near their village.

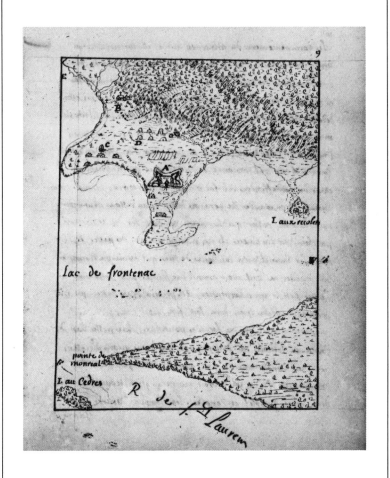

PLATE 3. Minet's map of the Fort Frontenac area, on the north shore
of Lake Superior, and its environs, with his description and key (facing page). (Courtesy of the Public Archives of Canada)

8

de serrer leurs marchandises et de les donner et de les
donner a leurs gens quand ils iroient a quebec. que
luy se rendroit a monreal dans le temps que les
peres s'inuoiroient qui les fairoient surprendre faisant
voir comme ces peres trafics mais la chose ne reusit
pas .

Il parti dela dans vn canot, et s'enfu au fort de
frontenac, il fu defricher des terres, semer, et raccom
moda son fort . qui est vn quarré de 50. Thoises de
costé, il y a les trois quars fait de massonnerie de
trois pieds d'espesseur, de hauteur depuis 12. Jusqua six.
et le reste de pieux, il y a dedans vn magazin
... vn corps
de garde, vne forge, vne maison pour les officiers,
vn puis, et vn autre endroit ... basse cour.
il y a des fosses tout au tour large de 20 pieds . il
y a vn couuent de recolets tout contre, vn habitations
de cinq familles de françois, et vn vilage d'Iroquois

A. fort de frontenac .   E. costé du lac de
B. les recolets   frontenac
c. habitations françoises   F. costé ou commence
D. vilages d'Iroquois   la fleuue de S.t Laurens
                                        G. fontaine

Minet's description and key to his map of the Fort Frontenac area.

A. Fort Frontenac   D. Shore of Lake Frontenac
B. The Récollets   E. Shore where the St. Lawrence
C. French dwellings   River begins
D. Villages of the Iroquois   G. Spring

this combat, which lasted until night, one Ilinois was killed and five Iroquois were wounded. Around ten o'clock at night, seeing that their women and children had gone down to the Misycipy [Mississippi] River, they decided to go join them there. The Iroquois, not finding them the next day, went after them overland by the route they thought was the shortest, to overtake them. Instead of the men, a hundred leagues away they found the women and children. Imagine their joy when they saw the wherewithal to feast sumptuously. They returned to their country, bringing with them nine hundred, as many elderly as women and children, every day feasting on the ones who could not walk and breaking the heads of the old men they did not find appetizing. It is thought that they ate five hundred of them on the way and some four hundred remained when they got home.[15] They burned some and made the rest slaves. I forgot to say that on their return they passed by way of the Ilinois, where they burned all their corn and set fire everywhere.

Monsieur de Tonty, seeing himself alone with those two priests and a few other Frenchmen in a large burned-out land, the country ruined and abandoned, they all returned to the fort, which is below the villages of the Ilinois where the battle had taken place.[16] There they held council, and they all deemed it necessary to return, having nothing to live on. They embarked in a canoe—seven that they were, with very little corn and powder—and took the road to Michelimaquina, on the north shore of the lake of the Ilinois. They slept four leagues from the fort and camped in a region where they thought they could find game. Father Gabriel moved apart before going to bed to recite his breviary, but there has been no news of him since. They ran in all directions looking for him; they shot many times; they called. Seeing that there was no way to find him, they suspected that some Iroquois or Ilinois had killed him.[17] The next day, around nine or 10 o'clock, food having run out, they left

15 Cannibalism was practiced among the Iroquois and other northeastern tribes but was usually confined to the ceremonial context: the heart and blood of a captive enemy who had died well following torture were consumed to absorb the courage of the parts eaten (see Cornelius Jaenen, *Friend and Foe*, p. 142–48). Minet refers to an incident in which the Iroquois were forced to retreat ignominiously with a large number of prisoners. The weight of evidence on attitudes toward cannibalism suggests that they would not have eaten prisoners in the manner described except in extreme circumstances.

16 Fort Saint-Louis of the Illinois, at Starved Rock on the Illinois River.

17 Father Gabriel de La Ribourde, in his seventieth year, was killed on September 9, 1680, by a Kickapoo party near the Illinois/Kankakee confluence (Temple, *Indian Villages*, part 2, p. 158); Isaac Joslin Cox, ed., *The Journeys of Réné Robert Cavelier, Sieur de La Salle*, I, 123–24n.

there and went to the portage of Chicagou.[18] They took days to go through it—it is a league and a half in length—to enter the lake where, after having navigated thirty leagues, bad weather overtook them. They lost their canoe, but they saved the rest of their corn and several beavers they had. He [Tonti] left Sieur de Boisrondel to take care of their beaver skins, and they took off across country to reach a village of the Poutouatamy, which was 20 leagues from there on the banks of the same lake. Since they did not know the roads, they passed through a forest of firs, where they got lost. They continued to wander around in the woods for 50 days. Having no more food, they were forced to eat grass and acorns. In the end, finding the savages' trail, they followed it and found some huts of Poutouatamy who had left their villages to hunt. They gave them some of what they had and afterward brought them to their dwellings. The Jesuits are established in this village.[19] They received them graciously, dressed them, fed them, and gave them good beds to rest on. Seeing themselves so well treated, they decided to spend the winter with them. These good priests also gave them a canoe to go back to their man and their beavers.

Spring having come, Monsieur de La Salle made them load what there was of merchandise in Fort Frontenac into a boat. They embarked and left for Niagara to a region called Le Cap Enragé.[20] A great storm overtook them. The boat was wrecked against the shore. They saved the merchandise. There was a village of Iroquois directly opposite the cape. He borrowed their boats, and the women helped him unload and reload the merchandise, which was brought to Niagara. From there he went in the canoes to Michelimaquina to pick up the people he had sent there to trade, brought with him 15 or 16 to join Mons. de Tonty and go on to make the exploration, but they deserted him on the way, [and] there were only nine when they arrived at the Ilinois, where they saw the unburied bodies, the country and the cabins burned. This upset him very much and even more so when, on descending to his fort, he found no one there. Half of the posts were knocked down, and the boat he had had started before he left was almost in the same state in which he had left it. Looking everywhere, he saw written on the trunk of a tree where

---

18 The Chicagou portage linked the southern end of Lake Michigan with the Illinois River via the Chicago River headwaters.

19 The Jesuit mission to the Potowatomis, founded in 1669 by Father Claude Allouez, was on the southern end of Green Bay.

20 Le Cap Enragé (the Mad Cape) is not shown on maps of the Great Lakes area; it seems to have been at the western end of Lake Ontario.

the bark had been removed, "We have withdrawn." He believed that M. de Tonty and the rest of his people had been made slaves or killed.

He returned to the village farther up since there were some ears of corn that had not been burned. They were ripe, so he had them harvested. Winter approaching, he saw that it would be necessary to spend the winter there, so he had them gather everything they could of foodstuffs.

Some Ilinois who had taken refuge in the woods came to gather the corn. He learned from them about their defeats and that the warriors had gone 150 leagues downriver to go back up another which was called the Missouris[21] from the name of a nation who lives on this river and who are their allies, and went upstream to go to war with the Pana[22] to take their women and children to replace those taken from them by the Iroquois. He told them that he had come to dry their tears and rekindle the fire of their villages, that they should go tell the others to return, that he would return with some Frenchmen, and arms and that together they would extinguish all the fires of the Iroquois [[Manner of Speaking]].

Spring having come, the Ilinois did not fail to go find their comrades. They found them with the Pana, whom they had defeated and whose women and children they had taken. This is a nation that is not warlike, besides being surprised. From there they went toward their lake, prowling around for two years [*sic*] from one side to the other. He [La Salle] took the path to Michelimaquina. Not having had news of M. de Tonty, he passed on to the Miamis,[23] where he met two canoes of Ouataouais who were coming that way to hunt. He asked them for news of his people. They told him that they had wintered at Poutouatamy. Knowing that, he left with joy and haste for Michelimaquina and at once sent a canoe to get them. After having thanked the Jesuit fathers for the linens, clothes, and good food, he [Tonti] went to meet Monsieur de la Salle. When they had arrived, he sent off three canoes

21 "Missouri" is an Algonkin (Illinois) name for a Chiwere Sioux tribe that referred to itself as the Niutachi. Though living on the Missouri as far north as the Platte (see Jacques Marquette, Map of 1673), they had originally lived around Green Bay (Hodge, *Handbook,* I, 911).

22 The Pana mentioned here are the Pawnees, a Caddoan group living on the Platte River. They had had contacts with the Spaniards since Coronado's time (Hodge, *Handbook,* II, 214).

23 The Miamis, originally an Illinois group, were located in two places at this time: south and east of the southern end of Lake Michigan, where they controlled portages to the Kankakee and Wabash rivers, and in the vicinity of Green Bay. It would seem that the former location is at issue here. See Temple, *Indian Villages,* part 2, 58.

with people to go trade with the Miamis and orders to wait for him there. He, the priests, and M. de Tonty left together, taking the path to Fort Frontenac. When they were at the portage of Tchiagon [near the fort], he left them there to wait for him at an Iroquois village, which gives this portage its name, and he went on to his fort to fetch people and merchandise for making the exploration. He remained a week at this fort and went secretly to Monreal to get merchandise, not wanting to be recognized because of the affair with his brother, for his enemies had put a number of spies in the country to try to nab him if he came to Monreal. He took only six days to go and return. He sent merchandise ahead, hiding the powder and lead in fabrics because the Iroquois did not want any brought to their enemies, with a letter to Mons. de Tonty to go in advance and wait for him at the Miamis. On arriving at the village named Tchiagon, he gave the chief a present of some axes so that the youths would help him carry the merchandise to the other side of the portage. At the same time he sent some of his men to fetch some canoes that he had left in the rushes when he passed. He embarked with his merchandise and his people on a small river that empties into Lake Taronteau [24] and from there down another small river, which has six portages and which empties into Lake Huron. Since it was not possible to carry much provision of food in these canoes during the voyage, they thought they would all starve to death without their dogs, which were a great help to them. On Lake Huron they found a village of Nepisingue[25] who were camped on the small islands on some rocks. They went to them to barter merchandise for food, which they refused to do. They were obliged to go 50 leagues from there to a village of the Ataouois named Manitoualin, who live on an island 30 leagues long.[26] They stayed there six days and traded much corn, or wheat of the Indies [*mays ou bled d'Inde*].

From there they went to Michelimaquina, which is 80 leagues from

24 Minet, on his "Carte de la Louisiane" (AN, Service Hydrographique C 4044−4), shows Lake Taronteau north of Lake Ontario; it is the lake now known as Lake Simcoe, directly north of Toronto and connected by streams to the southeastern end of Georgian Bay.
25 The Algonkin Nipissing Indians lived around a lake named for them, northeast of and connected to Georgian Bay.
26 The Ottawa village of Manitoualin, marked on some maps (e.g., Coronelli, *America settentrionale colle nuoue scoperte fin all' anno 1688,* plates IX, X, in Sara Jones Tucker, *Indian Villages of the Illinois Country,* part 1) as a "place of assembly" for the Indians, was on the island between northern Lake Huron and Georgian Bay. The "Parkman No. 4" map (Harvard University Library), c. 1670, has a cross marking the spot on the northwestern end of the island.

this village. He [La Salle] went to the Jesuits. They stayed there two weeks and always ate with them. Since the freezes were approaching, he bought some corn and canoes, his being worn out. There he obtained the five Loups[27] with their women, whom he brought with him. This is a nation that lives near the English. He left with six canoes, went onto the lake of the Ilinois, and went to the Miamis. He found M. de Tonty and the rest of his people, who were starving to death. Having dispersed around in different directions to hunt, they also found there a band of Loups, whom he asked to come with him to make the discovery. They all accepted the proposition in consideration of 100 beavers each at the end of the trip, but they would give the French half of all the game they would take on the way.

Here is how Mons. de La Salle set out to make the discovery with 18 savages, seven of their women, two small children and twenty-four Frenchmen. Since the portage of Teatequi[28] is two leagues long and very tiring, he sent his people to the portage of Chicagou, and he remained in this area where he buried the merchandise that he decided not to carry and came on foot to meet his people at the Chicagou River. Since it was frozen, the Frenchmen carried the canoes. The savages broke theirs up. Sleds were made to carry the merchandise the space of 40 leagues, as far as the fort that had been made for the Ilinois, named Pimiteouy, where we found the river not frozen.[29] We continued the trip as far as the place where the Ilinois River empties into the Micicypi. We stayed there twelve days because of the continual rains. The savages made themselves other canoes, and, since this river is very large, it carries a large quantity of ice floes, it being the end of December of the year 1681. A misfortune befell M. de La Salle, which one may call great since he had only one compass to make the discovery; it broke in this

27 The French applied the name "wolves" to the Mahican Indians, an Algonkin group living on the upper Hudson River (Hodge, *Handbook,* I, 786). Some of them moved in the 1720s to join the Miamis in Indiana. Other sources indicate that some Abnakis, whose homeland was Maine, were included in the group.

28 A clue to the identity of the Teatequi portage is found on a 1778 map by Thomas Hutchins ("A New Map of the Western Parts of Virginia, Pennsylvania, Maryland, and North Carolina") which shows the Kankakee River as the Theakiki. It would be the St. Johns/Kankakee portage.

29 At this point the narrative switches to first person; this may seem misleading, since the pronoun most frequently translated as "we" is "*on,*" as previously. The narrative also begins here its strong dependence on the account of Nicolas de La Salle, which is phrased the same way.

place.[30] Thus, during the whole voyage, we oriented ourselves with the sun. He took the latitude before leaving this area, with an astrolabe seven inches long, which he had acquired in Monreal. Latitude of 37° was found.[31]

We left in the morning and camped six leagues from there on the west side of the place where the Misourits [Missouri] River empties into the Micicypy River (but as all the names mean large river in the language of the savages or the name of a nation we know on the banks of these rivers, we will call it by the name M. de La Salle gave it, the Colbert River. For, as each small nation speaks a different language, it has different names that always mean the same thing: large river). Of that river where live the Misourits and the Panas we will speak later. Here we will simply say that it is very wide and deep and rapid and so muddy that it is unbelievable. Only this makes the Colbert River as muddy as it is.

The next day, after having again made six leagues, always descending, being near an island, we saw a village to the left. We went there but found no one, the inhabitants having gone hunting. This nation is called the Tamaroa.[32] We left them some glass beads and some knives hung on a rod to let them know that it was their friends who had passed their way. We went yet another two leagues that day. We camped on the right bank. Food becoming scarce, we stayed there two days to hunt. We killed seven buffalo [*boeufs*], four deer, and many turkey cocks, swans, and bustards.[33] The land is flat, elevated in some areas by small hills. The river is lined with large trees; and the area is full of walnut trees, oaks, elms, plum trees, etc., and everywhere tall grass the height of a man, very first-class.

The third day we left. After having traveled 10 leagues, we camped to the left in a flat area that floods. (It is to be noted that during the thaw all this land inundates this way. When we say a flat land, we mean

30 The breaking of La Salle's compass was doubtless the original source of his confusion in his thinking about where he was during and after the 1682 expedition. That his confusion was great can be ascertained from the so-called Chucagoa fragment (Margry, *Découvertes*, II, 196–203).
31 The latitude given from the mouth of the Illinois River is about 2° in error; 37° approximates the mouth of the Ohio River. This and other such miscalculations on the journey compounded La Salle's confusion.
32 For the expedition's contact with the Tamaroas at this site, a little below present-day St. Louis, on the return trip, see pp. 62–63.
33 The French word *outarde*, properly the European bustard, was applied by the Canadian French to the Canada goose (Antoine Simon Le Page du Pratz, *Histoire de la Louisiane française*, II, 113).

it is a country that floods, since it must be very elevated for it not to be inundated, and it is a silty clay [[It overflows from time to time like the Nile]] that spills over the whole land, this river being thick enough to cut with a knife.)

The next day we traveled fifteen leagues. We camped to the left in a place where the river is very narrow because of the elevated lands as it passes in this region between two mountains or rocks with another very high rock in the middle of the river, which makes an island. The whole [area is] full of large pines. We stayed there three days to hunt. We killed some bears and some deer, having found the inland country beautiful.

On the 4th day we left. We traveled fourteen leagues following a line of mountains on the right, and on the left a flat land that floods [and which is] full of cane and reeds. The next day we traveled eleven leagues more. That night we passed in front of the Houabache [Wabash] River, which they call the Choucagoua [actually the Ohio]. This river, part of which comes from the direction of the Iroquois, is beautiful, clear, large, and deep. (This is the river that made M. de la Salle believe that we could go that way to the Pacific Ocean.) [34] We camped one league below it.

The next day we left. After having gone six leagues, we came upon some hills on the left that rise as they get farther from the river. One could see in the ravines that the soil was a beautiful red color. We camped 5 leagues from there on the left after having passed three big islands full of trees in a flat land. Hunger pressing us onward, we made 20 leagues the next day to get to the hills to hunt. We camped on the left in a large bay in front of an island. Rain and wind overtook us. We were forced to stay there one day. We left on the second. M. de Tonty's canoe split, passing over a tree that could not be seen. This river having visibility only two inches deep, one could not see the bottom. We spent some time repairing it. Meanwhile, we were fasting. The food was all gone. After having traveled about 8 leagues, we came to some hills that rose on the left. We camped there. The savages went hunting. They killed two deer and two bears and said that the hills followed the river and that it would be better to hunt on this side. The next day we went

34 It was La Salle's information obtained from the Indians, not his exploration of the Ohio in 1669–70, that led him to believe that there might be a river route to the Pacific. See Nicolas de La Salle in Margry, *Découvertes,* I, 551. The French had not yet given up on such a route—perhaps via the Missouri River or Great Lakes—by 1682, but Marquette and Jolliet had demonstrated that it was not the Mississippi.

there after having rowed 5 leagues. First we went to hunt. We killed seven deer, which did the whole crew much good. The next day M. de La Salle's gunsmith [Pierre Prudhomme] got lost during the hunt. We sent the Loups to look for him. They went five leagues around without finding him, but they did find human tracks. They thought he had been captured or killed. That night we shot several times into the air. They again went to look for him in the country, which is nothing but hills and thick woods. The Loups came upon a savage hut whose inhabitants fled. They took from it what was good to eat and carried it to M. de La Salle with two blankets made of skins of deer, bears, and cats, with which he might cover himself. Seeing that his gunsmith could not be found and that the country was inhabited, he had an entrenchment made. He sent M. de Tonty with a canoe downriver to see if from the bank there might be news of him. The Sieur Barbier, while looking for him, found two savages who made as if they would flee. Barbier threw his gun on the ground, giving them a sign of peace. They approached. He pulled out a pistol from behind him and brought them by force to M. de La Salle, who took them with him.[35] Leaving the entrenchment, we camped three leagues lower, still on the left, where M. de Tonty met him without news of his man. We gave presents to the two savages. We made them understand the best we could that we had lost a man. We sent one of them to the village to ask them to give back this man [two words illegible]. We tried to find out the name of this nation. The savages answered when we made signs, "Chicacha." We believed that it was their name, and we called them Chicacha.[36] We waited ten days for news of our Frenchman. We did not hope for him any longer. We had killed much game and were preparing to leave when from far away we saw our gunsmith coming on two pieces of wood that he had bound together and let float with the current. From what he said, he had not eaten for eight days.

The next day M. de Tonty started ahead and waited for M. de La

35 This version of Barbier's capture of the Chickasaws, being more complete than others, must have come from Barbier himself. See John Stubbs, "The Chickasaw Contact with the La Salle Expedition of 1682," in Patricia Galloway, ed. *La Salle and His Legacy: Frenchmen and Indians in the Lower Mississippi Valley*, pp. 41–48.

36 The Chicachas or Chickasaws were a Muskogean tribe living—at least from Soto's time—in northern Mississippi. Although they ranged north as far as Illinois, their homeland was concentrated around the Tupelo/Pontotoc area. Their language was almost identical to that of the Choctaw, with whom they had many other affinities.

Salle at a little river we called Chicacha,[37] where the country is hilly and full of mulberry trees, walnut trees, laurels, and oaks. We joined up again and slept. The next day, 12 leagues from there on the right, there are some hills where we stayed one day to hunt. We told the Chicacha to go away, but he did not wish to. The day after that we camped 8 leagues from there to the right on flat land, not being able to go very far because of the rains. The next day we left during a big fog. The canoes could not be seen. After having gone about three leagues, we called to each other. There was a village of savages on the right. Hearing the cries they made the *saçacoie* and sent their women and children outside, thinking that it was their enemies. [[*Saçacoie* [is] a war cry [made] by clapping the flat of the hand against the mouth while shouting.]] [38]

We crossed in the canoes to the left at a sandy point. We entrenched ourselves the best we could with some small pieces of aspen wood [*bois de tremble*: probably cottonwood], which we cut and made into palisades. The fog lifted, and we saw a canoe of savages coming toward us. As soon as they were within bowshot, they shot one. If we had shot another at them also, they would have taken that for a sign that we were coming to make war with them. But, seeing that we did not shoot at them, they went back to say that we were men of peace. Six of them came back without arms with the peace pipe [*calumet du paix*], making signs for us to come to their dwellings. They offered the pipe to M. de la Salle and to all who were around him, always asking that we embark. The first thing they did when we arrived at their dwelling was to make a feast of corn for the whole group. The next day they [[the warriors and youths]] danced the calumet.[39] This is an assembly of everyone in the square. The warriors put their presents on rods as when one wishes to dry clothes. They brought two large calumets decorated with feathers of all colors and a large quantity of the hair of their enemies. They put all that in the hands of their chiefs, who are seated on the ground ranged around the square. [[The chiefs are the older people.]] They all have

---

37 The river here referred to as Chicacha, probably near present-day Memphis, may have been either the Wolf or the Margot. As was often the case, the French named it for the tribe to whose dwelling it supposedly led.

38 *Saçacoie* is one of several variant onomatopoetic renderings of the sound of the war cry used by the tribes of the lower Mississippi. Compare *sasacouest* in Tonti's 1682 letter (Habig, The *Franciscan Père Marquette,* p. 217).

39 The calumet ceremony, a precontact phenomenon, was used in several forms all over North America for cementing trade and other alliances. Anthropologists place its origin in the southwestern plains. See Donald J. Blakeslee, "Origin and Spread of the Calumet Ceremony," *American Antiquity,* 46 (1981): 759–68.

gourds full of small pebbles and drums, which are pots of clay. They begin a song, which they accompany with the noise of their instruments. While dancing, the warriors who have done great deeds hit a post with their tomahawks and tell of the great deeds they have done. If there are any in the company who know them to be lying, they take a skin and go wipe the post while apologizing to it for [its] having received some lying blows, and wipe off the untruth in a mourning style. Meanwhile, the chiefs, one after the other, smoked the calumet, and each one presented it to M. de la Salle and to all in the company. After he took it, they placed him in the center of the square, dancing all around him to the tune of the instruments and songs, each one putting on his body his present, which was skins of buffalo that have wool like our sheep in Europe. If the Frenchmen had not gradually taken away these skins, he would have smothered under their presents. He in turn presened them with gifts of axes, knives, and glass beads. We learned that there were four villages, which were called Accanseas [Arkansas] [40] by an Ilinois slave who was with them. At the end of three days, we spoke of leaving. They again presented us with chickens, which they have in great numbers, and some corn and dried fruits such as prunes, medlars, and raisins. For a beverage they crush the grapes in water and drink that.

We left, after having planted a post and raised the king's arms. This country is a little elevated, full of very large trees and good soil. Although it was the month of March, this country had healthy air. The trees were in bloom, especially the peach trees. [41] They gave us two of their warriors to conduct us by the shortest way to the home of their allies. I forgot to say that they presented M. de la Salle with a young slave of a nation named Mosopelea [42] and with a Chicacha woman.

40 This French name for the Quapaws (Dhegiha Sioux) corresponds to that given them by the Illinois. They apparently had moved to the Arkansas River vicinity from the Ohio region about the time of the Soto expedition and were designated "Pacaha" by the Spaniards. The Quapaws seem to have been the bearers of a Late Mississippian, mound-building culture, which had been diluted prior to French contact (Philip Phillips, James A. Ford, and James A. Griffin, *Archaeological Survey in the Lower Mississippi Alluvial Valley, 1940–1947*, pp. 429–31).

41 Peach trees, not native to this area, may have come through the Indians' western trade network from the Spaniards.

42 Minet's "Carte de la Louisiane" shows the Ohio River south of Lake Erie as "ancient country of the Mozopelea," but according to Marquette, Map of 1673–74, they were found on the east bank of the Mississippi south of the Ohio, possibly in Tennessee. Tonti's 1684 relation explains that the Mosopeleas had settled with the Taensas after being driven from this latter place (Margry, *Découvertes*, I, 610).

PLATE 4. Minet's drawing of a calumet (peace pipe). (Courtesy of the Public Archives of Canada)

We left at eight o'clock in the morning. After having made six leagues, we passed in front of one of their villages, but they had all gone hunting. We traveled four more leagues, and arrived at another of their villages where we slept, which is on the banks of a large river, named by their name, which comes from the west. It appeared to be beautiful and clear and seemed to come from afar. The next day we left. They asked us to wait to dance the calumet, but we did not want to. The two An-cancea embarked again and related on the way, while talking of the one who was with M. de la Salle, that they were at war against the Chicacha. The rain became heavy with a SSW wind, which obliged us to camp to the left in a flat region. The wind ceased. We left that night. After having made 10 leagues, we rested on a small island full of trees. At ten in the morning we left it. After ten leagues of paddling we stopped on a large island full of mulberry trees, laurels, and palms. [[These mulberry trees are like those in Virginia.]] We made a barricade [43] in the place where we camped for fear of being surprised. The next day, after five leagues of traveling, we came upon two deer that were swimming. We rowed hard and got to them. After having killed and skinned them, we traveled four more leagues where the Acancea showed us to the left a village of Tounica [44] who were their enemies, [saying] that it was neces-sary to disembark there and that we would conquer them easily with our arms. But we did not want to do this. This river, which had sepa-rated into three branches at Accanceas, rejoined here at this village of the Tounica. As this river and the land is very fertile in these places, it is densely populated with many different nations. [45]

We continued our journey and made four more leagues. We camped at the foot of some hills, which come from the Tounica. We wanted to

43 *Habaty* (abbatis) is here translated as "barricade." The French, in Roman style, built marching forts for overnight defense, throwing up a barricade fronted by a ditch for protection and shelter. A drawing of such a fort, built by Bienville on his way to the Chickasaws in 1736, is printed in Marc de Vil-liers du Terrage, *Les dernières années de la Louisiane française,* p. 24.

44 The Tunicas, whose wanderings during the French period were to lead them far south into Louisiana, lived at this date on the lower Yazoo River, principally at Haynes Bluff. See Jeffrey P. Brain, "The Archaeology of the Tunica: Trial on the Yazoo," National Geographic Society Research Re-ports, which describes excavations at the site. They probably were encoun-tered by Soto farther north and west, near his Mississippi River crossing.

45 This description of the Yazoo-Mississippi delta contains a misconception concerning division of the Mississippi into three branches, although the river does have several tributaries that flow into it from the Yazoo basin. The idea of dense population is probably based more on the Indians' oral reports and the Soto accounts than on observation, since it has been well established

go to the hills, but we found something like a pond between the hills and us. The next day, coasting along the big forest that is along the river, we came upon a furious crocodile [alligator], which M. de la Salle killed. We skinned it and ate it. It is a flesh that smells musky and is very tasteless. Seven leagues from there, where we camped, we did not fail to eat the rest. It was on an island, like the preceding one, where we again made a barricade. We started out early. We passed through a region full of mulberry trees and wild vines. We traveled eleven leagues; but as our route was along this river, which winds very much, we made no progress. We camped again on a rather large island. The next day we traveled ten leagues and stopped in a large bay where the Accancea told us to stay since here there was a nation of their allies called the Taensa.[46]

We sent them with three Frenchmen in a canoe to their village, which is situated on the bank of a lake made like a horseshoe [ox-bow] about four or five leagues long and one [and] one-half leagues wide.[47] It was two leagues from there to the village. It was necessary to make a portage of twenty paces to go to the lake because the outlet was too full of tree branches. The next day they returned, saying that they had been extremely well received. They were followed by some twenty canoes loaded with food, such as corn, dried fruits, and a paste composed of all sorts of fruits and corn flour with which they make all kinds of figures like the gingerbread in France. They also gave us salt. We asked them where they obtained it. They made us understand that it was toward the sun when it sets. We asked them if we could find salt water by going down the river. They made us understand that [the answer was] no or

that by this time Indian numbers had been drastically depleted. See Jeffrey P. Brain, "Late Prehistoric Settlement Patterning in the Yazoo Basin and Natchez Bluffs Regions of the Lower Mississippi Valley," in Bruce D. Smith, ed., *Mississippian Settlement Patterns*, p. 358.

46 The Taensa Indians have remained rather a mystery to history, as they have to archaeology. The most elaborate accounts of them come from the La Salle expedition, and on that basis they have been identified as being closely related to the Natchez. In 1706 they relocated among the Bayogoulas. Some years later they allegedly massacred the Bayogoulas and asked leave of the French to relocate east of the Mobile River delta. After 1715 they rarely appear in the historical record; the only lasting trace is the name of the eastern branch of the Mobile River. See George I. Quimby, *The Bayou Goula Site, Iberville Parish, Louisiana*, pp. 100–101.

47 The Taensa villages are believed, on the basis of later French mentions and meager archaeological evidence, to have been situated on a cutoff Mississippi River meander, Lake St. Joseph (Tensas Parish, Louisiana) (Stephen Williams, "On the Location of the Historic Taensa Villages," *Fifth Conference on Historic Site Archaeology Papers, 1965–1966* 1:2–13).

that they did not know. They made us signs that on going down the river one would find nations who would eat us. That frightened four of our Loups, who remained with them.

We stayed four days in this bay. They had some pearls[48] around their necks, but [they were] very small. M. de Tonty traded for about a dozen of them and one little slave, and a Loup also brought one [in exchange] for a cauldron. On the fifth [day] we left. We coasted along the land to the right because to the left the water goes crashing against a mountain and makes a violent eddy. We passed in front of an island and camped on another one farther down after having traveled seven leagues that day.

The next day, after having gone four leagues, we saw in the distance a canoe that was crossing the river and was going to the left. We rowed hard to catch up with it, but suddenly we found ourselves facing two hundred savages with bows strung and tomahawks in hand. First they gave the *saçacoye.* We stayed to the right. M. de La Salle sent M. de Tonty with three men, peace pipe in hand, to them in a canoe. The savages did the same, sending also three of their men. They smoked together and made peace and stroked M. de Tonty as a sign of friendship. (It is the custom of these savages to pass their hands over the whole body when they caress you or congratulate you for some good deed.) The whole crew crossed to the other side, where they [the Indians] were fishing. M. de La Salle went in a company of eight to their village, which was three leagues inland on a hill. He stayed there three days. When we saw that they were remaining there so long, we sent to find out why they were staying so long before returning. He returned and said they had told him to wait, to allow the chiefs from their other villages to come and dance the calumet. Seeing that they were not coming, he bade them farewell. We stayed two more days. They sent us a little corn, on which they live because, except for game, all the nations appeared not to have very much—at least they did not show us any. We found out that this nation was called the Corroa, or Corroua, and that the village was called Natché.[49]

The fifth day we left; two of these savages accompanied us. After

48 Throughout the southeast, Europeans, beginning with Soto, saw Indians using freshwater pearls for personal adornment and hoped the gems would prove valuable. Once examined, however, they were found to have been spoiled by the methods used to pierce them. See Tonti's comments in Margry, *Découvertes,* I, 602.

49 The indicated relationship between the Coroas and the Natchez is confused. They were two independent nations, more or less closely allied at this time but later separated when the Coroas moved to the Yazoo River. See Jeffrey P. Brain, "La Salle at the Natchez," in Galloway, *La Salle and His Legacy,* 49–59.

having made about eight leagues during a big rain, we arrived at another village of Corroua,[50] which is situated on the bank of the river at the top of a hill. We went to the village. It was very late. We were very well received; we found prepared the feast, which consisted only of corn, in bread, crushed, roasted, boiled, and fricasseed—and a few beans. We stayed two days in that region. The country is beautiful, full of hills. Their huts and their life-style is like the Tainsa.[51] They always have a torch made of lighted cane, which they take care to keep lit all night in each cabin. They also have dresses or blankets made with a sort of cotton. This resembles the hammocks of the Islands. That is what they cover themselves with, tying it with a large white cord that has large loops at the end, which they tie. They also have dresses of deer skins and copper of which they make discs, like covers of cooking pots, with which they decorate their cabins, and some sort of gun screw of the same metal, very large; and they put four or five of them in each ear.[52] The young M. de la Salle found a girl who had a necklace of eleven fairly large pearls. He took them from her and gave her his comb. The girl screamed, but he fled. The chief of the village complained about it to M. de la Salle, but no one knew who had done the deed. He did not keep them long since they robbed him of them. We left after having left two sacks of corn in the cabin of the chief since we were overburdened, letting them know that on our return we would pick them up. We camped five leagues from them to the left on a hill that is the continuation of the mountains of the Corroua. The next day we traveled five leagues more. We beat [our way] to an island. We killed a deer there. At daybreak we left and went eight leagues. That night we could not find a place to camp because the country was flooded. We saw higher ground, so we went and camped there. The next day we left early. After having gone three leagues, we found some mountains to the left. After again having made nine leagues, we camped to the right in a level region full of large trees. The slave who had been bought from the Tainsa was a

---

50 Brain (ibid., p. 55) has identified this village as the later Tiou village at the mouth of St. Catherine Creek.

51 George I. Quimby ("The Natchezan Culture Type," *American Antiquity,* 7 [1942]: 255–75) discusses arguments favoring a culture type including the Natchez and Taensas. Since the material remains corroborate the documentary testimony, the cultural similarities seem genuine.

52 The copper discs may have been native copper ornaments representing the sun circle (see Emma Lila Fundaburk and Mary Douglas Fundaburk Foreman, *Sun Circles and Human Hands,* plate 108), but the spring-shaped earbobs, usually connected with an English source at this date, must have come through some roundabout eastern route. See Peter Brannon, *The Southern Indian Trade,* p. 43.

Corroa, and he told us we were opposite the Ouma.[53] Monsieur de la Salle did not want to go there, since we had enough food.

The next day, after having gone five leagues, we passed in front of three large islands. We traveled eleven leagues that day. We camped in a flooded area where we made large piles of cane in order not to be in the water. At four in the morning we left. After having gone 6 leagues, we came upon some mountains to the left. After lunch we traveled five leagues more. We camped opposite a large river that was to the right, which came from the west, large and very clear.[54] Its mouth was half a league wide, and in the distance one could see some islands that were within. The next day we camped to the left ten leagues from there, after having passed in front of two small islands. We left the next day. We traveled fifteen leagues. Food was beginning to give out. We camped to the right on piles of cane that we made. We killed some cormorants. At daybreak we left. We did not come across any more islands. The river was much swifter than usual and the land more flooded. We made ten leagues and the next day 13. That day we came upon mountains to the left and a small river. That night we stopped on the left. At about five in the morning we left. We traveled 6 leagues. We camped to the left, still in flooded lands. The next day after having traveled three leagues, we saw nine canoes tied up on land on the right. We went there. We saw that the people had just left. We stayed there an hour. Seeing that no one came, we went on our way. At one league from there, we met some savages who were fishing.[55] As soon as they saw us, they fled to their village, but they [the Indians] shot at them. They [the Frenchmen] were obliged to return, seeing that they were continuing to shoot. We entrenched ourselves as best we could, but, seeing that they were not coming, we reembarked. At a league and a half from there, we saw a village

---

53 The Oumas or Houmas were a western Muskogean group related to the Choctaws and apparently speaking a Choctawlike language: their name is the Choctaw word for "red," and John R. Swanton (*Indians of the Southeastern United States,* p. 139) has suggested that they may have been an offshoot of the Chakchiumas ("red crayfish"). They were missionized briefly in 1700; in 1706 they may have been decimated by some supposedly friendly Tunicas, and the remainder settled near New Orleans.

54 The Red River.

55 Tonti and Membré identify these Indians as the Quinipissas, but certain identification may never be made. When Iberville came to found the Louisiana colony in 1699, he was much vexed by his failure to find a tribe known by that name. Only later, when a letter Tonti had left for La Salle with the Quinipissas in 1686 turned up with the Bayogoulas, did he realize that they were actually called the Mugulashas. They were living with the Bayogoulas, who turned on them in 1700 and killed many (Swanton, *Indians,* p. 177).

to the left;[56] we crossed. First we noticed something like many people; when we had landed, we saw that the crowds were crows, eagles, and other beasts that seek out carrion. We knew by this that the village had been destroyed. On approaching, we saw only carcasses of men and women, ruined huts, and others full of dead bodies, a coating of blood on the ground, and all their canoes broken and cut up with axes. We went to camp two leagues from there to the left, where we made a barricade of wood in order not to be surprised. The country was totally flooded, but the land did not fail to produce mulberries, laurels, oaks, and elms. This flooding enriches the land.

We left the next day. After having traveled four leagues, we met a canoe with three savages in it. As soon as they noticed people, they fled to the right; and, not being able to pass through the reeds and canes with their canoes, they landed and took to the woods. We went to the canoe. There we found some smoked caiman and the ribs of a man, which we took. We left as payment a *haleine* [*haillon:* a rag]. As hunger was pressing us, having only a little corn daily, we pounced on this meat. When we had eaten it, we knew that it was human by the bones and the taste, which was better than the caiman.[57]

We slept five leagues from there. The terrain was beginning to change. The canes, reeds, and palms became thicker, and the trees smaller, and the country low and flooded three or four feet deep. The next day we had not gone four leagues when we found ourselves as though on a great flooded plain. The tops of the grass and reeds appeared above the water. The banks of the river were higher and began to form a sort of embankment.[58] After having rowed two more leagues, we found a small grove of aspen [cottonwood] trees where we camped. Someone climbed one of the taller trees. He saw to the right something like a big tree. M. de La Salle went by land in a party of three through the reeds to see if it was the sea. He found, so he says, the water a little briney. In the place where we were camped there was a large quantity of land crabs, which escaped into some holes. They were as large as a

56 The Tangipahoas, probably a branch of the Choctaw-related Acolapissas, then living on the lower Pearl River (ibid., p. 190).

57 This passage, however grisly, authenticates a corresponding one in the account attributed to Father Membré by Chrétien Le Clercq (*Premier établissement de la foi dans la Nouvelle France,* II, 208–64). Membré's authorship has been questioned by Delanglez ("La Salle's Expedition of 1682," *Mid-America* 22 [1940]: 3–37), but this incident at least must now be seen as authentic, since Membré was with Nicolas at this time.

58 These embankments were natural levees formed by the flooding river as it deposited silt along its edges.

thumb. The next day, after having gone three leagues, we found that the river separated into three branches. We took the channel in the middle. After having navigated one league, we stopped in a place where the canoes had run aground against a large tree that was in the river, which the water had carried there; thus, the branches stuck out [of the water]. Not seeing a place to camp, we went back upstream and came down by the channel to the right. We traveled half a league, stopping opposite an island we found. We killed a quantity of birds there, white crows, red herons, pelicans, and a kind of bird that has only a little down on its body. It has the feet of a duck and lights on the trees. [It has] a short neck and a long bill.[59]

The next day Monsieur de Tonty went via the channel to the left. Monsieur de La Salle continued down the one where he was. They left around eight in the morning. After having rowed one league M. de La Salle found the river that continued to the sea, making embankments [levees] on both sides out of the wood it brings and cementing that with the mud it carries. These embankments continue a great distance. He crossed his canoe to the other side of one of the dikes to the right, tasted the water, and said that it was brackish. The 6 oarsmen he had with him said "No, it is not. It is not at all, since we drank a lot of it [and] it did not seem to us to be salty." He got angry with them, saying that it was a trick that they wanted to play on him to say that this water was not salty. "You will pardon us, Monsieur," they said to him. "We find it salty."[60] He went half a league away from there to a small island that was in the sea. On it there was a pool that the oarsmen found brackish. They took some in a cup to bring it to Father Zénobe, who had stayed at the place of three forks with the young La Salle and Barbier.[61] They also brought a canker crab and an oyster shell and returned at about five o'clock in the evening of the same day. M. de Tonty came back the next day at 9 o'clock in the morning. That mouth emptied into

59 Possibly the double-crested cormorant.
60 The argument about salinity, which would confirm that the river mouth had been reached, is mentioned by all the sources. The problem lay in the fact that the Mississippi, like other great rivers, dumps so much fresh water that it maintains its coherence as a current far into the Gulf of Mexico.
61 Minet denies the claim made in the "Membré" relation (in Le Clercq) that Membré this day accompanied Tonti down the middle channel; he could not have done so, since Minet says that exploration was not made until the next day, after Tonti had explored the left channel. This is an example of the embellishments in this source designated to magnify the Recollect's role in the exploration. No such claim is made in any other source, including the genuine Membré letter of 1682 (Margry, *Découvertes,* II, 206–12).

a large lake or sea of fresh water, seven leagues from where they had left to as far as the eye could see.[62] He had seen an island that appeared to be covered with big trees, but a strong wind had prevented him from going there. They had all drunk of this water, but it was not at all salty and [was] still muddy. We wanted to shoot birds that were passing over the water near us. As soon as they fell, a crocodile would pounce on them. Of six or seven that we killed, we had only one because of the numerous crocodiles.

He [La Salle] again sent M. de Tonty, [this time] via the middle channel. Meanwhile, we went three leagues farther upstream, where we camped, to the left, in a place where there were some small trees. M. de la Salle took the latitude at this place. He found 28 degrees 20 minutes,[63] the 6th [9th] of April, 1682. M. de Tonty returned and said that he had found the same as at the other channel, a large sea of fresh water,[64] but that this channel was shorter than the other. [[See the following figure.]]

At the place where we were camped, we cleared a place by felling the small trees that were there. We squared a large tree and planted it in the ground, nailing to the side of the tree three copper fleurs-de-lis made from a cauldron. We made a cross, which we also planted in the ground with this inscription on a lead plate: *Took possession of this land in the name of Louis XIIII, King of France and of Navarre.* We sang the *Te Deum* and fired three volleys. We were short on corn, having only a handful each for three days. We left after having stayed there one day. We went to camp four leagues from there. The country was more flooded than usual. We rowed six consecutive days, always camping on piles of

62 Although the distance is exaggerated, Tonti seems to have reached the vicinity of North Pass (at first called East Pass).

63 The actual latitude was about 29° 10'. La Salle, making no allowance for error—either his own or mapmakers'—concluded that this river could not be the Río del Espíritu Santo (Soto's Río Grande); indeed, there was no large bay extending above latitude 30°, as the maps indicated for the Espíritu Santo, and he had found that "all the mouths are to the east-southeast." He therefore visualized his river as flowing into the western end of the Gulf of Mexico, identifying it with the Río Escondido shown on maps since the mid-sixteenth century as entering the Gulf in the Texas coastal bend region, i.e., the Nueces River. La Salle's confusion emerges clearly in the Chucagoa fragment (Margry, *Découvertes*, II, 196–203). For a recent assessment of the fragment and La Salle's geographical conceptions, see Peter H. Wood, "La Salle: Discovery of a Lost Explorer," *American Historical Review* 89, no. 2 (April, 1984): 294–323.

64 Perhaps in the vicinity of Blind Bay; the water would have seemed fresh because of the volume of the Mississippi's discharge.

reeds that we raised to get out of the water, not traveling half the distance that we were able to make going downstream, living only on caimans that we killed.

The 8th [eleventh] day we arrived at the destroyed village. We camped there. We noticed a canoe on the other side. We sent someone there. He reported having seen four persons. We sent someone again. The next morning almost all of us went there. We met four women completely naked as they all are in that country. We tried to make them understand [that we wanted to know] whether there was a village on that side; they made signs to us that there was not. We brought them to the destroyed village. We asked them who had committed this destruction. We got no other answer but "Auma, Auma, Chiquilousa,"[65] who I think are two nations that live farther up.

We left the next day. We camped opposite the [Quinipissa] village where some arrows had been shot. After a heavy rain, the savages, upon seeing us, sent a canoe to identify us. It approached within bowshot. One person arose, showing us an axe with which he fenced, meaning that he wanted to fight. We put a canoe into the water to go to them, but they fled. Mons. de La Salle did not stop wanting to go to their side, showing them the peace pipe. About 30 canoes that left the woods came at him with bows strung. He returned and sent there two of their women with two knives, two axes, and some glass beads as gifts. They brought them halfway and swam the rest of the way. The savages, seeing that, sent two hostages, and we sent two. We camped on their side. They sent us a little corn, but only a little at a time, by their warriors. We paid them with iron for arrows [points]. Theirs are merely of pebbles or fish teeth.[66] The two men we sent as hostages returned that night. They said that they had danced and closed all their huts. One said that they had taken his cap and an old shirt, that they had made him a present of a human scalp and a dress or covering made of down from the turkey. As a beverage, they have a sort of herb they boil in water and drink very hot.

---

65 Of these raiders of the Tangipahoa village, "Auma, Auma Chiquilousa," the first can be identified as the Houmas. "Chiquilousa" probably refers to the Chickasaws, who had a major village of that name from earliest records and throughout the historical period. The area referred to is known to have been raided by the Chickasaws, who had evicted the Acolapissas from the lower Pearl River.

66 This is an accurate description of the Quinipissa arrowpoints, which, like those of all the tribes of the coastal region, would have been chipped from quartzite pebbles or made from fossil shark teeth or gar scales.

We placed a sentinel as usual and everyone retired. Around 11 o'clock it rained heavily. M. Dautree could not sleep.[67] He placed himself near the sentinel under his canoe. Around one o'clock they heard reeds breaking. We thought it was our dogs that were inside and were making this noise. All of a sudden we heard a loud shout or *saçacoye* all around us, and at the same time a rain of arrows on us. We cried, "To arms!" The sentinel shot; each one shot, even though the rain had soaked all our arms. We recharged and shot again through the reeds, since we could see nothing. Others of them came via the water to attack us. A canoe of these savages wanting to land, one who was in front mistook the barrel of a Frenchman's gun for a tree branch. He shot right away and killed two or three of those who were in this canoe. The rest jumped into the water. Fear having seized them, they floated with the current. We found the arms and the overturned canoe the next day in a backwash. Nevertheless, the battle lasted until daybreak, with shooting constantly from one side or another. As daybreak came, they all fled, leaving their tomahawks, bows, and blankets on the field of battle and their canoes in a small stream near there. We found two dead savages, much blood on all sides, and some tracks of men who had been dragged. We smashed their nine canoes. We cut off the heads of these two men. We lifted their scalps and we mounted the heads on some posts, the faces turned in the direction of their villages. The Loups opened the two bodies, which they found fat and appetizing. They would have eaten much of it without M. de la Salle, who forbade them. [[We did not know until [we reached] the Corroa that this nation was called the Kenipisa.]][68] They took out the hearts to dry to show that they had killed some men. After that they killed all their dogs to make a feast (it being the way of the savages that when they go to war they make a feast of dogs. When they are victorious, they again feast on dogs).[69] We all went to the feast.

We left there at about eleven o'clock in the morning. We went on for ten days, always forging ahead in a flooded country. Being short of corn, we ate skins of buffalo. We came upon hills to the right and

67 Jean Bourbon, Sieur d'Autray, who was commissioned a lieutenant in Valigny's company for La Salle's voyage to the Gulf. No indication is found that he went (Margry, *Découvertes,* II, 387).

68 See note 55.

69 The dog feast, a practice common to the Algonkin and Iroquoian tribes of the northeast and reportedly used by the Natchez, symbolized the warriors' fidelity to the war leader and was supposed to confer bravery and mettle (Charles Hudson, *The Southeastern Indians,* p. 290).

camped near a small river that we called the Rivière des Risques [River of Hazards].[70] We killed two bears, three deer, and some turkeys. After having stayed there three days, we left. We killed several crocodiles. For five days we found nothing but flooded country. We found the large river that comes from the west, which we named the Rivière de Seignelay [Seignelay River: Red River]. We found the mulberries good to eat. We lived on that. After seven days of canoeing we arrived opposite the Auma [Houma]. Going on that side, we found a road on the bank, some corn flour on the ground, and some sacks hanging on a tree. We interpreted that to mean, "Come to the village. We will give you full sacks of corn flour." We proposed to Monsieur de la Salle that we go there because of our need, but he did not want to go. We were obliged to live six more days on buffalo skins because for him we always killed some ducks. Seeing ourselves close to the Corroa, we cleaned our arms. We prepared ourselves even though we were extremely weak. We arrived at the foot of the hillocks of the villages, where I believe they had seen us come since the chiefs were there waiting for us. They fawned on [*fait mille caresses*] M. de la Salle and brought us corn, but we pretended not to be hungry, showing no eagerness to take any. They begged us to climb up to have a feast. We went. We found the feast of corn prepared in the middle of the square, which is built and cleaned like a mall. At first, there did not appear to us to be many people, but suddenly we saw ourselves surrounded by fifteen or sixteen hundred warriors, all daubed with red and black, with tomahawk and bow in hand. We saw very well that they had bad intentions. We ate, guns cocked, hatchets in hand, and knives in our stockings. Nevertheless, the little savage that the Loup had bought from the Tainsa, who was a Corroa, related to them how we had fought the Tenipisa or Quenipisa, who are their allies.[71] We made them a present of the two scalps. They rubbed them with plaintive cries. The chiefs told us to go away, that the young [men] had bad intentions. We took the food, which we brought to our canoes. During that time they counted us and our canoes. Seeing that we were still as many as when we left, they were surprised. This crowd of painted savages, seeing that

70 The Rivière des Risques is so named elsewhere only in the Nicolas de La Salle account. As the last small river from the east found south of the Red River, this one may be identified as the Iberville, which, as time proved, did have its hazards.

71 Alliances in these unsettled times in the lower Mississippi Valley could be very complex, and the Quinipissas quite likely had allied with the Coroas and Natchez, in spite of ethnic and linguistic differences, for protection against more numerous neighbors.

we were embarking, gained on us across the land to the village that had been called Natché. We camped opposite the Natché. We waited a long time to see if they would come to attack us. When they saw no one, they left after having made the *saçacoy* and the cries for the dead that we had killed at the Tenipisa.

All the people in this nation have flat heads. As soon as they are born, the mothers take great care to flatten them between two boards, which they put in front and in back.[72] They are tall men, well built. I think they worship fire because they have a temple in the middle of the square that is very well built. In this temple and in each house they have every night a lighted fire, which they carefully maintain.[73]

We had gone three leagues when we heard a voice to the right. We thought that it was some ambush. We continued the route, but from afar we saw a man who was coming toward us on a raft of cane. We went to him. He called himself a Tainsa and made us understand that while the Corroa were burdened with setting up an ambush, he had escaped. After three days' navigation, we arrived at the Taensa, who are only ten leagues from the Corroa. M. de Tonty went with his canoe to the village. One league from the village, the Taensa stood upright in the canoe and started to sing until we arrived. There were three cane torches that came to illuminate them, and some elderly men came to receive them. They went straight to the cabin of the chief. There was a cane torch in the center. The cabin was surrounded with sheets of polished copper, three old guns, and a Spanish sword.[74] The chief was seated in the corner on a mat raised a foot from the ground. He made them be seated around him. They brought some corn to eat and a little deer meat. We told him what we had done at the Tenipisa. He seemed happy about it.

72 Cranial deformation, by applying a constant gentle pressure to the infant's skull during the several cradleboard years, was common among the tribes of the lower Mississippi Valley and the Muskogean groups farther east. It apparently caused no ill effects. See Hudson, *Southeastern Indians,* p. 31.

73 The maintenance of perpetual fire was practiced by those groups who worshiped the sun. Its purpose is detailed in the Natchez creation myth, and documentary evidence attests to the practice among the Natchez, Taensas, some groups in the Mobile River valley, and here by the Coroas. This is another common trait supporting a Natchezan culture type, not considered by Quimby (see note 51). See Mardith Schuetz, "Ethnological Data," in the commentaries to the Talon Interrogations in this volume and note 13 anent the perpetual fire among the Hasinai Confederacy.

74 The copper sheets were probably cut from cauldrons obtained indirectly from the Spaniards through trade. The guns and the sword were probably obtained from the same source, but through theft.

All the elderly men who came into the cabin raised their hands above their heads, saying, "Hou, hou, hou," and the chief answered, "Negouder, negouder." When the one we had brought entered the cabin, he went to a corner after having saluted with great respect and stayed sitting on his heels as long as we ate, not ever speaking. When he saw that we were spreading mats to lie down, he saluted, "Hou, hou," and went away. All this nation is of a seriousness to be admired. They sleep on mats. The young [men] took the canoe and carried it into their temple.[75] [[That was to say that they esteemed it because the next day they put it back into the water.]] The chief had ordered them to bring refreshments to M. de La Salle.

The next day they walked all around the village. They gave them three large crates full of dried fruits, some corn [and] some bear oil. This village is one league long, along the lake. Only their temple, the home of the chief or king, and those of the elderly men are surrounded by palisades, where on the tip of each there is a skull of one of their enemies whom they have killed. Along the length of the temple is a roof like a sort of dome, the whole framework very efficiently covered with braided, woven bushes, the door painted red, and two sentinels in front. One of our Frenchmen entered. One of the sentinels followed him and wiped with his hands every place he put his feet and stroked his body. It is ornamented on the inside with canes and reeds, made like the baskets that our nuns make, and painted red. On the outside, the roof ridge is full of pieces of wood shaped like arrows, which stand out a foot and a half and are arranged neatly. In this temple they always have two torches lit during the night.[76]

Every morning at sunrise they carry their children to the shore of the lake and present them to the sun, taking water in their hand and throwing it on the child, extending their hands to the sun and again stroking the child afterward.

After having loaded the provisions, they came back to see M. de la Salle, to whom they had brought more than the canoes could hold. In the afternoon we saw some savages coming who were cleaning the road

75 Only Nicolas seems to have observed this veneration of the French canoe; Tonti, leader of the party, does not mention it.
76 This description of the Taensa temple with its perpetual flame accords well with similar descriptions of temples among the Natchez and Acolapissas. For the Natchez, see Antoine Simon Le Page du Pratz, *Histoire de la Louisiane française*. For the Acolapissas, see David Bushnell, "Drawings of A. De Batz in Louisiana, 1732–1735," *Smithsonian Miscellaneous Collections* 80, no. 5 (1921): 3–4, plate 1.

and spreading mats, and afterward we saw the chief appear, accompanied by two hundred savages. He and M. de La Salle saluted each other, sat on the mats, and said nothing; not understanding each other, they made signs.[77] He made him a present of his dressing gown, which had once upon a time been of painted linen cloth, and of the little Mosapelea slave. The chief made him a present of his blanket or cotton robe, as I mentioned previously, and they said farewell. After having stayed there three days, we left on the 4th [day]. M. de La Salle took the lead. M. de Tonty, who had stayed behind, met a Taensa and an Accansea. The latter embarked with him, seeing that they were going to their dwelling, and made him take the shortest [way], which allowed him to meet M. de la Salle seven days after he left him. The next day he again took the lead and arrived at the Accansea, where they feasted on dog, like warriors, and left the next day. M. de Tonty arrived a day later. They also made him a feast, calling us true warriors. We were waiting for them because they had some Ilinois slaves who explained what was said to us. This nation has no temple[78] or the customs of the Taensa. Their huts are round and made of tree bark. The second day we slept at the other village. The four Loups who had left us were very sad when they knew that we had killed some men. They swore that they would not return home until they had killed some also. We feasted the same way [we had]. The next day M. de Tonty slept at a river that comes from the hills to the right. [[On that side he met a canoe and eight Iroquois who were pursued by the Tamaroa, who had reached the River Houabache to go up to their country.]] Two weeks after M. de la Salle had left him, he [La Salle] fell ill with delirium. He left a note at the end of a stick where he asked M. de Tonty to make haste, since he was ill, to join him at the fort they had built when they had lost the gunsmith a month after he had left him.

He sent ahead to the Miamis to dig up the merchandise that they had stowed away for fear that it would spoil. At the end of a week they arrived. When the health of M. de la Salle returned, he left without seeing a Chicacha. Two weeks later we arrived at the village where we

---

77 Sign language was used by the North American peoples, who spoke many different languages, long before the coming of Europeans. It was quite natural that the same method would be applied to communication with Europeans. See W. P. Clark, *The Indian Sign Language*.

78 Minet errs; the Ouapaws are certainly known to have kept a temple (Dunbar Rowland, A. G. Sanders, and Patricia Galloway, eds., *Mississippi Provincial Archives: French Dominion* [MPA:FD], V, 175; AN, Colonies, Series C13A 39, 177–80, June 20, 1756). Evidence for other cultural practices held in common with the Taensas is equivocal.

had found no one on the way. We knew they were named the Tamaroa.[79] They made him a present of two little Pana slaves. They wanted to dance the calumet. He thanked them and left. We passed in front of the Missouris River and, leaving the Colbert River to the left, we ascended the Ilinois River. On ascending this river we killed a number of Canada geese, swans, and ducks with a stick. Because it was the time of molting, they were unable to fly. We also killed some buffalo, stags, and deer. The Ilinois not yet having returned, the animals had taken refuge there.

Fifteen days after having left the Tamaroa, we arrived at Fort Pimyteouy or Crevecoeur, which we found ruined and the boat burned. We arrived where the village of the Ilinois had been, on July 25, 1682. We could not find water to continue the journey. We were obliged to carry the canoes up to the island of the rapids. He left some of his people in that place with a little gunpowder for hunting, telling them he would return soon. And he went to the Miamis. He paid the Loups and left them there to spend the winter and went to Michelimaquina, where he found M. de Tonty, whom he sent back to the Ilinois with orders to make a settlement there, to assemble there all the French, to make there an entrenchment or fort, and he, who was going to France, would take the news of the discovery.

As soon as M. de Tonty arrived at the Ilinois, he established himself in a shanty in a small grove of trees on good land, where the French came to join him. The young La Salle had wintered at the Mascoutin and had endured cold and hunger. He was one of those whom M. de La Salle had left at the island of the Rapids. As soon as he knew that we were at the Ilinois, he came there. He persuaded M. de Tonty to spend the rest of the winter four leagues lower, where there was more game. At the end of the three days that we were camped, we were surprised to see M. de la Salle himself come with two canoes and some merchandise. He changed the place where we were camping and [we] went to settle opposite the village of the Ilinois, and [he] had his men construct there on a steep mountain a fort made of palisades measuring 30 fathoms in front.[80] He had corn planted. The Ilinois, knowing that the French were at their home, all came to reestablish themselves there. M. de la Salle welcomed them lavishly. He had them make peace with the Miamis, who numbered 800 warriors. There was another nation established near there named Chaouanons [Shawnee], whom the Spaniards of St. Augustine had chased from their land and whom the Iroquois had suc-

---

79 For the descent to the site, see p. 43, this volume.
80 This is the Starved Rock fort (Saint-Louis), which La Salle planned to use as the anchor for his Mississippi trading empire.

ceeded in ruining; there remained only 70 warriors. [[There were still 100 on the lands who were to come to settle.]][81] He took them with him also. He also put there the Mascoustin,[82] who are at least 200 warriors, and altogether made them pledge an offensive and defensive league against the Iroquois and [pledge] to notify and help mutually. But as all these nations are veritable savages who follow only their instincts, which closely resemble those of animals, thus he cannot trust them.

While all this was taking place a Pana who was with him had learned French and related that in their country there were some horses and they wore hats made of buffalo hides. They had near them a salty river, and west of them was a nation who lived near a large lake and had sabers. M. de la Salle asked about all these nations, one after the other. A chief of the Mascoutins told him that ten years ago, having gone to war 200 leagues inland to the west, he had brought a piece of iron whiter than ours[83] that the Jesuits had bought from him and had made of it a monstrance for their chapel of [name left blank in manuscript].

Some time after all these alliances, he [La Salle] left for Quebec with two Chaouanons, the young La Salle, Barbier, and L'Esperance.[84] On the way he met a man named M. de Baugis who was coming from that side to negotiate. One named M. Vital, who was of the company of this gentleman, returned with him to Quebec. He lent him 200 *pistoles* [gold pieces] after he had recounted all the discovery and the projects he was going to do in France. When he arrived at Michelimaquina, the Jesuits made him a present of a quantity of refreshments. He stayed a week

81 The Shawnees, an Algonkin tribe related to the Kickapoos, Sauks, and Fox, are better known for their wide travels than for almost anything else. The group mentioned here was living on an Ohio tributary, under attack from the Iroquois. They moved in with the Miamis south of Lake Michigan to await construction of the fort, then moved with them to Starved Rock in 1683 (Temple, *Indian Villages,* part 2, p. 174).

82 The Mascoutens were an Algonkin group probably closely related to the Kickapoos. During the 1680s they were living around southern Lake Michigan and Green Bay with the Miamis (ibid., p. 158).

83 This "white iron," apparently silver, could have come from the Mexican mines.

84 Denis Thomas ("Declaración de Dionicio Thomas," UT archives transcript, AGI, Mexico 616), the defector who, on being captured by Spaniards, divulged La Salle's subsequent voyage to the Gulf of Mexico, says he obtained his information on La Salle's plans and previous exploits from one of La Salle's servants named La Esperanza (during the first part of the voyage, before Saint-Domingue). This was undoubtedly the same L'Espérance mentioned by Minet. See Robert S. Weddle, *Wilderness Manhunt: The Spanish Search for La Salle,* pp. 8, 11, 11n.

with them and afterward he left by the Assiniboile River to Monreal [and] from there [went] to Quebec. He left from Quebec the first of November, 1683, in the ship *St. Honoré*. It took five weeks to make this trip from Quebec to La Rochelle and from there to Paris, where he first tried to form a company of merchants to go by way of the Gulf of Mexico to find the Colbert River and make a settlement near the Tainsa.[85] But, seeing that the merchants of Paris and Rouen would put nothing into it, he looked for people at the court to present him to Monsieur the Marquis of Seignelay.[86]

Notice of Things Omitted

I forgot to record in the discourse that M. Barbier saw a second mouth [Bayou Lafourche] marked on the map by the letter A,[87] that the Corroa savages had told M. de La Salle to take this mouth because it was the best but that, mistrusting them, he had done the contrary.

The young de La Salle and Barbier told me that in descending the river they almost always saw the sun set in front of them.

R: On that side he met a canoe and eight Iroquois who were pursued by the Tamaroa, who had reached the Houabache River to go up to their country.

85 La Salle spoke with merchants in Rochefort and La Rochelle—those already involved with the Canadian trade—and, finding no interest, turned to others in Paris and Rouen. See Margry, *Découvertes*, II, 294, 301, 451. Minet is the only known source identifying the site of La Salle's proposed settlement, sixty leagues up the Mississippi, as near the Taensa.
86 La Salle apparently obtained access to Seignelay through the Abbé Eusèbe Renaudot; Jean Delanglez (*Some La Salle Journeys*, pp. 80–83), argues that he was thus bent to the purposes of the Renaudot group, which supported a scheme for an offensive against Spanish New Biscay (Nueva Vizcaya) along the lines of the Peñalosa proposal. Such a theory loses its punch in view of La Salle's suggestion of such a possibility before he ever returned to France (Margry, *Découvertes*, II, 292–93).
87 The Coroas being the ones who gave advice concerning this distributary, it might be presumed to be the Atchafalaya (Choctaw: "long river"), which during the last hundred years has begun siphoning off the Red River discharge and trying to steal the Mississippi's main flow. See Jack Rudloe and Ann Rudloe, "Louisiana's Atchafalaya: Trouble in Bayou Country," *National Geographic* 156, no. 3 (September, 1979): 378–84. However, its proximity to the Quinipissa Indians on Minet's map (plate 5)—fifty-seven leagues from the Red, according to his narrative—suggests Lafourche Bayou, a quite navigable waterway that formed the Mississippi's main delta some two thousand years ago. See Douglas Lee, "Mississippi Delta: The Land of the River," *National Geographic* 164, no. 2 (August, 1982): diagrams, pp. 240–41.

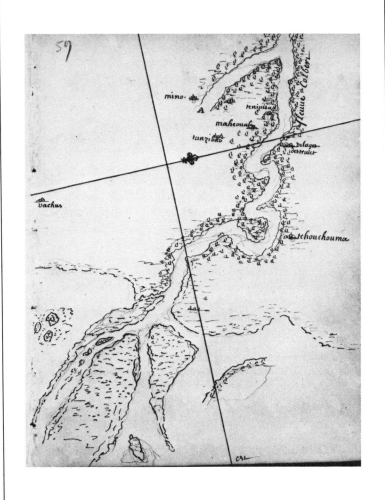

PLATE 5. Minet's "Mouths of the Mississippi."
(Courtesy of the Public Archives of Canada)

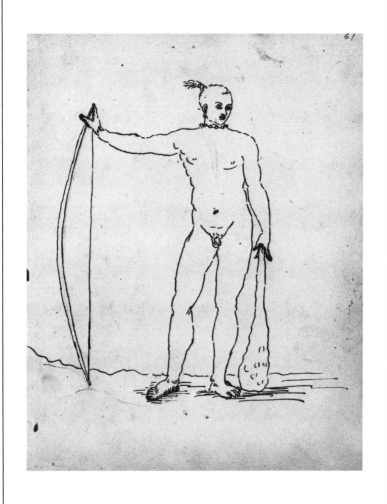

PLATE 6. Minet's drawing of a native warrior.
(Courtesy of the Public Archives of Canada)

Page 51. M. de Tonty met two or three canoes of Accanssa who were pursuing a canoe with Iroquois who had come to make war in that country via the Choucagoua River; but, their canoe being light, it soon reached the said river and left the Accança very far behind.

II. The Voyage to the Gulf

Minet's Journal:
The Cruise of the Joly

PATRICIA GALLOWAY

The little book that contains Minet's relation (Part I) does not end with the events of 1682; its second part contains the engineer Minet's own journal of La Salle's 1684–85 voyage to the Gulf of Mexico. Minet was but one of many in the large company on that venture, but he is one of the few whose observations have survived. With the exception of Joutel's journal,[1] his is the only continuous detailed narrative of the voyage. There are other sources, to be sure: the series of letters exchanged by La Salle and the naval captain Beaujeu, the formal record of their agreement and disagreement on the course the voyage was to take;[2] the several fragments written by the Abbé d'Esmanville, the only cleric of the seven undertaking the voyage who returned to France with Beaujeu;[3] the journal of La Salle's brother, the Abbé Jean Cavelier, the authenticity of which has been called into question by Villiers du Terrage and Delanglez fairly conclusively;[4] and, finally, a brief abstract of Minet's own journal.[5] Each of these provides a different view of events, but, as is the case with the 1682 portion of the Minet manuscript, we are vastly enriched by Minet's own story. In it we have a complete and detailed daily journal of the 1684–85 voyage that serves to amplify other sources and against which the other sources may be checked. Its special value is that it is not only the journal of a trained engineer, whose observations in

1 Henri Joutel, "Relation de Henri Joutel," in Pierre Margry, ed., *Découvertes et établissements des français dans l'ouest et dans le sud de l'Amérique septentrionale,* III, 91–162.
2 Mostly in Margry, *Découvertes,* II, 521–52; for the Atlantic crossing see pp. 485–99.
3 Ibid., II, 510–17, 584–88.
4 Jean Delanglez, trans. and ed., *The Journal of Jean Cavelier: The Account of a Survivor of La Salle's Texas Expedition, 1684–88* presents parallel French and English texts; Marc de Villiers du Terrage, *L'Expédition de Cavelier de La Salle dans le Golfe du Mexique (1684–1687).*
5 Margry, *Découvertes,* II, 591–601.

matters of geography are worthy, but also the only detailed record of events aboard Beaujeu's ship *Joly* after her departure from Santo Domingo. No claim is made that this is the first use of this source in La Salle studies; as will be seen, Villiers du Terrage used it extensively. But, until now, the researcher has had no access to its full text.

It is both odd and unfortunate that there is no similar journal from Minet's interlocutor, Nicolas de La Salle. Perhaps the keeping of such a journal was not considered to be connected with the younger man's duties and he simply lacked the time to record this voyage as he had the 1682 Mississippi River trip. It is quite likely that Minet kept him busy with questions regarding this early journey, too, for, when the engineer was not studying navigation or geography, it was doubtless his duty to pursue every avenue for obtaining knowledge of the country where a colony was to be planted—hence the first part of the manuscript, for which Nicolas was the principal source. (Reasons for believing that Minet worked on both narratives concurrently are discussed in the introduction to Part I.)

The only account of the 1684 expedition that can be compared with Minet's journal for completeness is the opening section of Henri Joutel's. From the July 24 departure from La Rochelle until September 28, when Joutel disembarked with La Salle at Petit Goâve (Haiti), Minet and Joutel were on board the *Joly*. During that time we would expect close agreement on dates and events, and, indeed, this is generally the case. Yet their latitude computations tend to complement each other rather than to coincide. Only three times do both journals give a latitude for the same day, and in those instances they disagree rather markedly. None of these observations is from the period when the two men were on separate ships.[6] The points of view of the two, quite naturally, are different also. Joutel was one of La Salle's most trusted men; although his view of La Salle is not blindly partisan, he did have a better chance to understand the explorer's behavior. Minet, on the other hand, claims to have been suspected by La Salle at the outset of having been sent on the voyage as a spy.[7] Minet's journal is far more informed by the attitudes and opinions of Captain Beaujeu, with whom La Salle was also at odds. After the departure from Petit Goâve the two narratives no longer are parallel, since Joutel embarked with La Salle in the *Aimable*

6 The dates are August 20, when there is a seventy-five minute difference; January 12, when there is one of twenty-nine minutes; and January 16, when the difference is forty-nine minutes.
7 Minet, "Journal de nostre voiage au golphe de mexique" (Public Archives of Canada, Microfilm reel H1022), p. 85 of the translation.

while Minet remained on the *Joly;* but again a comparison of the two has been useful in helping to establish where each ship actually went.[8]

The decision-making process during the course of the voyage and after the expedition's arrival off the Texas coast is illuminated by the series of letters that La Salle and Beaujeu exchanged from ship to ship after La Salle changed vessels. Beaujeu had made it a condition of his service that La Salle give him in writing all orders regarding the conduct of the voyage.[9] Each of these letters punctiliously lays down the points on which each of the two men based his judgments, so that responsibility for the various decisions would be rightly attributed. Before the pause at Petit Goâve, there is only one summary letter. It is addressed to Minister Seignelay by Beaujeu, who states that he is writing instead of La Salle because of the latter's illness.[10] The accuracy and intent of this letter can be gauged by the Minet and Joutel journals. Then, as the actual exchange of messages begins after the separation of the company on two ships, both sides can be monitored externally through the two officers' journals. Unfortunately for historians, these letters are devoted primarily to a lengthy argument over departure times, revictualing of the *Joly,* and the reasons for loss of the *Aimable.* Beaujeu's log for the *Joly* does not survive as far as we know, and that of the *Aimable* presumably perished with the ship.

The Abbé d'Esmanville, one of the seven clerics who accompanied the expedition, gives an account of the sea voyage that is fairly complete in its description of the highlights. (D'Esmanville remained on the *Joly* throughout the voyage.) But it is very much compressed in comparison with those of Minet and Joutel, relating little more than the bare facts. The "extract" from d'Esmanville's journal printed by Margry is said to have come from the collection of the Abbé Dangeau, contained in the correspondence of Cabart de Villermont in the Bibliothèque Nationale; but Margry also states that he was unable to relocate it, so it is presumably lost.[11] Its appearance among Villermont's papers—he was instrumental in securing the appointments of Beaujeu and Minet—implies that d'Esmanville was also not of La Salle's choosing. His journal states that he had been sent to evangelize Indians, not to participate in an at-

---

8 See the map reconstructing the route of the *Aimable* in Villiers, *L'Expédition,* facing p. 78. Although the *Joly*'s route is not shown here, Villiers used the Minet journal to aid in the reconstruction: see Villiers, *L'Expédition,* pp. 65–66.
9 Ibid., p. 11; See also Margry, *Découvertes,* II, 449–51 (Beaujeu to Villermont, July 10, 1684).
10 Margry, *Découvertes,* II 485–99.
11 Ibid., III, 631.

tack on the Mexican mines—"to make war on demons and not on Christians."[12] Minet characterizes the abbé as a priest of the St. Sulpice seminary who chose not to remain with La Salle.[13] Certainly his remaining with the ship to the end of her voyage does not appear to have been questioned. Beaujeu, in fact, refers Seignelay to d'Esmanville as a good source of information, noting that he "made this voyage with me."[14]

The account of La Salle's brother, Jean Cavelier, has been thoroughly discredited. Both Villiers du Terrage and Delanglez show at length that the "journal" demonstrates Cavelier's self-interest. Villiers does so with Minet's help but without access to the various versions of Cavelier, and Delanglez complements Joutel's testimony with other correspondence. D'Esmanville testifies that Cavelier wished to return to France with Beaujeu.[15]

Margry was able to locate the abridged version of Minet's journal that was prepared for Seignelay and a set of maps that Minet sent to the minister upon his return in the vain hope that his defection would be forgiven.[16] But for some reason the longer journal was not printed, perhaps because it was hidden away in a private collection, perhaps because of Margry's own bias. The brief version is as condensed as d'Esmanville's extract. Its statements about La Salle and Minet's reasons for leaving him, taken in the context of the cover letter from Minet to Seignelay (also printed by Margry), make it seem less truthful and more partisan. So clearly was this the case that Villiers, with a copy of the lengthier version at hand, doubted its authenticity.[17] Yet a careful collation of dates shows that it does not contradict the facts in the complete account, if indeed it does add some self-interested commentary. In any case, it is not possible to compare the handwriting with that of the longer version, of which Villiers was unable to re-locate a manuscript copy that he had seen previously.[18]

Minet's journal proper seems to have had, in a physical sense, an interesting career in its own right. It is obvious from examination of the existing manuscript in the collections of the Public Archives of Can-

12 Ibid., II, 515.
13 Minet, "Journal," p. 54.
14 Margry, *Découvertes*, II, 588 (Beaujeu to Seignelay, August, 1685).
15 Delanglez, *Journal*; Villiers, *L'Expédition*, pp. 202–204; Margry, *Découvertes*, II, 516.
16 Margry, *Découvertes*, II, 591–601.
17 Villiers, *L'Expédition*, pp. 60–61.
18 Margry (*Découvertes*, III, 647) states that it comes from the Dépôt des Cartes, plans et journaux de la marine, petites archives, 6ᵉ division. Villiers (*L'Expédition*, p. 60) says that he could not find the original.

ada—which was acquired from a private American collection[19]—that there is no separation between Minet's journal and the account of the 1682 expedition that precedes it; they were certainly always joined in the same small notebook. According to Villiers du Terrage, who quotes extensively from a journal of Minet entitled *Journal de nostre voyage au golfe de Mexique fait par le sieur Minet, Ingénieur du Roy,* there was a manuscript in existence prior to his writing in 1931 that also consisted of two sections. Villiers says that he examined this journal in a private French collection and remarks that it "remains unpublished."[20] A comparison of a few of the quotations in Villiers and parallel passages in the manuscript under discussion here shows that the quotations must have come from a more polished but practically identical version of our Minet journal (although one must be careful in making these comparisons, since Villiers quotes without distinction from both the long version of the journal that he saw in manuscript and the summary one printed in Margry).

Since Villiers's description of the manuscript clearly proclaims it to be the same as the one we are examining, we must consider the probability that, besides normalizing the spelling, Villiers edited these extracts for publication. If so, it would be a rather damaging indictment, for in this very work he makes serious criticisms of such practices by Margry. There is even a passage specifically quoted by Villiers as coming from the second part—the "Minet Journal"—of this manuscript, which has in fact been shifted from the end of the earlier section.[21] Villiers indicates that the manuscript he saw had several maps, not only those we have already mentioned in the 1682 portion but also several more, including probably the Minet version of the Franquelin map.[22] Although the manuscript we are discussing here has no drawings to accompany this section, there is reference in the text to several maps and drawings: surveys of the shore of Santo Domingo (fol. 6), a map of Petit Goâve

19 Victorin Chabot, "Journal inédit relatant les expéditions de Cavelier de La Salle," *The Archivist* 8 (1981): 8–9.
20 Villiers, *L'Expédition,* p. 13. On p. 163 Villiers describes what indisputably is our manuscript: "L manuscrit . . . commence par reconter tres brièvement les premiers voyages de La Salle au Canada et, beaucoup plus en détail, l'exploration du Mississippi, d'aprés les renseignements que lui avaient fournis le Père Zénobe, Barbier et le jeune Cavelier [*sic*]"; it contains "cartes du fort Frontenac et du delta du Mississippi."
21 See especially ibid., p. 32, concerning La Salle's efforts to finance the expedition.
22 Ibid., p. 39. Villiers refers to AN, Service Hydrographique 4014^c, *cartes générales* no. 3, but this seems to be the same map cited in Jean Delanglez, *Some La Salle Journeys,* p. 79, as AN, Service Hydrographique, C4044–4.

(fol. 7), and a drawing of the bay where the *Aimable* grounded (fol. 36). If Villiers is correct, then these maps probably did once form a part of the Public Archives of Canada manuscript. The last-mentioned of these and a companion map of the coast in the vicinity of La Salle's camp are reproduced with the journal from copies obtained by Mary Christine Morkovsky in the French National Archives. There are copies in the Woodbury Lowery Collection, Library of Congress. These maps correspond to Spanish copies obtained by Pedro de Ronquillo, Spain's ambassador to England, and forwarded in 1687 to the viceroy in Mexico. The soundings over the bar at the mouth of Matagorda Bay that are indicated on the maps correspond reasonably well to those given in Minet's journal, as the journal itself indicates. The two "Minet maps" printed by Villiers without clear attribution except the journal manuscript are near duplicates of the archival maps.[23]

Villiers also says that Minet indicates the longitude only once,[24] and this is true of our Minet manuscript also. (The abbreviated version of the Minet journal printed by Margry indicates neither latitudes nor longitudes, and those in Cavelier's works are almost entirely fanciful.) Another problem arises from the fact that in the manuscript at hand the title differs somewhat from the document cited by Villiers, the layout of which is approximated:

> Journal de nostre voiage au golphe
> de mexique. ~~fait par le sieur~~
> ~~Minet Ingenieur du Roy~~

It seems obvious that the short heading was written first, since it is nicely centered on the page, and that the additional part of the title was added later, then crossed out. The style of the crossing-out, which consists of a series of loops like a stretched spring, *eeee* is identical to that used in other parts of the manuscript (see ff. 5, 14, 22, 29, 51). Presumably, Villiers chose to ignore this expression of Minet's intention. It is

---

23 The Spanish copies are reproduced in Robert S. Weddle, *Wilderness Manhunt: The Spanish Search for La Salle,* as plates 3 and 6. They are nearly identical to the maps shown in Villiers (*L'Expédition,* 122, 130) and to the originals shown here (plates 7 and 8), except for an unexplained difference in the soundings. Both maps portray the entrance to Matagorda Bay where *Aimable* ran aground, and the "Plan de la Coste" shows Cedar Bayou (lower left), where La Salle first landed his soldiers. H. Dickson Hoese ("On the Correct Landfall of La Salle in Texas, 1685," *Louisiana History* 19, no. 1 [Winter 1978]: 6, 18) reproduces the maps from the Woodbury Lowery Collection.

24 Villiers, *L'Expédition,* p. 62.

also odd that Villiers encountered difficulty in establishing the identity of Nicolas de La Salle.[25] Minet makes it clear that Nicolas was not related to La Salle, and the 1682 account demonstrates that Nicolas indeed had valid claim to having served seven years in the New World. Yet Villiers fails to recognize that the account of the 1683 journey ascribed by Nicolas and published by Margry was recast by another hand. On several counts Villiers fails to interpret the evidence of this manuscript properly, so it is doubly fortunate that its complete text has become available.

The Minet manuscript in the Public Archives of Canada is easily recognized as an authentic, rough-draft journal. Not only does it contain numerous deletions, but there are also a number of marginal notes added, not as signals to the textual content, as was common in finished works of the period, but as commentary and afterthought. The notes amplify rather than summarize. Minet himself states, in the cover letter that accompanied his abridged journal, that he has written a detailed account of the places he visited and mapped, but that he will not send it until he has made a clean copy.[26] In the condensed version he compressed the material, leaving it in journal form but excluding latitude readings and much other detail. The original journal has a much greater immediacy, not only in its awkward phraseology and spelling but also in its reflection through several entries of his developing understanding of his subject matter.

It would be interesting to know what Delanglez would have made of the Minet journal, given his preoccupation with the political currents in France that surrounded the expedition. It is clear that neither Minet nor Beaujeu had anything to do with the anti-Jesuit, pro–La Salle cabal that Delanglez was so concerned with. On the contrary, it is clear from Beaujeu's correspondence to his friend Villermont before the departure of the expedition that Minet had been chosen for the assignment through the same agency.[27] His orders to serve La Salle came directly from Minister Seignelay, as he says repeatedly throughout the journal. By a technicality of these orders, which stated that he was to stay with Beaujeu as long as the *Joly* was "at sea," Minet argued that, since no harbor was found for the large ship, he was technically justified in not remaining with the colonial venture. He certainly thought it destined to fail, and doubtless his sense of honor was offended when La Salle repeatedly rebuffed him and rejected his offers of advice on strategic siting and for-

25 Ibid., pp. 156–58.
26 Margry, *Découvertes,* II, 602.
27 Ibid., p. 435 (Beaujeu to Villermont, June 15, 1684).

tification. But it is not possible to conclude with confidence that he intentionally provoked La Salle into sending him away. Seignelay's imprisoning him upon his return argues against his being a spy sent by the minister, as La Salle alleged; but his imprisonment was brief (July 22 to September 7), and his subsequent assignment to work with Vauban implies that he was not in disgrace.

Part of the worth of Minet's observations comes from our judgment of his access to sound information. From La Rochelle to Petit Goâve, La Salle was aboard the *Joly*. Minet's statements indicate that the two conferred from time to time but were hardly close associates, and here the fact that Minet's record of latitude observations rarely coincides with Joutel's may be significant. Villiers says that La Salle permitted no one to know what these observations were,[28] but they probably were made two or three times a day, weather permitting, by sun observation at noon and polaris sighting at morning and evening twilight. Joutel, as one of La Salle's more trusted officers, may well have had free access to them, whereas Minet may have made his own calculations independently and in secret or else obtained them from Captain Beaujeu or his pilot.

Minet provides interesting information from his activities on shore at Petit Goâve while La Salle lay ill. One item of particular interest concerns their destination, about which Minet sought to inform himself from everyone he met in the port town. He quotes at length from a Dutch buccaneer captain who quite likely was a henchman of Laurens de Graff ("Lorencillo" to the Spaniards), who was well acquainted with the Mexican coast from his various raids. Later, Minet reports that La Salle's party was to have sailed with the French pirate Michel de Grammont's fleet as it went to take Spanish Santo Domingo. This did not happen, however, since Grammont sailed before La Salle was ready to depart. Joutel says that La Salle had urgent business with the French officials from the Ile de Tortue (Saint-Laurent, Bégon, and Cussy). Later, Joutel reports that La Salle, Saint-Laurent, Bégon, and Beaujeu conferred privately on the route to be taken, calling in a privateer pilot to provide hydrographical advice on the Gulf of Mexico. Putting these facts together with the information that Cussy had received orders to "rehabilitate" Graff and Grammont and enlist their support for the taking of Spanish Santo Domingo, thus ending their depredations on the Spanish colonies,[29] there is room to speculate that their attack on Campeche on July 6, 1685, was intended to divert Spanish attention

28 Villiers, *L'Expédition*, p. 10.
29 Weddle, *Wilderness Manhunt*, p. 40.

from La Salle's endeavors. If so, it was to no purpose, since deserters from La Salle's company caught by the Spaniards with the pirates alerted them to the French incursion.

We have seen that Minet's observations from Petit Goâve to Texas are valuable for their information on Beaujeu's voyage. Villiers has used them in plotting the route.[30] Once arrived off the Texas coast, Minet took part in coastal explorations and depth soundings requisite to mapping the area of La Salle's camp. He turned his hand to helping the pilots set the buoys and landmarks that might have saved the *Aimable,* had her captain heeded them, and after the wreck he and others of the *Joly's* crew helped unload the store ship. Throughout, his view of the company's activities from offshore makes a useful contrast to Joutel's onshore view. In particular, one can see how Villiers, with access to Minet's journal, acquired his strong impression of Beaujeu's reasonableness. The portrait drawn by Minet is of an officer who was firm in his devotion to his duty to La Salle's mission but concerned as a commander with the welfare of his men and his ship.

Once La Salle had decided on a landing at Matagorda Bay, Beaujeu spent much time in his ship's boat and even on shore, seeking a suitable harbor for the *Joly* so that the settlement could proceed as planned. Even when it became obvious that no such port was available, the captain made every effort to help get the *Aimable* into the shelter of the bay before his departure, in spite of La Salle's refusal to accept advice from the *Joly's* pilots or help in lightening the store ship. Even after the vessel was wrecked, Beaujeu deployed all his forces to save as much of the cargo as possible. Although pressed by diminishing supplies of food and fresh water and unable to find either in the bay's environs, the captain awaited La Salle's decision as to the kind of relief he should send him, receiving nothing in return but veiled insult and threat. Finally, unable to wait longer without jeopardizing his return to France, Beaujeu yet consented to bear the expense of feeding the *Aimable's* crew so as to take them off La Salle's hands. Because of the extra men, he was unable to reach the so-called Bay of the Holy Spirit (Saint-Esprit or Espíritu Santo) and had to make instead for Cuba. Bad weather and an encounter with Spanish pirates forced Beaujeu to heed the advice of an English ship captain met at sea and sail for Virginia, where he could revictual his ship for the Atlantic crossing. This route offered the additional advantage of enabling him to reconnoiter the English settlement of Jamestown.

There is no striking new evidence here to suggest a sinister motive for Beaujeu's alleged desertion of La Salle; the accumulation of detail

30 Villiers, *L'Expédition*, pp. 59–111.

simply indicates that a combination of the provision shortage, bad weather, and apparent danger from Spain (Beaujeu had no way of knowing that peace had been made) forced his decision. It seemed that the best he could do for his ship and La Salle's enterprise was to return to France with a report as soon as possible. Minet's viewpoint does not suggest that he enjoyed Beaujeu's confidence in such matters; thus, these practical considerations assume greater importance in assessing the reasons for Beaujeu's course of action.

And what of Minet himself, and his relations with La Salle? Minet's report of the explorer's effort to have him join the company on shore suggests that he had been sent as a military engineer attached to the soldiery whose purpose was to seize the Spanish mines; clearly, Minet believed that he was to have been called upon to undertake siege works, rather than the building of a fort to protect a settlement. Yet it was obvious to Minet, as it is to us, that La Salle's soldiers, diminished by disease and weakened by malnourishment, could not have withstood a concerted attack by the neighboring Indians and certainly were not up to a long overland march to attack a settled Spanish garrison. Whatever Minet's failures of character or loyalty, he was obviously convinced that the expedition's prime motive was conquest; he knew that failure to find promptly the promised easy water route to the objective was tantamount to failure of the mission and the expedition itself, unless a more secure place for a settlement was found. And it must be admitted that, during the entire time that the *Joly* held her ground in the exposed anchorage awaiting La Salle's decision, no effort was made to relocate the encampment.

Unlike Minet, we are privy to other sources, including Joutel's journal and La Salle's letters to the Crown. In Minet's view, La Salle was reduced to hysterical and irrational behavior by the failure of his undertaking. Yet Minet's report allows us a three-dimensional view, since his attitudes doubtless reflect the feelings of the majority who watched mostly from the wings, unable to hear properly as the major actors in this tragedy worked out their fate on center stage. From this perspective, La Salle appears to have been misguided and mistaken in the involved interpretation of the circumstances confronting him and his own capacity for dealing with them.

The growing doubt was reflected in the faces and actions of all the supporting players. The leader's growing awareness that everyone, including himself, had forgotten his lines as he found himself playing to a hostile audience in an unfamiliar stage setting, and his realization that he alone must improvise to fit the altered script without changing the cast or the assigned roles, led, not surprisingly, to some desperate false starts. These were all that Minet saw before the *Joly* left the scene. But such behavior does not indict La Salle for madness, as Minet thought; nor does Minet's failure to pick up on the cues he was offered in the newly invented scene indict the engineer for desertion. The simple fact is that, once again, complex human beings failed to understand one another: history play or morality play, the theme remains the same.

Journal of Our Voyage to the Gulf of Mexico

MINET

[Translated by

ANN LINDA BELL

and annotated by

ROBERT S. WEDDLE]

After Monsieur de La Salle had made friends who introduced him to the Marquis de Seignelay, he gave him a map of the river and showed him how it flowed into the Gulf of Mexico. [He represented that] the reason they had not gone into it [the Gulf], even though it was very recognizable by the jetties it [the river] makes seven leagues into the sea, is that this country is low, disagreeable marshland and always flooded. Nevertheless, at its mouth it is 20 to 25 fathoms deep. Besides that, its being far back in the gulf where few boats dare to go, [and] being that [he] is the only one who had descended it, it has not been explored. What could be profitable from it to the king is to make a settlement in the direction of the Tainsa (not counting the one that would be made at the mouth of the river); from there all the fur trade would be attracted, the savages having only to descend the rivers to bring them to you. This land is extremely good, and all one can hope for in life will come from it.

The river that he calls Seignelay is the river of the north on which one could go on to New Mexico.[1] Even though there are rivers that descend from New Biscay [Nueva Vizcaya], one could go to the mines of Zacatecas, to Durango, and St. Barbe [Santa Bárbara]. Since the savages of Louisiana elected him chief of all their nations, knowing ten to 12 leagues of this country, he could do with them whatever he wanted. If his majesty wished to give him arms, cannon, gunpowder, and two hundred men, he would arm these savages and would go and attack

1 The Red River. The hydrographical description that follows reflects La Salle's erroneous concepts.

these Spaniards in their own country. The vessels could ascend the river up to the Seignelay, give him help, and he would ask of His Majesty at present only one *fluste* [flûte] and one bark to carry the food, arms, gunpowder, and men. When the flute returned, one could then send more vessels to do all that would be desired.

He was given 100 men—and would have to raise 100 at his own expense—powder, arms, some petard cannon, and the *Joly,* a third-class vessel, Monsieur [Tanguy Le Gallois] de Beaujeu, captain of the vessel, to take charge of it, and an engineer. The officers of this troop should be people who knew the savages. Nevertheless, he sold a portion of the commissions that Monsieur Morel had given him and gave the rest to his nephews or those of M. de Tonty, of a Canadian, and of M. de la Sablonnieres.[2] There was also an old officer of the infantry [Valigny] to whom a company had been given, but I do not count him in the number because of the inconvenience, besides which he left us at St. Domingue.

Having arrived at La Rochelle the second or third of June, we prepared to leave, but, Mons. de la Salle's business not being completed, we waited a long time to leave. During that time Monsieur de Beaujeu lent him a hundred *pistoles.* He also came to me and told me that if I had money he would repay me double in Louisiana. I told him I had none. "Ask for your salary," he said to me. I trusted him. Monsieur Arnoul, the intendant at Rochefort, had the goodness to give me twelve hundred *livres,* which I gave him.

We left from the *chef de bois* before La Rochelle the 24th of July, 1684, with four ships of our company: the *Joly,* the frigate *Belle,* which the king gave him instead of the little bark that was requested; a flute called the *Aimable*—which he chartered at his own expense [and] which carried the provisions and craftsmen's tools that had been given to him, seven cadets, and 40 hired workers—and a ketch [*Saint-François*] for which the intendant paid half the charter in order to carry the rest of the provisions, since we could put no more into the *Joly* or the other two ships.

The 26th the bowsprit of the *Joly* broke. We were obliged to return

2 The phraseology seems confused. As far as is known, there were no nephews of Tonti, or Tonty, or of Sablonnière on the voyage. On April 14, 1684, Tonti was given a royal order naming Sablonnière a lieutenant in his infantry company aboard the *Joly,* in port at Rochefort. (Tonti, however, did not make the voyage to the Gulf.) Similar orders were sent Valigny for the Sieurs d'Autray, Barbier (probably the Canadian Minet refers to), and Crevel de Moranget, La Salle's own nephew (Pierre Margry, ed., *Découvertes et établissements des français dans l'ouest et dans le sud de l'Amérique septentrionale,* II, 386–87.

and anchor before the island of Aix. I felt ill. I got off with Barbier on the island, where I let blood [*silé*] with a broken stone, like the savages. Since then I have felt fine.

[We] left August first.

The 8th we had gone ten leagues opposite the capes.

The 13th we were in latitude [*hauteur*] 37° N and S with Madere [Madeira], traveling the route to St. Domingue, making SE. At night we had calm, and the days were bright.

The 20th at midnight, being in latitude 33° 15', something like a piece of fire the size of a large barrel fell from the sky two cannon shots from our ship, which appeared all blue for the space of two minutes.

The 21st of August, latitude 32° 25', longitude 354°, Dutch; variation from the east side 2°.

September first, wind SSE, rain, bad weather. The flute and the ketch lost us.

The 2nd, south wind.

Monsieur de La Salle always had five or six spies on the bridge. One could not say a word that was not wrongly interpreted. As for me, since Monsieur le Marquis de Seignelay had ordered me to obey him with regard to my commission as engineer, and I had to keep within bounds with him, added to the promise he [La Salle] had made me that I would be forever rich, I said not a word and tried to calm his mind, which would become sour over nothing. But I was no more exempt than the others. He said that I was a spy on his actions, that they had sent me with him to see everything he was doing, that it was his enemies who had given me to the Marquis de Seignelay to go with him, etc. I had already had time to take his measure, but I succeeded in understanding the mind of this man who, with all the qualities of the country where he was born,[3] had mixed among the savages, and had a great esteem of himself.

The 5th in the morning, we were under the tropics [*sous le tropiques;* i.e., had crossed the Tropic of Cancer]. The sailors were preparing to christen [initiate] us, but Mons. de La Salle and his officers opposed them, saying that he did not want to be the object of ridicule of the officers of the ship. Monsieur de Beaujeu, to avoid trouble, made the sailors withdraw.

We came upon some grass floating on the water from 27° on [[Drawings follow]]. That is what amazed the crew of Christopher Columbus during his discovery.

3 La Salle's being a Norman, Minet thus indicates that he himself was not.

From the morning of the 18th until the 19th there was a strong wind with rain, lightning, and thunder. Our ships had rejoined us. This bad weather made us lose them once more.

The 22nd at six o'clock in the morning we saw the land of St. Domingue. From Cape Samaná to Cape Cabrón [northeast part of the island of Hispaniola], I took sightings [bearings] of the shore [[Drawings follow]].

The 23rd, latitude taken 19° 50′. Being opposite the mountains that are east of Monto Christo [Monte Cristi], we see by that that the Island of St. Domingue [Hispaniola] is 10 leagues too far north on the map, verified by several latitudes.

The currents and the wind favorable. It was said that the shores we were coasting were not exact, but different ways of seeing them sometimes causes this.

September 25th we passed before Isle de Tortue, which belongs to the king.[4] The night of the 25th we were opposite Cape St. Nicolas.

The 26th, opposite the Island of Guanabo [Ile de Gonâve], we went to see if we could take on water. Having calm, we were not able to reach Petit Goâve [Haiti]. The canoe went aground; but when we wanted to get out of it, we sank in a white mud that resembled lime. We returned on board without bringing on anything but a lot of mud. All that I noticed was that at one league from that island there are rocks on the surface of the water and that it is not good to approach them, at least not toward the part facing west.

The 27th anchored before Petit Goâve at 5 o'clock in the evening, in 25 fathoms, bottom of rotten boulders.

The 28th we ran farther into the bay, to 15 fathoms. Monsieur de La Salle still in a bad mood.

The 30th he became ill and delirious, believing that all those he saw were coming to prosecute him, saying that he had betrayed the Marquis de Seignelay.

4. Called Tortuga by the Spaniards, this rugged island off the north coast of Haiti served first as a refuge for English and French interlopers, then became the focus of a three-way struggle for possession until the first French governor with legal authority took charge and it became definitely French. It was on the Ile de Tortue and in the adjacent area of Hispaniola that the English term "buccaneer" and the practice of buccaneering as it was known in the West Indies in the late seventeenth century developed. The word evolved from a Carib-French combination, *boucanier*, applied to those lawless characters who hunted wild cattle and swine and smoked the meat by the *boucan* process—a pursuit often combined with piracy. Clarence Henry Haring, *The Buccaneers in the West Indies in the XVII Century*, pp. 58–67, 113–19.

[[October]] The 3rd, 4th, 8th, I drew a map of Petit Goâve.

The 12th, took latitude, found 18° 10′.[5] M. de La Salle's illness continues. We made an oven to bake some bread. Breaking an egg, we found yet another egg within it.

October 19, M. de La Salle's illness continues, always with dreams.

The 20th at night we saw ships from afar. We sent the longboat. We found out that it was Monsieur [Michel de] Bégon, intendant of the islands; and the commandant St. Laurent, the king's lieutenant for the islands and governor of St. Cristophe; Monsieur du Cussy [Tarin de Cussy]; and Monsieur de Franquenet, governor and lieutenant of St. Domingue.

We found out that the ketch [*Saint-François*] which had left us the 28th of August[6] with the flute during the bad weather, had anchored at Port de Paix behind La Tortue, whence these gentlemen came, [and] wishing to come and join us at Petit Goâve, [it] had been taken by a Spanish pirogue or galley. These are small, very long ships with 40 or 50 oars. They go from country to country and surprise the ships when they can. They [those on the ketch] had 25 barrels of provisions for Mons. de La Salle.

Description of the Part of the Island of St. Domingue That the French Own[7]

All the dwellings are scattered from one shore to the other. La Tortue is our first settlement. [[Tortue is an island.]] Opposite is Cape François and the Port de Paix and many other little spots scattered from one side to the other around these two places. Farther south, in the Yaguana Gulf [Golfe de la Gonâve], you have Léaugane [Léogâne], Grand Goâve, Petit Goâve, and Nipe [Petit Trou de Nippes]. All these lands are extremely good and fruitful, the country full of mountains and hills that are covered with trees that need to be cleared. Beautiful cotton grows

---

5 Short at least 15′.

6 September 16, according to Henri Joutel ("Relation de Henri Joutel," in Margry, *Découvertes,* III, 96).

7 French colonization of western Hispaniola (present-day Haiti) radiated from Tortuga, which was ceded to the French West Indies Company by Louis XIV in 1664. The French Crown included in the Tortuga governor's patent full jurisdiction over the settlement on western Santo Domingo, or Hispaniola (Saint-Domingue to the French), although Spain did not immediately recognize such claims. Clarence Henry Haring, *Trade and Navigation between Spain and the Indies in the Time of the Hapsburgs,* p. 249; William Edward Dunn, *Spanish and French Rivalry in the Gulf Region of the United States, 1678–1702: The Beginnings of Texas and Pensacola,* pp. 9–10.

there, good tobacco, cassia trees, sugar, corn, cassava, and cochineal. Among the fruits are pineapples, bananas, guavas, avocados, the nut and fruit of cashew and grapes the year round. The tuberoses are eaten when they begin to bud, as in France we eat asparagus. Nevertheless, commerce is mediocre. They all go buccaneering [*en flibuste*] like our corsairs of the Mediterranean Sea, and they return there to eat and drink the catch they have made. They do not take up cultivating the land at all. It would be necessary for France to make a good settlement by sending peasants, male and female, to establish a fort and a garrison somewhere in that area and make everybody work. But it would be necessary to grant them certain privileges at the beginning to encourage them. In the mountains there are horses, mules, and wild donkeys, which we take when we want to. Thus, there is nobody so poor as not to be mounted. In the lands behind the mountains there are plains 40 leagues long filled with all sorts of animals—cattle, pigs, turkey-cocks, guinea-fowls, wood pigeons, etc.

On the 24th [of October] Monsieur de Beaujeu fell ill and I also. After four days our fever left us. Mons. de La Salle was better, and there was talk of leaving. The 1st of November Monsr. de La Salle told the intendant that he wanted to buy a small captured Spanish bark that was at Petit Goâve. After Monsieur Bégon bought it for him, he retracted. Thus he [Bégon] was stuck with it.[8]

Monsieur Bégon and Monsieur de St. Laurent had come to arm the buccaneers and go to take the town of St. Domingue [Santo Domingo]. We would have been in the party, but they found the fleet commanded by M. de Gramont, composed of 25 vessels, gone.

They sent a message to the governor and intendant of St. Domingue concerning the limits of the island, to settle it among themselves; but they replied that they had no order from their king, and that they were going to write to Spain.[9]

The 11th, 12th, and 13th [of November] we loaded corn [*mays*] for M. de La Salle's 100 soldiers and for the crew of the *Joly*.

8 Joutel, "Relation," p. 104: Bégon offered La Salle a bark that had been taken as a prize by the *flibustiers*, but, since it had little freeboard and the Gulf was so rough, La Salle had to decline.
9 Spanish fears that the French intended expanding their claims to include the entire island of Hispaniola, from this indication, were well justified. Instructions of the French minister Seignelay to Cussy for using the pirate fleet to take possession of Santo Domingo were intercepted with the capture of a French vessel in the Windward Passage by a Spanish privateer late in 1685 (letters translated from French, UT archives, transcript, AGI, Mexico 616; Robert S. Weddle, *Wilderness Manhunt: The Spanish Search for La Salle*, pp. 39–40).

[[I forgot to say that every day they told Monsieur Bégon and Monsieur de Beaujeu that it was not necessary to load so much food, that when he arrived they would give us provisions, as much as we wanted. They got angry even about what we had taken.]] M. de la Salle's health is the same as it was when he left France. He says every day that he wants to leave but does not go aboard.

Those we ask who have been in the Gulf of Mexico are not familiar with Monsieur de La Salle's river. Some have been there [to the Gulf] five or six times. They say that at 40 leagues from land, as far as 30 and 27 degrees, there are 20 to 30 fathoms and that, approaching land, it is merely swamp. They landed. There are miserable savages who live on roots; but, as for rivers, they have seen none, but there are many large lagoons [lakes] in the land and some little outlets, but, as a general rule, one league from shore there is a fathom's depth. As for water at the entrance of the Baye du St. Esprit [Espíritu Santo or Holy Spirit], there are four fathoms up against the island; and, toward Pánuco, there is no way to approach the coast except by canoe; in addition, good weather and offshore winds are necessary. The north winds are extremely hazardous from the month of October to the month of January. Afterward, you have the south winds, so that if you approach the coast you are lost. These two winds are to be feared, one in the winter and the other in summer.

Le Sage, Dutch buccaneer captain, said that 20 years ago he went there with the Dutch, always following the coast, to search for a settlement. They were never able to find the least shelter for their vessels; and, after having searched thoroughly, a north wind took them and cast them on the Jucatan [Yucatán] reefs, and he saved himself. A Spaniard who took them to the pirate ship said that he had been on these coasts eleven times and that he shipwrecked six times. He had traversed all this country but never saw a large river on this coast, only a number of small ones. I forgot to say that everyone says that the land is low and nearly at sea level; there is always fog, which might cast one upon the shore; besides, the weather is always bad.[10]

The 24th. Mons. de La Salle did not embark in the *Joly* but boarded the *Aimable* because a part of the food and merchandise was on her, since there were some Norman cadets among the hired men, whom he feared could not handle his vessel.[11]

10 Concerning Le Sage, see Beaujeu to Seignelay in Margry, *Découvertes*, II, 488. This letter also gives an account of the pirate captain Du Chesne, who had raided Tampico the previous year.
11 Thenceforth, Joutel ("Relation," p. 166) and Minet chronicle the voyage from different ships, as Joutel goes with La Salle aboard the *Aimable*.

The 25th of November we set sail. We left Petit Goâve, where we left
M. de Valigny, an old officer who had been given M. de La Salle to command the first company of the four he was to have received. Many
others wanted to leave, but they were made to board. Only three boys
whom he had taken on as secretaries in Paris and at La Rochelle ransomed themselves with money.[12] Sickness cost him many. He was compelled to pay his debts by selling powder, flour, and cordage.

On the 26th we maneuvered to get out of the gulf [of Gonâve].

The 27th we reached Nipe [Petit Trou de Nippes, Haiti]. M. de la
Salle said that he wanted to anchor at the Isle of Pines [l'Isle de Pins].[13]
[[Drawing]].

The 29th at noon we saw the mountains of Cuba. The *Aimable,* as
usual, stayed behind. We were constantly forced to heave to and wait for
her. It is to be noted that from the time we left France we always navigated with only the two topsails, yet most of the time tacking because
never had a flute been so bad. It was always necessary to wait for her.

November 30th, always hugging the coast of Cuba, which faces
south. NW wind. When we first approached land, the wind shifted to NE
and then to E. There are currents, which carried us extremely quickly
along this coast [and] which go due west.

December 1st in the evening we saw Little Cayman west of us, tending a little toward the south.

The 3rd at midnight we hove to since we thought we were close to
land. At this place there are southerly currents. In the morning we
found ourselves against some rocks that are on the Isle of Pines. That
night we stayed at the cape, putting off until morning to look for an
anchorage on the Isle of Pines.

December 4th we set sail, coasting the island. The longboat went to
search for an anchorage. Not finding one in all the coves that we saw, we
continued west. That night we held the course.

On the 5th we tacked in order to anchor in a cove that the longboat
had found, sandy bottom. Anchored at noon in 16 fathoms at this place.

12 One of these, assuredly, was Denis Thomas, who joined the pirate fleet at
Petit Goâve and, when captured by the Spanish Armada de Barlovento (the
Windward Fleet) following the 1685 pirate raid on Campeche, disclosed to his
Spanish interrogators La Salle's enterprise (Denis Thomas, "Declaración,"
UT archives, transcript, AGI, Mexico 616.

13 The Isle of Pines, formerly known for its prison in which Fidel Castro was
confined, has undergone a name change under Castro's regime. As an indoc-
trination site for the young, it is called Isla de la Juventud (Isle of Youth). See
Fred Ward, "Inside Cuba Today," *National Geographic* 151, no. 1 (January,
1977): 43.

[[Drawing]] This is the Isle of Pines. The shores are lined with palm trees and are all full of rocks. The side of the island where we were runs SE and NW. The *Belle* came to anchor at three o'clock in the afternoon and the *Aimable* at midnight.

We disembarked. We killed a crocodile eight feet long. I wanted to eat some. It smells like old fish mixed with another wretched taste and a strong odor. There we also killed some wild rats, which are tasty enough [and] which are as large as rabbits and of the color of wolf fur.[14]

On the 6th we observed latitude 22°27'. We killed a wild pig and two crocodiles or caimans.[15] There is no fresh water in that place.

December 8th we weighed anchor in a north wind, that night NE.

The 9th we saw Cape Corrientes.

The 10th we posted watches. That night we approached this cape. The west wind having died down, we passed a league from shore. We no longer saw the rock or the reef that is marked on the map. Wind from the north.

The 11th we saw Cape St. Anthoine [Cabo San Antonio]. That night we posted watches and on the 12th also, between the two capes. The wind from N continued still. At noon we resolved to double Cape St. Anthoine with a NE wind that was blowing then. After that, when the wind turned N, it was necessary to fall back and look for an anchorage around this cape. After having found one, that night, we anchored in 30 fathoms in a large cove south of the island, east of this cape. We were swept away and took three hours to get back to the anchorage. At a quarter of a league from shore there were 30 fathoms on one side of the ship and 50 on the other.

On the 13th at 9 o'clock we weighed anchor with a NE wind. We doubled Cape St. Anthoine and set course NW. That night the wind from north. Bad weather setting in, we came about and fell back upon the cape.

On the 14th we set sail again from the same place we had left the day before.

On the 15th we went ashore to look for water. We found a pond (which is a league and a half around) 200 paces from the seashore, full

14 Muskrats (*Ondatra zibethica*) are a possibility.
15 Probably anchored behind Cabo Francés, the ships would have been in about latitude 21°31'. Minet is almost a degree in error. The pig was the domesticated kind brought to Cuba by the Spaniards and used to provision expeditions of conquest and exploration such as Hernando de Soto's. See Joutel, "Relation," p. 109. Although Minet might easily have confused crocodiles and alligators, these (being saltwater creatures) would have been genus *Crocodylus*.

of ducks and marsh hens. At noon we took latitudes with Monsieur de Beaujeu's quadrant, which has a radius of a foot and a half. We found 21°50' latitude.[16] That night it rained. On the night of the 16th, heavy weather.

On the 17th at 2 hrs. after midnight we were driven upon our anchor. The *Belle* was also and struck against the *Aimable,* breaking the main yard. The *Belle* discovered that her mizzenmast and main topsail yard were broken. That night heavy weather again.

On the 18th wind NE. M. de la Salle wanted to leave. We got under way at ten o'clock in the morning.

It is very difficult to determine the currents here. We observed them always going with the wind.

December 19th, wind NE. That evening, rain. That evening we headed NNW to fall in with the flute, which was drifting very much SW. That night we hove to, waiting for the *Aimable.*

On the 20th, calm. That evening, squall. Course NNW. [[A Squall is a storm cloud that brings a big wind and some rain, which lasts an hour and half at most.]]

The 21st calm. At noon a little wind. Latitude 25°09'. Eclipse of the moon. Its largest blackout at 5:20. Its end, which I most noticed, at 6:20 in the evening. We were here, according to the altitude [of the pole star] at the time of the eclipse, at 25°16' [[latitude, and longitude 288°]]. Having made four leagues NNW since noon, at Paris, according to the reckoning of time, it should end at 12:27. Thus, the longitude from here to Paris is six hours and seven minutes [of lunar travel], which are 91°45'.[17]

The 22nd, slight wind. Course [*Le cap au*] NW by N, wind NE by E.

The 23rd, calm, light wind, NE, E. That evening N, W, NNW.

The 24th, rain and high wind, N, N by NE. I forgot to say that at

16 Approximately the latitude of Cape San Antonio. Joutel ("Relation," p. 112) gives the latitude the preceding day as 22°02'. The Abbé d'Esmanville ("Journal," in Margry, *Découvertes,* II, 51) gives the latitude of the cape as 20°48'. Here Minet suggests that he himself participated in the taking of the latitude with Beaujeu's quadrant, though he uses the indefinite pronoun *on.*

17 Joutel ("Relation," pp. 114–15) gives no latitude between December 20 (26°40') and December 23 (26°18'). He makes no mention of the eclipse, as computation of longitude by the esoteric method mentioned by Minet would not have been attempted on any but the naval vessel *Joly.* That it was done on Beaujeu's ship is a testament to his competence as a navigator. See d'Esmanville, "Journal," in Margry, *Découvertes,* II, 511–12. The longitude arrived at (on the meridian of Louisiana's Barataria Bay) probably places the ships too far west but it did provide substantial correction to the estimated longitude of 288° (measured east around the globe from Paris), which would

Cape St. Anthoine M. de La Salle gave a declaration in writing to M. de Beaujeu that the river was at 28°20′, at the very end of the gulf.[18] One would know it by the great jetty it makes into the sea. Nevertheless, the rendezvous was in the Bay of Spiritu Santo (*sic*).[19] He must go directly there, and afterward we would follow the coast. If one were to get lost, the other would wait for him in this bay.

The evening of the 24th the *Aimable,* on which M. de la Salle was, took the wrong course. We were heading NW, NW by N. She [the *Aimable*] set course WNW. We noticed it only after midnight. Since M. Beaujeu suspected that M. de La Salle wanted to leave him and go alone to look for the river and leave him with the 100 wretched soldiers the king had given him on his hands without any food, we let out all sails from that side. After four hours we caught up with them. We asked him why he took the wrong route. He said that it was not wrong. We asked the same question of the little frigate *Belle*. The captain said that he was following the *Aimable.*[20]

The 25th, Christmas Day, slight winds. Course NW.

The 26th, night calm. The day wind NE, ESE.

---

put the expedition well out into the Atlantic Ocean. Joutel's longitude estimates are similarly in error, e.g., 288°35′ while standing off Cape San Antonio ("Relation," p. 112). No reliable means of computing longitude on ships at sea came into use until the invention of the chronometer late in the eighteenth century.

18 The declaration referred to is La Salle's letter of December 18, 1684, in Margry, *Découvertes,* II, 525–26. He had said essentially the same thing in his November 23 letter, before leaving Petit Goâve (pp. 521–23). The latitude taken by La Salle at the river mouth in 1682 was grossly in error, and this was a factor in his confusing the Mississippi and the Escondido. Latitude 28°20′ intersects land in the Gulf of Mexico just south of Texas' Matagorda Bay and just north of Tarpon Springs, Florida. The line runs some forty miles south of the present southernmost mouth of the Mississippi, which continued to extend itself into the Gulf for two hundred years before the process was reversed and the natural levees and deltaic wetlands began to erode.

19 The bay long presumed to be at the mouth of the river labeled Río del Espíritu Santo (the Mississippi) on the 1519 map sketch of Alonso Alvarez de Pineda (original in AGI, Mapas y Planos). La Salle, presuming the bay to lie northeast of the point at which he had reached the Gulf in 1682, took his failure to find such a bay as an indication that his river was some other (the Escondido). See Father Zénobe Membré's narrative of La Salle's 1682 descent of the Mississippi in Isaac Joslin Cox, *The Journeys of Réné Robert Cavelier, Sieur de La Salle,* I, 146; and the Chucagoa fragment, in Margry, *Découvertes,* II, 196–203. See also Minet's journal entry for December 29.

20 See d'Esmanville, "Journal," in Margry, *Découvertes,* II, 512. Joutel does not mention the incident.

The 27th, good SE wind. At 6 o'clock that evening soundings 40 fathoms, mud bottom, and the sea water clearer.

The 28th. That night hove to. That day after having gone two leagues, 17 fathoms, 15, 12 fathoms, without seeing land. That night we anchored in 10 fathoms, muddy sand.[21]

The 29th we weighed anchor. Course NW by N; 7 fathoms, 8 fathoms, 5 fathoms. The course WSW and W. The wind NE, NNE. That evening we saw fires NNE of us without seeing land. The pilots were not too sure where they were, saying that the currents bore to the east. They thought they were 50 leagues from the Baye du St. Esprit, on that coast. Monsieur de la Salle assured us that we were at Cape Scondido [Escondido], that he was sure that the current bore east and SE.[22] That night anchored in 6 fathoms.

December 30th, beautiful weather, fair, without seeing land.

Going SW. The *Belle* going into four fathoms to try to see land, and we went to seven and eight. Anchored that evening.

The 31st we coasted along the bank. Course NW at 8 and 6 fathoms, mud. It rained all morning. We wanted to go a little to the north. First we found 4½ fathoms. Thus, we did not dare advance farther. We went back to 8 fathoms.

[[1685]] January 1st, the *Belle* saw land. We boarded the longboat to see what kind of land it was. The vessels were anchored. By the plan and elevation you saw what that coast is. We were able to approach it no nearer than 150 fathoms from its shore. We had to portage. It is a dike of sand that the sea throws up and forms there, elevated some 4 feet; behind it is a muddy marsh, where there are small rushes. I wanted to go into it, [but] we sank [into the mud]. It seemed to be at the same level as the sea, not being flooded because of the sand banks that the sea forms there. We saw there four or five large trees that appeared old [and] that the sea had carried to the shores. One of them appeared to be 18 fathoms long. Looking toward the land as far as the eye can see, we

21 Joutel ("Relation," p. 116) gives noon latitude of 28°37' and says land was sighted half an hour before sunset. D'Esmanville ("Journal," in Margry, *Découvertes,* II, 512) gives latitude 28°, longitude 21° (from Petit Goâve).

22 Having been warned by the Saint-Domingue pirates of the eastward current, the pilots assumed they had been carried east of the mythical Bahía del Espíritu Santo. The direction of flow coincided with that of the effluent from the river's eastern passes observed by La Salle in 1682 (see Joutel, "Relation," pp. 116–17). The river's easterly course as it approached the Gulf was one of the factors in La Salle's identifying it with the Río Escondido, shown on maps since the mid-sixteenth century in a location about right for the Nueces River of Texas. See Chucagoa fragment, in Margry, *Découvertes,* II, esp. pp. 198–99.

could see nothing. It still looked like the sea from that side. The coast goes ENE and WSW. While boarding, as I was close to the longboat, I fell into the water. It was cold. Latitude 29°15'.[23] [[I think that we were near the Baye du St. Esprit, to the E.]]

The 2nd, cloudy weather, wind S, SSW. We made only a few tacks. There was a heavy fog. That evening the *Aimable* and the *Belle* strayed away from us. We anchored.

The 3rd we no longer saw the ships. We shot a cannon several times. They answered us. As we were still in a heavy fog, we could not see each other from a distance.[24]

January 4th at 7 o'clock in the morning we dragged our anchor. We weighed anchor and set course NNW and NW with slight sail in 8 fathoms. At 9 o'clock we came into 5 fathoms. We changed course to SW, WSW, found 5 fathoms again at 11. We again made SSW, but, always finding uneven bottom and sometimes mud, sometimes sand, without seeing land, we anchored at three o'clock. Our two ships were still lost. All night, without seeing land, we could see fires from the coast where it should have been. We shot the cannons several times to see if our two ships would hear us, but there was no answer. That night, strong north wind.

The 5th, at anchor, fog and strong NNE wind. There apparently is no current here. The ship was driven upon her anchor by the wind.

The 6th, still at anchor. We fired several cannon shots to see whether M. de La Salle would answer us. Still fog and cold.

The 7th and 8th, rainy, cold, foggy weather. We could still see fires on shore, one to the NE and the other to the N.

The morning of the 9th, wind south, we weighed anchor. We set course E by SE. Rain, fog.[25] We anchored at three o'clock in the afternoon. Calm and rain. This whole sea is full of whales [*de baleine*].

---

23 The latitude approximates that of the entrance to Barataria Bay, also of Point au Fer Island southeast of the point. The latitude given, however, is not presumed to be precise. Joutel ("Relation," p. 118) concurs on the date of this landfall but does not give a latitude until January 2: 29°20'. His more detailed record of the navigation, however, suggests that the first land sighted was the Isles Dernieres, some eighty-five miles west of the Mississippi's Southwest Pass. Marc de Villiers du Terrage (*L'Expédition de Cavelier de La Salle dans le Golfe du Mexique [1684–1687]*, p. 76) has the voyagers sighting Timbalier Island on the second and coming to anchor off the Isles Dernieres, a little east of Ship Shoal.

24 See Joutel's account of the separation ("Relation," p. 119). Minet and Joutel now describe the separate paths of the *Joly* and the other two ships.

25 The erratic course on the ninth and tenth evidently represents the *Joly's* search for the other two ships.

The 10th, calm and fog. At nine o'clock, clear weather, we weighed anchor, slight NNE wind. Calm. The wind WSW. Course NE proceeding in 7 to 8 fathoms.

As this land is full of marshes, we are not surprised at the fogs. A strong wind comes which raises them. Thus you have in that country fog or strong wind, or rain. You have only two kinds of weather: calm or high seas. At ten o'clock in the evening we anchored in 9 fathoms, mud. We kept firing, trying to be heard by the other vessels, that we might be found. We did not know if on the way to the Bay of Spiritu Sancto we had passed one another in the fog.

Our food began to run short. We were 18 at table, two priests, two Récollets, some officers, some cadets, and one hundred soldiers who are all ill, not counting the crew of the *Joly,* who are 80 persons more.

The 11th, heavy fog. Weighed anchor at 9 o'clock; dropped anchor at noon in 6 fathoms without seeing land.

The 12th we left in the longboat to see if we could not see land. We went NNW and made 4½ leagues without ever seeing land, finding always 6, 7, 5, 7, 6 fathoms. We returned on board that night. It had been seen from on board to the NE by N. Afterward I thought that the place where the vessel was anchored was a cove, which turns back inland after the Baye du St. Esprit, going SW. Latitude taken, 29°18′. Believing that this was the entrance to the bay, we rigged sail. That same evening we anchored (we wanted to anchor at the place where we had been) at midnight.

The 13th we saw land to the north. At sunrise we sent the longboat to reconnoiter the shore that we saw to the north and northwest. That evening it returned. They said that this coast appeared beautiful and inhabited because of the paths they had seen, that it runs ENE and WSW, that there were [the depth increased] five fathoms per league from the coast, and the going of the longboat was good. The pilots said that we were in the small bay of Matas del Salvador.[26] At five that evening we

26 Matas de Salvador as a place-name on early maps of the Gulf region is unique in that it appears on countless renditions of various nationalities, spanning almost two hundred years, without its location or orthography being appreciably altered. It is first noted on the "Salviati" map, c. 1525 (in W. P. Cumming, R. A. Skeleton, and D. B. Quinn, *The Discovery of North America,* p. 72) and is last found on Johannis Van Keulen's 1684 map, re-engraved to provide new information in 1717 (Historic New Orleans Collection, *Degrees of Discovery: From New World to New Orleans,* p. 13). On a dozen easily found maps, it is placed consistently just east of the imaginary features at the mouth of the Mississippi: Espíritu Santo Bay and Mar Pequeño. The name is traceable to no known expedition.

weighed anchor. The course was W by SW. The wind S by SE in six and seven fathoms.

The night of January 14th the wind was SSE. In the morning we were two leagues from shore. (A view of this coast is given later.) Still low land. At ten o'clock the shore was seen to the west. From eight, all of a sudden [the depth decreased to] six fathoms. We set course southwest, coasting the land, always keeping a close watch to see if we could see M. de La Salle and the ships. At two o'clock, calm. We dropped the anchor. At 9 o'clock that evening we weighed it during a little east wind. Course SW. That night the officers on watch saw some fires and something resembling a ship. We fired some cannon shots but got no answer. Beyond this coast we saw something like large lakes.[27]

The 15th at 4 o'clock in the morning we weighed anchor, believing that it was our ships. At 9 o'clock we weighed anchor in a north wind. Course WSW. At 11 o'clock in the morning, coasting along the shore, we passed before a river coming from the SW and some sandbars at the entrance, which ran N and S.[28] The coast runs NE and SW. The sandy beaches had no greenery except a few clumps of rushes here and there. The interior seemed inundated and marshy. At six o'clock that evening we anchored in 7 fathoms.

All the crew is nourished with corn and is in good health. The soldiers have eaten all their food and drunk all their brandy. They live at present on corn and water at the expense of the *Joly*'s crew. That night, wind N.

The 16th, wind N. At six o'clock we weighed anchor, coasting the land, latitude 29°09'. We wanted to go ashore with the longboat, but we could not approach the coast. It is low, and at 300 fathoms from it, the longboat, which draws only two and one-half feet, touches; besides, there are reefs and waves along the coast that rise and fall swiftly. Nevertheless, three sailors jumped into the sea and reported that at a quarter of a league inland there is another sea whose opposite shores they could not see, from either side, [and] that it was full of oysters.[29] They even brought some. They said that this sea had a tide. This coast runs NE by E and SW by W. That night we saw in front of us a large entrance and a broad sea or a large lake behind it. We anchored at six o'clock in the evening. We thought that it was the entrance to the Baye du St. Esprit

---

27 The Texas coast, inclining southeast, had been reached, evidently below the Galveston Bay entrance. Minet's lakes were the lagoons behind the barrier islands, such as West Galveston Bay.

28 Probably Oyster Creek, east of present-day Freeport, Texas.

29 Latitude 29°09' is in error by half a degree or more; the *Joly* now stands along Matagorda Peninsula, which encloses Matagorda Bay.

because we could see an island at its mouth, but we could see it was full of reefs and jetties that were thrown up far out into the sea.[30]

The 17th we weighed anchor at 6:30. The wind was east. At 8 o'clock in the morning, calm. We anchored. We were surprised to see that the opening seen yesterday more than four leagues before us was [now] three leagues behind us. Thus, the currents go rather strongly to the sw. We tried to go ashore to see a little of this mouth and a small point that extends seaward, but the reefs were so large that we could approach no closer than half a league from shore. So we went back aboard. We observed latitude 28°03',[31] by which we realized that it was not the Baye du St. Esprit, that, by the latitude and how the coast ran, we had passed it. Everybody wanted to go back to look for it at latitude 30°, saying that M. de La Salle was there at present and was waiting for us. But Mons. de Beaujeu opposed it, saying that M. de La Salle had wanted to leave us and had gone to search for the river and that it was necessary to continue, that we might find him. We wanted to return and to place ourselves opposite the entrance to the lake, but the currents and the wind allowed us to advance only half a league. Becalmed, we anchored.

January 18th we weighed anchor at 7 o'clock in the morning. Wind from N, course wsw. We coasted the land two leagues from it, always seeing the lakes behind it, like another large sea. We have been seeing the lakes five days now, so wide that we do not see the opposite shore and at other times very narrow.[32] These openings in the shore are the overflow channels of the lakes and links to the sea. This country being flat, the sea is enclosed in a cul-de-sac. Whenever it is the least bit high, it enters all this land and inundates it. When the sea is calm or when the wind is from the east, all the water of this flood returns to the sea, combined with the rivers that empty into it. The sea, always high on the coast, pushes sand and forms embankments.[33] Latitude 27°40'. Here

30 Minet's entry for February 13, plus his *Plan de la Coste de la Floride la plus occidentalle* (plate 7), fix the location as Matagorda Bay at Pass Cavallo. The "island" in the mouth is Pelican Shoal. Such a feature was sought because of the long-standing misconception that a similar one marked the mouth of the Río del Espíritu Santo. See introduction to Enríquez Barroto diary herein, p. 135, and note 15 to introduction. Note reference also in Joutel, "Relation," p. 121, and La Salle to Seignelay in Margry, *Découvertes*, II, 560.

31 Minet's latitudes now are shown to be erratic. Whereas the one given for the sixteenth is 30' too much, this one is about 20' too little; thus he indicates southward progress of some fifty nautical miles more than actually was made.

32 Matagorda, San Antonio, and Mesquite bays and the lagoons between the barrier islands and the mainland, which link them.

33 Minet describes the hurricane passes by which storm surge returns to the Gulf.

we have been, nevertheless, for three days in the latitude of M. de La Salle's river, and we do not find it. We passed the 28°20′ where it should be recognizable by the jetties and the island that goes ten leagues out to sea. On the map that he gave the king, of which they gave me a copy, he put the river at 25°50′. We will pursue this course to look for our ships and the river at that latitude. If we do not find it, assuredly it empties into these lakes. What makes me think that it empties there are the embankments and islands that he marks as being at its mouth. This lake is as salty as the sea and is more tranquil. So this river that descends with force forms the embankments and islands with the wood and the mud it carries, because this sea is too stormy and always too agitated to permit such jetties to form. The wind has boxed the compass for four days, in the morning north and in the evening south.

On the 19th we weighed anchor with a NNE wind. Course wsw. At 8:30 we saw from a distance two ships, which we thought were Spanish. We put ourselves under arms. When we were near we recognized that they were our vessels. So M. de Beaujeu was right in saying that, although M. de La Salle had given in writing that the rendezvous was the Baye du St. Esprit if we became separated, that assuredly he would not go and would go directly to look for his river. And he was not even at the [right] latitude, since we found him at 27°30′.[34] At 9 o'clock we anchored near them. He [La Salle] came aboard and said that the river led into the lakes but that there are entrances to go there and that he hoped to find some. He said that if he did not find any, he would return to France. He believed that La Rivière de la Magdelaine [Magdelaine River] was a branch of his river, the one by which he had not wanted to go.[35] That night he said that he believed that in the Baye du St. Esprit there was also a branch of the river or a portage that was not even 100 paces long. Nevertheless, we asked him for two months' provisions for the soldiers. He wanted to give us only enough for two weeks.

The 20th the longboat went ashore at 4 in the morning, loaded with soldiers, there being a small river or opening opposite us 15 fath-

34 Again too far south by more than half a degree, the latitude approximates that of Kingsville, Texas, south of Corpus Christi. La Salle gives the same latitude (*procés verbal*, March 4, 1685, in Margry, *Découvertes*, II, 559). A page from the log of the *Belle* (photostat from UT archives, AGI), gives the same for the latitude taken by Captain Moraud at noon on the eighteenth. D'Esmanville ("Journal," p. 514) gives 27°55′.

35 D'Esmanville ("Journal," pp. 511–12) and Joutel ("Relation," pp. 134–35) relate that the Chevalier d'Aire had first gone to the *Aimable* bearing Beaujeu's complaints and accusations concerning the separation. Rivière de la Magdelaine is shown on the "De Soto" map of Alonso de Santa Cruz as entering

oms wide and a foot in depth at low tide. (The sea rises 5 feet every 24 hours.) [[Drawing]] As we found some small ponds of fresh water, M. de la Salle wants to take on a little water in safety.

We went ashore with M. de Beaujeu. We took the latitude and found 27°54'.[36] We again ascended this river one league, seeing that it came from the lakes and that the whole shore appeared flat and marshy, full of oysters. We returned on board after having found an old broken canoe, some pumice stones, and a small path.

January 21st I went ashore. I found that M. de La Salle had gone to see in what country he was and if he could recognize it. That night he returned very tired, having found only lakes and marshes, where he said he thought he would perish.

The 22nd he asked M. de Beaujeu for his soldiers and dated his letter, "One of the branches of the Micicipy or Colbert River."[37] We sent him part. He said that his river is here and this is where the king had sent him, that the Magdelaine was not the river but that when we were to retrace our steps we would find at 40 leagues an opening where we would enter.

Until the 26th there were heavy seas, wind NE and ENE. Some of our sailors opened oysters and found some pearls. They have four or five very small ones.

---

the Gulf in the Texas coastal bend. Date of the map, though generally said to be 1544, is much in doubt, leaving room to suppose that the river name may bear some relation to the Médanos de Madalena, the name given the Padre Island sand dunes on Magdalen's Day, 1554, by salvagers of the three ships lost there in April that year (J. Barto Arnold III and Robert S. Weddle, *The Nautical Archeology of Padre Island: The Spanish Shipwrecks of 1554*, pp. 139–40; García de Escalante Alvarado, "Buceo de las naos que se perdieron en la playa de Magdalena," AGI, Contaduría 58). The Magdalena, Madalena, or Magdalaine usually is shown above the Escondido. Occasionally, as on the Pierre du Val map of 1663 (in Peter H. Wood, "La Salle: Discovery of a Lost Explorer," *American Historical Review* 89, no. 2 [April, 1984]: 300), it is shown as the same river. although Guillaume Delisle identified the Magdaleine River as the Guadalupe on his 1718 map, the name Magdaleine was not used extensively.

36 The drawing (plate 7) clearly depicts Cedar Bayou, 28°03.5'. The latitude taken on shore is somewhat more accurate than the one computed on shipboard. See Joutel "Relation," p. 136; he had gone ashore with La Salle: "We found M. de Beaujeu, who had come in the longboat with the Sieur Minet, engineer for our settlement. As they had some instruments for taking latitude, it was taken by them. They found 27°50'." The Abbé d'Esmanville ("Journal," p. 514) places the reunion at 27°55', "about thirty-five leagues from the Magdalain."

37 Letter of January 23, 1685, in Margry, *Découvertes*, II, 526.

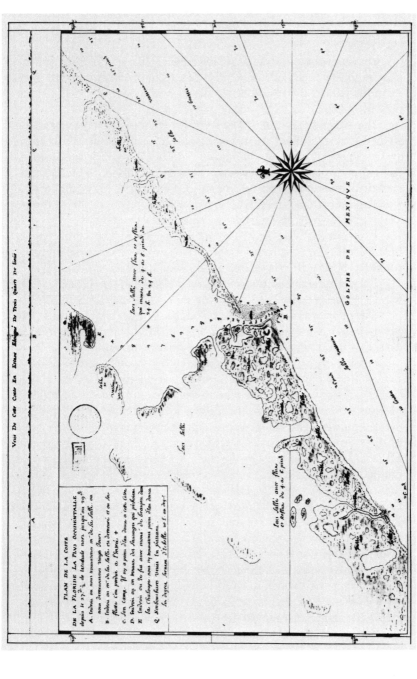

PLATE 7. Minet's "Plan de la Coste de la Floride la plus occidentale." (Courtesy of the Archives Nationales, Service Hydrographique, Paris) A. Where we found M. de La Salle and remained twenty days. B. Where La Salle has remained and where the flute was lost in the entrance. C. His camp. There is no freshwater source on this coast. D. Where we found some savages fishing. E. Where I went with Mons. de Beaujeu in the shallop. We found no freshwater source. Q. Mouths seen in passing.

One is unable to make more over the captain of the flute and the pilot than M. de la Salle does.[38] He has them eat with him and gives them his wine. So they are always in a good mood. The tide rises at present to five or six feet.

The 27th, calm weather. The longboat went to carry the rest of the soldiers, but it returned, the sea being furious on the coast. We weighed anchor to go to 8 fathoms. Thus we put ourselves nearly four leagues from shore. At 3 in the afternoon there arose a north wind, which kept increasing, and that night it became furious enough to lower the topsail.

The 28th it continued with considerable force, and a hard freeze. Water in some pails and tubs on the ship froze.

The 29th the wind shifted to NE and to the E. The soldiers again boarded the longboat to go ashore. He [La Salle] meant to send the soldiers ashore at this mouth to avoid giving them any more rations.

The 30th the rest of the soldiers were taken ashore. That night the wind turned SSE, with big waves. The ship was greatly tormented.

On the 31st the wind continued and the sea was very turbulent. The Spanish pirate[39] was right in saying that one must fear the south winds. The sea around our ship rose a fathom. That night, rain.

February 1st, rain, wind NW. The longboat came back that evening. They suffered much on shore. The sea had flooded nearly the whole country. There were only a few small sand dunes that were not flooded. Monsieur de la Salle was in the longboat on the lakes. It ran aground five or six times. The sailors were obliged to get out and push the longboat, [the water] being no more than two feet deep. When I saw that M. de la Salle insisted on staying there, I asked him whether he would not find it more beneficial to give food to Monsieur de Beaujeu to feed the soldiers and to go all together to look for his river or a mouth or bay to shelter the ships. [I told him that] he was running a great risk of perishing in going by land. He told me that he knew what he was doing and that he knew this country; that there was a large mouth 40 leagues from there that was four or five fathoms deep at the entrance and that he was going to board the *Aimable;* that Monsieur de Beaujeu could go away; that he had sent him word twice already and that I, too, could leave if I wanted to; that he was a good enough engineer to do what the king had commanded him to do.

February 2nd, beautiful weather. The *Aimable* was listing [while]

38 Captain Aigron and the pilot Zacharie Mengaud (Villiers, *L'Expédition,* p. 219).

39 Evidently the Spaniard encountered at Petit Goâve, who took the La Salle party to the pirate ship. See journal entry for November 11, 12, and 13, 1684.

going along the coast. One of the anchor cables broke as well as a piece of her bow. M. de Beaujeu sent to have her anchor dredged and sent some cordage. He told me that it was he who had told M. de La Salle that 30 or 40 leagues from here to the NE he had passed before a river that goes inland to the SW [NW] that he believed could be entered, but that he had not stopped to examine it, and his men had told him the same thing. I wrote to him to see if he would listen to reason. I pointed out that he said that he had been in these lands and that his river was here, according to three letters he had written to M. de Beaujeu; that this river was not the one that he boasted about [*vantoit*] so much in France; that he thought it very much more to the point that he and his men embark and that we leave to go search for a place to shelter the vessels, to search for the river from there, than to abandon the soldiers in unknown lands; that one could not go ten leagues without finding a river mouth that would forbid their passing, besides the fact that we no longer are able to find any—or very little—fresh water on this coast; that the marshes, the ponds, the food, the savages, the weather—none of that supported the rendezvous he had given them; that the first point one should pay attention to when one wants to make a foreign settlement is a port to shelter one's ships. Of what use are settlements in the hinterland where one cannot establish trade? I wrote that to him as courteously as I could, even though the Marquis de Seignelay [had] ordered me to obey him. But no one tells him anything. I saw a man who had made a mockery of the court and was making a mockery of us. I counseled Monsieur de Beaujeu that, if he did not find the river or a place to settle, he should return to France with his men. But he answered me, "I do not have an order to that effect, only to take him where he told me and give him all the help possible."

He [La Salle] gave me an answer full of invectives. I said to those who told me that the letter had angered him that I believed [that it was] in the service of the king to represent it thus to him. There was nothing against him, but this is a man who has lost his mind. I am no less his servant for all that, provided that he finds his river and carries out what he promised.

February 3rd the soldiers left with four young Normans who guided them. Weather cloudy.

The 4th, wind SE, ESE strong along the coast. M. de La Salle sent word to M. de Beaujeu that we had passed the river.

February 5th, weather cloudy, heavy seas, wind SE. The *Aimable*'s anchor is broken. We handed over to him all he [La Salle] had here of merchandise and food.

The 6th, wind NNE, NE, weather cloudy. We took an anchor to the

Belle, which had lost her own. She had spent the night with a small anchor of 150 *livres,* not having any other and having already lost all of her own. Bad weather.

The 7th, wind NNE, NE, cloudy.

The 8th, wind SW, calm at noon. The longboat wanted to go ashore but could not approach it. The sea on the coast was as high as the mountains.

February 9th. We weighed anchor at 7 in the morning with wind NE, N. Course E by SE. I believe that the current goes with the wind, but nevertheless today it is running W. The pilots told me that ever since we anchored it has borne almost southwest with considerable force.

That afternoon, calm. Anchored at 3 o'clock in ten fathoms, five leagues from shore. That night, rain and thunder.

February 10th. In the morning, rain and a little east wind.

The 11th we weighed anchor at 6 in the morning. The wind NNE, NE. We made several tacks. At midnight we anchored.

The 12th we weighed anchor with the wind SE at 9 o'clock. At 4 o'clock that evening we anchored. Heavy fog. At 8 o'clock we weighed anchor; at 9 we anchored. In the evening, lightning, thunder, and heavy rain.

The 13th we weighed anchor, and we arrived that evening before the mouth we had passed the 17th of January, which was 10 or 12 leagues from the little river.[40] We saw a white tent on the southern point, which our soldiers had pitched. We anchored.

February 14th, nice weather, wind from NNW. We left to go ashore with Monsieur de Beaujeu and a pilot in the longboat, always sounding when we wanted to approach land. We found no more than two feet. Wanting to go in the middle of the mouth, the longboat ran aground. We wanted to go alongside the island anyway. There being always two feet [depth] half a league from shore and in the channel, we were obliged to go to the coast on the NE side, where we landed. From there we went by land to the point to see the lake, which was full of *marcouin* [*maringouin* (?): mosquitoes]. We followed the coast on shore half a league. We made several stops there to draw the plan. We returned on board. The *Aimable* and the *Belle* were anchored west of us, closer to shore.

The 15th Mons. de La Salle sent the pilot of the *Belle* to tell Mons. de Beaujeu that he had found an entrance into the lake, that it was here that the king had sent him and that he wanted to settle. We asked the pilot how much [what depth] he had found. He said that on the bar there were 15 feet and, once inside, 24, 34 feet. At once Mons. de Beau-

40 That is, Matagorda Bay at Pass Cavallo, "10 to 12 leagues" from Cedar Bayou.

jeu, the pilot Gabaret,[41] and I embarked to see this entrance [and] whether one could enter in the *Joly* and winter here. Because that was done, the *Belle*'s pilot[42] was threatened and said afterward that there were only 12 feet at the shallowest. From the entrance we went to the *Aimable,* but M. de La Salle did not want to come and sound with us. We went to sound. The sounding lead, which is a foot long, found 25 feet, 15 feet, 8 feet; 8 feet a long half league from shore [[drawing below]]. On the side of the west point, on entering, 9 feet, 12 feet, 15 feet, 25 feet. The drawing shows you the soundings. We entered the lake. We descended to the left on the side of M. de La Salle's camp.[43] We found a country flooded with lakes. From afar we saw something like men, but someone said that they were big birds.[44] We reembarked without being able to find fresh water except a little puddle of rainwater. We penetrated farther into the lake, seeing smoke from afar. We said, "Let's go." After having traveled three more leagues, we saw from afar a higher land. We resolved to go there, always traveling NNW. When we were opposite it, night overtook us. We were unable to approach the coast nearer than 150 fathoms. We did not hesitate in landing and lit a fire. When we were a little warm, we wanted to go inland. Although it appeared elevated from afar, it was not, but very little higher than the place where M. de la Salle was camped, that is to say, six feet above the water. It was a sandy beach, and here and there it seemed to be good soil with many canes and a little grass and some small trees. At a quarter of a league from one side to the other there were vines in one area and a quantity of buffalo carcasses that seemed to have been killed at least 8 or 9 months previously.[45] We went inland two leagues without ever meeting anything but a doe that we saw. Fire had burned over all these places. The next day, the 16th, after having been very cold in spite of the big fire (as this whole coast is full of wood that the sea casts on the shores), without having been able to find one drop of fresh water, we left around six o'clock in the morning. There were a good 12 to 15 leagues from there to

41 Second pilot of the *Joly* (Villiers, *L'Expédition,* p. 218).
42 Elie Richaud (ibid., p. 219).
43 At the upper end of Matagorda Island.
44 Possibly the brown pelican, which still inhabits Pelican Shoal.
45 Interestingly, Cabeza de Vaca made no mention of the bison in this region a century and a half earlier; yet records of the La Salle settlement, as well as Enríquez Barroto's diary (entries for April 11 and 12, 1687) show the animals to have been quite numerous. Although the legendary great herds existed only in the Great Plains, bison were found in historic times along the Gulf Coast as far east as the Florida peninsula. The bison range is described by Tom McHugh, *The Time of the Buffalo,* pp. 23–26.

the ships, which were two leagues from shore. The wind was favorable to us. We sounded again. In this whole lake we found 8 to 9 feet, 7 feet, 6 feet, 9 feet. We sounded again at the entrance of the lake from the sea, and on the bar we found still the same. We arrived on board at 1 o'clock, very tired and with a big appetite.

That evening M. de La Salle sent one named Duhaut from Bayonne, who was the sergeant,[46] to say that he was going to have the *Belle* and the *Aimable* enter the lake behind the island that he had sounded, that on the bar there are eleven feet at low tide and it rises five feet, and he begged him [Beaujeu] to give him powder. He also gave a summons to Sieur du Val, the king's scribe, to the effect that Monsieur de Beaujeu was to deliver me into his hands, that it is here that his majesty is sending him, having gone ten leagues from the other mouth of the Colbert River for reasons for which he would answer only to the court.[47] I said that Mons. de Beaujeu had an order to keep me on his vessel as long as he was at sea, that I was making no resistance to the service of the king. Proof of that was that I had written him a letter, which was all for the service, but that from this place he could not arrive at the river, that it could be 200 leagues west of there, that all he was doing appeared to be rather against the service instead of for it, that I no longer wanted to have a hand in that, and that I was amazed at his manner of acting in my behalf, I who had lent him my money, who had always given evidence of my respect for him, that even yesterday when I saw him he told me nothing and today he sends me a writ or summons. There must be something behind it that I do not understand.

His food is diminishing every day. He has nothing left but flour and some wine. He ought to have 200 soldiers. Only 100 are there, and two or three of them die every week. In the region where he is, there is only rainwater, nothing else. In the region where he is, there is only rainwater, nothing else. He says that the river is muddy; the lakes [on the other hand] are beautiful and clear, very salty.

February 17th, the pilots of the *Joly* and the *Aimable* again went to sound on the bar to make an official report of it. Monsieur Du Hamel, ensign of this vessel, came on board again in the longboat to bring Du-

46 Pierre Duhaut, the elder of the two brothers whom Villiers (*L'Expédition,* p. 218) identifies as merchants. It was he who assassinated La Salle.

47 Which is to say, La Salle thought he had passed the true mouth of the Mississippi "ten leagues" farther up the coast, where Galveston Bay had been sighted from the *Aimable* on January 11, while sailing apart from the *Joly.* Joutel ("Relation," pp. 123–24) says that La Salle wanted at the time to reconnoiter the bay to see if it was the Baye du Saint-Esprit but was dissuaded by the pilots.

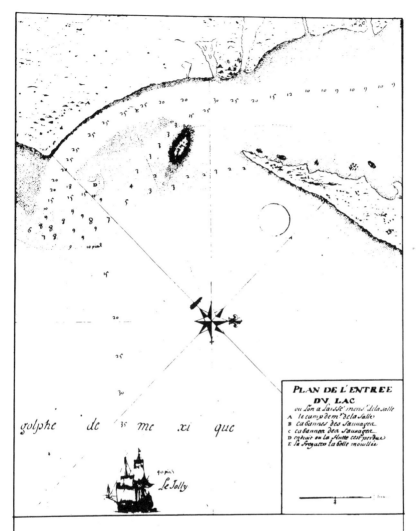

PLATE 8. Minet's "Plan de l'entrée du lac."
(Courtesy of the Archives Nationales, Service Hydrographique, Paris)

A. La Salle's camp.
B. The savages' huts.
C. The savages' huts.
D. Where the flute was lost.
E. The frigate Belle anchored.

haut to carry a second summons, two pages long, for Monsieur de Beaujeu, saying that he was to put me ashore, that it was here that the king sent him, and that he wanted to build a fort here.

We sent him the powder.

That evening again a third summons in which he declared that his river is here, that he wants to make fortifications. Whom does he want to build these fortifications? Does he have masons? Some laborers? He had about 20 hired men [*engagés*], of whom half are dead. Of 100 soldiers there are still 80 ill. With that, what fort does he want us to wall up without bread or water? And the floods.

The pilots and the king's scribe who made the official report of the soundings with M. de La Salle have returned, and he made them wait for high tide, according to what they said; but it is very irregular. They found one more foot than we did, but it is because they counted the lead.[48] They said that he argued over an inch. He said that [it was] so much the better that there be only nine feet. Only merchant ships would come. The king's ships came only to torment and make demands.

He told me several days ago that all the northern country at present was frozen. That is why there was no water in the lakes, but all summer where we were seeing only eight feet of water there would be 20.

February 18th, wind SE. Monsieur de Beaujeu did on his part all that the court had ordered him. He offered him all that he and his men could do to go into the lakes to look for the river with the longboat and canoes, and to hold a council of arbitration to see what could be done for the success of his affairs; but he wanted to listen to none of that.

The 19th, wind SE. We sent him his iron today. We sent him the longboat to help unburden the *Aimable* so she could enter. The *Belle* has entered.

February 20th, wind SE. At 10 o'clock we left in the canoe with M. de Beaujeu and the pilot Gabaret. We went as far as the breakers. The sea was heavy there. We had sent word to the *Aimable* that she was going to enter as soon as M. de La Salle had a fire lit on the coast [as a signal]. We saw the buoys that the pilots had placed when sounding. Monsieur de Beaujeu and Gabaret asked him [Aigron, the *Aimable*'s captain] how much water [the ship] drew. "Eight to eight and a half feet," he responded. They said to him, "I advise you not to enter. You draw too much water, and then there are waves." He answered, "Mons. de La Salle wrote me to enter, and we will enter." As soon as we were [back] on board [the *Joly*] we saw the lighted fire, which was the signal

48 That is, they included the length of the sounding lead, about one foot, in the measurement.

that had been given him, and she got under way. She spent some time following the markers and buoys, there being a league to the point south from the place where she was anchored. But when she came to the bar she grounded. She furled her sails, fired a cannon, and put her flag at half mast. Since our longboat had gone to help her if she were in need, we had only the canoe, which we sent him with an officer, some cordage, and our best sailors, who did what they could to save her. But she was too solidly aground, and the wine that M. de La Salle left for the captain and the pilots had rendered them more daring than necessary, so that night the flute stuck fast in the sand. M. de la Salle had sent word the day before to M. de Beaujeu that he could leave, since he did not want to make the *Joly* enter, and that he was going to make the *Aimable* enter fully burdened. The response was that he advised him not to make her enter, that, as for himself, he was awaiting the letters and a certificate to the effect that he [La Salle] no longer had need of a ship to depart.

The 21st. The flute kept sinking and contorting herself very much, being in the reefs. The longboat and the canoe had helped all night in the unloading. Monsieur de Beaujeu went there. He returned that night, which means that he wants to believe our sailors. They all say that they wanted to lose the flute. They saved the flour, corn, some meat, and a good portion of the wine and brandy.

After dinner, when the soldiers went to look for wood, they saw some savages and came to sound the alarm at the camp, saying that they had seen more than four hundred savages; that they had surprised them; that they had seen them only when they were upon them; that they could not flee; that first they approached them, took their hands, and felt their pulse to see if they were afraid. The savages, who numbered 50 in the canoes approaching the camp, came with caution up to M. de la Salle, who gave them some tobacco to smoke. They found it so good that they swallowed it all, not breathing out the least smoke. They were naked, having only a buffalo skin, which serves them as a coat or blanket.[49]

The 22nd, wind SSE. Monsieur de Beaujeu and the Chevalier d'Hear [d'Aire], lieutenant of the *Joly*, again went to the *Aimable* to make the sailors work to save something. That night the wind increased.

The 23rd, wind SSE, billows. The longboat and canoe could not come in this bad weather.

49 These natives were Karankawan (Clamcoëhs), of independent linguistic stock, connected most closely with the Coahuiltecans (John R. Swanton, *The Indian Tribes of North America*, p. 320). Concerning the Karankawas' fondness for tobacco, see the Talons' answer to question 12 of the Interrogations.

When we entered the lake we went ashore. We thought that what we were seeing were birds. It was the savages, since they have their huts in exactly that area,[50] and they say that if they had wanted to, they could have killed us, being hidden in the rushes. The flute began to break up.

The 24th, rain, fog, wind N, NNE, foul weather.

The 25th, wind NE, high waves. Our sailors who are ashore are exchanging all their knives and a little tobacco for the savages' blankets of buffalo hides. This skin has a short fur like sheep's wool, of a brown color. They are from the last hunt. They search for small roots in the dirt and live on that. They come to the camp and give their hides for a little corn. We see no caiman or crocodile here,[51] or heron or other birds that live along the river.

The 26th, good weather. Monsieur Beaujeu has returned. The powder, the cannons and the food have been saved and a portion of the merchandise. The longboat of the *Aimable* is also lost.

February 27th. The longboat has returned to shore to see if they are in need. The savages came, painted all over, with their arms—that is to say, bows, arrows, tomahawks—to camp, but we went to them to tell them to withdraw. They had some evil design. M. de La Salle made them understand that he was looking for a large river and named for them the nations that we had passed, but, except for an old man, they did not know any of them. When he made him a sign that there were some with flat heads, he made a sign that he knew them and showed with his bow that they had gone to war with them. They speak pleasantly enough, clapping the tongue against the palate like when we talk to a horse.[52]

The 28th, wind east. We went to the flute to see if we could take off something else. There was water up to the waist between decks.

50 For the location of the Indian camp in relation to La Salle's, see plate 8. With the French camp on the eastern point of Matagorda Island (Enríquez Barroto's Punta de San Francisco [diary entry for Thursday, April 3]), the native huts were situated to the north, on Siluria Bayou, about where the town of Siluria once stood and the ruins of the "hurricane proof" U.S. Coast Guard station still stand.

51 There were, nevertheless, alligators in the freshwater inlets, for Alonso de León, on finding but three bodies at Fort Saint-Louis following the massacre, concluded that the rest had been thrown into Garcitas Creek to be eaten by alligators (Alonso de León, "Autos y diligencias," April 22, 1689, UT archives, transcript, AGI, Mexico 616). See Del Weniger, "Natural History," in the commentaries on the Talon Interrogations. The absence of water birds in this locality also is remarkable.

52 Flatheads—Chinook, Choctaw, Salish, and Waxhaw—a name given various tribes for their custom of deforming the head, but none with which the Ka-

March 1st, wind SE, SSE, heavy sea. The *Aimable* sinks deeper, every day more and more. Captain Aigron of the flute has a letter from M. de La Salle in which he commands him to enter as soon as he will have lit a fire on shore, and that he was not able to go there because of the savages we had seen, and had sent word to Mons. de Beaujeu the day previously in answer to his own in which he instructed him to take care, that he did not think that the *Aimable* could enter, there being only 8 to 9 feet and furious breakers; that that did not scare him; that the flute would enter anyway. Besides, he understood the sea. He said 20 times to M. L'Abbé Baudrand and M. de Cartigny and in the memoirs that he provided, and to me, that he knew the sea and that he would conduct the ships into the port. At present he retracts, saying that he does not understand the sea, that he is not a pilot.[53]

The 2nd, no wind. The sea very heavy.

March 3rd, wind SE. The sea still agitated. The longboat and the canoe are still ashore. They cannot come.

The 4th, nice weather. The longboat and the canoe have returned. Wind NE. Monsieur de Beaujeu wrote Monsieur de la Salle asking him whether he has some hope that his affairs will yet succeed; as he has orders from the court to give him all the help he needs, he is looking for ways to render him service. If he wishes it, he will go to the Windward Islands [Isles de Vent] to fetch him food and everything he will need, that he should not be sparing, that he decide as soon as possible because the water and the food are diminishing. He answered that he would carry out what he had to do without involving the king in greater expenses or him [Beaujeu] in so much trouble.

He had the king's scribe draw up an official report on the loss of the flute. He plays at present another role. He is abusing Captain Aigron, makes him fast, threatens him that it is his fault if his business does not succeed, that it is his enemies who have paid him to lose the flute.

As for me, I will be the cause of the king's business not succeeding because he must build forts and there are no engineers, that he must attack strongholds and he cannot do all that because I do not want to go with him.

---

rankawas might have come in contact. Minet, in his account of the 1682 journey, says the Coroa all had flat heads. See p. 60 and accompanying note 72; also p. 119. Concerning the Karankawas' manner of speech, see note 43 to the Talon Interrogations.

53 The row that went on over the loss of the *Amiable* is told in a series of documents published in Margry, *Découvertes*, II, 564–73. Baudraud and Cartigny are not included in Villier's (*L'Expédition*) list.

March 5th, Monsieur de Beaujeu wants to leave. He no longer has water or food. The crew grumbles to see that we are not leaving and that all is finished.

The 6th. Mardi Gras is lean Tuesday for us. Luck has not been with me. My friends were right not to approve of this voyage.

> To murmur against it and lose patience
>   is not apropos,
> Wanting what God wants is the only learning
>   that gives us repose.

The greatest doctors are not always the greatest men. Common sense accompanied by a great steadfastness of soul and an inviolable attachment to one's duty is worth incomparably more for the service of God and the state than all the learning in books and colleges together in a spirit without honor, without courage, and without integrity.

The 7th, wind E. We no longer see the flute. She has completely sunk. Many things are happening on the shore. The savages have found a bundle of blankets. They have divided them among themselves. Monsieur de La Salle was aware of it. He wants them [back]. Mons. Du Hamel was ashore with the longboat during that time. The savages were scattered from one side to the other. They were in three villages on the lake shores. "It is necessary," he [La Salle] said, "to go and take their canoes if they do not want to give them to us. I am going to one of their villages. An officer will go with you [Du Hamel] in the longboat with some cadets and soldiers to the other village." He commanded them especially not to harm them or to take anything from them except their canoes [and then only] if they did not return the blankets. He went to a village. He took a canoe that was there and all their skins, nets, and food. As for M. Du Hamel, seeing that they had only two blankets, which they had cut in two, he took from them three canoes; and told them that when they returned the blankets their canoes would be returned, and they left. As it was getting late, M. de la Salle's officer [Crevel de Moranger], a young man who was his nephew, said that he could go no farther with the canoes. It was a long way to camp, and, being halfway between the savages and the camp, they could stay there, that M. de La Salle would send them help. M. Du Hamel went away with the longboat, and the sailors say that he had left his nephew there with seven cadets and hired men. As soon as he was gone, the nephew went ashore with the men, secured the canoes, made a fire, and went to sleep while waiting for help. The savages who saw a fire came there. Finding them asleep, they shot arrows at all who were there. They killed two outright and seriously wounded three who returned to the camp badly injured and again sounded the alarm. Those who were not wounded shot several times while fleeing. Because of that, the savages did not take their canoes. They have not been seen since.[54]

The 8th, foul weather, wind NE, N. That night the wind grew stronger.

The 9th, wind the same. M. de la Salle again told M. de Beaujeu that he could leave, and said loudly that if he had not been there the flute would not have been lost, that for a long time he had been sending him word that he no longer had anything to do with him, that nevertheless he still stayed, that he wanted to see what he would do but that he would not serve him.

The 10th M. de Beaujeu sent a receipt to M. de La Salle for the letters he would give him.

All the soldiers have dysentery. It is because of the salty water they are drinking.

The letters were brought.[55] He [La Salle] told Monsieur du Hamel that we were all like lice on his gown. He brought the crew of the *Aimable* and the captain of our crew said that they would reduce rations to feed them.

The 11th we thought we could leave, but the wind was against us. We had resolved to go to the Baye du St. Esprit to see if there we could take on water and hunt to have something to live on.[56] We again went ashore

54 Joutel ("Relation," p. 161) attributes to this episode the "disgust" that caused Minet, the Abbé d'Esmanville, "and some others" to abandon the enterprise and return to France with Beaujeu. As we have seen, Minet's disgust had a number of causes. His status, and whether he should go or stay, was bandied back and forth in letters between La Salle and Beaujeu, dating from February 17. Beaujeu maintained that the decision was Minet's alone, that he himself had no authority over him (Margry, *Découvertes,* II, 542, 544, 547, 548, 550–51). D'Esmanville, on the other hand, perceived La Salle's design of sending troops to conquer the Spaniards of Nueva Vizcaya. He protested that he had been sent to make war on demons, not Christians (D'Esmanville, "Journal," II, 515).

55 These included La Salle's *procès verbal* of March 1, 1685, and his letter to the Marquis de Seignelay of March 4, in Margry, *Découvertes,* II, 555–63.

56 La Salle and Beaujeu had discussed the possibility that the *Joly* might reconnoiter the Baye du Saint-Esprit (Espíritu Santo)—which was still perceived as shown on the maps, at the mouth of a different river from the one La Salle had explored—and send back a boat to inform La Salle of its location and advantages. Beaujeu offered to fetch supplies for the colony from Martinique if La Salle would give him a letter declaring the necessity. The letter never came, and both plans were ultimately abandoned (Margry, *Découvertes,* II, 564–65). Just where Beaujeu intended to look for the bay is not clear. La Salle and Joutel had at first thought it to be the one passed on Janu-

to take on several barrels of water to cook the corn. Soldiers are dying every day. Two have deserted.[57]

The 12th we rigged sail on a SSE wind. We left at 9 o'clock, the course ENE, and the 13th, wind favorable.

The 14th at 3 o'clock in the morning, wind from the north. Food and water were diminishing every day. That night the wind was still against us. We held a meeting to see what was best to do. The crew all said that they preferred to be reduced to one *chopine* [a measure nearly equal to an English pint] of unboiled [*sans chaudiere*] water and to go to Cape St. Anthoine, that this coast always had foul weather, that all the winds were dangerous, that no one had been to the Baye du St. Esprit, that one was not sure of taking on water or food, that there one would be better set up for St. Domingue and other places where one might wish to go to take on some food. Monsieur de Beaujeu, who had always been for the Baye du St. Esprit, told them, "Since you want it, I am willing, and, besides, the winds are contrary for going to the said bay."[58] We set course E by SE.

The 15th, wind S by SE. Course E by SE.

The 16th, wind N with violence, rain, thunder, lightning.

The 17th, wind chilly, NE, ENE.

The 18th, wind S by SE. Course E by SE. That evening calm. That night good wind S by SE.

The 19th, same wind. At noon calm. Endured severe thirst. The salt meat cooked with seawater.

The 21st calm. At noon, wind E.

The 22nd, light wind SE by E to S by SW. The crew ate the meat raw, and we ate ours cooked with seawater or roasted a little, as we were also lacking wood.

The 23rd, wind ENE. Course SE by S.

The 24th, wind ESE, SE by E. The currents west. Latitude 24°59′.

---

ary 11 (Galveston Bay), and La Salle finally concluded that they had passed the principal mouth of the *fleuve* Colbert, or Mississippi, on January 3, about the time the *Joly* became separated from the other ships (Margry, *Découvertes,* II, 539, and III, 121).

57 One of these deserters probably was Jean Jarry (or Géry), whom the Spaniards found living among the Coahuiltecan Indians in present-day Kinney County, Texas, and who played a part in Alonso de León's 1689 expedition to find Fort Saint-Louis. See Weddle, *Wilderness Manhunt,* pp. 132, 151, 175–78, 189.

58 For 150 years Spanish sailing instructions had prescribed a course from Mexico to Spain that took advantage of prevailing wind and current, leaving the Gulf through the Straits of Florida. Beaujeu, without such advice, chose the more difficult route, running contrary to the Caribbean current coursing into the Gulf through the Yucatán Channel.

March 25th, calm. That evening, light wind ESE. Course NE, tacking. Wind E by NE. Course SE by S.

The 26th, wind south. Course ESE. That evening, wind SW.

The 27th, wind to the N. Rain, foul weather. At noon [wind] NW. It rained. We caught a little water. At two o'clock we saw land. We did not think we were so close to shore. The current was E and NE. We saw very high mountains. We were not sure what it was, but, on approaching, we recognized to our left, 7 or 8 leagues east of us, the mountain of Havana, Cuba. At 4 o'clock we set course to the west to reach Cape St. Anthoine.[59]

The 28th, wind N and NNE. Course WSW. Sighted some coasts 9 leagues away. The currents N. That evening we set the same course because the night was dark and we wanted to recognize Cape St. Anthoine.

The 29th we set sail in the morning, but at four good leagues from shore we failed to miss some rocks and shoal cays. While going to the cape, north of it, we tacked about. From all sides we saw shoals, which amazed us since we were surrounded by the bay.[60] We came out of it as best we could to reach the open sea. That evening we went to anchor at the place where we had anchored previously; but a land breeze drove us into the offing, so we tacked about all night.

March 30th we again tacked about. Finally we anchored a league closer to the cape than where we were. We went in the longboat to look for water. We weighed anchor to anchor farther up [because] we thought we might fall upon some shoals. That evening we anchored close to where we had weighed anchor.

The 31st we wanted to go ashore to see if we could find a place to take on water besides the three small holes that we had already found. M. de Beaujeu set the departure for next day, saying that we would go together. That night he sent Captain d'Avines[?] with five men and some arms to make a little guardhouse at the place where we had found the springs so that when the longboat got there it would find the casks filled. The water flows into the holes slowly. It rained all day. We caught a lot of water.

April 1st, *1685*. The longboat left to go to the three holes to get

---

59 The mountains first sighted probably were the Cordillera de los Organos. The recognizable feature farther east may have been the Pan de Cabañas. The current already had carried the *Joly* east of her charted course. Had Beaujeu been knowledgeable of these waters, he would have turned northeast at this point and followed the Gulf Stream through the Bahama Channel and into the Atlantic—which he was to do later with English help.

60 Bahía de Guadiana. See Enríquez Barroto diary, June 23–25, concerning coastal navigation west of Havana.

water that the guards had taken in. This place was farther NW than our boat, by about half a league. I embarked with M. de Beaujeu in his canoe to go to the opposite side to see if we could not take on some water. We landed and dug among the rocks that are there to see whether or not we could find a little water to take. On our way we heard cannon shots. We returned to our canoe. We saw a Spanish galley pursuing our longboat and firing on it, and we thought all our people would be killed. We returned on board. There were 24 [men] ashore. Some were hunting; the others were taking on water, and still others were at the longboat. When they saw the galley, or pirogue, 18 embarked, thinking they could reach the shore; but it [the galley] was soon upon them. Two of our sailors were killed, and 16 were taken prisoner. The others came opposite our ship, and we rescued them with the canoe. That night they sent one of our men from the galley opposite the ship to say that they wanted to have a meeting. We fetched him. He was carrying a letter to Monsieur de Beaujeu by which the captain of the galley asked if he wanted to ransom our people; otherwise, they would all be killed. We sent M. d'Esmanville, a priest from the Seminary of St. Sulpice, who had not wanted to stay with M. de la Salle. They demanded 100 *ecus* [300 francs or 100 crowns] for each one, a thousand-weight of powder, and six swivel guns.

The 2nd they returned with M. de Beaujeu's last offer. (It must be noted that we believed we were still at war with Spain.[61]) Finally, after they had negotiated that evening, they agreed on what we would give for the 16 prisoners: two swivel guns, 200 crowns, a thousand-weight of powder and two casks of brandy, which we sent right away and on the longboat and our people with all the precautions we could take.

The 3rd we saw two vessels from afar. Right away we rigged sail. When we saw nine of them, we did not hesitate to go to them, ready to fight; but we saw that they were English.[62] We went aboard their ship to ask them for water and food. They gave us a little. Another large English ship arrived, which was their flagship, all merchants who gave us more. We came out of the Bahama Channel with them [[having missed Matanzas because of the calm]].

The 14th, observed latitude, 30°; thus we had cleared the channel.

---

61 Minet here clears up a point long in doubt: La Salle had not learned at Petit Goâve of the Treaty of Tregua, signed at Regensburg on August 15, 1684, restoring peace between France and Spain. Whether or not the Spanish captain was aware of it made little difference; the Gulf was held to be exclusively Spanish, and any foreign ship entering it was an intruder.

62 England and France were closely allied during the reign of Charles II. Charles, initially deposed by Oliver Cromwell, had found refuge with Louis

We went to the English. They again gave us food and water and advised us to go to Virginie [Virginia] instead of St. Domingue. We took this route.[63]

April 15th we took on much water through the rudder bands. We hove to in order to repair it.

The 16th, wind N, NNE. Monsieur de Beaujeu wants to go to St. Domingue.

The 17th, wind against us to go to Virginie. We set course ESE.

The 19th, wind NE, ENE. That evening the sailors represented to Monsieur de Beaujeu that, having neither food nor water, the shortest way would be to go to Virginie.

The 20th, wind ENE. The course SE. We saw two ships from afar. We approached them, but they were two of our English ships.

After dinner the wind E by NE. Course north to go to Virginie.

The 21st, calm.

The 22nd, Easter Sunday. Good wind E by NE. Course N by NE.

The 23rd, slight wind, ENE. Course N. Calm that evening and all night.

The 24th, calm. At noon, wind fresh, NE, ENE. Water is beginning to run low. We have a pint a day.

April 25th, slight wind. After dinner, wind fresh. It is a breeze that comes this way every day when there is no strong wind. At night, rain, wind NW.

The 26th, strong NW wind. Wind NNW. Rain. Course NE. Observed latitude, 33°54'.

The 27th, the wind a little calm but always in the same direction. Course NE. That night the winds changed to SE, to ESE. Light wind, heavy sea.

The 28th, slight wind E, SE, ESE, changing; heavy sea. Still cloudy weather. Again the kettle is empty. There are no more than four swallows of water. Today we are in 34° latitude and Dutch longitude 302°, and always the wind against us to go to Virginie.

April 29th, wind still violent. That day we set course not knowing whether we were near land. Even though we sounded, we could not find bottom. Heavy rain. Sea extremely agitated. That night, hove to, wind SE.

XIV and during his exile came under Louis's influence. The *Joly*'s officers, therefore, recognized the English vessel as friendly.

63 The *Joly* now had reversed course, traversed the Straits of Florida, and exited the Bahama Channel. Latitude 30° places her a little north of St. Augustine, Florida, well on the way to Virginia.

The 30th, weather still stormy, heavy rain, violent wind straining the sail. Wind SE, SSE. That night, hove to. The wind a little calmer.

The 1st of May, good weather, wind SE, SSE. Heading W, searching for land. That evening wind N, NW, latitude 37°40'. So here we are farther north than we thought. We set course SW by S to go along the shore and at the same time get to it.

May 2nd, sounded. The night of the first to the second, 50 fathoms, slimy sand bottom. In the morning, 20 fathoms. Course S by SW, wind ESE. At noon we could not see land but many birds, straw-colored marsh hens. Sounded 17 fathoms, bottom of fine sand. At 3 o'clock in the afternoon, we saw land about four leagues from us. Heading W, 17 fathoms, 16 fathoms. We thought that they were the islands that are south of the bay. That evening, sounded 12 fathoms, muddy sand. At 9 o'clock that evening we anchored three leagues from shore. The currents in this place run south with great force.

May 3rd at 6 o'clock in the morning we set sail, course N by NW, land to the W and NW. We sounded 12, 13, 14, 12 fathoms, bottom of fine sand and shell, a little ooze. Weather overcast, fog, wind E. We approached land, entering Chesapeac Bay a league and ½ from Cape Henry; 11, 13, 10 fathoms, heading NNW. We followed a ship that was entering. This gave us great pleasure since we had followed it up to an English flute that was anchored at the entrance and which was awaiting a W wind to depart. We sent a canoe to their side, asking them to give us a pilot to achieve our entry. They gave us one. We ascended and passed through 7, 5, 4 fathoms, bottom of muddy sand. Then after 5, 6, 7 we anchored at 4 o'clock that evening. The pilot then left. He was afraid of losing the W wind, should it come. We sent the longboat to the right, where we saw some ships, to ask for a pilot for going to anchor at a place to take on water. In truth, it was time to come to Virginie, as we were all very low, with neither water, wine, brandy, nor wood, burning our framework, tormented by bad weather.

The 4th, the currents and the tide are so strong that the longboat could not return until today at one o'clock in the afternoon with a pilot and a sailor from a revenue boat [*patache*] of the king of England that is here to collect the taxes and prevent fraud.

We set sail right away. We ascended another two leagues in the bay through 5, 6, 7 fathoms, NNW. After that we entered a large river to the W, WSW through four fathoms, 5, 7, 9. We anchored a league and a half upriver in eight fathoms at 5 in the evening. There is a regular tide here like on the coast of France, in that, although it rises only three or four feet, it has furious waves.

The 5th the longboat took to the water. The captain of the revenue boat, who is an old navy officer they put there in recompense for his services, came to see Mons. de Beaujeu.

This river where we are anchored is called the Hiems [James]. One can ascend it with ships 40 leagues farther. In this Chesapeac Bay there are 30 navigable rivers. The trade here is tobacco. There are always 40 or 50 ships scattered from one side to the other, loading it. They have a large number of apple trees from which they make cider, which is their drink. This country is flat, full of large trees such as pine, oak, elm like in Touraine, and a tree of which there is a great number that they call sassafras, known by our surgeons; a large number of bears and deer; turkeys, and savages. The rivers are quite full of fish.

The Iroquois come this far to make war, plunder the dwelling places, and make war on the savages who are tributary to Virginie and who live in higher country 150 leagues to the NW.[64] There are mountains like the Pirennes [Pyrenees], always covered with snow. Those mountains have never been crossed. I questioned one of the inhabitants of the country. He told me that all of Virginie believed that behind these mountains there was a Spanish town, but I do not believe it. There is a nation of savages to the NW whom they call the Flat Heads on whom they make war. I saw one, a slave, at the home of a colonel where we dined. The back of the head, which to us seems raised up, is very flat, and it seems that they try to flatten it between two planks, which they set, one at the forehead and the other at the opposite side, in the back.[65]

The country of Monsieur de La Salle is Apaches of the *vaqueros*, and Quivira, by way of the Pana [and] Panimaha.[66] All the coast on the south side is sandy bottom from 36½°. Those who do not want to enter the bay, who need only to take on fresh provisions, go to this coast behind. Within gunshot there is a great lake of fresh water, and all the country is inhabited [by people] who at a fair price will furnish you

64 The Iroquois of the central Mohawk Valley and the lake region of central New York gained, with French firearms, an influence over the natives from Maine to the Mississippi and between the Ottawa and Cumberland rivers. Their population in 1685 has been estimated at sixteen thousand. In the next century they were allied with the English in wars with the French (Swanton, *Indian Tribes,* pp. 33, 40).

65 See note 52.

66 The Vaquero Apaches were the Jicarillas (Athapascan linguistic stock), who ranged principally in Colorado and New Mexico, nowhere near La Salle's settlement. How word of them had come to Jamestown at this early date is a mystery. Minet seems to wander. The Panis (Wichita) and Panismaha (Pawnee), closely related tribes of the Caddoan linguistic family, at this time were living in Oklahoma, Kansas, and Nebraska (Swanton, *Indian Tribes,* pp. 370–72, 305–306, 289–90).

with necessities, except for wine and brandy. Food is cheaper by half than in France. There is no wheat bread but plenty of good corn.

May 6th we left the shore to go to Jamestown [La Ville d'Hiems] to ask the governor's permission to take on water. We arrived there with the Chevalier d'Heer [d'Aire], lieutenant of the ship, in two days because of bad weather, being able to go there by the tide, even though it is ten leagues inland. We found there the legislative assembly [*assemblé de estat*] of the country. Lord Howard, governor of the country, was not there. His wife was sick. He was at home with her. This town consists of 15 houses of wood and brick. It is a place fixed for the assemblies, nothing but that, because the inhabitants are scattered on the lands; and each one has his property. As the country has an infinity of small rivers, the greatest *seigneurs* are those who possess one of these rivers because commerce goes better with them. A property of 100 *arpents* [old French measure, roughly an acre] with the lodging, all built on the banks of a river, would cost only two thousand *livres*. Horses, cows, and sheep are a great bargain, so a man with a thousand crowns [*ecus*] can live like a king in this country.

To return to this town. It is on an island in the river of the same name. We stayed there three days. The gentlemen of the assembly gave us the permission in writing that we requested, and then we left. Bad weather overtook us. We again slept outdoors in some plantations that are on the banks of this river.

In the Council or the Estates [legislative assembly] it is the lord and a counselor of the king who preside. They elect for the people a president and some counselors and judge there the affairs of the province twice a year. It is 100 leagues in length, inland, and 50 leagues of coast comprising only Virginie and Marilande without counting Caroline. There are 49,000 plantations populated with Negroes, savages, and tenants. There are 40,000 men bearing arms. The revenue and the currency of the country is tobacco. They have no fort. Formerly there was one, which is now in ruins, at the entrance of the Hiems River. In town there is a battery made of brick where there are seventeen cannon, of which four are of cast iron. They all rest on end, without gun carriages.

I saw three savages who came to the council. They were allies who were coming to render homage. They had blue blankets, which covered them, plumed headdresses, and glass beads. Their only trade is fur, but very little.

The people have been rebelling against the governor for eight years. This town was larger. They went there and burned it entirely. These are obstinate people, and every day they seem to want to revolt. In Marilande, which is as large as Virginie, there is a lord who is the magistrate.

They are all quasi-Catholic. The king of England[67] gave this country to this lord and gave permission to all the Catholics of his kingdom to go live there. They render a certain tribute to the king, but it is believed that three or four lords who are powerful in that country will rise up and will become masters of all of Virginie and Marilande.

May 10th we arrived on shore with some letters for the captain of the ketch and permission to take on water and wood, even though they were half done already. We found out about the death of the king of England.[68] They were wary of us, thinking that we were coming to take over the country and saying that there were at Cape Henry, behind the coast, 15 or 16 French ships. But that did not last. They saw very well by the frank and free manner that we used and our necessity that we had come simply for our needs.

There are many small animals here as big as rats, which they call flying squirrels. They are gray like rabbits, with white stomachs. They have pockets on the side, which they spread by stretching their feet and flapping these said feet like a bird does its wings, and [they] fly in this manner from one tree to another.

There are many white mulberry trees here, but they cannot import silkworms. There is a tariff of a hundred *livre* for anyone who does. They were never able to grow more than 80, [and those] with much difficulty. These mulberry trees are like those in the Tuileries.

There is a Frenchman here from La Rochelle named M. Servant who seems to be a very honest man. He has been away from France 40 years and is married to a Frenchwoman from Paris. She was brought from France to England at the age of twelve. She is said to be of the Fouquet family[69] and is called Louise Fouquet.

---

67 Charles I (Stuart), whose reign began in 1625 and ended with his flight to Scotland in 1646 in the face of Oliver Cromwell's victories. In 1649 he was delivered up to the English Parliament, condemned as a public enemy, and beheaded.

68 Charles II, son of Charles I. He was proclaimed king by the Scots in 1651, only to flee to France with the defeat of his army by Cromwell. Cromwell's death in 1658 and popular dissatisfaction with the commonwealth form of government enabled Charles to return and assume the English throne in 1660. His allegiance to Louis XIV of France seems to have been based on more than gratitude for having been given refuge; the Sun King made a practice of buying his friends, and the English monarch is said to have been in his pay. Charles's death signaled a change in the relationship between the two crowns.

69 Nicolas Fouquet (1615–80) was the French superintendent of finance. His excessive power and driving ambition had led to his downfall (W. J. Eccles, *France in America*, p. 60).

The 22nd we celebrated with a 21-gun salute the Duke of York's being named King of England.[70]

The 26th, after having satisfied all our needs, we left with a WSW, W wind. At noon we were 5 leagues out to sea.

May 30th, rain, thunder. We saw St. Elmo's fire on the weathervane.

The 31st. The [compass] variation here is NW 10°; latitude 38°30′, estimated 200 leagues from departure.

[[June]]

June 5th we caught a shark eight feet long.

June 16th, latitude 42°15′.

June 18th we were half way.

The 1st of July, latitude 46°20′, longitude 3°.

The 2nd, 3rd, 4th, good wind from NW and w. The 4th we met a ship from Bourdeaux [*sic*] that told us we were 10 leagues from Isle Dieu. We saw Belle Isle and that evening Isle Dieu. Course ESE. Arrived at Rochefort the 6th of July, 1685.

I stayed with Monsieur Arnoul, naval intendant, while awaiting news from the court and from Paris.

July 28th the intendant received an order from the court to have me put into the St. Nicolas Tower in La Rochelle until further notice and an order to M. Millet, governor of the region of Aulnis and lieutenant-general of the king's armies, to have me held by force and well guarded.

I went there Sunday, July 29th.

Monsieur de la Salle had written against me and against Captain Aigron, who also is a prisoner here. Several have been sent to question him.

I would like to be able to make an interrogation of Sieur de la Salle about what I would ask him. While I have spare time, here are some questions for that:

70 Charles II was succeeded by his brother, James II, who asserted his independence of French influence, sought to restore Catholicism to England, and manifested a new friendliness toward Spain. The new stance enabled Spain to obtain through its ambassador, Pedro de Ronquillo, reports on La Salle's colony and copies of the maps prepared by Minet. James's reign, however, was short-lived, as he was forced to abdicate in "the Glorious Revolution of 1688." Fleeing to France, he was cordially received by Louis XIV, and William and Mary (James's son-in-law and daughter) took the English throne. The Spanish versions of two Minet maps are reproduced in Weddle, *Wilderness Manhunt,* plates 3 and 6, from hand-drawn copies in the J. P. Bryan Collection, UT archives. See also Pedro de Ronquillo, "Copia de la relacion hecha al Rey Xpmo tocante a la Bahia del Espiritu Santo," UT archives, transcript, AGI, Mexico 616.

—What is his religion?

—Why [did he] borrow money on all sides in La Rochelle and in Paris for whatever interest they wanted, up to 150%?

—Why [did he] take young men as officers, as soldiers, like little boy clerks taken out of their shops?

—Is it not true that he promised a river?

—Why [did he] bring three priests and three friars [*recolets*] and so many church ornaments?

—Why [did he] bring women and small children?

—Why [was he] always at variance with M. de Beaujeu?

—Why [did he] have four spies on board who listened to all we were saying?

—Why [did he] have young and handsome valets and make them sleep with him?

—Why [did he] speak so much on board, he who spoke so little on land?—And at Versailles they had trouble extracting a single word from him.

—Why [did he] go back on his word so many times and on so many subjects?

—Why [did he] say that the intendant had not said I was to choose a room on board after M. de Valigny because he was old and feeble?

—Why [did he] say bad things about me to all the Normans?

—Why [did he] say that I was a spy of his actions and that it was his enemies who gave me to Monsieur the Marquis de Seignelay?

—Why [did he] say that he did not need an engineer and that he knew as much as all the engineers?

—Why [did he] say that he wanted to send me back?

—Why [did he] find fault with everything?

—Why [did he] quarrel with everybody?

—Why [did he] forbid his surgeon to help the ones on board care for the sick, since it was his own who were ill?

—Why [did he] lie so much about his voyage, an infinite number of lies which would be too long to report?

—Why [did he] not get along with the three persons who were in the discovery party [of 1682] so that at least they all four would be able to say the same thing?

—Why [did he] make us keep his voyage a secret since he spoke of it to all those who wanted to lend him money?

—Why [did he] say that he never wrote when in the meantime he had someone keep a journal of everything we said and did on board?

—Why [did he] speak so much evil of the Jesuits?

—Why [did he] tell us that the Jesuits had asked the intendant at

Rochefort to delay this voyage as much as possible and [say] that Monsieur the Intendant tried to do it because he was awaiting the abbot [M. l'Abaÿe]?

—Why [did he] say that M. de Beaujeu did all that he could to prevent the success of this voyage because the Jesuits had promised a benefice to his son?

—Why [did he] tell everybody that he was sending M. de Beaujeu to France as soon as he arrived at St. Domingue?

—Why [did he] get sick at Petit Goâve and in his delirium say that he had betrayed the court?

—Why [did he] sell gunpowder at Petit Goâve?

—Why [did he] dismiss the good men he had and let them go in a pirate ship as soon as they offered him money?

—Why [did he] have Englishmen with him?

—Why [did he] get angry when we took food and say that he would furnish some when we were on the river, 100 times more than was needed, and repeat it 20 times to M. de Beaujeu and to M. Bégon, the intendant of the islands?

—Why [did he] then take some himself?

—Whether the pirates did not tell him that he would not find the river along that coast, or food or fresh water, etc., [but] only swamps, and that we would perish?

—Why [did he] put them on board the flute if it were not true that he had given a rendezvous in case of separation at the Baye de Spiritu Sancto?

—Whether it is not true that he had given in writing that the river was at 28°20′?

—How did it happen that he twice took the wrong route?

—How did it happen that, having lost us, he was not at the rendezvous?

—How did it happen that he did not stay at the latitude of the river, that he passed it, and that we found him anchored at 27°48′?

—How did it happen that he told us that he had made a mistake, that the river led into the lakes that we saw, and that he wanted to return to France?

—How did it happen that he gave no food to M. de Beaujeu for his soldiers he took on his boat to take them where he wanted and that he let them go on foot at the mercy of all the evils that are in a wilderness, without food or water?

—Why the next day he sent word that the little outlet where he was anchored was one of the branches of the river?

—Why [did he] tell us afterward that he had not promised a river?

—Why [did he] remain 20 days before this little outlet of the lake?

—Whether it is not true that he told us at the end of this time that the river was 40 leagues from there at the NE?

—Why [did he] stop in front of an outlet of the lakes that were only 8 or 9 leagues from the place whence we had departed?

—Whether it is not true that he told us that the river was here?

—Whether it is not true that he told us that he had never promised a river and that he knew what the king had ordered him to do and that it was for [these] reasons that he had taken all these steps?

—Why he gave his wine to the captain of the flute and to the pilot in the midst of the dangers they were facing along that coast?

—Why he sent word to us that there are 14 feet of water on the bar at the entrance to the lake and there are only 8 or 9 feet?

—Whether it is not true that the pilots of the *Joly* and those of the other ships sounded again (even though it had already been done twice) in his presence and at the hour that he wanted, that with a pike they found only nine feet minus a few inches.

—Whether it is not true that we sounded three or four times again?

—Why [did he] not bring the captain of the flute and the pilot to sound, since he wanted to make the flute enter, so they would see what this sounding was?

—Why [did he] say and send word that the tide rose four feet, since every time we sounded we always found eight or nine feet at the most?

—Why [did he] want to make the flute enter this opening, since it would serve for naught in a flooded land where there is only sand and mud without fresh water?

—Why [did he] wait until after noon to make the flute enter, since his wine was at the command of the captain and the pilot who got drunk every day and fought with their crew, added to the fact that he rarely gave any to his officers, the wine being ours besides?

—Why he who said that she would enter and that he had helped plant the buoys and that he had so well noticed the hour of the tide did not himself go aboard the flute to make her enter?

—Why [did he] write for them to enter when he was not able to go in, having business on shore, that is to say, a matter of greater importance than saving a vessel and those who were in it?

—Why [did he] forbid the captain to open the hold to lighten the vessel, and command him in writing?

—Why, before the tide rose, [did he] light the fire or smoke that was the signal for the flute to enter—he who said he had such beautiful notes—and that was the cause of the flute's grounding and being lost?

—Why [did he] make so many fine promises to the captain, making over him and making him his confidant while he had the flute and mistreating him after he had lost it, since all he did was to follow his orders exactly on every point?

—Why during the whole voyage [did he] forbid the said captain to see or speak to M. de Beaujeu or to any person of the *Joly*?

—Why [did he] starve the soldiers to death by giving them only flour while he stuffed himself with wine and meat with the monks and did not let the officers eat with him, giving them only a little corn?

—Why [did he] say that it was the provisions of the king that were taken and lost and that his own were the ones that were saved, and for that reason make people fast, leaving them weak and unable to serve?

—Why, after having said several times that this river was the Colbert River, even though we saw only large lakes, did he afterward say that he had not promised a river? What was the use of saying and retracting every day?

—Having found some savages, why, out of malicious convictions, did he quarrel with them who had offered to go fight against their enemies when with kindness he could have done with them whatever he wanted?

—Why [did he] go steal their food, canoes, and nets to have war with them?

—Why [did he] tell me a hundred times that I could leave, that he had no need of me and afterward stand against me?

Everything that I put here a hundred people will sign, for not only I but all on board heard it, and his letters say it.

Got out of prison September 7, 1685, by order of the king addressed to Monsieur Arnoul. Stayed at La Rochelle to wait for Monsieur Ferry and Monsieur de Vauban.[71]

71 Sébastian Le Prestre, Marquis de Vauban, Louis XIV's commissary-general of fortifications and a member of the inner group of military advisers to Louis and Jérôme Pontchartrain, successive secretaries of state for the marine after 1690. Vauban in 1698 made an eloquent plea for a new Gulf of Mexico expedition. Pierre Le Moyne, Sieur d'Iberville, undertook his first voyage the following year (John C. Rule, "Jérôme Phélypeaux, Comte de Pontchartrain, and the Establishment of Louisiana, 1696–1715," in John Francis McDermott, ed., *Frenchmen and French Ways in the Mississippi Valley*, pp. 180–81, 188).

III.   The Spanish Search

The Enríquez Barroto Diary: *Voyage of the* Piraguas

ROBERT S. WEDDLE

News that La Salle had penetrated the Gulf of Mexico—historically an exclusively Spanish sea—provoked consternation on the part of Spanish officials in Mexico. The word came from a pirate crew captured in flight following the sack of Campeche. Among the captives were six deserters from La Salle's company who had jumped ship at Petit Goâve. Questioned before hanging, they betrayed the French plan to establish a colony on a river called Miscipipi.[1] The name meant nothing to the Spaniards; they surmised that the river was the one shown on various maps as the Espíritu Santo, the actual location of which was in doubt.

Admiral Gaspar de Palacios, planning the search for the French invaders, chose two senior pilots of the Windward Fleet (Armada de Barlovento) to carry out the initial phase. Juan Enríquez Barroto and Antonio Romero were to scan the wilderness coast west from San Marcos de Apalache (St. Mark's, Florida) to "the bay of Miscipipi or Espíritu Santo," said to lie somewhere between Apalache and Tampico.[2]

1 Denis Thomas, "Declaración de Dionico Thomas," in "Testimonio de los autos y diligencias fechas por el govierno de la Nueva España sobre el reconocimiento de poblazón de francesses en la Bahía del Espíritu Santo," UT archives, transcript 67, AGI, Mexico 616. Thomas, one of the French defectors, claimed he had been informed of La Salle's previous exploits and his current objectives by a "servant" of the explorer named La Esperanza—doubtless the L'Espérance who Minet says accompanied La Salle to France in 1683.
2 Gaspar de Palacios, "Ynstrucción y derrota," Veracruz, November 13, 1685, in ibid. The Río del Espíritu Santo first appeared on the 1519 map sketch attributed to Alonso Alvarez de Pineda (AGI, Mapas y Planos). It has been widely published. The Alvarez sketch, as well as accounts of the Soto expedition some twenty years later, appeared to have escaped the notice of those concerned with the La Salle quest. Most useful in connecting the name with the location of La Salle's intended settlement were the memorial of Fray Alonso de Benavides (*Benavides' Memorial of 1630*, Peter P. Forrestal, trans.)

Enríquez Barroto, "a person of recognized intelligence, adept at solar observations and coastal mapping," was assigned to overall command.[3] He was to become one of the principal figures in the search that lasted more than three years. A key participant in three voyages, he contributed maps and diaries that advanced geographical knowledge and aided colonization. Yet little is known of him. At the time, he was serving as chief pilot of *Nuestra Señora de la Soledad,* a ship of the Armada de Barlovento, the fleet charged with guarding the coasts of America. He was a former student of the noted savant Carlos de Sigüenza y Góngora, professor of mathematics and chief cosmographer of New Spain, with whom he shared his nautical data and who turned the information to his own advantage. Enríquez Barroto, however, apparently did not mind; he was "a modest, unassuming individual, greatly beloved by his former professor, and it did not occur to him to capitalize on the discoveries that he had made in the performance of his duty."[4]

To carry out the initial search voyage, Enríquez and Romero embarked at Veracruz for Havana and there were assigned a frigate of the Armada de Barlovento. On the eve of sailing they received news that added a new concern to this voyage and foreshadowed the next. Three crewmen from a Spanish "trading galley"—a euphemism for something closely akin to a pirate ship—reached Havana from St. Augustine, Florida. Having sailed with Captain Juan Corso in search of a rumored French settlement at Espíritu Santo Bay, they had been marooned with half a dozen companions on the western Florida coast.

Corso's galley was a participant in the unofficial Anglo-Hispanic maritime war that went on in the Gulf of Mexico and the Caribbean Sea during the latter part of the seventeenth century. The licensed English privateers of wartime had escaped legal authority to continue their depredations on Spanish shipping and coastal settlements after peace was made. Nesting in the Laguna de Términos, the freebooters varied the pursuits of logwood cutting and cow killing with occasional forays on the Mexican coastal towns from Campeche to Alvarado. Spanish officialdom retaliated by countenancing the operations of "trading galleys" like Corso's, whose activities are described by the three castaways.[5]

---

and a 1685 proposal by the pilot Martín de Echagaray to explore the river mouth (Report of Junta General, Mexico, March 28, 1686, UT archives, transcript 67, AGI, Mexico 616).

3 Officials of Veracruz to Viceroy Paredes, November, 1685, in "Testimonio de los autos," UT archives, transcript 67, AGI, Mexico 616.

4 Irving A. Leonard, trans., *Spanish Approach to Pensacola, 1689–1693,* p. 24.

5 This rivalry is described from the English point of view by William Dampier (*Dampier's Voyages: Consisting of a New Voyage round the World, Two Voyages to*

During the preceding three years, the vessel and its crew had preyed on English ships all across the Caribbean. Then, in April, 1685, with news that "the enemy" was settling at Espíritu Santo Bay, they proceeded to Tampico to look for an Indian pilot who might take them there. Finding none, they steered east toward Apalache. Near the Mississippi Delta, they heard from Indians that a large band of people with muskets like the Spaniards' had landed there and gone inland, but they could find no sign of them. On May 19, the vessel sought shelter in an unknown inlet; the nine-man foraging party was left stranded when a sudden squall drove the ship to the offing. The castaways, seeking Apalache Bay on foot, wandered about the wilderness for two weeks before a Panzacola hunting party took them in tow and conducted them to the Mission Santa Cruz de Sabacola, where the Flint and Chattahoochee rivers join. The Franciscan Fray Juan Mercado directed them to Apalache. No news of their ship awaited them. Reaching St. Augustine, three of the wanderers took passage for Havana, where Enríquez Barroto and Romero heard their story secondhand just before sailing on January 3, 1686.[6] The missing galley became an objective of their quest.

The voyage was to turn up no real news of Corso's ship or the fate of the crew. The sequel appeared more than a year later, on the voyage conducted by Captains Martín de Rivas and Pedro de Iriarte. It is related in Enríquez Barroto's diary, beginning with the entry for April 17, 1687.

From Havana, Enríquez and Romero proceeded to the Apalache port of San Marcos. After taking on two Apalachino Indian guides, they sailed west along the coast and rediscovered Pensacola Bay, site of Tristán de Luna y Arellano's abortive settlement more than a century previously. Their description of the large, deep harbor was to inspire Spanish occupation of the site some years later.

After a pause at Mobile Bay, the mariners probed west and south along the islands bordering Mississippi and Chandeleur sounds until

Campeachy, a Discourse on Winds, a Voyage to New Holland, and a Vindication in Answer to the Commercial Relation of William Funnell, John Masefield, ed., II, 144–45). See also Robert S. Weddle, *Spanish Sea: The Gulf of Mexico in North American Discovery, 1500–1685*, chaps. 20, 21.

6 Diego de Castro, Jorge Nicolás, and Manuel Munibe, "Testimonio," UT archives, transcript 68, AGI, Mexico 616. I have altered my previous conclusions concerning this episode (Robert S. Weddle, *Wilderness Manhunt: The Spanish Search for La Salle*, pp. 41–44), particularly with reference to the location of the "bay" they were seeking and the place the men were marooned. The territory of the Panzacola Indians and the location of Father Mercado's mission provide the key.

they reached the first mouth of the Mississippi River. The location, given by the pilot as 29°03′ north latitude, actually was at North Pass, in about 29°12′. The river mouth was choked with logs and surrounded by mud lumps, and the Spaniards chose appropriate names: Río de la Palizada (River of the Palisade) and Cabo de Lodo (Mud Cape). While the pilots pondered the advisability of attempting to enter the river, a storm arose and drove the ship across the Gulf. With provisions running low, they made for Veracruz, arriving March 13, 1686.[7] The pilots reported to Admiral Palacios, and the ship's log and Enríquez's chart were forwarded to the viceroy.

Although plans for a second maritime expedition were held in abeyance, land marches were directed from such diverse points as St. Augustine, Florida, and Cadereyta, Nuevo León. Neither proved any more successful than the Enríquez-Romero voyage. In the spring of 1686 a special dispatch vessel from Havana carried news of the La Salle expedition to Spain, where Crown resolution called for "the greatest force and effort" to remove the foreign threat from the Gulf.[8] The following September the Conde de la Monclova reached New Spain to succeed the Marqués de la Laguna, Conde de Paredes, as viceroy. Within little more than three months of his arrival, a complete coastal reconnaissance of the Gulf was planned and launched.

When the new viceroy summoned ranking officers of the Armada de Barlovento to a planning session, Enríquez Barroto and Romero found themselves at center stage. On their advice Monclova ordered the building of two small ships of the type ordinarily used by pirates. These shallow-draft vessels, called *piraguas,* carried oars as well as a single large sail and were highly maneuverable. They could cross bars too shallow for larger vessels, seek refuge from foul weather in meager coves, and even be hauled up on the beach. By early December the craft were finished and manned with the best soldiers and sailors the Armada de Barlovento had to offer.[9]

7 Juan Jordán de la Reina, "Diario y derrotero del viaxe," Veracruz, March 16, 1686, UT archives, transcript 68, AGI, Mexico 616. The Jordán diary is translated in Irving A. Leonard, trans. and ed., "The Spanish Re-exploration of the Gulf Coast in 1686," *Mississippi Valley Historical Review* 22, no. 4 (March, 1936): 547–57. The voyage is summarized in Weddle, *Wilderness Manhunt,* pp. 46–52.
8 Report of Junta de Guerra de las Indias, April 8, 1686, UT archives, transcript 68, AGI, Mexico 616.
9 The term "*piragua*" may designate either of two types of vessel: the one just described (see John Esquemeling, *The Buccaneers of America,* p. 89), or a

The two small ships, with keel lengths of fifty-four and sixty feet and carrying sixty-five men each, were crowded and uncomfortable. Captain Martín de Rivas commanded the larger vessel, *Nuestra Señora del Rosario* (*Our Lady of the Rosary*) and was in overall charge of the expedition. Pedro de Astina was his second-in-command, Miguel Barroa his ensign. Enríquez Barroto, as chief pilot, was assisted by Pedro Biñales. Captain of *Nuestra Señora de la Esperanza* (*Our Lady of Hope*) was Pedro de Iriarte, with Antonio de Ibarra as second-in-command, Francisco de Aldama as ensign, and Romero as chief pilot, assisted by Gerónimo de Acosta. Additionally, there were the two Apalachino Indians who had joined the Enríquez-Romero voyage the previous winter at San Marcos de Apalache, now being returned to their homeland. There was also Juan Poule, an English pilot—or artilleryman, as he is variously described—one of the pirates captured in April, 1684, in the act of sacking Tampico. Poule offered expert knowledge of the northern coast, especially the bay that was to become the focal point: Matagorda. Each ship carried two *prácticos de la costa,* persons with expert knowledge of a given section of coast, here translated as "coastal pilots" or "native guides."

Each vessel, provisioned for three and one-half months, had twenty oars per side and towed a canoe for exploring shallow coves. The two "ladies," *Rosario* and *Esperanza,* were mounted with six bronze swivel guns each and carried incendiary grenades, hand grenades, cutlasses, pikes, and fetters on loan from the San Juan de Ulúa prison for restraining any Frenchman apprehended. There also were spare sails and cordage; pitch for caulking; grease for protecting masts, hull, and rigging; cases of pharmaceuticals and linen for bandages; carpenter's hatchets, nails, tacks, and spikes; and tallow for candles. Besides the *bizcocho* (ship's biscuit or hardtack), which was standard shipboard fare, there were earthen jars of wine and aguardiente (spiritous liquor). Fresh meat would be boarded at Tuxpán and Tampico.[10]

Attention given the preparations reflects the urgency of the mission. The orders specified that there was to be no turning back before the coast was surveyed to latitude 30°, the supposed parallel of Espíritu

boat propelled only by oars, specifically, a dugout. Concerning the viceroy's order, see Monclova to the king, December 30, 1686, UT archives, transcript 68, AGI, Mexico 616.

10 "Relación de las dos piraguas," undated; and "Razón de lo que llevan las piraguas," Veracruz, December 24, 1686, both in UT archives, transcript, AGI, Mexico 616.

Santo Bay or "Micipipi." At Tampico, the mariners were to obtain native guides to the region beyond. Proceeding northward within sight of land, they were to sail only by day, entering all "bays, bars, and river mouths" to take soundings and sketch the coastal contours. If they located the French colony, the explorers were only to gather intelligence, avoiding confrontation.[11] Nothing in the orders called for complete circumnavigation of the Gulf, yet that was to be the extent of the voyage.

The *piraguas* sailed at nine on Christmas morning, 1686. Enríquez Barroto began his log, which encompasses not only the first complete circuit of the Gulf but also the first exploration of Galveston and Atchafalaya bays and Sabine Pass, delineation of the Mississippi Delta, and description of the various Mississippi River passes.

The diary presents a rare close-up view of coastal navigation in the seventeenth century. The concern with the weather—even to the point of noting the slightest wind change—though of only passing interest to the present-day reader, was of vital importance to the mission; likewise the water depth and nature of the bottom, the record of which, with the pilot's description of the shoreline, was designed to guide future voyagers. The character of the bottom had a dual significance. Samples of the material brought up by the wax-filled lower end of the sounding lead indicated whether or not it was suitable for holding an anchor. The nature and color of the substance clinging to the wax also provided a record by which mariners of the future could determine their position, for the deposits in a given locality usually had some distinguishing quality. An experienced pilot could read these samples with amazing accuracy.[12]

The *piraguas,* experiencing a stormy nightmare as they sailed north in winter, were in constant peril. A sudden squall in the middle of the night could cause a poorly secured vessel to drag anchor and crash on a lee shore. It was the pilots' duty, therefore, not only to ascertain whether the bottom was suitable for anchoring but also to observe the wind's behavior.

Enríquez also was alert to other hydrographical factors, including tides and currents; witness, for example, his description of the tide's peculiar behavior inside the Calcasieu River of Louisiana on April 19, and the struggle with the Caribbean current while crossing the Yucatán Channel.[13]

In keeping with the orders, Enríquez, who was noted for his skill in

11 Francisco de Navarro, Instructions, Veracruz, December 12, 1686, in ibid.
12 See J. H. Parry, *The Age of Reconnaissance,* pp. 97–98.
13 See Enríquez Barroto's diary entries for April 19 and June 25, 1687.

this regard, made daily celestial observations, weather permitting, to compute the latitude. He employed an astrolabe to measure the sun's declination, or angle from the horizon, at its meridian. Polaris sightings also were made, and on one occasion (April 16) he went ashore to observe the sun with "a geometric quadrant with a radius of three spans." Observations taken on shore were more accurate than those made aboard ship, especially when the sea was rough and the vessel small.[14] Enríquez's latitude computations for known points were extraordinarily exact, considering the limitations of his instruments and methods. Accuracy is presumed, therefore, for the rest of the voyage; the course along the unknown coast may be tracked with reasonable certainty. Still, the voyage was influenced at times by erroneous preconceptions.

The previous year, Enríquez and Romero, standing at North Pass, had failed—just as La Salle had in 1682—to recognize it as the Mississippi River or Río del Espíritu Santo. The French defectors had described La Salle's river as emptying into a "bay or port" that had a small island in the mouth, forming two channels. However they derived such a description, it had developed in part from the 1519 map sketch of Alvarez de Pineda, who, from his failure to delineate the Mississippi Delta, seems to have perceived the river only from its mighty discharge, rather than close observation.[15] Enríquez was still looking for such a feature when the *piraguas* arrived on April 11, 1687, at the Texas river called Río de Zívoras (Cíbolas). Because the island was not in evidence, the river was judged to be of no importance.

Enríquez Barroto also misjudged the nature of the Tamaulipas-Texas coast, which is embraced by a string of barrier sand islands enclosing a continuous lagoon. He assumed the extenuated body of water inside the sand beaches to be a river paralleling the coast, from the Río Maupate (Las Palmas or Soto la Marina) to the Sabine. Spanish mapmakers, in consequence, were slow to recognize the barrier islands. Even after French cartographers (notably Claude and Guillaume Delisle) began showing them, Spanish maps continued to represent the coastline as being unbroken by such features.

As the two *piraguas* sailed north from Veracruz on Christmas Day,

---

14 Ibid., April 16. The quadrant, depending on a plumb-line hung from the apex of a quarter circle to indicate the polestar's angle of elevation, had an obvious shortcoming for shipboard use. The astrolabe was more suitable for use at sea (Parry, *Age of Reconnaissance,* pp. 107–108).

15 Veracruz officials to the viceroy in "Testimonio de los autos," UT archives, transcript 67, AGI, Mexico 616; Alvarez de Pineda map sketch. The island in the mouth of the Río del Espíritu Santo may have originated with an inkblot.

the voyagers assumed a calculated risk. The winter winds, barring an extraordinary stroke of good fortune, would be against them. Yet the mission's urgency required the attempt. Their haste proved wasteful indeed; the weather turned sour at Tuxpán, and more than two months elapsed before they were able to proceed beyond Tampico.

Just before leaving Tuxpán on January 8, Captain Iriarte received an interesting passenger aboard the *Esperanza:* Diego de Castro, one of the three castaways from Juan Corso's galley. Strangely, the diarist accords Castro no further mention, not even when two of his erstwhile shipmates turn up to relate the bizarre sequel to his own tale of the galley's adventures.[16]

After Tampico, the voyagers had numerous encounters with natives. Among the Pelón Indians (the Bald Ones) of the Tamaulipas coast, they witnessed the exemplification of an old custom: the stripping of white captives. These natives, having first perpetrated this indignity on the occupants of one of Pánfilo de Narváez's boats in 1528, continued the practice—often as a preliminary to murder—until their final conquest in 1749.[17]

At the mouth of the Río Grande (Bravo) the voyagers encountered naked Indians armed with bows and arrows but avoided a confrontation. And, ascending Padre Island, they witnessed a constant parade of natives on the beach, probably the ancestors of the Malaguitas encountered almost a century later when Diego Ortiz Parrilla explored the region. At Corpus Christi Bay, they again found bald and tattooed (*pelones y rayados*) natives like those of Tamaulipas. Beyond lay the Karankawas' country. It was they whom the voyagers pursued at the Río de Flores (Cedar Bayou) and who left behind remnants of La Salle's lost ship *Aimable.* But the most significant contact with the Karankawas occurred at Matagorda Bay, after the finding of the French bark *Belle,* just a few miles from La Salle's Fort Saint-Louis of Texas. Enríquez Barroto's description of the Karankawas from this meeting bears out information from Alonso de León's *entradas* of 1689 and 1690 and to some extent that given by the Talon brothers: they were of impressive stature, inclined to be hostile, and terrified of firearms.[18]

As Corpus Christi Bay marked the division between Malaguita territory and Karankawa, Galveston Bay separated the Karankawan range

16 Enríquez Barroto diary entries for April 17 and 18.
17 Weddle, *Spanish Sea,* pp. 199, 207, 250, 300, 301.
18 Diary entry for April 7. See Talon Interrogations, question 12; and Mardith Schuetz, "Ethnological Data," in the commentaries thereto. See also Jean Béranger, *Béranger's Discovery of Aransas Pass,* p. 21.

from the Atákapan. The friendly natives encountered just west of Galveston Bay probably were related to the Karankawas of Matagorda Bay. Those encountered on the Calcasieu River of Louisiana, who offered to guide the Spaniards on their search for the lost ship and the rumored white colony on a river to the west, were Atákapas. These were the friendly hosts of Pedro the Apalachino and the Mexican boy Nicolás de Vargas, castaways from Juan Corso's galley. Nicolás, like the French captives among the Hasinai (Cenis) and the Karankawa, was tattooed, testifying to the universality of this practice.[19] More remarkable is Enríquez Barroto's statement that his hair "had a circular cut like a lay brother."

Although Enríquez may have been the first explorer since Cabeza de Vaca to describe the Atákapas, he gives little information on their customs. He perceived them as being rather backward, observing that "not even by the moons do they know how to reckon time." The pilot was more astounded by Vargas's revelation that the crewmen of Corso's galley had been so driven by hunger that they cannibalized their dead shipmates. Never before, says Enríquez, had he heard the like of it, "anywhere in the world." He evidently did not know of the parallels related by Cabeza de Vaca, on or near Galveston Island in the winter of 1528–29 and, later, near the Texas coastal bend.[20]

On hearing the Indians' tale of the lost ship and white men, the explorers were uncertain whether they were speaking of Corso's men or of La Salle's colony. The natives probably were repeating rumors they had heard about both groups and were joining them in their own minds. Indeed, if the Atákapas had seen a wrecked ship, it was the missing Spanish galley, not La Salle's. The description of white people hunting on horseback and living among the Indians in the natives' own habitation may well have referred to the deserters from La Salle's company who had joined the Hasinai (Cenis) of eastern Texas and taken Indian wives.[21] The natives' confusion, no doubt, was compounded as the stories were related through an interpreter.

19 Schuetz, "Ethnological Data."
20 Enríquez Barroto diary entry, April 18; Alvar Núñez Cabeza de Vaca, *The Journey of Alvar Nuñez Cabeza de Vaca and His Companions from Florida to the Pacific, 1528–1536,* trans. Fanny Bandelier, pp. 63, 85.
21 At least three French deserters lived among the Hasinai from the time of La Salle's first visit until after his death; Jacques Grollet, Rutre, and a man from Provence. All remained with the Indians after the remnant of La Salle's party departed for Canada. Both Henri Joutel, in his "Relation," and the Talons, in the Interrogations, make it clear that these men hunted and went to war with the natives; the Provençal and Rutre took Indian wives.

In the end, Enríquez judged the Atákapas harshly. He suspected them of having murdered the Spanish freebooters, then lying to cover up the crime. But it may have been the Karankawas, west of Galveston Bay, rather than the Atákapas, who finished off the starving remnants of the galley crew. The Atákapas and the Karankawas ("the Indians to leeward") were at war with each other, according to the natives' testimony.[22]

The Indians' tale, whatever the source, caused the *piraguas* to backtrack to make the first known exploration of Sabine Pass and Galveston Bay. Thus, it was indirectly responsible for the voyage of Francisco López de Gamarra and Andrés de Pez, sent to look for the *piraguas* three days before they returned, overdue, to Veracruz.

Exploring Atchafalaya Bay and River while looking for fresh water, the assistant pilot, Gerónimo de Acosta, described this major distributary of the Mississippi as "only a large lake . . . with a long, low island in the middle."[23]

The declining latitudes after May 14 indicate the *piraguas'* descent of the Mississippi Delta from the vicinity of Barataria Pass. Two days later, after passing two smaller mouths, they stood among the shoals at Southwest Pass, the river's most southern outlet (Río de la Aguada), discharging a great volume of fresh water and driftwood. From then until the twentieth, when the ships reached North Pass and stood north toward the Chandeleur Islands, the mariners limned the birdfoot subdelta and registered the various capes and river mouths.

It was a high point of the voyage and a landmark discovery. Never before had European navigators been able to approach this, the continent's greatest river, from the sea closely enough to describe it. The Rivas-Iriarte expedition, the magnitude of its accomplishments three centuries in coming to notice, now looms large in the annals of North American discovery. The subdelta, with the Mississippi River discharging 134 billion tons of land-forming material per year, has changed appreciably during that time.[24] Yet Enríquez's account of the navigation from Southwest Pass to North Pass—his Río de la Palizada of the 1686 voyage—can be followed on a present-day sea chart.

From North Pass to San Marcos de Apalache the way was known.

22 Enríquez Barroto diary entry for April 23.
23 Ibid., May 8.
24 Richbourg Gaillard McWilliams, "Iberville at the Birdfoot Subdelta: Final Discovery of the Mississippi River," in John Francis McDermott, ed., *Frenchmen and French Ways in the Mississippi Valley*, p. 129. See also Douglas Lee, "Mississippi Delta: The Land of the River," *National Geographic* 154, no. 2 (August, 1983): 226–52.

Although Enríquez Barroto and Romero had stayed two weeks at Mobile Bay the previous year, no extant account relates their activities during that time. On the second visit, one day (May 23) was spent reconnoitering the bay. It was the only one on the northern Gulf Coast—excepting Pensacola, which the Apalache garrison had under constant surveillance—that would accommodate a ship drawing two fathoms. It also had the requisite island (Sand Island) in its mouth. Here, the captains reasoned, must be the bay the French had sought. Instead of the great river providing a link with New France, however, they found a shallow estuary, the Río de la Mobila, discharging through half a dozen silt-laden mouths. *Rosario* grounded in four spans. Nevertheless, Mobile Bay was thenceforth identified in many minds with the Bahía del Espíritu Santo, the bay that actually existed only as the figment of a mapmaker's imagination.

At San Marcos the captains reported on their voyage to Pedro Aranda y Avellaneda, who had assumed the Florida governorship under bizarre circumstances. At a port in latitude 28°23', 150 leagues to leeward of Mobile, they related, a wrecked French war vessel with keel of twenty-four cubits had been found, fitting the description of La Salle's frigate: "We judge it so to be, and that its people have perished at the hands of the Indians and from hunger, like those of Juan Corso, of whom we have definite news from a Mexican boy and an Apalachino Indian whom we found on a river among the wild Indians and brought with us." From the wrecked vessel and the gear from the larger ship, the captains concluded that the French settlement had aborted as a result of severe storms, "because they left Petit Goâve at the beginning of winter." Only by a miracle had the *piraguas* escaped a similar fate.[25] The circumnavigation of the Gulf, nevertheless, was completed without loss of life.

Reasons for adhering to the southern Gulf Coast on the return voyage rather than sailing directly for Veracruz—where the *piraguas* were long overdue—are not spelled out. It is clear, however, that the La Salle intrusion had heightened concern over the presence of other foreigners in the Gulf, notably French pirates who might be in league with La Salle. Also an irritant were the freebooters, principally English, who throughout this period harbored in the Laguna de Términos, cutting logwood, killing wild cattle, and periodically raiding the coastal towns.

25 Martín de Rivas and Pedro de Iriarte to Pedro de Aranda y Avellaneda, San Marcos de Apalache, May 27, 1687, UT archives, transcript 68, AGI, Mexico 616. Concerning Aranda, see diary entry for May 26 and note 61.

Yet Enríquez reports no sightings of suspicious vessels in this area, and he saw no need to describe the coast in detail; it had been known since the 1518 discovery voyage of Juan de Grijalva.

The *Rosario* made port at San Juan de Ulúa, adjacent to Veracruz, the evening of July 3, the *Esperanza* the next morning. The circumnavigation was complete. The chief pilot credits the feat not to his own superlative navigation but to the ships. The close coastal inspection, he notes, would have been impossible with vessels of deeper draft. The statement was to be proved by the voyage already begun by Captains López de Gamarra and Pez.

Out of concern for the *piraguas,* not heard from since leaving Tampico, these officers had been dispatched four days previously in two frigates. A bark sent to call them back reached Tampico too late; the Rivas-Iriarte voyage as far as Cape San Blas, Florida, was to be repeated, including inspection of the Mississippi passes, but without the close reconnaissance of bays and shoaly coast.

In the meantime, Viceroy Monclova summoned Captains Enríquez, Romero, and Iriarte to Mexico for debriefing. (Rivas remained too ill to make the journey.) With them went the two survivors from Juan Corso's galley, Pedro the Apalachino and Nicolás de Vargas. The officers reported "with great lucidity." Coincidentally, the viceroy received, on the day the captains arrived, information on La Salle's undertaking, obtained through diplomatic channels from French sources. The *relación* from Pedro de Ronquillo, Carlos II's ambassador to England, included the report of Captain Beaujeu, who had returned to France from La Salle's colony, and Spanish copies of Minet's maps of the Texas coast. The three officers read the report and wrote their comments in the margin of a copy to be sent to the king with Enríquez's diary. The viceroy, in his cover letter, exulted: the two documents affirmed that the vessels found at the Bahía de San Bernardo were La Salle's. It seemed evident that the French threat had been eliminated. So vital was the diary's information that the viceroy restricted its circulation. "I keep for myself a copy of the diary and letter that I send to Your Majesty. . . . I have ordered Juan Enríquez Barroto not to make any other letter or copy of the diary."[26]

This prohibition, according to Enríquez's closing statement, also included his sea chart. Yet the chart, before its final disappearance, was used on at least two occasions. As Captains Pez and Rivas prepared to

26 Viceroy Monclova to the king, Mexico, July 25, 1687; "Copia de Relación" and notes affixed thereto, both in UT archives, transcript 68, AGI, Mexico 616.

embark on the fifth and final voyage of the La Salle quest, they wrote to the viceroy, "The map that Juan Enríquez left in the custody of Dn. Andrés de Pez will be taken on this voyage." Florida governor Diego de Quiroga y Losada, describing the location of the Apalachicola River in conjunction with a plan to fortify that region in 1691, wrote, "All these distances are taken from the map drawn in 1687 by the pilot Juan Enríquez Barroto, who was with the *piraguas* on the reconnaissance of Espíritu Santo Bay, this map being taken as the most precise from the standpoint of being the most up-to-date, specifically of the entire Seno Mexicano."[27]

When López de Gamarra and Pez returned on September 4, 1687, from their voyage to Cape San Blas, Enríquez, Romero, and Iriarte again were summoned. They studied the diary of Luis Gómez Raposo, pilot of Pez's frigate, the *Santo Cristo de San Román,* and affixed their comments. Because the frigates could not sail in shallow water, the officers observed, they had examined only the mouths of the rivers; they encountered no Indians and failed to find the wreckage of the two French ships seen by Rivas and Iriarte. From Río Bajo (Galveston Bay) to Cabo de Lodo (at North Pass of the Mississippi) they were forced by shallowness of the coastal waters to sail out of sight of land most of the time. Four days of cloudy weather, as well as the size of the ships, hampered their exploration of the birdfoot subdelta. They failed to find the main entrance to Mobile Bay and passed up Pensacola because of slight wind and contrary current. In short, the López-Pez voyage and Gómez's diary[28] pale considerably in the light of Enríquez's record of the Rivas-Iriarte expedition.

Despite the seemingly conclusive evidence provided by the latter, the search had not yet ended, nor had Enríquez Barroto's part in it. In the spring of 1688 he accompanied Captain Pez in the *Santo Cristo de San Román* on a voyage to Mobile Bay—now confusingly called Espíritu Santo—in response to a pack of lies told by a captured English pirate named Ralph Wilkinson. Juan Poule went along as inter-

---

27 Martín de Rivas and Andrés de Pez to Viceroy Monclova, Veracruz, July 24, 1688, in UT archives, transcript 69, AGI, Mexico 616, Diego de Quiroga to the Crown, UT archives, transcript 136, AGI, Santo Domingo.

28 *Colección de diarios y relaciones para la historia de los viajes y descubrimientos,* IV, 149–50. Gómez's diary is in *Colección de diarias,* IV, 114–48. For want of Enríquez Barroto's record of the Rivas-Iriarte voyage, that of López de Gamarra and Pez has been accorded a significance that is not warranted (Weddle, *Wilderness Manhunt,* pp. 108–17; Jack D. L. Holmes, "Andrés de Pez and Spanish Reaction to French Expansion in the Gulf of Mexico," in Patricia K. Galloway, ed., *La Salle and His Legacy,* pp. 106–28).

preter. Enríquez and Pez, pursuing Wilkinson's claim that he had visited the French colony in this vicinity, explored Chandeleur and Breton sounds, which afterward appeared on certain maps as Laguna de Pez (see plate 9).[29]

After Alonso de León, on a land march from Coahuila, had found La Salle's ruined Fort Saint-Louis on April 22, 1689, Enríquez and Pez were called upon to examine his diary and witness the interrogation of the two French prisoners (Jean L'Archevêque and Jacques Grollet) he had brought. The bay called Saint-Louis by the French captives and Espíritu Santo by León, the captains affirmed, was indeed the one named San Bernardo on the Rivas-Iriarte voyage, where the wrecked French vessel had been found. Carlos de Sigüenza y Góngora drafted a map showing León's route across southern Texas, labeling the rivers with the general's names. The coastal features were those described in Enríquez Barroto's diary, and the toponyms were the ones he had applied.[30]

The French geographer Claude Delisle is known to have obtained a copy of the map and used some of its place-names on his own 1703 map. He also used names from Enríquez's diary that do not appear on Sigüenza's work, including "Río Boho" (Bajo), the first known European designation for Galveston Bay. Nicolas de Fer, the French royal family's official geographer, also used some of Enríquez's toponyms on his 1705 map, including a few that do not appear on Delisle's work. Somewhat later, the royal British geographer Thomas Jefferys used some of them on his 1775 map entitled "The Western Coast of Louisiana and the Coast of New León," as did several others.[31]

In 1691 Enríquez Barroto returned to the Bahía de San Bernardo (Matagorda Bay), which he had visited with Rivas and Iriarte four years previously. In the interim the bay had been explored and mapped by

29 Wilkinson's various declarations are in AGI, Mexico 616. The incident is discussed in Weddle, *Wilderness Manhunt,* pp. 118–31.

30 Andrés de Pez and Juan Enríquez Barroto, "Paracer," Mexico, June 12, 1689, UT archives, transcript 68, AGI, Mexico 616. Depositions of L'Archevêque and Grollet are translated, with related documents, in Walter J. O'Donnell, trans., *La Salle's Occupation of Texas.* A copy of the Sigüenza y Góngora map showing León's route with Enríquez's toponyms is reproduced in Weddle, *Wilderness Manhunt,* as plate 8.

31 The 1703 Delisle map is reproduced in Historic New Orleans Collection, *Degrees of Discovery,* p. 16; the others in J. P. Martin and Robert Sidney Martin, *Contours of Discovery: Printed Maps Delineating the Texas and Southwestern Chapters in the Cartographic History of North America, 1513–1930—A User's Guide,* map portfolio. Concerning Delisle's use of the León-Sigüenza map, see Jean Delanglez, "The Sources of the Delisle Map of America, 1703," *Mid-America* 25, no. 4 (October, 1943): 298.

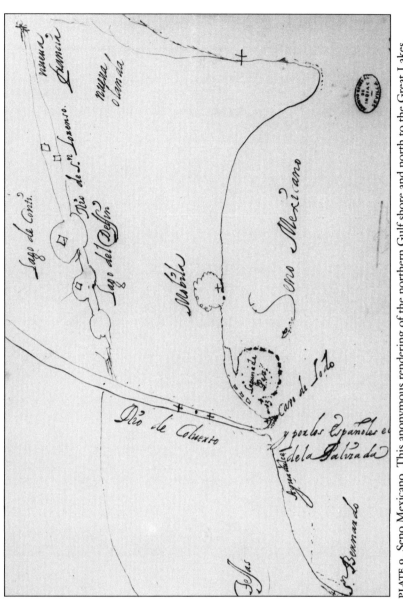

PLATE 9. Seno Mexicano. This anonymous rendering of the northern Gulf shore and north to the Great Lakes, c. 1690, shows Laguna de Pez (Chandeleur Sound) and the Mississippi River by both its French and Spanish names. The projection labeled Cabo de Lodo is perhaps the earliest known rendering of the peninsular Mississippi Delta. (Courtesy of the Archivo General de Indias, Seville)

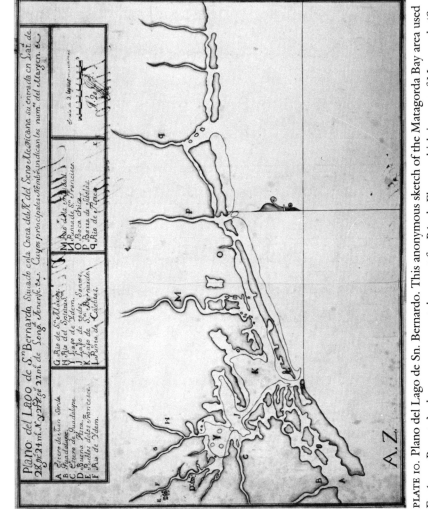

Plano del Lago de Sᵗⁿ Bernardo. Situado en la Costa del Nᵗᵉ del Seno Mexicano. su entrada en Latᵈ de 28. pˢ 24. mᵗ. N. y 278ᵍ. 35ˢ 21mᵗ. de Longᵈ. Tenerife. &ᵃ. Cuyos principales Nombᵉˢ indican los numᵗⁱ del Margen. &ᵃ

A Estero de Juan Sorda.
B Ygualdapa.
C Estero de Guadalupe.
D Buena Mira.
E Pueblos de los Franceses.
F Rio de Ydem.

G Rio de Sᵗⁿ Marcos.
H Rio del Spiritu.
Y Lago de Ydem.
J Lago de ledro Sanve.
K Lago de Sᵗⁿ Bernardo.
L Punta de Culebra.

M Boca de la bahia.
N Ponta de Sᵗⁿ Francisco.
O Boca chica.
P Barra de la bahia.
q Rio de Flores.

A. Z.

PLATE 10. Plano del Lago de Sn. Bernardo. This anonymous sketch of the Matagorda Bay area used

Francisco de Llanos and Manuel José Cárdenas y Magaña. Enríquez, as captain of Pez's former ship, the *Santo Cristo de San Román,* was charged with transporting troops and supplies to support Governor Domingo Terán de los Ríos in his effort to relieve the East Texas missions, which had been established to counter the French threat. Assisted by Joseph de Aramburu, commanding the bilander *San Joseph,* Enríquez made two voyages from Veracruz, ferrying supplies. Additionally, he transported to the Texas coast troops commanded by Gregorio de Salinas Varona, who also had been in charge of land forces with Llanos and Cárdenas. While the ships lay in an exposed anchorage off Punta de San Francisco, six men drowned in a boat accident.

Terán, at the end of a frustrating trek that extended to the Red River in present-day Miller County, Arkansas, boarded the *Santo Cristo* in late March, 1692, leaving his troops to return overland to Coahuila with Salinas. The governor then directed a voyage to the Río de la Palizada to determine the great river's potential as a navigable waterway. The two ships—unlike the *piraguas* of the Rivas-Iriarte expedition—sailed well away from the Louisiana coast until the Mississippi Delta lay on their port beam, then turned north to anchor "in view of the western branch and the island that stands in its mouth." While the captains conferred, a storm arose that forced the ships to leave the shoal-studded coast and run before the wind.[32]

Although Spain turned away from the vital Mississippi, both French and English vessels found their way past the mud lumps and drift logs to explore regions not glimpsed by Spaniards since Soto's time.

Enríquez was denied a part in the occupation of Pensacola Bay; yet his contribution to that project was substantial. His retiring nature, it has been said, caused him to fade into the background, leaving the task and its glory to Pez and Sigüenza. Thus, he has been dismissed from the pages of history. In truth, there is another reason for his "withdrawal." In 1693, the same year that Pez and Sigüenza made a joint reconnaissance of Pensacola Bay, Enríquez was lost at sea.

The French threat in the Gulf having abated for a time, Spanish officialdom turned its attention to the English menace to Florida. Royal orders focused on the need to dislodge the English from their Carolina base.

32 Alexandro Bruno, "Derrotero que hizo el Alférez Dn. Alexandro Bruno piloto de la fragata Santo Cristo de San Román desde el dia 27 de Marzo de el año de 1692," UT archives, transcript 345, AGN, Historia 27. Although the pilot Bruno is the author, the document is signed by Terán as part of his own report.

On September 18, the Armada de Barlovento cleared the Bahama Channel and sailed north into an Atlantic hurricane. "Fifteen leagues" from the mainland coast, on the Carolina Banks, two frigates went down with all hands: *Santo Tomás,* captained by Francisco López de Gamarra, himself a key participant in the recent search for La Salle; and *Santo Cristo de San Román,* Captain Juan Enríquez Barroto.[33]

Long in controversy has been the so-called Pez Memorial, which Captain Pez took to Spain (at the same time he conducted the two French captives, L'Archevêque and Grollet) and laid before the Crown early in 1690. It was this document that led eventually to the Spanish settlement at Pensacola, just in time to keep it from falling to the French. If Pez was not guilty of outright plagiarism, he at least was not too particular about setting the record straight concerning authorship of the memorial and the origin of its data. Sigüenza later sought to do so by attaching a note to at least two copies of the document:

> I drew up this memorial with the data concerning the port of Pensacola furnished me by my former student, Captain Juan Enríquez Barroto, who discovered it. As he did not wish to sign it because of his modesty, Don Andrés de Pez, captain of the presidio of Veracruz, did so and, upon presenting it to the viceroy, the Conde de Galve, he was able to go to Spain and give it to the Council of the Indies; and by this means he became general of the Armada de Barlovento. In order that this may be on permanent record, I attach my signature. Carlos de Sigüenza y Góngora.[34]

By capitalizing on Enríquez's achievements, Pez was able to accelerate his career, which culminated in his selection as secretary of state and navy in January, 1721.[35]

Enríquez showed no potential as the architect of empire. Yet he did what he could to meet the obvious challenge to Spain's control over the Gulf of Mexico, enriching the pages of history in the process. Quite simply, his diary contains the perceptions of an alert observer, recorded objectively and nonpolitically, as he stood at history's crossroads. Here made known for the first time, it illuminates a facet of Spanish colonial endeavor that has been much neglected: the maritime exploration on

33 Andrés de Arriola, "Ynforme," Mexico, August 20, 1706, UT archives, transcript 76, AGI, Mexico 61-6-25 (old number).
34 Irving A. Leonard, ed., *Documentos inéditos de Don Carlos de Sigüenza y Góngora,* p. 45.
35 Holmes, "Andrés de Pez," p. 123.

which all the colonies depended. Although numerous diaries of land marches have been translated into English and published, they have had no real counterpart in narratives of voyages like the one here given. In that sense Enríquez Barroto's diary provides a new dimension to the historiography of the Gulf region. The voyage it relates was known previously only from various correspondence, which failed to disclose its full significance.

While the importance of the La Salle invasion as a catalyst to the Spanish occupation of Texas and Pensacola—as well as later territorial disputes between Spain and the United States—is well known, Enríquez emphasizes a less obvious result: the rebirth of Spanish exploration. From the French intrusion, Spain's lack of knowledge of certain territories that it claimed came into sharp focus. The Rivas-Iriarte voyage represents the first—if not the only—complete Spanish circumnavigation of the Gulf. It set the stage for a century of exploration, by land and sea, that concerned itself increasingly with scientific observation and the expansion of knowledge.

The Enríquez Barroto Diary

Translated and annotated by

ROBERT S. WEDDLE

Diary of the voyage and navigation that by order of the Most Excellent Lord Count of Monclova, viceroy, governor, and captain general of New Spain, was carried out in two *piraguas,* built for coasting and reconnoitering all the Mexican Gulf [Seno Mexicano] by order of His Excellency in the port of Veracruz and here named *Nuestra Señora del Rosario* and *Nuestra Señora de la Esperanza,* Captain of Sea and War Don Martín de Rivas having gone as commander of one, with Juan Henríquez Barroto as pilot, and, of the other, Captain of Sea and War Don Pedro de Yriarte, with Antonio Romero as pilot, each one manned by a crew of sixty.

The said pilot Juan Henríquez Barroto has written this diary and drawn the map that goes with it, begun 25 December 1686, when they left the port of Veracruz, until 3 July 1687, when they returned there with every good fortune, without having lost a single man on the entire voyage.

By the grace of God we left Veracruz in the two *piraguas* commanded by Captains Martín de Rivas and Pedro de Yriarte, who are going to discover Spíritu Santo Bay, on Wednesday, 25 December 1686, a little before nine in the morning. Sailing with a somewhat fresh southeast wind, we arrived at six in the evening at Punta de Piedras [Rock Point], 21 leagues from Veracruz.

Thursday the 26th. From 6 last evening to almost midnight we navigated, with fresh southeast wind, northwest by north, running close to shore until this wind calmed and the land breeze came with slight surf from the southwest, west-southwest, and west. Dark clouds covered the sky, threatening from three in the morning till sunrise, which cleared everything. We proceeded with the land breeze thus until 2 in the afternoon, as with a calm. The northeasterly current bore us away from shore about three leagues, leaving no hope for the northeasterly sea breeze; seeing that it was not coming, we determined to reach the Río de Tecoluta [Tecolutla], 4 leagues to leeward, where we arrived under oar and sail (to avoid risking another night at sea in this weather).[1] A little wind already was coming from the north. At 5 in the afternoon we crossed the bar, which is of sand. It has two mouths now, of 11 spans of water. The entrance of one is toward the south-southeast and the other to the southwest. The mouths of this river are formed by banks in the middle, in front of two somewhat distant round hills. The one farthest north is larger, and both are some distance inland, their median bearing southwest from the river mouth.

Río de Tecoluta   Friday the 27th. The norther has been blow-
Latitude 20°30′   ing all day, although here it is more like north-
northwest. It has not been very strong, but some swells washed the coast. Tonight the two captains wrote to the royal admiral Don Francisco Navarro and to my admiral, Don Antonio de Astina, informing them how we arrived here, in view of the concern with which they would be viewing the norther. They also wrote to the chief justice of Tampico, that they might have meat prepared when we arrive there, if possible.

Saturday the 28th. Until 3 in the afternoon the wind has been fair from the north; later, it shifted to north-northeast and at night to northeast.

Sunday the 29th. At half past 10 in the morning we sailed from Tecoluta with an easterly wind. Although we had wanted to do so at dawn, it was not possible with low tide, because the whole bar was awash. We went on running the coast. The wind was fair, and by afternoon it was from the southeast. The coast from Tecoluta to the Río de
Río de   Cassones [Cazones] runs northwest by north. It
Casones   is low, almost level, and full of timber. The coastal
pilots count it seven leagues from one to the other, but in my judgment it is no more than six. From Cassones to Chaparral Point there is a league of coast that runs north-northwest. The Río de Cassones has within its mouth an outcropping covered with trees. The bar is bad and of slight depth. A little past sunset we passed Punta de Piedras, according to the coastal pilots, 3 leagues from the Río de Casones, but it is

1 The Río de Tecolutla is in latitude 20°28′, approximately. "Leeward" and "windward" as used in the diary do not refer to the actual wind direction. Ships coming from Spain rode the northeasterlies; hence "to windward" came to mean "in the direction of Spain," north and east. Tecolutla, to leeward, was south of the ships, which had already passed it and had to fall back.

only a little more than two. The coast goes north-northwest and, running it so, we passed at nine by the bar or river of Tuxpa [Tuxpán], which has to the south-southeast a long, smooth mesa. We navigated thus until three in the morning, when the wind died and we anchored in 8 fathoms half a league from shore in front, or east, of the Sierra de San Juan, which is somewhat more than 4 leagues from the northern part of Tuspa. The bottom along the whole coast is of sand with some slime in places.

Monday the 30th. It dawned with wind from the north-northwest. At 11 the wind changed to north and, although it was gentle, we got under way for Tuxpa to secure our ships until there is suitable weather for pursuing the voyage. After noon we made sail, and a little before 3 we entered by the Tuxpa bar, the entrance now being to the southwest, and certainly very good with 14 spans of water. We then proceeded one league by river, west-southwest, to the salt warehouses, where the pueblo was situated previously.[2] This river is very pleasant and has, from its bar to eight leagues within, an average of 10 fathoms of water with somewhat steep banks. This afternoon the norther blew quite briskly, with some rain. With that drawback, and it being wintertime, these weather changes are not surprising to me. The captains had news that dispatch and order had come to the alcalde of this jurisdiction from the Most Excellent Lord Count of Monclova for giving them the necessary provisions for the voyage. They therefore decided (seeing that the provisionment was more prompt here than in Tampico) that the meat and honey should be obtained here, so that on arriving at Tampico they would have only to receive the Indian interpreters and then sail.

Tuesday the 31st. The butchering of meat was begun, making it into jerky because it keeps better dried.

[January, 1687]

Wednesday, 1st of January. We went almost a league farther up the river and from there to Tabuco Pueblo to hear mass.

Thursday the 2nd. The wind, as in days past, was from the north, with rain most of the day.

Friday the 3rd. There was also water and wind from northwest and north, the weather having been such during these four days that we have not seen the sun; not good for drying meat.

---

2 Tuxpán, says Antonio Vásquez de Espinosa (*Description of the Indies [c. 1620]*, nos, 543, 854), was a *corregimiento*, or judicial district.

Saturday the 4th. It dawned clearer, and from 9 in the morning it was a good day. By afternoon we had north-northeast wind.

Sunday the 5th. It was a good day for curing the meat, and therefore the rest was butchered. Today there was east and southeast wind in the afternoon, and we had mass on board.

Monday the 6th. At 8 in the morning the wind arose from the north and was quite bitter all day. The captains wrote to the Most Excellent Lord Count of Monclova and to the Lord Admirals, giving account of the voyage to date. Persuaded by the captains, the assistant curate of this village said mass for us on board.

Tuesday the 7th. The wind has been from the north all day, but more moderate.

Wednesday the 8th. We went to the mouth of the bar, where we anchored at 3 in the afternoon, because the morning was spent packing the meat and putting it on board. Here Diego de Castro,[3] who came with the assistant curate by order of His Excellency, embarked with Captain Pedro de Yriartte. Today we had calm and from time to time a wind from the shore.

Thursday the 9th. At 7 in the morning we crossed the bar with the westerly land breeze and sailed northwest, running the coast until it *Description of the* calmed a little past 10, and we anchored west *Sierra de San Juan* [east?] of the Sierra de San Juan. The day has been very cloudy, and at 11 the wind shifted to north, upon which we made sail before noon and arrived across from Tuxpa, where we entered at two with the wind much fresher. The Sierra de San Juan has on the southern part a great gap with which it forms a loaf similar to that of Guajaibón on the coast of Havana. The rest of the mountain range, which extends from the north part of this loaf, is very high, almost like that of Villa Rica.[4] It is 7 leagues from the coast in front of Tami Agua [Tamiahua] and is similar to what I have drawn in the new description of this coast made on this voyage.

Friday the 10th. The wind has been from the north-northwest and north all day.

Saturday the 11th. There was moderate northwest and north-northwest wind all day.

3 One of the castaways from Juan Corso's galley who had been marooned in the Florida wilds in 1685. See introduction to diary, p. 131 and note 6.
4 The site of Hernán Cortés's first settlement, Villa Rica de la Vera Cruz is some thirty-five miles north of the present-day city of Veracruz, near the mountainside archaeological site of Quiahuitzlan. The area's dominant landmark is a loaf-shaped peak called Bernal Grande, overshadowing the ancient Totonac town.

Sunday the 12th. We had very strong northwest wind with much rain.

Monday the 13th. The sky, which each day has been so cloudy that it did not allow us to see the sun, has cleared somewhat in the afternoon. The wind came from north-northeast and with it hope of good weather.

Tuesday the 14th. At one in the afternoon we sailed from Tuspa with east-northeast wind (which could not be done previously because of the tide). We navigated northwest about 3 leagues to Tanguiso; two north by northwest; and two north to Tamiagua (counting seven leagues from Tuzpa). From there, with east-southeast wind, we proceeded north-northwest until sunset and from the topmast was seen the Ysla de Lobos, bearing approximately northeast. The wind was slight, and at 9 it calmed. We therefore anchored in 5 fathoms, near shore. The bottom was fine brown sand. The land breeze then arose from west-northwest, causing much concern, because the ideal is from the southwest, which brings good weather. In effect, we made sail and navigated northeast and east-northeast one league to go to 8 or 9 fathoms; then north; setting course north-northeast. Since the wind would not allow us to conduct our navigation, we anchored again in a bit more than 9 fathoms at half past two in the morning.

Wednesday the 15th. At dawn we were next to the estuary of Pie de Palo[5] with a strong northwest wind and within view of the Ysla de Lobos, bearing east-west, where we then went to take shelter. We anchored southwest of the island in a small cove formed by a point of sand running out west-southwest from the island and another to the *Ysla de* south-southwest. The bottom, of clean, white *Lobos* sand, is 8 or 9 fathoms. Much of this island is flooded at high tide like San Juan de Ulúa. It is somewhat larger and the middle part is covered with a wood distinguished by its palm trees and figs of the Indies. It has on the northeast part, in the wood, a freshwater spring, and whoever might go to look for it should follow these *Landmarks to* directions carefully: Being situated on the beach *the water* on the eastern shore of the island, he will see many carefully spread-out rocks next to the wood, which serve the fishermen for catching fish. One will enter through the wood and, in a few paces, will see the site where the fishermen have their *ranchería* with many little racks that serve them as beds, and then to the north a path

5 Pie de Palo (Peg Leg) was Cornelius Corneliszoon Jol, a Dutch raider who operated in the Gulf of Mexico in the 1630s and probably anchored in the estuary.

that leads to the spring, which will be found at the foot of a large fig tree that has a cross cut in it. In front there are some banana trees, of which the island has no others. This Ysla de Lobos is surrounded on all sides

Ysla Blanca and by reefs. To the northwest it extends more to a
the other reefs point; between this and Cabo Rojo, which is northwest, is Ysla Blanca, extending lengthwise half a stone's throw. It is of white sand, is much washed by the sea, and on all sides has reefs and also another reef a little less than a quarter league long. Among them all

Latitude of there are channels of 12 and 14 fathoms. The Ysla
Ysla de Lobos de Lobos is 3 leagues from the cape and is ob-
and Cabo Rojo served in latitude 21°29', and thus Cabo Rojo is in 21°36'.[6] The coast between the Río de Tuxpa and this cape makes the aforementioned large cove. I consider the said river to be north-south with the cape, with which the island and the shoals of Tuzpa are also on the same meridian. The wind today was north-northwest.

Thursday the 16th. A little before one the northwesterly blew very strong and with much water, and all day the wind was increasing. I mean one at night.

Friday the 17th. By night and day the northwesterly has been blowing, always with water, and the fierce storm obliged us to put the mainmast and the yards on the half deck.

Saturday the 18th. Before dawn the wind moderated and stayed in the northwest.

Sunday the 19th. At 10 in the morning, with the land breeze from the southwest, we sailed from the Ysla de Lobos. We went to Cabo Rojo, from there running the coast, which is low, the shore marked by hump-backed dunes of white sand. The coast runs, from the cape to the

Captain last *ranchos*[7] of the watering place, northwest by
Pedro de Yriarte north, which is, according to the native pilots,
ill with fever 3 leagues from the south side of Tampico. These are known by a landmark of a narrow strip of sand inside the dunes. The Laguna de Tamiagua, which is formed by the Río de Tuzpa, reaches this place. Above all this land, if it is clear, rises the Sierra de San Juan. From different directions it presents a different appearance. This afternoon

6 Isla de Lobos is in latitude 21°27', Cabo Rojo in 21°34', as indicated on a small-scale chart. Enríquez's calculations were approximately two minutes, or two nautical miles, in error—remarkably accurate for his instruments and methods.

7 There appears to be no distinction drawn between *ranchería* and *rancho*, the one meaning "settlement," the other, "camp."

the wind was fair from the southeast. At 9 it shifted to northeast and at 12 midnight to north, upon which we anchored near shore in 5 fathoms, dark sand, in front of the last *ranchos,* which I have mentioned, because the wind was gentle.

Monday the 20th. We were anchored with the wind from the north until past 9 in the morning, waiting for the other *piragua,* which had anchored some distance away by our stern. Then we got under way, sailing to windward with the purpose of making good the 3 leagues that separated us from Tampico, and we went toward the offing. With increased wind and sea that was coming up, it was such that by 10 we were obliged to fall off to leeward to take before nightfall the shelter of Ysla de Lobos, where we arrived at 3 in the afternoon, sailing 18 leagues in 5 hours (surprising matter, so furious was the wind). The sea tired us severely. Captain Martín de Rivas arrived at the island with fever and was painfully afflicted.

Tuesday the 21st. Until afternoon we had north wind, then northwest, more gentle. Today we found part of the provisions in the *piraguas* to be damaged. The larger one had the most damage.

Wednesday the 22nd. All day the wind was gentle from the northnorthwest.

Thursday the 23rd. In the morning we had a land breeze from the west; at 9, northwest; and thus, little by little, the wind was going around the compass until night, when it came to the east, but so gentle that it was little more than calm. Today I observed the rising sun on the horizon with compass needle and found that the variation was 13 minutes northeast, with which I can say that my needles were virtually correct in this place, since the variation is so slight as *Here the needles* to be of little consequence. During these days *are correct* the captains and some of the people have been convalescing in cabins that they ordered built on the island. Somewhat improved, they came aboard this afternoon and at 9 in the evening we sailed from the island.

Friday the 24th. Since sailing from the island until 7 in the morning, we navigated from time to time with oars during calms and then again under sail with slight wind from the west. We came to anchor a little less than 5 leagues north-northwest of Isla de Lobos in 26 fathoms, mud bottom. Then a little wind came from the northwest and at noon changed to north-northwest. Seeing by two in the afternoon that the northeast breeze did not come, we fell back again to the island, that the ships might be assured of its shelter. We arrived with little wind at sunset.

Saturday the 25th. A little past noon, with slight east-northeast wind, we sailed from the Ysla de Lobos and navigated thus until four in the afternoon, when we were becalmed. We proceeded under oars all night, clinging to the shore.

Sunday the 26th. At dawn a gentle north wind blew upon us, and still we proceeded with oars until noon, when it changed to north-northeast. We slackened sail and with the help of the oars navigated thus until sometime past two in the afternoon, when we anchored in front of the watchtower a league from Tampico. The coast from Cabo Rojo, as I have already stated, runs northwest by north; somewhat more toward the northwest; to the course of 39° [*sic*]; between north and northwest until near the last *ranchos;* from there, north by northwest to the Tampico bar, which has a small cove near it. Because of the advice of the two resolute coastal pilots concerning the anchorage, we were here all day, with some sea and wind, and until midnight, not having borne away sooner because of the risk involved in running the shoals between the cape and Ysla de Lobos before day. If after midnight it should become necessary to get under way, we would proceed with little sail till dawn, so as to recognize the shore near the cape and, with day, take the shelter of the island until 11 at night. After sunset the wind and the sea were increasing, with much water, but from then till day God was served that it should greatly moderate, the wind changing to north-northwest. Thus, finding ourselves with fewer hardships, we awaited the day. With these winds the current rose southeast, violently.[8]

Monday the 27th. At 6 in the morning the wind came off the shore, northwest and gentle, with which we improved our position in relation to the bar, half a league by oar and sail. The wind then came to the north again and we anchored. At 9 it moderated somewhat and was thus until midnight yesterday. Today we were seeing the bonfires and lights that they were making for us in the mouth of the bar, and the people traveling on horseback along the coast.

Tuesday the 28th. At two in the morning with an offshore wind, west-southwest, we proceeded under sail and oar to anchor at three in the morning in front of the south part of the bar in order to enter with day and the coming of wind from the sea. The current along this coast, as I have said, runs violently to leeward, with the winds varying from northwest to northeast. Today dawned with the wind almost calm, and a little before 11 it came to the east-northeast, very gentle; and then we went in under oar and sail. There was little tide and therefore, with

---

8 The ships here encounter the eddying shore current, flowing southeast, or "to leeward," under the influence of seasonal or local conditions such as winds and river discharge.

flood past the midpoint, we entered quite gladly at noon and went to anchor about two leagues upriver in the mouth of the shrimpers' harbor. One league to leeward of the mouth of this river is the highest *Tampico* ground of all this coast. Near the beach, from *landmarks* Cabo Rojo to windward, what I could see is low and flat. Therefore I saw that, to come by sea in quest of this river, one should come to its latitude, which I will give upon observing it; and then will be seen the high land that I have mentioned (which there they call the lookout or watch). For this navigation one has to keep completely to leeward. The mud channel now lies west southwest with three fathoms of water. The bottom on this coast is completely clean and open, so that, navigating from the cape in search of the bar, it is possible to come, even by night, in nine or ten fathoms until finding mud, which would be in front of the mouth and in the channel. This river is like that of Tuspa, quite pleasant, and on the average it has 8 or 9 fathoms of water and in most parts has steep banks.

Wednesday the 29th. At midnight the wind arose from the north and had blown furiously all day with much water. Today we took the *piraguas* toward the shrimpers' harbor, to the lagoon and through it to the site of Tampico, which now is depopulated and in almost total ruin.[9] From the mouth of the bar to the shrimpers' harbor it is two leagues, and to that point the river runs west-southwest, southwest, south-southwest, and south, turning in a circle. The shrimp harbor comprises 21 cays. Mouths are formed with small man-made islands of oyster shell and are extended in a line approximately northeast-southwest. Through these mouths the water enters the Tampico lagoon, which runs some four leagues southeast and south-southeast from the shrimpers' wharves. The site of San Luis de Tampico is on the bank in front about a musket shot or a little more.[10] With the pilots and native guides gathered before the skippers of the galleys, they had a meeting with some citizens of the place to find out the best procedure for the navigation ahead (having experienced frustration in the effort so far). Everyone agreed that we

9 Tampico's devastation was from pirate raids. A French pirate named Du Chesne, from Saint-Domingue (Haiti) revealed to Captain Beaujeu of the La Salle expedition his strike against Tampico in the spring of 1683 (Pierre Margry, ed., *Découvertes et etablissements des français dans l'ouest et dans le sud de l'Amerique septentrionale*, II, 488–89). The "Testimonio" taken by Spanish interrogators from a motley band of various nationalities following their capture of Tampico in May, 1684, is in AGI, Mexico 560, ramo 1.

10 San Luis de Tampico was the mission founded in 1554 by Fray Andrés de Olmos for the Olive Indians from the Río de las Palmas (Soto la Marina) region.

should wait in this port until February has passed; the weather will improve with spring. At this, the captains sent to His Excellency, that he might order that which would serve him best.

Thursday the 30th. The captains wrote to His Excellency, giving account of our navigation from Tuzpa here and of the meeting of which I have told.

Friday the 31st. The letters were dispatched for Mexico with the mail.

[February, 1687]

Saturday, 1st of February. The captains wrote to the admirals on the same matter as to His Excellency.

Sunday the 2nd. The letters were delivered to the deck petty officer of *Reglita*, who carries a pass for going to Veracruz for treatment.

Monday the 3rd. The petty officer left at dawn for Tamiagua, to proceed from there through the mountain chain to Veracruz. Today has boded change; the norther, which has been blowing with continuous rain since the 29th of last month, has moderated.

Tuesday the 4th. The sails were dried and unloading of the *piraguas* commenced. There was a northeast breeze here. Some of the crew became ill.

Wednesday the 5th. A large part of the bread was found to be damaged. We had a breeze from the southeast.

Thursday the 6th. We had a strong north-northeasterly and, because of the high wind, the removal of the bread could not be finished.

Friday the 7th. There was fair weather, with which the unloading
Latitude of the *piraguas* was completed. I observed the
of Tampico sun in this place and found latitude 22°16′, which
puts the bar in 22°23′.[11]

Saturday the 8th. We had quite a strong norther but without water.

Sunday the 9th. There was fair weather and slight wind, north-northeast.

Monday the 10th. There was northeast wind, very gentle.

Tuesday the 11th. We had a very strong north-northwest wind, with water.

Wednesday the 12th. In the afternoon the north-northwesterly moderated somewhat.

Thursday the 13th. There was south wind all day, and before midnight the north wind came with great force.

---

11 The error here is about five to seven minutes.

Friday the 14th. The norther was blowing all day with great fury.

Saturday the 15th. The wind moderated somewhat, but was from the north all day.

Sunday the 16th. There was calm with some rain almost all day.

Monday the 17th. The north wind arose at dawn, strong, with water.

Tuesday the 18th. The norther has been blowing all day.

Wednesday the 19th. It was calm, winds off the shore most of the day.

Thursday the 20th. In the morning we had west-northwest wind and by afternoon a gentle breeze and tonight some water. The mail arrived from Mexico.

Friday the 21st. In the morning we had calm and by afternoon south wind.

Saturday the 22nd. There was also south wind. Tonight, after 11, the mail arrived from Veracruz.

Sunday the 23rd. There was light, variable wind, with water.

Monday the 24th. The mail for Veracruz was dispatched in early morning, and we had a gentle breeze.

Tuesday the 25th. In the afternoon we had a very good breeze from the southeast. Today Pedro Viñales[12] brought me the description of the river, beginning at Pánuco, with three lagoons.

Description
of the river.
It is properly placed
in very different
position.

Wednesday the 26th. At dawn the wind came from the north and was very strong all day.

Thursday the 27th. There was a norther all day but more gentle and with much water.

Friday the 28th. Like yesterday, with north wind and water.

[March, 1687]

Saturday, first of March. There was considerable west and west-northwest wind with water all day.

Sunday the 2nd. The wind returned again to the north and was strong.

Monday the 3rd. There was also a norther with much rain. The repairs the *piragua* needed, which have been delayed so long by the bad weather, were finished today.

Tuesday the 4th. The norther had calmed by morning, and a little past noon the wind became a northeasterly breeze. This afternoon the

---

12 Viñales, or Biñales, was Enríquez Barroto's assistant pilot.

sea biscuit that His Excellency had sent at the request of the captains arrived at the wharf of the Laguna de Tamiagua, which is two leagues from here.[13]

Wednesday the 5th. At dawn the *piragua* was taken from the lagoon to the river and all the biscuit was boarded, which was the only thing we were waiting for. Today there was a good breeze.

Thursday the 6th. Very early we went to anchor at the bar, there to wait for a norther to subside before sailing. Two Indians of Tamaolipa [Tamaholipa] came on board the *piraguas* as interpreters. The one on the *piragua* called *Nuestra Señora del Rosario* is named Alonsso Ramires, chief of his pueblo, a man of valor and ability and quite expert in the Castilian language and other languages of the nations of this coast. The one in the other [*piragua*] is Antonio Payta, who is adept in the Spanish idiom. They say that he is well known all along the coast from Tampico to a province called Ysmutli. Today we had a very good breeze, and it continued all night.

Friday the 7th. At 8 in the morning the captains placed letters for His Excellency in the mail that is going to Mexico, and those for Vera-cruz were dispatched through the mountain range. Seeing the breeze so steady, it was resolved to sail today to pursue our voyage. Thus at 10 we were already outside the bar, and we navigated with east-southeast wind more than a league and a half north by northwest, close to shore. This section of coast is of high, humped dunes of white sand. Above them, a little inland, is a hill, not very high, that is called Cerro Gordo. To this point comes the saline that is hardly more than two leagues from the Tampico bar. Then we went north two leagues and north by northeast.

Cerro de Metate   To the west the Cerro del Metatte was staying with us. It is high and 7 leagues from the coast. After this, north-northeast something more than 5 leagues, is Trinidad Bar, which is 12 leagues from Tampico. Through this the water enters the salines of Tampico and Tamaolipa. This bar has so little water that they are accustomed to crossing it on horseback. Thus far, the coast is low with some dunes that stand out. Then, along similar coast, we navi-gated north-northeast one league and north by northeast three [leagues] until sunset, always within view of the Cerro del Mettate and of another small, round [hill] more to the north [in the area] called Valle de San-

---

13 The Laguna de Tamiahua is enclosed by the thin strip of land that forms Cabo Rojo, south of Tampico. The distance indicates that the wharf was on the narrow upper end, now called Laguna de Pueblo Viejo, near the village of Tampico Alto, one of the sites occupied by the Tampiqueños fleeing pirate raids.

tiago, and of another long mountain range with many gaps that is a
Sierra del Fraile   little farther north called Sierra del Fraile. Above
[and] de Malenchen   the peak of the southern point is seen the Sierra
de Melenchen, which is quite high and very far inland. It has a large gap
in the middle that is shaped like a saddle. The lower slope of the Sierra
del Fraile is 5 leagues (according to what Alº. Ramírez, our interpreter,
has told me) from the coast. The said Alonso is the one who has given
me the names of these mountain ranges. Here, as I say, at nightfall I saw
that the Sierra del Fraile was remaining west by northwest. Tonight we
traveled north about four leagues, near shore, and anchored after eleven,
with calm.

    Saturday the 8th. Before dawn we got under way with very slight
wind and thus at 6:30 in the morning we should have gone something
like half a league, to a sparse palm grove that is on the coast. One of the
palms is higher than the others and some are bare of leaves and fronds.
Until noon we navigated from here along the coast (which is like the rest
that I have mentioned, with great savannas) north by northeast, about
three and one-half leagues. I observed the sun and found latitude 23°38′
and saw a river mouth not far away. We went to sound it and found in its
channel eight spans of water. The citizens of Tampico say this river is
Río Maupatte in   called Maupatte, but our interpreter Alonsso
latitude 23°40′   says that it is Río de las Palmas; the land to windward, the province of Maupate, whose inhabitants are called the Pelones
because they have their heads shaved. Being in the mouth of this river, I
noted some mountain ranges bearing west by southwest. They are high
and about four leagues from the coast. According to what Alonsso says,
they are called Las Minas de Caravajal; according to others, Sierras del
Maupate.[14] I am putting them and all the rest in their places on my
new description. From here we went along the coast (which is as I have
said) north by northwest, about 8 leagues, until sunset, when we an-

14 Latitude 23°38′ is about five miles south of the mouth of the Río Soto la
    Marina, the Río de las Palmas of colonial times. The name Pelón, meaning
    "hairless" or "bald," was applied by the Spaniards to as many as eight groups
    in northeastern Mexico that were noted for shaving their heads (T. N.
    Campbell in Eldon Stephen Branda, ed., *The Handbook of Texas*, III, 718).
    The word was used as a descriptive term rather than as a tribal name (see
    diary entry for Thursday, March 20), but on the Tamaulipas coast it seems to
    have designated a specific group, probably Coahuiltecan-related. Las Minas
    de Carávajal refers to Luis de Carvajal y de la Cueva, who was granted colo-
    nization rights to an area extending up to two hundred leagues north and
    west of Tampico in 1579 and who opened silver mines near present-day Ce-
    rralvo, Nuevo León. See Robert S. Weddle, *Spanish Sea: The Gulf of Mexico
    in North American Discovery 1500–1685*, ch. 18.

chored near shore in 5 fathoms, fine brown sand. From here to windward, very near the coast, runs an arm of a river that is seen inside
Branch of river   the dunes. The Río de el Maupate, according to
behind the dunes   what I have heard from persons who have been
here by land, has two very extended branches. One goes southeast, the
other northwest.

Sunday the 9th. Before sunrise we got under way and with south-
southeast wind went about 6 leagues north by northeast and about 4½
north-northeast until noon, when I observed the sun and found latitude 24°40′. At this time some Indians appeared on shore and we anchored. The canoe of Captain Pedro de Yriartte went with the two Indians of Tamaolipa to obtain news of the coast, but the great breakers
prevented their reaching the beach. The canoe came back aboard, and
we got under way with the wind, now southerly, some two leagues until
3 in the afternoon, when it calmed. Then the wind shifted to north-
northwest, and we anchored near shore in 5 fathoms, brown sand. Captain Pedro de Yriartte ordered his canoe ashore again (because it was
larger and better than ours). It arrived and they talked with the Indians,
who were the Penoles [Pelones], and they brought one of them aboard
who said he had been in Tampico and that his name was Andrés and
that he was companion of that Perico whom His Excellency ordered us
to take away from there. They left as hostage an artilleryman named
Juan Poule.[15] This Indian said that two days' journey from here is the
Río Bravo and that the first mouth is the Laguna de Ysmuth, 20 years
[leagues] from this cove. The captain regaled him, but, because a high
north wind arose, he was not then put ashore. The wind being of great
force, we were forced to take down the mainmast and put the yards on
the deck, but, as the coast runs north-northeast/south-southwest, we
were severely mauled by the sea. The branch of the river was still in view
behind the dunes.

Monday the 10th. All morning there was much wind. In the afternoon it moderated a bit, and all night it was almost calm.

Tuesday the 11th. At daybreak Captain Pedro de Yriarte sent ashore
the canoe with the Indian and they took Andrés. Only with difficulty
did they get away from the Indians, who already were more than 200, all

15 Juan Poule, an Englishman whose rightful name probably was John Poole or
John Powell, is described later as a pilot with the pirates who were captured
in the act of sacking Tampico, evidently in 1684. Perico (diminutive of Pedro:
"Pete") evidently refers to one of the native interpreters from Tampico, although the Apalachino Indian from Corso and Castro's galley later found
living among the Atákapas also was called that (see diary entry for Thursday,
April 17).

armed wth bows and arrows. The breakers were many, and on leaving the shore the canoe was swamped. They were able to get out no more than three of the eight muskets. One lad swam for shore alone and, before the rest could get there with the canoe, the Indians ripped all his clothing to pieces. The ensign threatened them with a musket and they withdrew. The canoe came on board, and we got under way with west wind and went two leagues north-northeast as far as the mouth of the *Laguna de Ysmuth*, Laguna de Ysmuth, where a moderate norther again presented itself. We anchored in 4 fathoms, sand bottom. This lagoon, from what I could see, is large, with two islands inside, in front of the mouth. The river branch that I have said runs behind the dunes arrives here. In places it is so wide that the other bank can scarcely be seen. The mainland is made up of level savannas and is subject to flooding. The mouth of this lagoon is closed with a sand beach, now somewhat high.

Wednesday the 12th. At dawn we got under way with the land breeze and navigated one league north-northeast, at the end of which there are another three closed mouths like the previous one. To all of them I give the name of Las Bocas de Ysmuth. We navigated another league on the same course with very little wind until the calm forced us to anchor at 10. The captain ordered the canoe ashore to fetch water and, at a *casimba* the people made on the beach, they filled 4 barrels. They came back on board at noon. A northeast wind arose and it was therefore not possible to go back for more. Here the river branch runs about two leagues from the coast, which is made up solely of somewhat high, humped dunes with no timber whatsoever in all that could be discerned. I observed the sun and found the latitude to be 24°55'.[16] The bottom along the coast is all sand, and there are always about 5 fathoms half a league from the beach.

Thursday the 13th. Starting at dawn, we went a league northnorthwest, then northeast by north with east-southeast wind 3 leagues more to another closed mouth like the others. This one has two small hills a bit higher than the dunes and near them, without trees but with smaller plants like many of the dunes. The branch of its cove extends inland and the coast runs northeast by north as far as latitude 25°27', which is the latitude I observed today. North-northwest of here, about two leagues, there is another closed mouth with many lagoons and estu-

16 Laguna (or Las Bocas) de Ysmuth represents the Laguna Madre of the upper Tamaulipas coast. A *casimba* is a hole dug in a sandy beach for fresh water. Enríquez Barroto mistook the arms of the lagoon for the river branch that he believed ran along the Tamaulipas-Texas coast.

aries inside that enter the river branch running inland from this mouth.
Río   It goes, as I have said, north by northeast a league
Bravo   and a half to the Río Bravo, where we anchored at
three in the afternoon. Captain Pedro de Yriarte's canoe then went to
sound the bar, but they could not because of the heavy sea. During the
first night watch we were hindered by much rain, and past the middle
[of the watch] it cleared. The wind was always southeast. At daybreak
the two canoes went again to sound and found—although with great
difficulty because of the sea—six spans of water in the mouth, and that
of the river is fresh. Here there are three *rancherías* of Indians, one on
the high dunes to leeward and the others down on the river banks.
Many Indians came down to the beach, all armed with bows and arrows
and all naked. With these winds, the current is strong to windward.

Friday the 14th. Seeing at 9:30 in the morning that we could not
enter to take on water in this river, we got under way and, with southeast wind, ran the coast north more than one league, in which sector
there are three closed mouths like the others. These I called the Dry
Bocas Secas   Mouths of the Río Bravo. I observed the sun to-
de Río Bravo   day and found latitude 25°55'. To 26° the coast
goes north, then north by northwest, between north-northwest and
north about four leagues, where the coast is very low with some knolls
and some dunes as long and large as those of Veracruz, and always we
saw Indians on the beach. A league farther on, the coast goes north-
northwest, and 3½ [leagues] north by northwest and after that north-
northwest to latitude 26°45', which I observed during the evening
watch.[17] The large, long, and barren dunes that I have mentioned extend this far, and there are some knolls among them at intervals. In this
latitude the sun was setting on us, and we anchored in four fathoms
near shore. The wind was southeast. About three leagues before arriving here, in a *ranchería* of Indians, they showed us a small boat [*chin-
chorro*], which they carried aloft between two of them.

Saturday the 15th. We got under way at daybreak and went north by
northwest one league, where we saw 3 huts [*bujíos*] of Indians and not
many breakers on the coast. Here, with the canoes, we finished watering, for which purpose we anchored near shore in a small lagoon not far
from the huts [*chozas*]. There were five Indians, and they presently fled

17 Latitude 25°55' is just a little south of the present mouth of the Río Grande.
The turns in the coast described here are accurate within a few minutes. The
voyagers proceed thence along the present-day Padre Island National Seashore, between Port Mansfield and Corpus Christi, Texas.

behind some large and extended dunes like those I have mentioned. The river that flows within still is seen but very far off. At nine we got under way again and went coasting north by northwest with east-southeast wind until noon, when I observed 26°56' latitude. Here end the dunes that I say are like those of Veracruz, and again the knolls follow with tall grass. On the whole shore there are no high ones, nor any with trees. The river still runs within. We traveled two leagues farther north by northwest, four north by northeast, and north-northeast about 5 or more with fresh southeast wind until sunset, when we anchored in 5 fathoms near shore. Before midnight the wind changed to north-northeast and became gentle.

Sunday the 16th. At dawn we got under way with north-northeast wind and went shoreward to anchor in four fathoms and take our meal on the beach as the other *piragua* was doing, but at this time the wind increased and Captain Martín de Rivas did not wish to risk the canoe. Finally, at half past eight, the wind shifted to northeast with great force that scarcely allowed the canoe to be brought on board. In the afternoon it came to the east-northeast and with the force it was blowing raised such great waves that we found ourselves quite miserable and, worse, unable to get under way to go to deeper water. From four in the afternoon till 5, it ranged the entire compass with great claps of thunder, lightning, and much water. After 5 the wind returned to the northeast and from sunset till nine at night blew with greater force. The current was so violent to leeward that it never permitted turning the prow seaward but only to the north-northeast as the coast runs, and thus the waves bathed us each instant from prow to poop, breaking on the sail. After nine God was served that it be moderated, and tonight the sea should be placated.

Monday the 17th. At dawn, with the calmness of the sea, we departed under oars to more than 7 fathoms, the bottom brown mud, where we anchored and refitted the mainmast that we had placed on the deck yesterday. Today I observed the latitude, 27°33'. All day there was gentle northeasterly wind and still strong current to leeward.

Tuesday the 18th. Until 6 in the evening we had gentle northeast wind. At that hour the wind changed to north-northeast, very strong, and lasted until 10 at night, after which time it was moderating.

Wednesday the 19th. At noon the north-northeasterly had cleared everything, and tonight there was a land breeze from the southeast and, near daybreak, the west.

Thursday the 20th. Before sunrise we got under way and went coasting with the land breeze from the west until 9, when the wind went around toward the north. At 10 it was already from north-northeast; we therefore stood inshore, to the northwest, and, at 11, to the north, with east-northeast wind. At 11 : 30 we discovered a river mouth, then went to anchor before it. Captain Pedro de Yriartte's canoe went to sound the bar. It was half sand, and they found 7 spans in the channel. We therefore went inside the entrance a little northwest to take the breakers more to windward, then another little way southwest, falling off well to the leeward shore, which is steep, with three fathoms of water. Thence we went north-northeast to anchor inside a small cay of white sand that is in the mouth, so flat that the sea almost washes it. Between this small cay and the windward shore there is no channel; nothing but breaking waves. To this point the coast still runs north-northeast. In the mouth of the river I observed the sun and found 27°46′ latitude, and, everyone *Río de* agreeing, I named it Río de San Joseph. The *Sn. Joseph* branch that I have said runs within enters this river and from here continues north. From the height of the dunes, I could discern no other, nor whether it has any that runs into the interior, west or southwest. From the small cay toward the inside, it has little water and many sand banks. I discovered some at low tide. The river is of saltwater and has another small lagoon that runs behind the leeward point. The mouth of this river, coming from the sea, is easily recognizable by the large gap between the windward shore and the leeward, with the body of the river.[18] To leeward it has a high, white, knoll-shaped dune that stands out more than the others, and from afar it looks like a great fortress. From the beach it is about the distance of an artillery shot. To windward there is another, but it is neither as high nor as far away, but by far the best sign is the latitude. After we had entered, the two canoes went with the ensigns in charge to talk with the Indians who were waiting upon the dunes. They took the two interpreters from Tamaolipa and arrived at the foot of the dunes. The Indians came down and each one presented an arrow as a peace token, most of them without the flint point, which they purposely had removed. Most of them

18 The latitude given is about four nautical miles (minutes of latitude) south of Aransas Pass, the present entrance to Corpus Christi Bay. The name San Joseph survives in San Jose Island, which extends north from the pass. Lac de St. Joseph is shown on the 1703 (Claude) Delisle map, Rivière S. Joseph on the 1718 (Guillaume) Delisle map. Nicolas de Fer's map of 1705 has Baye de St. Joseph; Thomas Jefferys's of 1775, Lago de San Josef. The two Delisle maps are reproduced in Historic New Orleans Collection, *Degrees of Discovery*, pp. 16, 21; Fer's, Jefferys's, and the 1718 Delisle maps in Robert Sidney Martin and James C. Martin, *Contours of Discovery*, map portfolio.

are bald and tattooed [*pelones y raiadas*], but the interpreters did not understand their language.[19] Therefore, communicating only by signs, we could understand nothing. The sign for water having been given, they guided us to a lagoon, where we watered.

Friday the 21st. We had a severe storm from the south-southeast and southeast from 7 at night till 10—much water, terrible thunder, lightning, and more wind. At midnight it changed to northwest and then to north-northwest.

Saturday the 22nd. There was north-northwest wind until noon, when it blew from the east, gently. It cleared completely, and the meat was brought out [to dry]. The Indians came to the beach to play games next to the galley today. I went ashore with the captain [Rivas], who gave all of them some leaves of tobacco. They were about two hours with our people, who gave them some old clothing, and then went to their *ranchería* because they saw that he [it] was [word illegible]. He met the canoe of the other *piragua*, in which was going Captain Pedro de Yriarte, whom the women went to receive with presents of fish, and he divided some beads among them. Then came the Indian men, who ordered them [the women] to withdraw and made signs to our people that they should go. They did so, and they began to take up their few belongings to move their pueblo or *ranchería* to another site, having little security here. As our interpreters did not understand them, we had asked them nothing, nor could we make them understand anything.

Sunday the 23rd. Until almost noon there was a land breeze from the southeast. The wind changed to south and then to southeast and blew considerably until night. Today the coastal pilot went to sound the bar but could not do much because of the heavy sea.

Monday the 24th. Dawn came with the land breeze blowing from the southwest. At 9 it went to the west, at 10 to the northwest, and after 11 to the north, where the wind was not very strong until near midnight, when it came with great force.

Tuesday the 25th. At 7 in the morning the wind went to the north-northeast, stronger, and at 3 in the afternoon to the northeast, already much calmed. At midnight it was east-northeast. During these days we saw the Indians no more.

Wednesday the 26th. Dawn came with the wind in the east, quite

19 Possibly the Malaguitas, believed to have been Coahuiltecan speakers, who ranged the Texas-Tamaulipas coastal region and some of whom later entered missions in Texas and northern Mexico.

strong. Past noon, it went to the east-southeast, where it remained all day and, since that is at right angles with this coast, it·put much sea upon it.

Thursday the 27th. All day we had strong southeast wind, and, during the three days in which the flood tide has not subsided, dense fog that looks like smoke.

Friday the 28th. There was very strong south-southeast wind until 11, when it went directly to north-northwest with great force and dissipated the fog to our [word illegible]. At three in the afternoon it calmed somewhat and was thus the rest of the day.

Saturday the 29th. At one in the morning the north-northwesterly blew again with great fury and at 7 in the evening the wind calmed and came to northeast, gentle.

Sunday the 30th. Dawn came with gentle wind in the east and, with yesterday's bluster quite subdued, the sea, from the southeast, upon the bar. Thus, at 9 in the morning we sailed outside. With the east-southeasterly we ran the coast northeast by north, about 5½ leagues of dunes that are not very high but are knoll-like and without trees, like the others. From here the land forms a little cove and continues half a league from white and very flat beach, where goes the river that runs within, very near the coast, the distance of an artillery shot from this beach in terrain also very flat but humped with some dunes. It appears like a river mouth. We anchored on it and the coastal pilot of the other *piragua,* Mateo de la O, went in the large canoe to sound it. Although not in the channel, he found ten spans of water and we therefore went inside. We saw that it was a bay or large lake that had two river branches, the one that comes through the coast from the Río de San Joseph and another from the north, which runs up from this river like it has to this *Río de* point. Because today is Easter [Pasqua Florida], *Flores* I named it Río de Flores [River of Flowers]. From the mouth the channel goes north until passing to windward by a small cay of white sand that is midway between the two shores, from the mouth toward the inner part about a quarter of a league or a little more, and has 2, 3, and 4 fathoms of water. From the small cay the channel goes northwest and northwest by north until it meets the shore. Of two fathoms, it is full of marshes with many islands and estuaries, the end of which could not be seen in most places. We arrived there pursuing a canoe of Indians, who then entered one of the estuaries, and Captain Martín de Rivas sent our own in its pursuit with the ensign in charge. This obliged this one and another that was seen to unload the wood they carried and to pass through branches by a reef to another lake, through which they escaped. Ours returned because it was almost night.

Captain Pedro de Yriarte sent the large canoe with his ensign in charge to some Indians who were on the windward shore, and at 7 in the evening it came back aboard with two canoes from which the Indians had fled. In one of them came a woman who without doubt was more than a hundred years old. In both were found some large and fresh *corbinas* [a kind of fish], a small fishnet, a chain hinge, a chain with deadeye, a hoop, and a pump lever, all from a ship of up to 300 *toneladas*.[20] There *Signs of lost ship* were also another three or four smaller hinges, hammered to a point like chisels by the Indians' hands, and for such a purpose they undoubtedly served them. There were also wool and a French hatchet, some gun carriage irons, and other trifles, all of which indicated that a ship had been lost on this coast. From the bar to the mouths and estuaries, this bay or lake is two leagues across, and its shape is almost round. We anchored there because the southeast wind and the current toward the inside did not permit us to reach the small cay.

Monday the 31st. All day we had strong south and south-southeast winds. The incoming tides, which on all this coast are of no consequence, rise and fall with the winds that impel them. Here I observed latitude 28°03'.[21] Captain Pedro de Iriarte ordered that the canoes and what they contained, except for the irons, be taken back where they were found, with the Indian woman, to whom he gave a blanket and a string of beads. The woman was to be put ashore with a ration of biscuit, that she might eat.

[April, 1687]

Tuesday, 1st of April. Quite early in the morning we came by oar with gentle south wind to the small cay, where the wind went to the west-northwest and we anchored. The canoe went to take on water at a small lagoon that is east-southeast of the small cay on the mainland to wind-

20 In this context, "*toneladas*" is used to express the ship's carrying capacity in wine tuns and is not to be confused with tons displacement. The vessel here described was La Salle's storeship, *Aimable*, lost at the entrance to Matagorda Bay (Pass Cavallo) in February, 1685, and pillaged by Indians who, like those now found with the ship's gear, were Karankawas. Concerning these natives, see the Talon Interrogations (questions 4, 11, and 12) and Schuetz, "Ethnological Data," in the commentaries thereto.
21 The latitude is precise for Cedar Bayou. Although the Río de Flores clearly is Cedar Bayou at Mesquite Bay, it has been shifted about by mapmakers. The anonymous *Plano del Lago de Sn. Bernardo* (plate 10), for example, shows it far up the coast, and Jefferys puts it just west of the Sabine (Río Dulce).

ward. On this entire coast, water will be found where there are Indians and, where not, in *casimbas* in the very good sand. At 10 at night the wind came around to the north with considerable force.

Wednesday the 2nd. At 10 in the morning the norther calmed. Past noon the calm wind came to the south, and we put to sea at three in the afternoon through the channel, which I found was 12 spans deep. We navigated one league northwest by north; two and one-half northeast, where there is an opening through which discharges the river that comes along the coast. I therefore named the place el Desaguadero [The Outlet]. We went northeast a league and a half more, running the coast, [which was] always flat with small dunes and knolls. Here we anchored at sunset in 5 fathoms, fine, brown sand.

Thursday the 3rd. From daybreak we went some 3½ leagues northeast by east, somewhat farther northeast, and two almost east-northeast. The coast is flat, of low dunes and knolls, here somewhat higher where the shore makes a point with more than half a league of sandbank of little water that runs east. We proceeded through 12 spans more than a quarter league from shore. From here I saw to the north more than a league another point and between it and the other a small, flat island of white sand, nearer the leeward point than the other, the seaward side made quite shoaly with a shallow sandbar. Somewhat distant, toward the north, it is deep, but there is a channel between it and the windward point. Upon the sandbank of the leeward point we awaited the passage of the other galley, and shortly the wind and water carried us across the mouth upon the shoals of the island, where we narrowly missed scraping bottom; and, sounding always between the two sandbanks, the most water I found was 16 spans, which was in the channel between the other galley and ours. Always falling back to the windward shore, and from the bar toward the inside, I found 4, 5, and 6 fathoms in places until reaching the windward point. From leeward the shore goes northwest, north-northwest, north, and north-northeast, forming a large bay, until arriving about a league and a half to the north-northwest of the windward point, where we anchored. From here the coast runs a little to the northeast and then toward the interior, which, like the adjoining coast, has many estuaries and lagoons, but none goes to the sea. From the north-northwest to northeast by north, land cannot be seen, and thus, between the leeward point and the windward is formed a very large lake or bay, the principal channel of which is the one I have mentioned. All this land is very flat, of great savannas without any timber whatsoever. On the windward point there are many lagoons of deep, fresh water. Here I observed the sun and found the latitude to be 28°23′. We found on the beaches some trifles from ships that the sea has washed

Río de   up. I named this Río de San Bernardo [Saint
Sn. Bernardo   Bernard's River], it being his day; the leeward
point, San Francisco; and that to windward, Culebras, for having found
some [snakes] there.[22] This afternoon Captain Pedro de Yriartte sent his
canoe with the ensign to see if he could find any Indians. He went
about a league by the windward shore and then across the bay to the
point to our north-northwest. They returned saying that in most parts
there was no more than twelve spans and two fathoms of water. With
this the captains decided to send the canoes tomorrow to sound the bay,
one along one bank, the other along the other, to meet in the middle 3
or 4 leagues from here.

Friday the 4th. Before sunrise the canoes went out with the native
guides and the two assistant pilots. They returned after 5 in the afternoon, saying that 3 leagues from here, east-northeast, inside the bay on
the windward shore, they had found a lost ship that has 3 fleurs-de-lis
Lost   on her poop; six pieces of artillery, mounted,
ship   woolded, and hove down; two iron swivel guns
without chambers, which they brought in our canoe. The masts have
fallen into the water (because the shipworms had eaten them in two at
the holes) with all the rigging. Even though they were ruined, the yards
resting among the rocks, holding up the topsail sheets, we recognized
by these things that she was a warship. On the beach they found some
barrels of powder, full but ruined by the weather; other broken ones;
and other things that the captains wished to go see tomorrow. They
found the channel, from here to the shipwreck close to shore, of four
fathoms, sometimes more and others less, and, half a league north of
this Punta de Culebras, a sandbank with two and three spans of water in
places. It is large and the channel goes between it and the shore.

Saturday the 5th. At 7 in the morning we got under way and went
along the inner shore, northeast by east and east-northeast, to the ship,
which we recognized as being French and of war by the things mentioned. She has all the starboard side, the deck, and the prow under
water. All her tackle (from what I saw in what was being appraised) was
very fine, new, and mostly of four strands. She had eight portholes and
as many other flues. As for swivel guns, five pieces that fire a ball of up
to four *libras* [pounds] were still upon their carriages, lashed to the

22 Again the latitude is accurate within less than one minute; the "windward
    point," Culebras, is the western end of Matagorda Peninsula; the "leeward
    point," San Francisco, is the upper end of Matagorda Island. Whether En-
    ríquez was aware that Guido de Lavazares had given the name San Francisco
    to the adjacent bay in 1558 is problematic.

ship's sides. The others perhaps had fallen into the water. The double tackle was rotten because, from appearances, she has been here more than a year. We gathered up some cordage that still might be serviceable for us and embarked the 5 pieces for ballast, two of them in our galley. We also took an anchor of up to 6 quintales and some 30 fathoms of 8-inch cable [*cable de 8 pulgadas*], half of which was divided into strands for yarn. The other *piragua* took half. On the beach were found the other gun carriage and the main yard, which was measured and found to be 16 cubits. Therefore I am saying that the ship's keel is 24 cubits.[23] We brought this yard and that of the fore topsail for making oars, and from that of the foresail a boom was made for ours. Captain Pedro de Yriarte took that of the mizzen also. There were found some large smith's bellows and some other very small ones of hand type, a large cooper's plane, some leaves torn from an arithmetic and artillery book in the French language with a piece of map, from which I conclude that she was a French ship. Notice that the irons that I have told of finding in the Río de Flores are not from this ship but of another considerably larger. The launch of this one was not found; perhaps the people saved themselves in it, having left this ship with all their equipment except the manual arms.[24] There have been diverse opinions; and, because they are so various, I write none of them so as to refrain from extraneous matters. I named this place Navío Quebrado [Wrecked Ship]. This afternoon we arrived again at the Punta de Culebras.

Sunday the 6th. Quite early in the morning the captains dispatched the two canoes with the ensigns in charge that they might go with Juan Poule to reconnoiter the estuary where he careened his ships when he was here previously. This Juan Poule, whom I mentioned the 9th of last month, was pilot of one of the two [ships] that our armada seized in Tampico. They made port on this river when they came to this coast in search of diving [salvage]. This afternoon they returned after having seen what we believe was the place. Here tonight the captains, with the concurrence of the other officers, resolved to go and see the end of this lake or bay, since beyond Navío Quebrado we have found sufficient water for it.

23 This was La Salle's bark *Belle,* a gift from King Louis XIV. Enríquez calculated the length of keel from its customary ratio to the main yard. A cubit usually is eighteen inches, indicating a keel of thirty-six feet.
24 Enríquez's conclusions are close to the truth. The ship's boat and six men had been lost while seeking fresh water prior to the wreck of the *Belle,* probably in late February, 1686. The rest of the crew escaped in a derelict canoe (Henri Joutel, "Relation de Henri Joutel," in Margry, *Découvertes,* III, 227–31).

Monday the 7th. At 6 in the morning, with east-southeast wind and the favorable current, we went northeast by east until arriving to windward of a point that is about 5 leagues approximately northeast of Punta de Culebras.[25] It is very low with a long reef toward the west, and behind this one runs another branch of the river from the interior. The channel, ever narrowing, goes between this shore [of the bay] and that of the [outer] coast. Here it is about two and one-half leagues wide and 3 fathoms deep in the middle, soft mud bottom. We went another 5 leagues, beating to windward until near a small island with some low woods, and I have seen no other place anywhere on the shore that is so flat and marshy in the extreme. To this point the water has been constantly diminishing in depth, but with many intermissions, and the channel here is 14 spans. On the two shores it is little more than one league to fairly fresh water, and it is therefore certain that this is the river branch that runs along the coast, as it has come continuously from near Maupate. The other shore, beginning between the northeast point and that which I have mentioned, is north-northwest of Punta de Culebras. Juan de Poule has told me that it is 7 or 8 leagues from the mouth and that it is in the form of an arch, the interior abounding in estuaries and lagoons, like the rest that we have seen, with two fathoms of water throughout the lake and in parts less,[26] and that behind the north-northwest point enters the branch that comes along the coast from Río de Flores. [He says] that when he was here the first time, his people many [times] went that way to kill buffalo and deer. Finally, the form of this bay or lake is approximately as it goes in my new description with the depths indicated by numbers, although few are significant.[27] Past 3:30 in the afternoon, having seen some Indians gather among the mottes on the mainland, a little to leeward of the small island that I have mentioned, the ensigns went to them in the canoes and reached the Indians, who then made them signs that they should lay down their arms. They left their muskets and went to talk with them. One came and, lifting their coats, told them that they should leave their pistols and cutlasses. Ten did so, and they received them in friendly fashion. Making signs and questioning them on what they wanted to know, the interpreters could not understand anything for certain. They left 4 men as

25 Palacios Point.
26 Reference apparently is to Sand Point, at the end of the archlike peninsula enclosing Keller Bay and forming the entrance to Lavaca Bay, an extension of Matagorda.
27 Enríquez's map of Matagorda Bay and vicinity, in his "new description," second only to Minet's, has not surfaced in recent times. The Minet map (plate 8) shows only the area around the mouth of the bay.

hostages and went down with as many other Indians to the beach to bring them aboard to the captains, but they did not wish to be embarked. They therefore sent the canoes to ask the captains for some trade goods with which to regale them until tomorrow, that fair winds might blow another day, for certainly there was good accord as we had seen at the Río de Sn. Joseph. Captain Marttín de Rivas sent to our ensign some beads, knives, and tobacco, and Captain Pedro de Yriarte went ashore with others. Then the four Indians saw the large canoe go (ours was already there) with many more people. They departed, retiring to the *ranchería,* and the ensign Francisco Aldama, without arms, with them, trying to persuade them to wait, but he was benumbed and therefore arrived with them at the *ranchos.* He returned then at the time that his captain already was going there with his two Indian interpreters, Anttonio of Tamaolipa and Phelipe, one of those whom I brought from Apalache. They went naked and with their bows and arrows, the rest of the people being without arms. Reaching the *ranchería,* he persuaded two or three of the Indians and regaled them with *álagas* [yellow wheat] that they should come aboard. Seeing that they did not wish to, he ordered Juan Poule to take hold of one and make him do so, and the ensign and another together, but the three could not subdue him, because all these Indians are of great stature and very robust of limb.[28] With the knife he had he wounded the three who had taken hold of him and thus freed himself. To his shouting many others came out who had concealed themselves in very tall grass and commenced shooting arrows at the captain and the rest, defenseless but for the two Indians, who fought to defend them until our Ensign Miguel Barroa came with his people and arms. After a few musket shots all of them fled across the savanna and our people came back aboard. One Indian was seen to fall among the grass and two were wounded by our Indians' arrows.

Tuesday the 8th. Very early in the morning we came through two fathoms and 20 spans of water to Navío Quebrado, where we anchored, and a meal was prepared for the people. Then we went to Punta de Culebras. Tonight we had much wind from the south-southeast with water and, near day, it strengthened.

Wednesday the 9th. In the morning the wind calmed and remained out of the south all day. As that is a beam wind on this coast, it made a heavy sea.

Thursday the 10th. Almost all day we had calm and a little west

28 These were the Karankawas, noted for their great stature, described by Jean-Baptiste Talon in the Interrogations, question 12, and discussed by Schuetz, "Ethnological Data," in the commentaries.

wind. This afternoon there was found near the beach at Punta de Cule-
Note   bras a rudder pin whose shank was two spans
and three fingers long and seven inches thick,
with one span of groove, and each flange with eleven nail holes. Those
of our flagship [*capitana* (of the Armada de Barlovento)] are not as
large.

Friday the 11th. After two in the morning, the wind came strong
from the west-northwest. At dawn we got under way and sailed out
through the leeward channel by which we entered, because in the other
there were heavy swells. The shallowest water was two fathoms. At
seven in the morning we cleared Punta de Culebras and navigated until
noon, about 17 leagues, when I found latitude 28°45′, the coast always to
the east-northeast, tending slightly northeast, extremely flat, and without woods. There are only three or four high, knoll-like dunes 5 leagues
from Punta de Culebras and 3 leagues farther another with a gap in the
middle, others 6½ leagues. We proceeded to a small mouth through
which empties the river that runs along the coast, and I named it Boca
Chica.[29] Two and a half leagues farther, there is another mouth of a
large river with many shoals of sand to windward and leeward with a
channel in the middle, doubtless 10 to 12 spans deep, like the other bars
we have seen. The inner shore has many woods and they appear to be
pine groves. A little before arriving here I saw more woods on the other
bank of the river that flows within. To this mouth I gave the name of
Río de   Río de Zívoras [Cíbolas], because of having seen
Zívoras   five [buffalo] on the coast just before reaching it.
The captains did not detain themselves to take soundings, believing it a
matter of no importance since it had no island in the mouth and no
more than two fathoms of water outside the channel. We sailed four
leagues more to another mouth similar to the previous one. It was already 6 in the evening. Since we could not enter because of the contrary
wind—already from the northwest and so strong that all day we were
forced to carry the sails without bonnets—we proceeded about a league
and a half to windward and anchored in four fathoms, sand bottom, to
separate ourselves from the swells on the bar. All this coast is as I have
said, very flat, smooth, with neither dunes nor woods. Since noon, it
runs northeast by east, somewhat more to the east.

---

29 Latitude 28°45′ approximates the mouth of Caney Creek (Boca Chica),
which then flowed directly into the Gulf, rather than into East Matagorda
Bay, as at present. The name Boca Chica, later designating a mouth of the
Río Grande, is shown on the upper Texas coast by Delisle (1718) and Jefferys
(1775). Plate 10 shows it correctly.

Saturday the 12th. It dawned with the wind in the north. At 9 in the morning we entered through the channel of this bar, which lies east-west, to the two points of the mouth. The least depth from the mouth toward the inside, a musket shot, is 12 spans. There are three fathoms and more in parts, but farther in there are many banks and little water. The branch of the river that comes from leeward enters this one. There are many mouths and estuaries, forming many small islands, and it has another branch that runs to windward. Here we found no fresh water *Río de* and therefore made *casimbas* from which very *Sta. Suzana* good water was drawn. I named this river Santa Suzana because it was her feast day. This morning the people of the other *piragua* killed a large buffalo [*zívora*], bigger than a cow and very similar except for having longer hair that looks more like wool. The wind has been constantly from the north, quite strong. I observed here 29°09' latitude.[30]

Sunday the 13th. In the morning we had gentle north wind, then northeast, east, southeast, south, and southwest at night. Today our people killed two small buffalo like veal calves, which they brought aboard in quarters.

Monday the 14th. At sunrise we sailed from this river with land breeze from the northwest, and a little before 6 we were outside the bar. Until noon we navigated more than 6 leagues northeast a quarter east, a bit farther to the northeast, running along the shore, which in every respect is similar to that seen on Friday. At 9:30 the land breeze calmed and the two canoes went ashore with our ensigns and Antonio Romero to talk with some Indians who were on the beach. They received them in friendship without becoming excited at seeing the muskets and other arms. They asked them by signs whether they had seen other people like us. They replied that they had no chief and thus they so called whomever they might choose.[31] After giving them some trade goods and seeing that they were saying nothing of substance, we got under way at 10 with the wind from the sea, south-southeast. At noon I observed 29°22' latitude, and afterward we sailed with a south wind half a league

30 Since leaving Boca Chica the *piraguas* have passed Cedar Lakes (Cedar Lake Creek) and the mouths of the San Bernard and Brazos rivers. Río de Zívoras, or Cíbolas, may have been the San Bernard. Santa Suzana probably represents San Luis Pass, at the west end of Galveston Island. The observed latitude 29°09' is about three minutes too much for the anchorage inside West Bay.

31 The nonsensical response reflects that the Spaniards and the Indians were not communicating. Again, the natives would have been Karankawas, various groups of which ranged eastward to Galveston Bay.

Boquilla   to a small mouth, which I named Boquilla [Little Mouth]; a league and a half, all on the course mentioned, to a point of very low white sand; a league north of this, another wiith a small cay of white sand.[32] A little way off and between these two points is a river mouth that forms a sand bank of very little water a little less than two leagues to the east. Then, almost as far, we passed through two branches. From more than a league off the east side of the white point to the coast that runs from the mouth to windward, this one runs east-northeast about 6 leagues, forming a little bay, to some groves of trees, three larger and four smaller. The one to wind-
This one is   ward, being southwest of them, is larger than all
called Río Bajo   of them, round, and more apart. The rest of the coast is very flat and smooth, without dunes. It is very shallow, since one league from it there are no more than 3 fathoms, mud bottom. I
Matas de   named these groves Santa Casilda. Here the sun
Sta. Casilda   set on us, and we proceeded to 4 fathoms and anchored.

Tuesday the 15th. We navigated from dawn with the land breeze from the northwest, coasting approximately east-northeast until noon, about 4 leagues. I observed the sun and found latitude of 29°40'; another two leagues with the *virazón*, the wind from the sea,[33] we continued to a large round thicket of timber and four small ones a league and a half farther on (always on the aforementioned course). We discovered a river mouth through which fresh water was flowing into the sea, but we did not reach it because there were no more than 2 fathoms a league offshore. To this one I gave the name Río Dulce [Pleasant River]. From here we went another two leagues in which there are 11 quite small mottes and as many as four large ones, with good division between the first two and the last two. The river that comes along the coast may be part of it. A little before arriving at Río Dulce, we anchored in 3 fathoms, mud bottom, south of these mottes. The whole coast is very flat, as I have said, and therefore the thickets stand out.

Wednesday the 16th. From dawn until 8 we went under oar with slight south-southeast wind and calm about two leagues and anchored to prepare a meal on shore. I went ashore to observe the sun with a geometric quadrant with three spans of semidiameter or radius and found the latitude to be 29°47'. From here the coast, all of savannas,

---

32 Latitude 29°22' indicates the Galveston Bay entrance.
33 Enríquez almost never uses the word *virazón* without defining it in these terms. The latitude approximates Texas Point at the mouth of the Sabine River (Río Dulce).

runs east.[34] The soil is doughlike and brown, as I saw in a *casimba* we opened in search of water, but [the water that] came up [was] very brackish. The bottom up to the beach is ooze, and, under the sand, all is black mud on the mainland coast. Here I saw few signs of breaking sea because the herbage is near the water and the driftwood three paces from it, the shore being so low. This has appeared better to me than what lies between the Maupate and Río Bajo, all of which is filled with swamps, saltwater lagoons and sand dunes, estuaries, and islands without woods and is good for nothing. The coast is severe in the extreme and bad for shipping, especially in winter, since there are no ports for ships, nor any more relief for those who suffer shipwreck than to suffer at the hands of the barbarians.[35] From one o'clock until sunset, with southeast wind, we made four tacks in which we made good about three leagues east and anchored in three fathoms, ooze, in front of a small river mouth where we saw Indians on the beach. Here by observation I saw that the compass needles were virtually in adjustment.

Thursday the 17th. Quite early the coastal pilots went in the canoes to sound the river mouth and they found, a little outside, a not-very-large sandbank with 8 spans of water and from there to the river 12 and 16. We were near the leeward point. The wind was fresh from east-southeast, contrary for our navigation. We therefore entered this river, which is deeper within, with two and three fathoms, as far as the Indian *bujíos* [huts] and *rancherías* half a league from the mouth, but it is not very wide here. We anchored so as to speak with them with greater ease. Then there came aboard some whom the captains regaled and, upon their return to shore, others came. To all were given trade goods with which they remained so happy and grateful that all day they were admitting our people to their *bujíos,* giving them living quarters. Sixty comely women, with their few ornaments, were made to attend them.[36] At three in the afternoon three Indians came in a canoe from the east bank

34 Between the Sabine and the Calcasieu rivers, the Louisiana coastline levels out, running almost east-west. The apex is in latitude 29°47′, approximately.

35 The foregoing passage is an example of the "bad press" that was partly responsible for the Spanish failure to develop ports in the region described, from the Soto la Marina River to Galveston Bay. Enríquez's description was quite accurate, as proved by repeated shipping disasters attended by the massacre of passengers and crews.

36 The Indians were Atákapas, whose various bands extended along the Gulf Coast between Galveston and Vermilion bays. They were of the same family as the Chitimacha, their eastern neighbors, and probably the Tunican group on the Mississippi. The name Atákapa means "man eater" in Choctaw and Mobilian (John R. Swanton, *Indian Tribes of North America,* pp. 197–98).

to the *ranchería* on the west, among them one who knows the Castilian language fairly well. They informed the captains of this, and I went ashore with them and noticed that he told them that his name was

Pedro the Apalachino Indian   Pedro and his homeland San Luis de Apalache, whence he had been taken by the corsairs previously mentioned, who went thence to rob Tampico; that from there his master, called Gaspar, who now is in Pánuco, fled with others. This was about 6 years ago.[37] From there Captain Pedro de Castro took this Indian for his interpreter. According to what he says, after losing their provisions, they navigated with great labor (each one searching every day on the beaches for mollusks and fish to eat) until, much farther to windward than this river, they left the 9 men on shore and fell off to leeward. A little to leeward from here, the people went ashore as always to look for their daily sustenance, and, to avoid dying of hunger as many others already had, he decided to remain on shore with a Spanish boy and be delivered to the Indians in a nearby *ranchería*. They did so and they took them in and regaled them most mercifully. He says that they have lived with them to this day without any unpleasantness whatsoever. They asked him whether or not the boy was near and when he would be able to come. He replied that he was living in another *ranchería* on the other bank of the river a day's journey from here. The captains asked that he be brought, and they gave a bundle of tobacco to an Indian to go and look for him. Pedro told us that one Indian was saying that not very far from here he had seen a

News of white people   wrecked ship and white people with firearms who traveled on horseback, killing buffalo to eat. They asked him if they had large ships or small ones, white women, or any settlement, and he replied that they had no ships, not even canoes, and that they had no white women, and that they were living with great friendship in the *rancherías* with the Indians without having built houses for themselves. The matter was put to rest till tomorrow, when the boy should arrive whom Pedro says was a native of Mexico, and, in commemoration of such a pleasing discovery, we named this the Río del Mexicano.[38] After 10 in the morning the east-northeasterly blew with

37 "The corsairs previously mentioned" were the 1684 raiders captured by the Armada de Barlovento three years previously. Either Pedro had been left at Tampico by a previous pirate raid or the time is exaggerated.

38 This first European name given the Calcasieu River appeared thereafter on numerous maps, including those of Fer (1705), Delisle (1718), and Jefferys (1775) (Martin and Martin, *Contours of Discovery*). This is one instance in which Fer used one of Enríquez's place-names not found on the 1703 Delisle map—proof that he had a different source for the Spanish pilot's toponyms.

such force that if we had been at sea it would have troubled us greatly.

Friday the 18th. The Indian who gave this news said that, being paid, he would go with us to show us where he had seen the people, and that he was a native of that place, although he was married here. The captains now talked with him at length, promising that he would be paid liberally. At sunset the Indians arrived on the other bank of the river with the boy and were asking the others for a canoe for crossing. Ours went and brought them. Coming on board, he wept with joy at seeing himself among Spaniards. His face has tattoos like these Indians, with a black line that goes down the front to the end of his nose, another from the lower lip to the end of the chin, another small one next to each eye and, on each cheek, a small black spot. Like the nose, the lips also are blackened, and the arms are painted with other markings. His clothing consisted of the deerskin that girded the waist, and the hair has a circular cut like a religious lay brother's, with one line going down the neck to encircle the breasts like the other Indians of this nation. They asked him his homeland, and he said that it was Mexico, that his name was Nicolás de Vargas like his father, and that his mother was Josepha de Rojas, widow, who was living on the Calle de la Misericordia Piedad. He told me [that he is] nine years old, but it appears that he is older. He speaks the language of these people with perfection. Therefore the captains, with such a good interpreter, asked the Indians who came with him and the other one about the news that was being given: whether it was true that there were white people on this coast, what they were doing, how they were living, and whether they had ships. The Indian who had taken in the boy, whose name was Itanjas [?], and others who had come with him confirmed all that the first one has told, although they had not seen them but had only heard the story from others. They asked them how much time had passed since such men had been seen in this region, which they did not know because they live so much like animals that not even by the moons do they know how to reckon time. Seeing this, Captain Pedro de Astina asked them whether it was before or after taking in the boy. They replied that it was before, by which we gathered that it was more than two years ago. They asked them whether they were still there, whether they had built a fort, how they dressed, whence came their horses, in what region they were, and whether the place was far. They replied that the captain of those, with more than the people's friendship, had gone inland on horseback quite a while ago, and that they judged the rest would be with them, that they had made neither fortification nor any houses whatsoever, that their dress was like ours: wide trousers covering the whole body like our people, the shoes like ours, and that some wore hats and others cloth caps, and that they brought other clothing wrapped in bedding. They said the horses were from the land of Spaniards and that each day the Indians who inhabited the interior brought them, indicating that the place was to leeward and adjacent to the first river, which we inferred was the one I called Río Dulce. The old one and various others told me that the Indians already had burned the ship to recover the nails.[39] The captains coaxed the two Indians to go with us to show us these people, promising them very good pay and to return them here. They replied that they were satisfied [with the arrangement] and would do it. With this they left them until tomorrow, for today we have had much east-southeast and southeast wind with thunder and rain. We asked the boy about Captain Pedro de Castro, Juan Corso, and the other people, and he told us that Juan Corso had died of weakness that he suffered in the breast and that when he [himself] remained here with Pedro the Indian, most of the people

Hunger that forced them to eat the dead

already had died of hunger and that those who lived (terrible thing) ate the dead without wasting even the heads, rendering the cut-up corpses in the stewpot. I asked him if they had killed anyone just to eat and whether at any time he had eaten of them. He said that they had killed no one but that he had eaten many times of ours. He told me that Captain Pedro de Castro remained alive with 30 or 35 men of the 130 he had taken from Nueva Veracruz.[40] Thus the curious reader may ponder this thing, the likes of which I have never heard, anywhere in the world, until today.

Saturday the 19th. Until 9 in the morning we had east-northeast wind and then it went around the compass, with water. In the afternoon it remained southwesterly, and it cleared, giving sign of good weather

Strange tides

until tomorrow. At 8 I saw that the tide, ebbing, suddenly rose about two fathoms in less than two *credos*, running in with great noise and small, bubbling waves, and at nine it returned to empty out. Finally, almost every two hours, it flowed and ebbed, a thing that I have never before seen, which means that on all this coast I did not find tides of consequence but all of them like the winds that impel the waters, as they do in the rest of the Indies.

The old Indian and several others have been on board all day. After

---

39 A common practice accounting for the failure in recent times to find on this coast a great number of ship remains from the colonial period.

40 The city of Veracruz at its present site, adjacent to the San Juan de Ulúa fortress, occupied in 1599 and called Veracruz Nueva to distinguish it from the previous location some fifteen miles up the coast, referred to as Veracruz Antigua for many years but now called Antigua.

sunset his two nephews and his brother arrived, and the captain regaled them also. Another twenty went to the *ranchería*. There are so many, and the captains tried anew to convince the Indian who first gave the news that they should embark to show us the place and that they would be well rewarded. They replied that they [the white men] were not still there, having gone inland, and that they [themselves] feared the other Indians. With this reply I seriously doubted that it was the truth, and I feared (as I always suspected) that the people of whom he spoke were those of Captain Castro [and not La Salle] and that the Indians had finished killing the few who, dispirited, remained; and that they lied concerning the horses. Nevertheless, the captains again urged them to show us where they had seen them, saying that, with them [the Spaniards], they need not fear the Indians or any other people whatsoever. With this they stayed to be embarked tomorrow, with Pedro the Apalachino. He told us and various others that tonight more Indians were coming from other *rancherías* and that we should beware of them because they were thieves. This we have experienced among those who came on board these days, with whom there might have been trouble. Pedro the Apalachino says that these are the Chisca nation and that they live without superior law or government, like bandits, that they only have captains who lead them in affairs of war and that no fealty or devotion whatsoever has been recognized in them.[41]

Sunday the 20th. Early in the morning Captain Pedro de Yriartte sent to the *rancherías* for the Indians and found that they had hidden themselves. They had done so from fear, the others said. [The messengers] therefore came on board with Pedro the Apalachino and an Indian friend of his who returned ashore to look for the others and was delayed. We waited a little while to see if he would come back to hail [us] with another Indian who would want to come. He returned, saying that they were afraid, and everyone began taking up his bow and arrow to go to the savanna, taking among four [others] a woman; that they were afraid to take the risk, seeing that they would accomplish nothing worthwhile by the effort; and that it might be impossible to overtake them running. We put to sea a little past nine with slight easterly wind, which past noon changed to south-southeast. We arrived at three in the

41 Swanton (*Indian Tribes,* pp. 117–18) identifies the Chisca (Chiska) with the Yuchi and places them in eastern Tennessee. The Chisca are mentioned by the Soto chroniclers in that location in 1540. In the late seventeenth century they harassed the Apalache missions in Florida and were attacked by a Spanish-Apalachino force near the mouth of the Choctawhatchee River in 1677. I have found no other mention of them west of the Mississippi in this period.

afternoon at the mouth of the Río Dulce. The coastal pilots went in the canoes to see if we could enter and found a channel of 8 spans, more toward the leeward point than the windward. And, as the whole mouth was free of breakers, we entered at will and went north about half a league to anchor where the river makes a northwest bend and is much narrower than at the mouth. There are many very shallow oyster banks and among them good channels for these ships, but great care is required in looking for them because the water is turbid and they cannot be seen. Here we suffered as much from the mosquitoes as we might in any other part of the Indies. Today each one may be given ration of 14 ounces of bread, but evenhandedly.

Monday the 21st. Early in the morning the coastal pilots went to sound the river one league and returned saying that in many places there was little water with many banks and shoals, but by the leeward shore there is a channel of 3, 4, or 5 fathoms. We therefore went with the *piraguas* to reconnoiter all of it. Note that we navigated somewhat more than a quarter league northwest, more than a half north, and more than two west-northwest until we touched the mud bottom in four spans. Therefore, we then sailed downstream and went under oar to anchor in 12. The captains sent the coastal pilots in the canoes to sound beyond with orders to make a fire on the savanna, that upon this signal the Indians might come. They did so and went about two leagues west-northwest and west. Always they found very little water, in places not even enough for the canoes. Here the river widens, and I believe that it connects with the branch that has always come along the coast, since I saw it approaching this place. This afternoon we had much south wind and all night it was stronger with much rain and thunder.

Tuesday the 22nd. Until 10 in the morning the water and south wind continued. Then it changed to southwest and west, with which it cleared in the afternoon, and at four we made for the mouth. Having gone about a league, we heard shouts and yells of an Indian who stood on the leeward bank. The canoe of Captain Pedro de Iriartte, being closer, then went to bring him. He was embarked, and we anchored. Arriving on board, he said that he had gone out alone on the savannas to hunt deer and that, having seen us, he hailed us to detain us because we might need fish; in his *ranchería* he had some that he would exchange for trade goods. At this moment a canoe was approaching with five Indians. The captains asked him if he knew of any lost ship and whether he had seen any pass along the coast or any white people in these parts. He replied (in the presence of the other 5 who had just arrived; they were from the Río del Mexicano and had come overland; among them came the friend of Perico [Pedro] the Apalachino who went to call the others) and now gave his acquittal, saying that he was innocent of the intention of the others, that he had heard it said to others that on the next river, two days' journey from here, there was a lost ship; that he had seen no others pass along the coast; that he had heard also that there were white people and that they must be going inland because they were no longer there and that he had never seen or heard of this from anyone. They asked him if he might know the river and if he would show us this place. This gave rise to many difficulties, and the friend of Perico said that he had seen the river and the ship and, were it not for fear of sailing on the sea, he would go with us. (This Indian and the others from the Río Mexicano always had said that this ship was like ours.) They told him that our vessels did not rock or roll and that they always sailed near the shore, with which he resolved to go and encouraged others to go. They asked the captains, who secured their canoe, and all of them remained on board. We went toward the mouth until a little while later the other galley grounded on a bank. So violent was the current in the channels, the tide being out, that it could not be floated off until our [evening] prayers. We then anchored and brought on board the Indian who came alone and the other one, and the captain regaled them. This shore is very flat and marshy, like that to leeward, without woods, and I believe that with high water the savannas would be flooded because in many parts of them I have seen large trees carried there by the waters.

Wednesday the 23rd. At 10 in the morning seven Indians arrived in front of the galleys. Captain Martín de Rivas went ashore with the boy [Vargas] to see whence they came and what they wanted. He found that the captain of the *ranchería* and the father of the Indian who had come alone were among them, and they related that, since he had been missing the night before, they had come looking for him, for he was married and had children to support, and that he knew nothing concerning the affairs of the Indians to leeward because he was at war with them. With that the captain grudgingly had the Indian taken to them on shore, and all of them promised to bring him a little fish. A little past noon, the galley sailed at high tide, and we came to anchor near the leeward point, the wind being strong from the west, although today it was northwest.

Thursday the 24th. At 11 in the morning we sailed from the Río Dulce and in two tacks on a southeast wind from the sea, we proceeded to anchor next to the Mata Redonda [Round Grove] so as to utilize the land breeze next morning, the wind having shifted more to the west.

Friday the 25th. With the land breeze from the northwest and north until 8, when it calmed, the *virazón* or wind from the sea came at 9:30

from south-southwest, then south, with which we came to anchor after sunset a little to leeward of the Matas de Santa Casilda.

Saturday the 26th. With calm, we proceeded under oar about two leagues until 8. At 10 the *virazón* came from the south, and in two tacks we arrived after four at the mouth of Río Bajo, which is flat, as I said on the 14th of this month, and now I saw that, between the shore that goes out from the white cay and the coast that goes to windward, there is a long reef of sand running east-west, with very little water by the windward point. We proceeded from this, and I therefore did not see how much water there is between the two reefs but noted that the one that goes out from the small cay extends almost to the other. Then, between the two, until passing the cay, there are 3 fathoms and 2 fathoms, sand bottom in places, ooze in others. More than half a league inside there is similar bottom, and afterward 12, 10, and 8 spans. We therefore anchored until sounding farther inside the white cay tomorrow, with the canoes. Toward the west I saw a long reef and southwest of this another. The mouth of this river is about a league and a half wide, almost north-south, and the cay more toward the northern point than the one from the south. The shape of this river is similar to that of San Bernardo.

Sunday the 27th. Very early in the morning Captain Pedro de Yriarte came to our *piragua* with Perico and the other Indians for us to tell *Gradual calming* them what was being said and thus to ask them *of an Indian* again where the lost ship was. The friend of Perico replied that it was under the water and could not be seen. They asked him why he was saying one thing one day and something else the next. He replied with great naturalness that his mind was blown [*tenía quebrada la cabeza*] with so many questions and that the first time he had been telling the truth and the second time they asked him for the place where he had seen the white people, a lie; and he said that from here to there was two days' journey. Thus they determined that we would go to the area he was indicating, as far as the *piraguas* could go. At nine they brought from shore the food for the people. Then we went north about a league and a half and northwest a half as far as a point that is northwest of the mouth and has a large grove of trees that from afar looks like a small island. This [point] has six or seven small white cays that run in a northeast-southwest line until it approaches the shore that forms the branch that runs along the coast to Río Dulce. Since the galleys could not pass between these cays, we anchored next to the point with the grove in 10 spans. Northwest of these cays is another bay about a league and a half from them, its shape like a bow, as the shore appears to me.[42] Seeing that we could not proceed farther, the captains dispatched the large canoe with good people in charge. Ensign Aldama took the Indian to show them the place, and the boy for interpreter. The Indian said that tomorrow at nightfall they would be able to return here. All day we had very strong south-southeast and south wind with much rain, thunder, and lightning until near midnight, when the wind went to the northwest, and then it cleared. Beginning today, the bread ration will be reduced four ounces and only one meal is eaten each day.

Monday the 28th. Until 9 in the morning we had northwest wind, which remained calm. After noon, the canoe of the other ship arrived, and the ensign said that the Indian had told him that on the point of the grove he had seen the white people and that they were encamped there, killing buffalo. They therefore examined everything and found no signs whatever of Indians' even having been there; buffalo and deer, yes. Then he said that he would go to the pueblo or *ranchería* to obtain news of this people, upon which the canoe went about two leagues northwest of this point to a river by which they went to the *ranchos*. They found that they had forsaken them a great while ago, since there were no fresh signs but only sticks and arches still arranged in the shape of their *bujíos*.[43] Seeing this, the Indian said that he had come this far and that he had already shown the promised place. With this the canoe came back, and we went toward the mouth of this river, southeast with northwest wind, which was rising, through 10 and 12 spans to reach the midpoint between the windward point and the white cay, for thus goes the channel; then 2 and 3 fathoms, up and down. But, on leaving at 6 in the evening, I found between the two reefs no more than 12 spans. I therefore point out that to enter this river a ship requiring 8 or 10 spans should anchor east of the cay in two fathoms and with the launch sound the channel, and even mark it with buoys, because seldom does the sea break on the reefs. The northern point of this mouth is in latitude 29°26'.[44] Today the boy has told us that what the Indians said about the horses is false, that they never knew what a horse was until he showed them how the Spaniards used them—mounting on a limb on which he

---

42 The point evidently was Eagle Point, northwest of which the shoreline extends in the shape of a bow. The cays run northeast to Smith Point, forming East Bay, "the branch that runs along the coast to Río Dulce."

43 It is not at all unlikely that the aforementioned deserters from La Salle living among the Hasinai had come to this area on a hunting expedition. The voyagers may well have had from the Atákapas news of their quarry that they failed to recognize. *Bujío* is an Arawak word applied by the Spaniards to any hutlike native dwelling.

44 Actually about 29°22.5'.

placed a goatskin for a saddle—and the use of stirrups and bridle. With this I conclude that it was the galley of Captain Pedro de Castro and that the Indians of this river put an end to it and the few people who remained, in which destruction some of those of the Río del Mexicano also may be implicated. All night we navigated, with north-northwest wind until nine, then north, with which we were forced to make two tacks before day.

Tuesday the 29th. Dawn overtook us east of the leeward point of Río Dulce. The wind was northeasterly and we made two more tacks before afternoon, when, being in 5½ fathoms, we could not see land. With the wind already in the east, since the turn in the coast, it came at 3 to the south and later to the south-southwest. We ran along the coast until 7, when we anchored about 3 leagues to leeward of the Río del Mexicano to examine the mouth, because the land is so flat and hard to recognize that it made me doubt whether I actually was in that place.

Wednesday the 30th. After 7 in the morning the wind arose from the east, somewhat fresh, although it had been blowing offshore since last evening. At 7 (seeing that it was increasing and that there was a weather change) we fell off to leeward to the shelter of the Río Dulce, where we entered at noon and anchored inside the mouth. This afternoon the wind came to the southeast, more gently.

[May, 1687]

Thursday, 1st of May. From midnight to noon we had very strong east wind, then stronger southeast.

Friday the 2nd. All day we had so much southeast wind that the intruding sea obliged us to withdraw from the mouth.

Saturday the 3rd. At dawn the wind arose from the west with great force, rain, thunder, and lightning. At 7 it calmed and at 9 it came to the northwest, very gentle, with which we sailed a little before 10. Past noon, the wind returned to the west, then to the west-southwest, and in a few hours to the north; at midnight to the northwest, always gentle. At 11 we arrived upon the mouth of the Río del Mexicano and saw the fires of the *ranchería*. At 3:30 in the morning the wind rose somewhat, and we proceeded with slight sail until dawn. Since we knew through the Indians and the boy that in many leagues of these environs there is no settlement of white people, sailing until daybreak caused the captains no anxiety, and we therefore proceeded through 20 spans.[45]

---

45 Enríquez alibis a minor violation of the orders, which stipulated that the mariners should sail only in daylight along the unknown coast.

Sunday the 4th. Dawn broke upon us about two leagues to windward of a large motte that is two leagues east of the Río del Mexicano. About one league to windward of this motte is the Río del Tocail, which (according to what the boy has told me) has two lagoons on the east shore, one near the mouth and the other, which is called Tainons and has another river branch, well upriver.[46] He says that he has fished on it with the Indians and that the river's water is fresh. From the motte the coast runs about 3 leagues east-southeast, in which direction there are many other large and small mottes. Then dense woods follow with some gaps not far from the beach on a very flat shore; the coast goes southeast by east another 6 leagues, where I observed 29°31′ latitude.[47] From noon to sunset we navigated with gentle west wind two leagues east-southeast and three southeast by east along similar coast but with the woods farther away. We anchored in three fathoms, ooze bottom, a league from shore.

Monday the 5th. With wind from the east, east-southeast, southeast, and south-southeast, we made good about 5 leagues, tacking on the eastward-running coast to 8 mottes, some larger than others, where we anchored in 20 spans of water, in mud. In these 5 leagues the wood is about 2 leagues from the coast, which is extremely flat and therefore all of brown mud with some sand on top in places. On the savanna all the land is subject to flooding. They went in the canoe today to look for fresh water. The servants made a *casimba,* but it flowed very brackish water.

Tuesday the 6th. In a matter of about a league, we advanced eastward, beating into the southeast wind to the western point of a wood of very dense timber about half a league long. From the western point to the middle equals [the distance] from there to its edge. It has five gaps, which from afar look like mouths. To this I gave the name of Monte de San Juan [St. John's Wood]. To leeward it has four or five mottes, not very large, and in places the trees of the woods come to the water's edge. Because the wind was very strong, we anchored at noon in three fathoms, ooze bottom, more than a league from shore. Here I observed latitude 29°22′.

Wednesday the 7th. Tacking eastward from dawn to noon, with southeast wind more gentle in the morning, we made good about 2 leagues. Near 12 the main yard of the other *piragua* broke, and we an-

---

46 This was the Mermentau River; the lagoons suggest Lower Mud Lake and Upper Mud Lake.

47 The distance indicates the area of Big Constance Bayou, the latitude a position about 3.5 miles offshore.

chored in 14 spans, ooze, a league from shore. From the Monte de San Juan a shallow reef, in places mud and in places sand, extends seaward. In some places the shore, which is very low with some groves at intervals, cannot be seen from two fathoms.[48] They gave our main yard to the other galley, and for our own another was made from the yard that we brought from the lost ship in the Río de San Bernardo. By afternoon we had strong wind, but, as we went farther upon the reef, it did not bring much sea.

Thursday the 8th. After sunrise we got under way and with the southeast wind went two hours from the turn of the tide. Coming from the shore, we discovered a river mouth. We turned the prow toward it and, until entering between the points, the least water was one fathom, and then four and five. It is of salt water and is east of the Monte de San Juan; to leeward, three divided mottes, and to windward, others, and one large one a cannon shot distant. This being Ascension Day, I gave this name to the river [Río de la Ascensión].[49] Here some *casimbas* were made and the water that came up in them was little better than brine.

Friday the 9th. The two canoes went upriver to look for water and, meanwhile, the people opened other *casimbas,* one below the black mulberries of the large motte, which I have said is to windward of the river mouth, but all flowed saltwater. Here there are many blackberries and large mulberries. All day it has been blowing very strong from the south-southeast without moderating at night.

Saturday the 10th. I observed the sun and found the latitude to be 29°26'. Shortly after noon the canoes came back without water because all they found was salty and the land was flooded. Gerónimo de Acosta told me that this river had no inland source and that it was only a large lake that runs northwest-southeast from the mouth with a long, very low island in the middle. After eating, all the people went down to look for water, without anyone being kept back by the captain. After more than 30 *casimbas* had been opened, at four in the afternoon, others were opened farther to windward of the large motte, where sand was found,

48 The *piraguas* may have been the first European vessels to sail within sight of this shallow coast. Adhering to the two-fathom curve, they lost sight of land as they crossed Atchafalaya Bay east of Marsh Island.

49 A Louisiana river or bay called Ascensión is mentioned in several documents, some of them antedating the Rivas-Iriarte voyage. It seems clear, however, that the name designated the Mississippi and stemmed from a confusion of the two religious occasions, nine days apart; the Festival of the Holy Ghost, or Espíritu Santo, and Ascension Day. It appears on the 1703 Delisle map as Lac de Ascension, reflecting Gerónimo de Acosta's description of it as "only a large lake."

arid water as good as and very similar to that of the holes of Campeche,[50] with which the people were quite satisfied, and today we made the whole watering. All day we had southeast wind, less strong than yesterday.

Sunday the 11th. All day it blew strong from the southeast, and, because it was the day of Conjun.[on] we did not sail.[51]

Monday the 12th. Before dawn we sailed from this river with southeast wind. I marked a very dense wood of live oaks that was (according to a coastal pilot who went there yesterday) something more than a quarter of a league long. The sea breaks among the trees, and I saw that it was about two leagues from the mouth of the Río de Mora, southeast by east, somewhat farther east. Today we made 6 tacks, and since three in the afternoon with the sea breeze from the south-southeast. After sunset we went to anchor in two fathoms near three cays of white sand, two of them very small and the other larger, which are about 3 leagues south-southeast, a bit more to the southeast of the wood that I named *Monte de Santiago* Monte de Santiago [St. James's Wood]. Between this and the cays is the very low shore and it forms a bay with some small, scattered mottes. I named these San Natal. This coast is very shallow and, more than a league south of the Monte *Cayos de Sn. Natal* de Santiago, there is much driftwood upon the oyster banks. From the Monte de Santiago to the cays we have seen the sea covered with countless logs brought by the wind and the current, perhaps from the Río de la Palizada, since that of La Ascensión does not bring them out to sea.[52]

Tuesday the 13th. Tacking with east and southeast wind, we made good about two and one-half leagues, east, to two mottes, one long but not very high. The rest of the coast is very flat and low, since more than

---

50 On the Yucatán peninsula there are few streams; in many places the only water source is the natural sinks providing access to underground reservoirs in limestone. The first two European voyages to explore the Yucatán coast—those of Francisco Hernández de Córdoba and Juan de Grijalva in 1517 and 1518—watered from Campeche's *cenote,* incurring the enmity of the native Mayas.

51 This religious occasion has not been identified.

52 The bayous and rivers of this region, including the Atchafalaya, make up a distributary network for the Mississippi, operating to drain floodwaters from the big river. The highly complex nature of this section of coast makes it impossible to track the voyage with precision. For an understanding of the delta system, see Douglas Lee, "Mississippi Delta: The Land of the River," *National Geographic* 164, no. 2 (August, 1983): 226–52; and Jack Rudloe and Anne Rudloe, "Louisiana's Atchafalaya: Trouble in Bayou Country," *National Geographic* 156, no. 3 (September, 1979): 377–96.

a league from it there is much driftwood on the banks. Here we anchored in 10 spans, and only with difficulty could the shore be seen from the masthead.

Wednesday the 14th. Sailing to windward with the said winds quite strong, we advanced eastward about two leagues, to where there is another long but not very high motte. At 3 in the afternoon a squall from the south obliged us to anchor in 14 spans of water south by southeast from the motte and northwest of the other 6 small, close-together ones, about a league from the one and more than a half from the others. At this end the shore forms a large bay toward the northeast. Today I observed latitude of 29°16'. The coast and the bottom are still as I said yesterday, and I observed that outside, in 20 spans and 3 fathoms, there is mud, and also between the banks.

Thursday the 15th. At dawn we got under way and with southeast, south-southeast, and south wind we navigated, making some tacks along the coast, which runs a quarter of a league southward to a very small motte; southeast one league; east-southeast two; and east one. It is low and flat in the extreme, with some small, scattered mottes. Today I observed the latitude, 29°07'.[53] Here we anchored.

Friday the 16th. Since dawn we sailed (with gentle southwest wind and, in the afternoon, south) south-southeast 3 leagues to eight small cays; the two to leeward run northwest-southeast, the other 6 eastward, and all of them cover something more than a league. Here the shore forms a cape, and, because it was so shoaly that it was not possible to reach it with the ship to see it, I called it Cabo *Cabo Bajo* Bajo [Shoal Cape] and the cays San Isidro. Then *Cayos de Sn.* we went northeast 3 leagues; east by northeast, *Isidro* two; and east, one, to an opening; southeast by east, two; and east by southeast, one, to another mouth that forms an island, this being 3 leagues. By the windward point, between it and the mainland, there is another small one. A little to windward of this mouth is that of another river, and in these two last ones I saw the sea breaking somewhat and, running toward the coast, white water, almost fresh. The shore is like the rest, very flat with some small, low groves. Today I observed the sun a little to windward of the 8 cays; latitude 28°52'. South of this last mouth, we anchored in 3 fathoms, ooze, near shore. From the cays the deeper part is to windward, at the first of these mouths. I called it Boca Escondida [Hidden Mouth] because it is seen with difficulty; the next

53 On Wednesday the latitude of 29°16' and the large bay to the northeast indicate a position near Barataria Pass. Thursday's latitude of 29°07' marks the descent of the delta to a point just short of Grand Pass.

Boca Escondida   one, Boca de Guerrero [Guerrero's Mouth], so
Boca de Guerrero   called by the lad who saw it from the masthead;
Río de la Aguada   and the other, Río de la Aguada [River of the
Watering], because much fresh water and some driftwood comes out of
it. On the points it has a few breakers. Here the water runs violently to
leeward.[54]

Saturday the 17th. Quite early in the morning we got under way
with northwest wind and went about a quarter league to another small
mouth that is formed with a point that the shore makes here and a narrow, low beach or thread of sand in which there are innumerable drift
logs. Between this and the mainland there is a large lake with many estuaries and some logs on the inner banks. We went about half a league
farther, east by northeast and east-northeast, until 9, when the wind
came to the east. With that we made 4 tacks and at 3 in the afternoon
went to anchor in front of the mouth of Río de la Aguada, almost
where we left it, so strong was the current in this river. Today we made
almost the whole watering. I observed the sun and found 29°52′ [28°52′]
latitude. The other galley arrived to anchor half a league on our lee.

Sunday the 18th. The watering was finished and all day we had
southeast and east-southeast wind with which the other galley tried to
come to us, but the current carried her farther to leeward, and she returned to anchor.

Monday the 19th. Beginning at dawn, we navigated with west wind
four leagues east-northeast to a wood that has a gap toward the western
end. In length and height it is similar to the Monte de Santiago. This
one, I named Monte de San Pedro. We then went 4 leagues to a point
that is southeast of the aforementioned wood. In the interim there is a
large bay to the northeast. West of this point, well out to sea, there are
no more than 2 fathoms of water. I therefore named it Punta de Placer
Punta de   [Sandbank Point]. We sailed south-southeast,
Placer   southeast, and east-southeast to round said sandbank, until 7 in the evening. With little wind, we went one league farther, southeast, for fresh water, to another point, where we anchored at
Punta del   8, so as to pass the mouth from which it extends,
Palo   believing it would be the Río de la Palizada. This
last point I named Punta del Palo [Timber Point] for a large log it has.[55]

54 Although the Mississippi passes in 1687 differed somewhat from the present
ones, latitude 28°52′ and the violent discharge "to leeward" suggest the vicinity of Southeast Pass. The current was so strong that the *piraguas* had to
await a west wind to carry them beyond the stream.
55 Navigation is in an area corresponding to East Bay, the two points near the
mouth of South Pass.

Tuesday the 20th. Very early, with west wind, we navigated one league east-southeast with bay toward the north to a point that has 6 cays on one side. They are of mud, as is the shore also. On doubling this Punta de los Cayos [Point of the Cays], eastward, there is a small river,

Punta de los Cayos which I named San Bernardino; thence east one
Río de league to another point that has two small cays
Sn. Bernardino of mud toward the north. Nearby and between them and the coast there is a bar with much driftwood. Here also there is a bay toward the north with two small cays inside. I named this Punta de la Restinga [Bar Point], We went one league farther east-northeast to

Punta de another point on which there is also much drift-
la Restinga wood. It was a good stretch. This is the one to leeward of the mouth of the Río de la Palizada and I therefore named it

Punta Punta Deseada [Desired Point] because of the
Deseada great desire we had of arriving at this place, seeing that the provisions were running out and that the people were lamenting the short rations so much that everyone was coming to eat as with equal status at one mess. We then went northeast 4 leagues to Cabo de Lodo, passing by the two mouths of the Río de la Palizada before 9. At this hour the wind shifted to northwest, upon which I put the prow to the north-northeast and at noon observed 29°15' latitude. And, when expecting to arrive momentarily at the Cayos de San Diego,[56] I could not see them except from the masthead, and then not well enough to distinguish the water from the western shore, so violent was the current toward the east-northeast. Past noon, with wind diminished, I pointed the prow northeast and northeast by north to 6 and 8 fathoms as far as latitude 29°40', where we anchored after 6 to await the other galley, which was somewhat distant.

Wednesday the 21st. From dawn until 8, with north-northeast wind, we went east about two leagues, where it calmed, and we anchored in 16 fathoms. Here I observed 29°38' latitude at noon. The men put their lines in the water as they did each day and in less than 2 hours they took more than 200 red snapper. At three the wind arose from the west, and I turned the prow north. At 8 I observed 30°10' latitude, a matter that caused me to wonder because the natural movement of the ship with the gentle wind would not be so far. At 9 we came to anchor in 9 fathoms so

56 Punta Deseada (Desired Point) was at the right of North Pass, the "two mouths of the Río de la Palizada" discovered on the previous voyage. The Cayos de San Diego, evidently named by Enríquez Barroto on the 1686 expedition but not mentioned in the Jordán diary, may have been the Grand Gosier Islands.

as to observe the shore in the morning. Here the easterly current was felt most violently.

Tuesday the 22nd. Before sunrise we got under way and with west wind proceeded along the coast until about 9, when we arrived at the mouth of a large bay. I went aloft and recognized, by its course and the bars it made, that it was the Laguna de Mobila [Mobila Lagoon]. Because the mouth to leeward had no more than 8 and 10 spans, I proceeded outside the bar south of the island and entered by the windward channel,[57] although they went in the canoes, sounding the other, and we came to anchor in the shelter of Punta de Venados [Deer Point]. The other *piragua* went to a bonfire that the Indians had on Punta del Pina [Pine Grove Point] but could overtake no one, as they quickly fled. At nightfall she came to anchor next to us so as to examine the bay tomorrow, because only this one is similar to what the declarations prescribe as adequate for large ships, since the channel has six fathoms of water and, from the Punta de Venados north more than one league, six to three fathoms, ooze bottom. With a fortress on the island, entry could be impeded because the channel passes near it. Here there is a great abundance of fish, although the water is fresh.

Friday the 23rd. Early in the morning we went north along the leeward shore, fresh west-southwest wind. Having gone about a league and a half, we arrived in 20 spans of water. It was diminishing little by little and, after 4 leagues, we came to the mouth of the Río de la Mobilla (according to what the Indian interpreter who came with me from Apalache says) and four spans of water in which the *piragua* grounded. This river discharges through 6 or 7 small mouths that have many reefs and shoals. They went in the canoe to sound them and found none through which we might pass. Through these flows water that makes fresh that of the bay and lagoon. Past noon we went down to windward. By sunset we made good two leagues to a point that runs northwest to the mouth of the river, and it is the one that had been seen from the mouth of the port. Between this point and the river mouths, almost halfway, there are two large, red clay pits. At 9 the wind rose from the west, upon which we went to Punta de Venados.

Saturday the 24th. Just at dawn we sailed from La Mobila with gentle west wind and at 2 in the afternoon arrived at Bahía de Panzacola, where the captains did not enter (it seeming to them a matter to be avoided, knowing that each day these Indians were going to Apa-

57 The two channels lay on either side of Sand Island, off the eastern end of Dauphin Island. The *piraguas* followed the course to the present ship channel, passing near Mobile Point.

lache). Here I have perceived that from the Bahía de Mobila to that of Panzacola is twelve leagues less than was ascribed to it when I navigated it last year, since I sailed it with very strong head wind and current, tacking along a little-known shore, often obscured by clouds, so that I could never know the distance made good on each tack. Thus this error is no matter of wonder for anyone who understands the circumstances and modes of navigation; for example, on the 17th of the current month, when I saw myself navigating with a fresh wind, we fell back another five or six leagues. Additionally, I consider the longitudinal difference between the meridians of Mobila and Cabo de Lodo to be less than I had given by 8 leagues. With the difference of longitude between Veracruz aand Havana, all these [corrections] make a difference of 26 in the description I made last year from the meridian of Cabo de Lodo to here. I will do what seems proper with all the rest of the coast. From Panzacola we went coasting with fresh wind until 3 in the morning of the following day, when I came near the Médanos de Pacara [Pacara Dunes][58] (where, the wind being in the west-southwest and our having Cape San Blas to double) I turned the prow to the light.

NOTE: Today I heard it said to the Mexican boy that the sash that Captain Pedro de Castro wore, a pack of needles from his storekeeper, and some musket and pistol barrels from which they forced Perico to make them knives, had been seen in the custody of the Indians of his *ranchería*. Thus I have come to believe that the few spared by starvation were finished off at the hands of these barbarians.[59]

Sunday the 25th. Although with the day the wind came to the southwest, we rounded the cape with two tacks at 12, well favored by the current. Here I observed 29°33' latitude. At 6 in the evening we passed Ysla de Sn. Ignacio and at 11 at night we anchored in six fathoms, sand bottom, about two leagues to windward of Ysla de Candelaria, that we might double Punta des Abiñes in daylight because of its reefs.[60]

Monday the 26th. At 7 in the morning we passed by Punta de Abiñes between the reefs that are near shore and those about a league from it, in nine and ten spans of water. At 9:30 we reached Punta de la Cassina and, a little past noon, Bahía de Sn. Marcos, to proceed among the many oyster banks that make the entry difficult. There we had news

58 St. Joseph Peninsula.
59 Meaning the Atákapas.
60 Cape San Blas is in latitude 29°39'. To clear the shoals on which Enríquez's ship had come close to grounding in 1686, he gave it a wide berth. Passing the islands rimming St. George Sound, the *piraguas* approached Punta de Abiñes, identifiable as Lighthouse Point.

that the Sargento Mayor Don Pedro de Aranda y Vellaneda [Avellaneda] is governing Florida because Governor Don Juan Márquez de Cabrera has absented himself in the galley he took from Monsieur Gramon [Grammont], without revealing why or where he went.[61]

Tuesday the 27th. Considering that here there are no royal coffers, the captains wished to exchange the remaining trade goods for some meat and beans, but they then received a paper from the lieutenant offering them, on the account of the treasurer of Mexico, all the supplies that they might need. And thus they answered him, requesting 12 beeves, 12 fanegas of beans, and 12 of corn and one and one-half of salt, as expeditiously as possible. Today the commander of the infantry here told me that after I left this port on the discovery of Misipipi, the lieutenant who was of this province, Antonio Matheo, had made two expeditions by land almost to Mobila, in search of the new settlement. Never was he able to obtain news of it.[62] I therefore believe that it does not exist and that the ships that came for this purpose have been lost.

[There are no entries for May 28–June 1.]

[June, 1687]

Monday, 2 June. Everything has been boarded and paid for with trade goods except the meat that they gave. Yesterday the captains returned. These days we have had moderate winds.

Tuesday the 3rd. In the afternoon the meat was received and boarded,

61 The pirate leader Michel de Grammont, who had figured prominently in the 1683 Veracruz raid and the 1685 assault on Campeche, approached St. Augustine with three vessels on April 30, 1686. His plan to take the fort aborted when one of his ships ran aground. Following a bloody battle in which forty-three pirates were killed, the Spaniards, led by Aranda y Avellaneda, captured the unfortunate vessel's captain, Nicolas Brigaut. Brigaut, after giving information that paralleled the account of Denis Thomas at Veracruz, was hanged. Thus Márquez Cabrera was moved to send westward an expedition under Marcos Delgado to seek La Salle's colony. Planning a coastal reconnaissance and a second land expedition led by Antonio Mateos, his lieutenant at Apalache, the governor had the captured pirate galley outfitted and built two *piraguas* for the voyage. But then his own officers, galvanized by Aranda, rose in opposition, protesting the great expenditure of royal funds. Threatened with mutiny, Márquez abdicated. Aranda assumed his post. See Weddle, *Wilderness Manhunt,* pp. 66–86, for an account based on documents in UT archives, transcripts, AGI, Mexico 616. William Edward Dunn (*Spanish and French Rivalry in the Gulf Region of the United States, 1678–1702,* pp. 70–75) offers a briefer summary.
62 This is the only indication I have found that Mateos actually followed up Delgado's expedition as Márquez Cabrera had planned.

and we went to anchor at the banks in preparation for sailing in the morning.

Wednesday the 4th. We put to sea and, once clear of the banks, proceeded with southwest wind, steering northeast about 12 leagues until 5 in the afternoon, when the shore obliged us to go south-southeast, the wind already westerly, until 9, when it calmed. A little past 12 we resumed sailing, always in three fathoms, on the same course with slight west-northwest wind. At three in the morning we encountered the land breeze from east-northeast and proceeded thus until we came into 6 fathoms at dawn.

Thursday the 5th. At 6 in the morning, being in 7 fathoms and not seeing the shore, I went southeast from eight in the morning with calm that lasted all day. I observed the sun and found 29°09' latitude.[63] At 7 in the evening we anchored in 8 fathoms and had a severe squall from north-northeast with much thunder, wind, lightning, and rain that lasted until midnight, when it cleared and the wind went to the east. At four it was southeast. Since it began we have gone south-southeast and south-southwest to 10 fathoms.

Friday the 6th. We went south-southwest until 6 in the morning, when we turned the prow landward, east, navigating thus to 5 fathoms. The wind then came from the sea in such a manner that we were forced to go southeast to 3½ fathoms. A little past noon it calmed. I observed the sun and found 28°55' latitude.[64] At four a slight north wind came, with which I went south until 7 and came to two fathoms. I then went west-southwest to 3, where a squall from the southeast obliged us to anchor.

Saturday the 7th. Before sunrise we got under way and, with the land breeze from the east and east-northeast, we coasted southward. At noon I found latitude 28°12'. Afterward, with the wind from the sea, or *virazón,* [we sailed] until 5, when a squall obliged us to anchor; at six we proceeded under oar toward shore through 5 fathoms to 20 scant spans and anchored again to look for water. They went in the canoe and, it being night, did not pass beyond the beach. They opened *casimbas* and brought up brackish water. All the vessels were filled with it. At four in the morning, with the land breeze, I turned the prow southward until daylight, but the coast from here goes south-southeast.[65]

---

63 The latitude approximates Cedar Keys, adjacent to Wacassa Bay.
64 Near the mouth of the Crystal River.
65 The noon position, 28°12', was near Anclote Keys and Tarpon Springs. The bend in the coast places the watering at Sand Key. The brackish water taken on there was at least partially responsible for the illness that followed.

Sunday the 8th. From dawn to noon and latitude 27°34' we went southeast by south and from the other galley a little before nine in the morning was seen Spíritu Santo Bay, which they say is in latitude 27°45'. [[This Espíritu Santo Bay is not the one we are looking for because this one is well known, and each day the ships from Havana that are going to Apalache enter it to trade with the Indians for amber.]] We then sailed southeast about five leagues and south-southeast to latitude 26°46', and there we were becalmed about midnight.

Monday the 9th. Until noon we were becalmed in 11 fathoms. The sea breeze arose and we went to the other galley and asked them where they were going to water, since there are many watering places on the mainland and we were suffering with the extreme heat and great thirst. Captain Pedro de Yriarte answered me: Cayo de Guesos [Huesos, Key West]. I therefore went toward shore to see the Bahía de Carlos. I observed the sun and found 26°45' latitude and saw this bay to the east, then coasted south-southeast until 6 in the evening. Running the coast, I saw the Cayos de Muspa, where I turned the prow south for Cayo de Guesos, believing the other galley is going likewise.[66] At midnight we were becalmed.

Tuesday the 10th. At sunrise we did not see the other *piragua,* nor all day long. I therefore believe they have changed course, because we always come with the sail necessary to keep ourselves with her. Although last night we put out a signal light four times, they did not answer with theirs. Today, until 4:30 in the afternoon, we had calm, then slight north-northwest wind until 11, when the land breeze came from the keys to the south and we anchored in 14 fathoms, coarse white sand.

Wednesday the 11th. Quite early, with slight west-southwest wind, almost calm most of the day, we went south. At 11 at night, with the land breeze from the keys, south-southwest, we anchored in 7 fathoms, coarse white sand, in latitude 24°45'. From this [position] and the bottom, it was evidently near the keys.

66 Enríquez's identification of the Florida bays is in accord with age-old consensus, disputed in recent years. He sighted Tampa Bay near Long Key (27°45') and called it, after Hernando de Soto, Espíritu Santo. Becalmed at Gasparilla Island, he proceeded another minute of latitude to the Charlotte Harbor entrance (Boca Grande), between Gasparilla and Lacosta islands. He called it Bahía de Carlos. For different interpretations, see Weddle, *Spanish Sea,* pp. 53, 214, 240–41, 329–30. The sixteenth century cosmographer Juan López de Velasco (*Geografía y descripción universal de las Indias,* pp. 85–86) places Point Muspa in latitude 25.75° but gives a description that suggests Cape Sable. Enríquez Barroto, on the other hand, indicates Cape Romano as Point Muspa.

Thursday the 12th. At dawn I saw the keys that are approximately northwest of Cayo de Guesos, but since it was doubtful that they were these, I did not go west-southwest to look for the Cayo del Marqués, which is the last of them. We arrived there early, and the people went ashore and made *casimbas* but, although they were between some palms, only saltwater came up. We then went east-southeast about a league and a half to Boca Grande Key (according to what was told me by an artilleryman who has come here other times). We anchored and I took him with me in the canoe to see a *corral,* which he told of having made on the eastern point, and I found that it was true, that with the canoe, following his direction, we could go by way of the south shore of the key to Cayo de Huesos.[67] I have not come this way previously. On this Boca Grande Key I opened more than twenty *casimbas* and always drew saltwater. I then went to two other keys of white sand but grounded and therefore returned aboard with the disconsolation of seeing and suffering thirst in sight of land because these ships did not bring enough vessels for an 8-day water supply without rationing, which is a sorrowful matter in the great heat in which we have entered and will cause the people to fall ill.

Friday the 13th. In early morning we proceeded under oar for the western shore of this key and three others. Then, with south-southwest wind, we arrived at 10 at Cayo de Guesos and anchored on the west-northwest point, where we found the *casimbas* with brackish water, upon which we determined to remedy our lack because we did not know what else to do. At 3 in the afternoon a canoe of Indians came to the key and two of them came aboard. [[Today Captain Martín de Rivas became ill with fever and since yesterday four more.]] They spoke the Castilian language and gave us news that the governor of Florida is in Havana[68] and that behind this point a quarter league (north of the key) from our wood is a hole of very good water. The captain regaled them and told me I should go with them to see it. I went and found that it was true and thus the watering was begun. At 5 in the afternoon the other galley arrived here and did its own, in water almost adjacent to the anchor.

Saturday the 14th. We left the Cayo de Guesos a little before 11 and

67 Boca Grande Key is approximately eleven miles west-southwest of Key West (Cayo de Huesos). The artilleryman who had been there previously must have been Juan Poule, described by Enríquez both as an artilleryman and as a pilot. *Corral* in this case means "fish pond." Here the word *cayo* is translated as "key," rather than "cay" as elsewhere, because the reference is to the Florida Keys.
68 Governor Márquez Cabrera. See note 61.

at noon passed to leeward of Cayo Blanco, which is an edge of the shoal and is south-southwest of that of Guesos; then southwest by south in quest of the Mesa of Marién on the coast of Havana. The wind was east-northeast and east.

NOTE: Here I give notice that I have found between the meridians of Havana and Apalache less difference of longitude than had been placed in my new description previously from information of the native pilots. Thus, in another regard this Seno Mexicano [Gulf of Mexico] shall have correction and perfection. Captain Pedro Yriarte is ill with fever.

Sunday the 15th. In very early morning I saw the Sierras de Jaruco. Although near daybreak there was little wind, the current worked with increased violence. We then proceeded south-southwest and south by southwest to take the shore more quickly, and a little before noon we arrived near El Morro, so that we were seeing the fortress from the point. We let fly the bunting and turned the prow westward, running along the shore. At six in the evening a squall from south-southwest obliged us to take shelter from the storm in the port of Marién, and at 11 we sailed with the land breeze and went west, coasting until dawn.

Monday the 16th. Day broke about a league to leeward of Cabañas. With little wind until 10, we were carried a league east of this port. The wind then came from the north, and, although it was quite gentle, we arrived at one opposite Cabañas, where we entered and took on water. In the afternoon the wind went to the northwest and west and, at night, to the south, but so slight that I dared not sail for fear of the current.[69] On our galley there are the ten sick and on the other 17, with no remedy for them in the medicine chests (according to what the surgeons say). Since it was decided, in someone's moderation, that the voyage [would be] forty days, the care was not given that should have been, considering [that it was] six months, as I have said many times, concerning certain experiences.

Tuesday the 17th. The wind was always gentle from the northwest. Today a little before noon Captain Martín de Rivas was found so afflicted by the fever that it might be necessary to go to Havana to seek treatment to save him. I therefore was sent with Captain Pedro de Astina to the other galley to notify Captain Pedro de Yriarte of his indisposition and to determine whether they had anyone similarly ailing and with like desires. Thus, they resolved that upon return of the large canoe, which had gone for some fresh oranges, we should leave. Then, at

69 Sailing west along the Cuban coast, the *piraguas* confronted head-on the Gulf Stream, which gathers its force in the Straits of Florida before flowing north through the Bahama Channel into the Atlantic Ocean.

three in the afternoon, seeing Captain Martín with greater affliction, crying out under pain of the fever, we got under way without waiting for the other *piragua*. At 7 we anchored beneath El Morro until 9, when orders came permitting us to enter. Then the captain went to the home of Juan de la Rasquita, paymaster of our fleet. Tonight Captain Pedro de Astina had high fever, and the whole expedition was exhausted by very poor health, although I stayed on my feet.

Wednesday the 18th. The storekeeper of our armada told me that a Frenchman who 8 months ago was imprisoned in this city's jail made a declaration to its governor saying that, of the French ships that entered the Seno Mexicano with Monsieur de Salas [La Salle], the only one saved was the pink [*pingue*] that received the people from the others [vessels], which were lost.

Thursday the 19th. The captains of the two *piraguas* asked of this accountancy, for each vessel, six slabs of sea biscuit, 12 jars of honey, four sides of pork, and the medicine list that the surgeons presented. Yesterday the sick ones went to the hospital except our assistant pilot, Pedro Viñales, who went to the home of his kinsmen.

Friday the 20th. We took on a completely new water supply here.

Saturday the 21st. At 10 in the morning the requested supplies were received. The biscuit was taken from El Morro and, although they chose the best, it was very old and to some extent damaged.

Sunday the 22nd. At 6 in the morning the captains came aboard, somewhat improved, but Captain Pedro de Astina sicker. At 7 the people came from the hospital, also with considerable improvement, and then we went to El Morro to await the governor's license for sailing. It came at 8 and we sailed with the land breeze, running the coast until 10, when the *virazón* or wind from the sea came from the north. In the afternoon we had three squalls from the southeast and south, after which we passed by the mouth of Marién. After 6 it was calm, and we therefore proceeded under oar to Cabañas, where we arrived at midnight. This afternoon we saw four ships come toward this shore, executing the tack not far from us, and we therefore recognized that the one ship was a medium-sized hooker, one a pink, another small one, and a sloop. It seemed they were going to disembark at Cabañas. We anchored and the empty water vessels were filled. Today Captain Martín de Rivas told me that in Havana there is a dispatch for the Most Excellent Lord Count of Monclova asking that he return to Veracruz with all possible haste. They answered him that for his purpose a frigate was being made ready.[70]

70 The meaning here is unclear. The wording suggests that Rivas had written the viceroy asking permission to return to Veracruz, a move that would have

Monday the 23rd. At 9 in the morning they took Captain Pedro de Astina to the other galley for treatment by its surgeon, because he was still very weak. At 10, with the sea breeze from the north, we sailed from Cabañas. After 3 in the afternoon, the calm and current by the prow obliged us to anchor next to the reef in 5 fathoms, more than a league to leeward of Bahía Honda. A little before 7 we got under way with the land breeze from the south-southeast and southeast, somewhat fresh. I went west until midnight, then west, southwest, and southwest by west. Day broke upon us in sight of the cays 3 leagues to leeward of Río de Puercos, and presently we escaped the steady current, which tonight was strong.

Tuesday the 24th. At sunrise we espied two ships going toward the sea. Today, with slight northeast and east-southeast wind, we came at 6 in the evening (navigating west-southwest and southwest by west with shore current) quite near the Cayos de Santa Isabel. From there we went west until 11 to escape the shoals, then west-southwest and, near daybreak, southwest by south, with south-southeast wind somewhat longer.

Wednesday the 25th. Since dawn I have gone southwest by south with the said wind until noon, when I observed latitude 22°05', and then southwest by west. Shortly the wind came to the southeast and at nightfall to the east-southeast, quite gentle, until two in the morning, when it freshened. We always came with less sail than we could have carried to avoid putting ourselves too far ahead of the other galley, which was coming a little way by our stern. At one at night I observed latitude 22°08'. Seeing, [as] we navigated on the said course, that it was not possible to diminish latitude (such was the violence of the current), I turned the prow to southwest by south. Here I put the sounding lead into the water, believing myself within soundings, but, as the draft was slight and the leadline somewhat heavy, I could not sound adequately and therefore left it off until it seemed we were in 20 fathoms. At 5 in the morning I observed latitude 21°47'. I sounded and found slightly less than 18 fathoms, fine, white sand. I then turned the prow southwest.[71]

Thursday the 26th. At sunrise the wind remained almost calm, and we could not spot the topmast of the other galley. Until noon, with the

---

been wholly unnecessary. Actually, two days prior to this, on June 20, the viceroy had ordered Admiral Francisco de Navarro at Veracruz to outfit two ships to search the northern Gulf shore for the two overdue *piraguas* (UT archives, transcript, AGI, Mexico 616).

71 The ships, having fallen off to escape the shoals rimming the Golfo de Guanahacabibes, are crossing the Yucatán Channel. The Caribbean current, pouring out of the channel into the Gulf of Mexico, sets them northward until they fall behind the Yucatán shore, then carries them westward.

calm, the current carried us very much westward. Thus I ran, entering in soundings. Then came the wind from east-northeast, with which I made for shore, southwest by south. At three in the afternoon I came into four fathoms a little more than a league to leeward of the cay. Then I proceeded along the coast in three fathoms. The wind was very fresh. Past 4 in the afternoon we espied in the offing the other galley, which was coming shoreward under sail. We furled our foresail to await her, and at midnight she was already with us. At dawn we arrived off Río de Lagartos[72] and then, with lessening wind, made for shore, east-southeast.

Friday the 27th. Dawn overtook us two leagues to windward of Chubusna [Yucatán]. Until noon we had gentle wind, then northeast as strong as yesterday. At sunset I saw the cone of the salines.[73] Here we had calm until 10, upon which we anchored. Afterward, with the land breeze, we went to the Morros de Taina, where dawn overtook us.

Saturday the 28th. We navigated with the land breeze, which was little more than calm, until noon; then, with the sea breeze, we arrived at 2 in the afternoon to anchor next to the Campeche wharf to take on water more quickly and, with the Indians whom the *sargento mayor* sent, it was finished a little past 3. At this hour came a severe squall from the east, which lasted until five. At six we weighed anchor and proceeded to Lerma, to anchor next to the other galley, which I found taking on water. Because of the squall, she still had not been able to finish it. Tonight, because Captain Pedro de Astina was considerably more ill, they took him to Campeche. We got under way before sunrise with the land breeze.

Sunday the 29th. We navigated south by southwest until noon, when we arrived off Canpeton [Champotón], and then southwest with the sea breeze from north-northwest until 5 in the afternoon, when our coastal pilot, Joseph Guzmán, ordered the prow turned west-southwest, following the coast. Since Campeche, the ships have been in his charge. At six we arrived off Puerto Real. We proceeded thus all night and stood at dawn some distance off the Tabasco bar.[74] By what they say, this is fifty leagues from Campeche.

---

72 Río Lagartos, on the northern Yucatán coast, so named in 1517 by Yucatán's discoverer, Hernández de Córdoba, for its alligators.

73 The Campeche salines are described by William Dampier (*Dampier's Voyages*, ed. John Masefield, II, 244–45) as being twenty leagues north of the town of Campeche. See Weddle, *Spanish Sea*, p. 408.

74 Just why Guzmán had taken charge is not clear. Puerto Real, now only a ferry landing at the mouth of the Laguna de Términos, was the hangout

Monday the 30th. We went southwest with slight offshore wind until noon. The current from the rivers carried us away from the shore, which we lost from view. The sea breeze came, and after 2 we came back within its view. From 13 fathoms we went quite near, coasting west by southwest all night. I observed latitude 18°, and at daybreak we stood upon Tonalá.

[July, 1687]

Tuesday, 1st of July. At sunrise the wind blew upon us from north-northwest. This being contrary, at 11 we took the shelter of Guazacualcos [Coatzacoalcos], whence the captains sent word of our arrival to Veracruz.

Wednesday the 2nd. At 4 in the morning we sailed with calm that lasted until 11 and the northerly current carried us some distance from shore. Then came the sea breeze with which we navigated along the coast, which runs northwest until the Punta de Zapotitlán, till four in the afternoon. Then it remained calm until seven, when the land breeze came upon us, with which we navigated all night, northwest by west, to Roca Partida.[75]

Thursday the 3rd. At dawn we were about 3 leagues to leeward of the Río de Cañas but somewhat to sea because from the Rock toward Alvarado the coast runs approximately west. The land breeze, hardly more than calm, lasted until 10, and at noon the *virazón,* or wind from the sea, came from the northeast. We arrived at 3 in the afternoon off the Río de Alvarado and then sailed along the coast toward Veracruz, where the entire circumnavigation that we have made of the Seno Mexicano was finished, a feat that would have been impossible with ships drawing more water than these. At 5 in the afternoon the city came within view, for which I give infinite thanks to God. Finally, this is how much we have seen and done since we sailed from San Juan de Ulúa that may be worthy of mention.

[Lettered in a different character]

Be advised that this is a rough-draft copy that I have made during the navigation and delivered to the Most Excellent Lord Count of Mon-

---

during this period of English logwood cutters and buccaneers. The Tabasco bar refers to the mouth of the Río de Grijalva.

75 "A point of land on the coast extending from the Sierras de San Martín into the sea, with a gap so low that at high tide it appears to be separated from the shore. It is therefore commonly taken for an island" (López de Velasco *Geografía,* p. 122).

clova, viceroy of this kingdom, which I have examined and corrected to the letter. I advise also, for better understanding of the coast that I have sketched, that what is colored green (from Apalache to Cabo de Lodo and Río de Palizada) is what I and Antonio Romero discovered in the year 1686 on orders given us by Admiral Gaspar de Palacios in Veracruz. Because of not having carried sufficient provisions, and bad weather, we did not finish the reconnaissance, having arrived at Veracruz from Cabo de Lodo, as shown by the diary and map that I made then and sent to Spain.[76] That which is sketched in red is what has been reconnoitered on the present voyage and which previously was unknown to everyone, between Tampico and Cabo de Lodo. All the rest that I included on the chart has been examined with such care that the defects contained in the others have been corrected in this one. And I declare that it has been ordered that I make no other chart or diary copy until His Majesty, God keep him, so orders. Mexico, 22 July 1687.

Juan Enríquez Barroto
[rubric]

The captain of sea and war Don Pedro de Yriarte and the pilot Antonio Romero depose that we have read this diary and examined the chart that Juan Enríquez Barroto has prepared, and we as eyewitnesses declare that it conforms entirely with what we have seen on all the reconnaissance. In confirmation thereof, we sign it. Mexico, 22 July 1687.

Pedro de Yriarte [rubric]
Antonio Romero

76 Reference is to the map and the diary Enríquez prepared during the voyage with Romero in 1686, neither of which has come to light.

IV. The French Survivors

The Talon
Interrogations:
A Rare Perspective

ROBERT S. WEDDLE

In 1704 La Salle's brother, the Abbé Jean Cavelier, wrote to Pierre Le Moyne, Sieur d'Iberville, to inquire whether there might still be survivors of La Salle's Texas colony living among the Indians. In reply, the founder of Louisiana, emphasizing the completeness of the Fort Saint Louis massacre, referred the abbé to information given by the Talons: "Enclosed, Monsieur, is the extract from the report of Pierre and Jean Talon, natives of Canada from a village near Quebec, who were returned here from Mexico and whom I had two years in Mississippi in the King's pay. They came back two years ago and at present are in the prisons of Portugal."

Iberville's excerpt from the transcript of the Talon interrogations was published more than a century ago in the original French.[1] Yet few have recognized it as the extraordinary document that it is. The extract, however, makes up less than one-third of the complete text; where seventeen questions were answered by the Talons, the published version treats only six. But neither has been used extensively. Charlevoix and Parkman, with a few paraphrased lines, indicate that they saw the full document. Yet neither accords it any real significance; nor has anyone since, until the last decade or so.[2] An explanation of such oversight

1 "Interrogations faites à Pierre et Jean Talon, par ordre de M. le compte Pontchartrain, à leur arrivée de la Vera-Cruz," erroneously dated September 14, 1698, instead of February 14, in Pierre Margry, ed., *Découvertes et établissements des français dans l'ouest et dans le sud de l'Amérique septentrionale*, III, 610–21. The Iberville letter is on p. 622.
2 I drew from the extract (ibid.) and other French sources in developing the Talons' story, published in 1972 and 1973. See Robert S. Weddle, "La Salle's Survivors," *Southwestern Historical Quarterly* 75, no. 4 (April, 1972): 414–33, and *Wilderness Manhunt, The Spanish Search for La Salle*, pp. 252–62. The full text of the interrogations enables clarification of nuances and correction of some errors.

might well become long and involved. Parkman himself was a noted intellectual snob, with scant interest in persons of low station, as the Talons decidedly were. His work on La Salle, so masterful in its broadstroke delineation that few since have dared think of enhancing it with fine-line detail, may actually have been a deterrent to further investigation. Yet the Talon document contains the only eyewitness account of the Fort Saint-Louis massacre. It is filled with anthropological and natural history observations that offer interesting comparisons with other sources, as well as new insight. Besides the early historians, only a few linguists appeared cognizant of its existence. Taking note of its Indian word lists, they evidently delved no further into the document, their perspective limited to the concerns of their own discipline.[3]

Even the Spaniards who rescued the Talons from the natives—so diligent in taking depositions from all the other principals—failed to consider that these children might have worthwhile information. Yet, when the two young men who had been with La Salle reappeared in France just as Iberville was preparing to renew La Salle's undertaking in the Gulf of Mexico, the marine minister's interest was unbounded. He assigned the brothers a part in the enterprise that probably was of greater importance than can be proved, one that extended at least until 1715.

Pierre and Jean-Baptiste Talon were the sons of Lucien Talon, native of the bishopric of Beauvais, in Normandy—about seventy kilometers east of La Salle's native Rouen—and Isabelle Planteau of St. Méry Parish in Paris. The couple is believed to have married about 1671 in Quebec, where these two sons and two older daughters were born in the next eight years. Whether or not the family was related to the Jean-Baptiste Talon who was intendant of New France from 1665 to 1672, and who later occupied a prominent post in the French cabinet, has not been established. Lucien Talon's father, however, was named Jean.[4]

The Talon family, returning to France about the time that La Salle was organizing his voyage to the Gulf (1684), joined the expedition a short time later. It was the only sizable family in the company, which probably had only one other. (The paymaster had his young son with him and, presumably, his wife.) Probably before the Talons left Canada, a third son, Lucien, was born. When the family joined the expedition,

3 See Rudolph C. Troike, "Karankawa Linguistic Data," in the commentaries that follow.
4 Cyprian Tanguay, *Dictionnaire généalogique de familles canadiennes depuis la fondation de la colonie jusqu'a nos jours,* I, 558. A footnote states, "It is said that he was a nephew of Talon the intendant." If so, then Lucien's father and his father's brother both had the given name of Jean.

Madame Talon again was pregnant. She delivered during the voyage; the fourth son was named Robert. Thus the mother, destined for early widowhood, arrived on the wilderness shore of Texas with six children ranging in age from a few months to twelve years.

The Talons, from all indications, occupied no prominent place in the colony. Their sole distinction lay in being the only large family. Although Lucien Talon *père* was a carpenter by trade, Henri Joutel—the principal chronicler of the episode and La Salle's trusted lieutenant— calls him a soldier.[5] Most of what is known of the family comes from the Interrogations, which somehow failed for almost three hundred years to attract significant notice. The father, according to Joutel, died before October, 1685; he does not say how, and his children never knew the circumstances of his death—only that he had been "lost in the woods" while on a march with La Salle. The widow Talon later entered into a controversy with the Sieur Barbier who, having married one of the young women of the colony, asserted for their unborn child a claim to the special perquisites granted by the king to the first child born in each American French colony. Madame Talon contested the bid on behalf of her youngest (Robert), born during the voyage. The matter resolved itself when Madame Barbier miscarried,[6] although it may have surfaced again with her second pregnancy. From the Interrogations we learn that Madame Talon's grief over the loss of her husband was compounded by the death of her elder daughter, Marie-Elizabeth, who succumbed to an illness (apparently during the winter of 1686) at about age thirteen. Then came the separation from her eldest son, whom she was never to see again.

When La Salle left Fort Saint-Louis of Texas in January, 1687, to seek his Fort Saint-Louis on the Illinois River, he took young Pierre Talon, not quite eleven. He planned to leave the lad among the Hasinai (Cenis or Tejas) Indians to learn the language; "likewise," says Joutel, "Father Anastase and some others."[7] By this means La Salle hoped to build a relationship whereby these friendly natives would sustain the twenty-odd men and women left at the settlement on Lavaca Bay. Father Anastase Douay, whose narrative is not noted for strict adherence to truth, claimed a more elaborate design: he was to begin a mission among the Cenis, and Father Zénobe Membré was to come from Fort Saint-Louis to join him, "while awaiting from France a greater number

5 Henri Joutel, "Relation de Henri Joutel," in Margry, *Découvertes,* III, 191.
6 Ibid., pp. 257–58.
7 Ibid., pp. 260–61. Concerning the Hasinai, see Mardith Schuetz, "Ethnological Data," in the commentaries.

of gospel laborers."[8] Whatever the plan, its course was diverted by tragedy in both groups of the now-divided colonists.

The sadness of the parting—never, said Père Zénobe, had he experienced one more sorrowful—touched everyone; perhaps Pierre and his
mother most of all, for each must have realized that it could be their last.
Yet, what a blessing that they could not see into the future.

Pierre surely remembered his eleventh birthday for the rest of his
life. It came the day after La Salle was felled by an assassin's bullet in the
East Texas wilds, the aftermath of three previous murders in a hunting
camp. Pierre's account of this and the subsequent bloodletting among
the Frenchmen in Cenis country is at variance with Joutel's. That the
young man might confuse the ages of the Duhaut brothers, thus at-
tributing La Salle's slaying to the wrong one, is understandable. It
is even understandable that he had forgotten the name of La Salle's
nephew, Crevel de Moranget, whose conduct is said to have provoked
the whole affair, and that he tells of four murders in the hunting camp
instead of three. But when he denies the surgeon's part in it and ascribes
an entirely different role to him, questions arise. So far as is known, the
only surgeon with the group was Liotot, named by Joutel as the das-
tardly, venomous butcher who committed three axe murders and in-
dulged in mockery over the fallen La Salle. Joutel, on the basis of what
was told him by one of the participants, relates a conspiracy involving
Pierre Duhaut (the older brother); Liotot, the erstwhile English buccaneer called Hiems (a French corruption of James); L'Archevêque
(Joutel's informant); and the pilot Tessier. The plot, as he tells it, culminated in the murders of Moranget, Saget, and the Indian hunter Nika,
with Liotot wielding the axe. Joutel accuses L'Archevêque of luring La
Salle into ambush, Pierre Duhaut with firing the fatal shot. More than a
month later, the assassins, still in Cenis country, had a falling out among
themselves, he relates; Duhaut died by Hiems's gun, and "Ruter"
(Rutre)—one of three deserters from the previous Cenis expedition
who had rejoined the group following La Salle's death—killed Liotot at
the same time.[9]

Pierre Talon, on the other hand, says the younger Duhaut (Dominique) found only one other, James, who would side with him in aveng-
ing his brother's death; the two of them then killed the four others—

8 Anastasius Douay, "Narrative of La Salle's Attempt to Ascend the Mississippi in 1687," in Isaac Joslin Cox, ed., *The Journeys of Réné Robert Cavelier,
Sieur de La Salle,* I, 266–67. Joutel ("Relation," p. 191) disputes Douay's
claim that there were nine or ten families among the French colonists and
challenges his accuracy on several other points.
9 Joutel, "Relation," pp. 327–30, 369.

Nika, Saget, and two whose names he cannot remember—evidently to keep them from leaking word of the plot to slay La Salle. Then, he says, James and Duhaut lay in ambush for La Salle as the leader approached the hunting camp with Père Anastase, and Duhaut shot him.

Pierre tells of the second blood purge as though it occurred after the departure of Joutel and his six companions on their march toward Canada. Duhaut, having seized command over those who remained, was slain by James two or three days later. Several days after that, James was slain by Rutre, and, somewhat later, Rutre died at the hands of "a surgeon," whose name is not given.

Such a different version might be written off to scrambled childhood memories but for Pierre's claim of a subsequent relationship with this surgeon. Fearing that he would be slain as the others had been, Pierre says, the surgeon fled to the Indians called Toho, whom he accompanied on a raid against their enemies, the Paouites and the Temerlouans.[10] Pierre claims that he himself went on that raid, riding a horse that the surgeon had provided. It is implied that he saw the surgeon fall in battle; he says that he escaped a like fate by fleeing on the surgeon's horse.

Joutel has generally been accepted as the most reliable of the chroniclers of La Salle's somewhat confused and mysterious last venture. From La Salle's own accounts, his brother's, the Abbé Cavelier, and Father Anastase Douay's, one is apt to suspect motives of concealing, rather than revealing, what actually happened. Although Joutel was not privy to all of La Salle's schemes and maneuvering, his veracity in relating events of which he was knowledgeable has never been seriously questioned. Whether it should be so now is problematical.

Certainly, the answers recorded for the Talons in response to the interrogations are not entirely reliable. The interrogator at one point takes note of their vagueness, and they err in details such as the time spent with the Indians and in Mexico and the number of soldiers of the various Spanish expeditions. There are several factors, aside from the radically different version of La Salle's death, that may raise doubts as to the complete credibility of this record: (1) being quite young, they may not have understood all that they saw and heard, and their memories may have become confused; (2) their entry into Indian life was traumatic, especially that of Jean-Baptiste, who witnessed his mother's death in the Fort Saint-Louis massacre; (3) having lived almost a decade among Indians and Spaniards, their facility in French may have been impaired; (4) the answers were given orally and written down by some-

10 Concerning identity of these natives, see Schuetz, "Ethnological Data."

one else, possibly with some distortion in the process. Questions inevitably arise, therefore, as to how much of what is recorded in the Interrogations actually reflects what the Talons intended.

Joutel's "Relation," like Bernal Díaz del Castillo's history of the Mexican Conquest, was written to set straight the record put forth by other chroniclers. Besides a spurious account attributed to Henri de Tonti, there was Father Douay's narrative, published in 1693 in Father Chrétien Le Clercq's *Premier établissement.* Joutel took issue with some of the misstatements therein.[11]

Pierre Talon seems to settle in Joutel's favor one of the points of disagreement. Where Douay claims to have buried La Salle "as well as I could" and to have raised a cross over the grave, Joutel says the body was left to the ravages of wild beasts.[12] Pierre's statement that the Indians brought to the Cenis village the gold pieces La Salle had on his person when he was slain suggests that the body was not buried.

Finally, seven Frenchmen, headed by Joutel, departed for the post on the Illinois while at least seven others remained alive among the Cenis: Pierre Talon, Pierre Meunier, James, Rutre, L'Archevêque, Grollet, and the man from Provence; if Talon is credited, the surgeon also was alive. In any event, the number quickly dwindled. James and Rutre were killed[13]—and the surgeon, as Pierre tells it. The Provençal either died or, having become thoroughly Indianized, did not associate with the other Frenchmen. The other four, although living in close proximity to each other, paired off, L'Archevêque with Grollet, Talon with Meunier. It was the first two whose longing for civilization led eventually to the Spanish rescue of all the Frenchmen among both the Hasinai and the Karankawa, except the Provençal.

The Hasinai, L'Archevêque and Grollet later recalled, had offered to take them and two other Frenchmen, not identified, to visit the Spanish priest among the Jumano Indians in the Big Bend of the Río Grande. Passing near Fort Saint-Louis on the way, the Frenchmen asked leave of the natives to go there to see how their countrymen fared and thus came on the scene of the massacre. Claiming to have buried fourteen bodies,

11 Joutel, "Relation," pp. 190–91.
12 Douay, "Narrative," p. 224; Joutel, "Relation," p. 331.
13 While looking for a mission site among the Cenis in 1690, says Fray Damián Massanet (letter in Herbert Eugene Bolton, ed., *Spanish Exploration in the Southwest, 1542–1706,* p. 379), the Spaniards were shown by the Indians "two dead bodies of Frenchmen who had shot each other with carbines." Alonso de León ("Diario," in Lino Gómez Canedo, ed., *Primeras exploraciones y poblamiento de Texas [1686–1694],* p. 114) says they were shown the graves, rather than the bodies, and does not mention the cause of death.

they returned to live among the Hasinai without ever visiting the Jumanos' country. By those natives, L'Archevêque and Grollet dispatched to the Spaniards of Chihuahua a plea for rescue.

The area of the Spanish search, meanwhile, narrowed to the bay where the Rivas-Iriarte expedition had found the wreckage of La Salle's ships in 1687. Alonso de León, marching from Coahuila and guided by a French deserter, found the devastated French fort on April 22, 1689, a few months after the Karankawa had massacred all the adult occupants. In response to a letter the Spanish officer sent to the Indians, L'Archevêque and Grollet surrendered themselves to León and duly gave depositions in which La Salle's murder was attributed to "an English gunner"—James.[14]

On reaching Mexico, the two Frenchmen were sent to Spain aboard the ship of Andrés de Pez, who carried the famous "Memorial" advocating settlement of Pensacola Bay to safeguard it from the French. Reaching Spain in January, 1690, they spent the next thirty months in the royal prison awaiting dispotion of their case. The French captives posed an enigma for the Junta de Guerra, which was fearful that their knowledge of Spanish territory would be damaging if carried to France. The council at last granted their request to return to America in the service of the Spanish king. Yet, the Talons reveal, the two men were still in irons when they saw them upon their return to Mexico.[15]

Officials of New Spain, meanwhile, moved to secure their own claim to the region later known as Texas. León and Fray Damián Massanet again penetrated the Tejas land in 1690, established a mission among the natives, and returned five more French survivors from among the Hasinai and the Karankawa: Meunier, age twenty; Pierre Talon, now fourteen; Talon's older sister, Marie-Magdelaine, sixteen; and their two younger brothers, Lucien (birth date not known) and Robert, who was not yet six. Like L'Archevêque and Grollet, all of them were marked with grotesque Indian tattoos on their faces and various parts of their bodies. The two smaller boys had forgotten their native language; only their older sister could converse with them.[16]

14 Alonso de León, "Declaración," in Canedo, *Primeras exploraciones,* p. 109; Weddle, *Wilderness Manhunt,* p. 196. L'Archevêque here substantiates Pierre Talon's assignment of a part in La Salle's murder to James. It is possible that L'Archevêque misled Joutel concerning the murders in the hunting camp.
15 Concerning L'Archevêque and Grollet's trip to Spain and their later life as New Mexico soldier–settlers, see Weddle, *Wilderness Manhunt,* pp. 235–37, 249–52.
16 Ibid., p. 214; Alonso de León to the viceroy, Río Grande, July 12, 1690, in Canedo, *Primeras exploraciones,* p. 157. Birth dates of the four older Talon

At the flooding Río Grande, Meunier was sent ahead in the custody of Captain Gregorio de Salinas Varona, that he might proceed to Mexico and give his deposition. The document, although remarkable for its clarity, does nothing to dispel the confusion concerning the French settlement attempt or La Salle's murder; which he seems to attribute to Duhaut. Meunier was sent back the following year to San Francisco de Coahuila, the present Monclova site, to serve as interpreter for a new expedition to Texas, led by Governor Domingo Terán de los Ríos. It was this *entrada* that brought out Eustache Bréman, the paymaster's son, who seems to have been taken in by the Talon family, and Jean-Baptiste Talon, age twelve.[17]

Strangely, there is no indication that the Spaniards interrogated any of the Talons. There is no evidence of official concern that they would ever transmit information to France that would be inimical to Spanish interests. It was a serious oversight. The children were taken as servants into the household of the viceroy, Gaspar de la Cerda Sandoval Silva y Mendoza, Conde de Galve. Not until Pierre and Jean-Baptiste returned to France was the latter's eyewitness account of the Fort Saint-Louis massacre recorded.

From Jean-Baptiste we learn that there was dissension among those persons left at the settlement, as well as those proceeding toward Canada. The Karankawa, finding the French without a strong leader and so caught up in their own squabbles that they were heedless of the possibility of Indian treachery, fell upon them at Christmastime, 1688. Jean Talon saw his mother slain before his eyes as the Indian women, moved by the thought of the French children's tender years, carried them away to their village. The Indian women also sought to spare Madame Barbier, who, after her previous miscarriage, had conceived again and was nursing a three-month-old infant, the first European child born in Texas. The Indian women's compassion for the mother and child was not shared by the native men. The mother was slain first. The baby, counterpart of the English Roanoke Colony's Virginia Dare, died at the hands of a Karankawa warrior who held it by a foot and bashed its head against a tree.

Mystery still surrounds the Italian whom the Talons say was taken

---

children are given in Tanguay, *Dictionnaire généalogique*, 1, 558. Pierre Meunier ("Declaración," UT archives, transcript 69, AGI, Mexico 616) gives his own age as twenty.

17 Terán's diary of this expedition is printed in Canedo, *Primeras exploraciones*, pp. 169–223; Massanet's is on pp. 229–54. Concerning Meunier's (Pedro Muñi) service as interpreter, see p. 245.

by León on the 1690 expedition. Spanish sources fail to mention him. The Talons, who manifest clear understanding of Spanish territorial jealousy, say that the mistrust of the adult French captives, L'Archevêque and Grollet, extended also to this Italian. He was imprisoned in San Juan de Ulúa's dungeons, where the Talons later saw him. He died there before the brothers' final departure from Mexico.

The Talons, understandably, are less than precise in describing the route followed from Texas to Mexico City, and they continue to be confused about time spans. In less than a month (rather than two) from the rescue of Marie-Magdelaine and the two younger boys, they reached "Caouil"—San Francisco de Coahuila, or Monclova. They had crossed the Río Grande at one of the prominent fords near present day Guerrero, Coahuila, and paused briefly at the missions of San Salvador and San Bernardino at Candela. Passing within sight of high mountains, they proceeded on horseback to San Luis Potosí, which they likened in size to La Rochelle; and thence to the capital, probably arriving in late summer.

A search of documents pertaining to the viceroy Conde de Galve for mention of the French children who were his household servants for the next several years has been fruitless. The Talons observed a populous and well-built city of *casas de terrada,* the flat-roofed masonry houses for which the Spanish colonies were noted. The streets swarmed with horse- and mule-drawn coaches, the visible status symbols that set the ruling class apart from the masses. Beneath this pompous façade, however, lay a seething cauldron of resentment that, on June 8, 1692, boiled over in a rock-throwing melée. The oppressed *indios,* aggravated by hunger resulting from a small corn crop, put their Spanish overlords in fear of their lives.

A writer of the next century [18] relates that the viceroy and his wife, Doña Elvira de Toledo, at the time were at "San Francisco" and remained there, out of harm's way, while the rioters burned the viceregal palace and municipal buildings. The Talons, however, reveal that the count and countess escaped through a palace window to take refuge in the archbishop's palace, while the prelate and his clergy staged a peace march through the streets, only to become the target of the rock throwers. Somehow mollified by the Creole Count of Santiago, without use of force the natives were banished to the suburbs, our eighteenth-century writer relates, and they were forbidden their native drink, pulque. The Talons report a more severe punishment, at least for the pri-

18 Pedro Alonso O'Crouley, *A Description of the Kingdom of New Spain, 1774,* p. 134.

mary instigators: flogging and death sentences. The brothers voiced no prediction as to the result of such unrest. Yet they observe that the spirit of revolt was nurtured among the Creoles no less than among the Indians and mixed bloods, for the ruling classes deprived them of all civil and military offices. It was information in which the French ministry was vitally interested.

As the Interrogations bring out, their entry into Spanish service as soldiers in the Armada de Barlovento, or Windward Fleet, came a short time before the ailing Conde de Galve ended his term (early in 1696) and embarked for Spain. Pierre, Jean-Baptiste, and Lucien, ages nineteen, sixteen, and probably fourteen, respectively, proceeded to Veracruz for assignment on the *Santo Cristo,* the *almiranta* (admiral's flagship) of the armada.[19] The count, succeeded in office in February, sailed for Spain with Doña Elvira, Marie-Magdelaine, now twenty-two, and Robert, who was only eleven.

Patrolling the Gulf of Mexico on January 7, 1697, the *Santo Cristo* was captured on the approach to Havana by the French warship *Bon,* whose captain was Patoulet, of Désaugiers's squadron. The three young Frenchmen from the Spanish ship were taken first to Saint-Domingue (Haiti), where the squadron commander presented his amazing captives to the intendant. The brothers were by no means pleased at these developments. Their thoughts were of Marie-Magdelaine and young Robert, who had proceeded to Spain with the count and countess. The boys demanded to be taken there also, but Désaugiers and the intendant vetoed the idea. Instead, they were sent to France in the charge of Sieur de Boissieux, a marine lieutenant.

Boissieux, probing for whatever information the three brothers might reveal, found them less than cooperative. They described their rescue from the Texas Indians by the Spaniards and revealed their sojourn in the viceroy's household but knew "nothing of the [Spanish] mines that they wish to tell." Eustache Bréman and Pierre Meunier, they disclosed, were still in Mexico. It was exactly a year after the capture of the Spanish ship that the lieutenant reported to the minister of marine, Louis Pontchartrain. It appears that in the meantime the brothers' initial anger had been mollified with a promise that every effort would be made to reunite them with Marie-Magdelaine and

19 A 1685 list of warships of the Armada de Barlovento shows three frigates called *Santo Cristo: Santo Cristo de San Román,* with eighteen guns, which as noted previously (p. 146), was lost in the 1693 Atlantic hurricane; *Santo Cristo,* ten guns; and *Santo Cristo de Leso,* six swivel guns (AGI, Mexico 91, ramo 3).

Robert. Boissieux, however, insisted that Pierre and Jean-Baptiste enlist in the French marine service, and they were assigned as soldiers
in Feugerolles's company, in which he himself was serving. Lucien,
still too young for French military service, was placed as a servant
at Oléron.[20]

On receipt of Boissieux's letter, Pontchartrain responded immediately with instructions to Desclouzeaux, the intendant at Brest, to in-
terrogate the brothers, and he included a list of questions to be asked.
There was good reason for his interest. Pierre Le Moyne, Sieur d'Iberville, was shaping up a new voyage to the Gulf of Mexico, designed to
renew the enterprise initiated by La Salle.

Joutel's prolix journal already had come to the attention of the minister, who studied it carefully. Despite his promise to return it within six
weeks, he sent it on to Iberville, and Iberville took it with him on his
first voyage to Mississippi. Not until five years later was it returned
to Joutel—who, preferring not to "incur new risks," had declined
Pontchartrain's urging to make the voyage.[21]

Iberville also must have had on his first voyage a transcript of the
Talon Interrogations, but not the Talons. Pontchartrain had hoped to
send the brothers on the voyage, for the information they had given indicated their potential usefulness. There was still some confusion in
French minds over the location of La Salle's settlement in relation to the
Mississippi, but the Talons held the distinction of having traveled overland from the settlement to the City of Mexico. "It would not be too
difficult for them to make this trip [again] if they could find the same
nations with whom they had lived, for they still remember enough of
their languages to make themselves understood . . . not only by the nations with whom they have lived but even by other nations, by means of
signs." In the minister's view, that passage from the transcript, translated in the following pages, contained the crux of the whole inquiry. It
also portended the Talon brothers' role in French exploration and settlement of the Gulf region for years to come.

Yet Pontchartrain was frustrated in his design to embark the repatri-
ates with Iberville on his first voyage. The brothers were on their way
from Brest to La Rochelle aboard the ship *Ville d'Embden,* and the minister instructed the intendant, Michel Bégon, to send them to Iberville
upon their arrival. Bégon did not act promptly enough; Iberville failed
to seize the initiative, and Pierre and Jean-Baptiste transferred to the

20 "Lettre du sieur de Boissieux," in Margry, *Découvertes,* IV, 43–44.
21 Weddle, "La Salle's Survivors," p. 423, and sources cited therein.

Gironde and sailed from the port on June 7 without Iberville's having talked with them.[22]

Iberville departed from La Rochelle on his first voyage to Louisiana on September 5, 1698, with neither the Talon brothers nor Joutel. He did have Father Anastase Douay, who, having witnessed La Salle's futile quest for the Mississippi, celebrated mass on March 3, 1699, on the occasion of Iberville's discovery of that river. Douay, however, was a source of aggravation, especially when he lost his breviary and made a petulant scene, accusing the Bayogoula Indians, who were hosts to the French, of having stolen it. When Iberville returned to France, the priest chose to return to his monastery in Paris and to have no further involvement in the American colony.[23] Thus he fades from history.

In the meantime, Pierre and Jean-Baptiste Talon had been placed in one of two Canadian companies to be held in readiness for Iberville's second voyage. Their company commander was Louis Juchereau de Saint-Denis. They sailed on October 17, 1699, aboard the *Gironde* and anchored in Biloxi Bay on January 8, 1700.[24]

The part the brothers played at Fort Maurepas and in various expeditions from there during the two years before their return to France is left to conjecture. They may have been among the twenty-two Canadians who accompanied Saint-Denis and Bienville on their overland trek in March and April, 1700, from the Taensa village at Lake Saint Joseph on the Mississippi to the Red River near present-day Natchitoches, Louisiana. The journey was made with a view to establishing contact with the Hasinai with whom Pierre had lived for three years. The brothers may have been among the fourteen Canadians who in August that year followed Saint-Denis up the Red River to the Natchitoches village and thence to the Cadodacho (Kadohadacho), but again the record fails.

Reference to them is found in the journal of Father Jacques Gravier, who had come down the Mississippi from the Illinois late in 1700 and remained at Fort Boulaye (on the Mississippi below New Orleans) until Iberville's arrival on his third voyage. The priest mentions two Frenchmen at Fort Biloxi who had been members of La Salle's expedition and were captured by the Spaniards: "It is from those two Frenchmen that

22 Ibid.; Margry, *Découvertes,* IV, 63.
23 Carl A. Brasseaux, trans. and ed., *A Comparative View of French Louisiana, 1699 and 1762; The Journals of Pierre Le Moyne d'Iberville and Jean-Jacques-Blaise d'Abbadie,* pp. 40 n., 67, 68, 73.
24 Sieur de Bégon, "Rolle des canadiens passez de Plaisance en France pour servir sur les vaisseux que doivent aller à Mississipy pendent la putz, Anée 1699 avec leur solde par mois" Rochefort, May 5, 1699, manuscript copy, UT archives.

our people learned what had become of the sorry remnants of that great expedition of Monsieur de la Salle." [25]

Iberville, returning to France from his third voyage in the spring of 1702, evidently had the Talon brothers aboard his vessel. Jérôme Pontchartrain, having assumed his father's duties as minister of marine, had written to Michel Bégon the previous August: "There are in the department of Port-Louis [*sic*] two soldiers who are returning from the Mississippi to look for their woman. I am ordering the Sieur Hocquart to send them to La Rochelle. It is necessary that you have them embark on the vessel that the Sieur d'Iberville commands." [26]

The woman referred to, it would seem, was their sister, Marie-Magdelaine, who had gone to Spain with the Condessa de Galve in 1697. Marie-Magdelaine, from all indications, had returned to France shortly afterward but had failed to make contact with her brothers. The record shows that she had married Pierre Simon of the Saint Paul section of Paris and, in 1699, bore him a son. [27]

Two years later, after their return from Mississippi, according to Iberville, Pierre and Jean-Baptiste Talon were "in the prisons of Portugal." How they happened to be there is not explained; nor is it known when they gained their liberty. This is the last mention we have of Jean-Baptiste. Pierre reappears some years later on the banks of the Río Grande in company with his brother Robert and his old commander, Saint-Denis. He at last has been called on to retrace the road linking French territory with New Spain.

The year was 1714. Saint-Denis, guided by Pierre Talon, whose facial tattoos from a quarter century ago still served as his passport, had crossed Texas from the Natchitoches village in quest of Spanish trade. In late September the previous year, Saint-Denis had left Mobile with twenty-four Canadians and a number of Indians. Crossing Lake Pontchartrain by canoe, they ascended the Mississippi River, then the Red River as far as Natchitoches, where they left their canoes and set off into the land of the Hasinai. There they sought the Spanish priest Francisco Hidalgo, who in 1711 had written a letter to the governor of French Louisiana to inquire of the possibilities of renewing the Franciscan mission-

25 Jacques Gravier, "Journal," in Reubon Gold Thwaites, ed., *The Jesuit Relations and Allied Documents: Travels and Explorations of the Jesuit Missionaries in New France, 1610–1791*, LXV, 175. Thwaites (p. 270, note 33) erroneously concludes that "the Frenchmen at Biloxi were probably deserters from La Salle's forces, who had gone to live among the savages."
26 Minister of Marine to Michel Bégon, Versailles, August 10, 1701, in Margry, *Découvertes*, IV, 496–97.
27 Tanguay, *Dictionnaire généalogique*, VII, 187.

ary effort among those Indians. More than two years later, one copy of the letter came to the hands of Antoine de La Mothe, Sieur de Cadillac, who was vitally interested in renewing trade relations with the Spanish colonists. Such was the motivation of the Saint-Denis expedition.

The episode has been badly garbled by those interpreters who have attempted to follow the spurious relation of André Penigault. Penigault claims to have been a member of the expedition himself, a matter denied by the commandant at Presidio de San Juan Bautista del Río Grande. Captain Diego Ramón reported the arrival of Saint-Denis and his companions to Father Hidalgo, then at Querétaro: "I communicate to Your Reverence that in this presidio are four Frenchmen: a captain called Luis de Sn. Dionisio, another Pedro Talon and the other Roberto, who were among those rescued by General Alonso de León. The captain does not speak Spanish, nor does his other companion [Médard Jallot]." The presidio's treasurer, who spoke French, examined the visitors as to their purpose. "I say," Ramón continued, "that if His Majesty does not intervene and the villages of the Naquitoies are not settled, the French will be masters of all this land."[28]

By such a threat the Spaniards again were moved to action. In response, the 1716 expedition to renew the moribund missionary effort in Hasinai country was mounted, with Saint-Denis, newly married to Ramón's granddaughter, Manuela Sánchez Navarro, as a key participant.

The Talon brothers had long since slipped back across the Río Grande to follow the dim Spanish trail to eastern Texas, proceeding thence by wilderness streams and tidal lakes to Mobile. They carried their captain's report—a written message, dated February 21, 1715, to be supplemented orally. Saint-Denis, whom the Spaniards still regarded suspiciously, advised Cadillac, "I do not wish to write you fully of all that has happened here; the bearers, whom I have sent away in secret, will tell you the better part."[29]

The "better part" is not specified, but it must have had to do with the map Cadillac sent to the minister, showing Saint-Denis's road from the Red River to the Spanish settlement of San Juan Bautista. It showed, sixty leagues from San Juan Bautista, the silver mines of Boca de Leones (Villadama, Nuevo León), where, it was said, wealthy merchants were eager to purchase French goods with unmarked silver.

28 Diego Ramón to Francisco Hidalgo, July 22, 1714, Archivo Santa Cruz de Querétaro, K, legajo 1, no. 7 (typescript, Bancroft Library, University of California, Berkeley); Weddle, "La Salle's Survivors," p. 431.
29 "Extrait des lettres de Lamothe-Cadillac, gouverneur de la Louisiane et de Saint-Denis" (1716), in Margry, *Découvertes,* VI, 195.

A later report was brought by a French sailor who had encountered Saint-Denis in Mexico City. It told of rumored Spanish plans to re-occupy Texas, possibly with settlements on Espíritu Santo Bay, the Madelaine River—"called Guadalupe by the Spaniards"—and even the Red River. Cadillac sought geographical clarification from "the two men named Talon," who had just "returned from the discovery." They reported that the Madelaine was navigable by pirogue a hundred leagues inland. "If the Spaniards have not settled the Baye du Saint-Esprit," says the summary of Cadillac's letter, "it would be a politic move to keep other nations from knowledge of their riches."[30] For the French, the politic move was to block Spanish expansion as best they could, which they sought to do by occupying the Natchitoches site in January, 1717.

Implicit in the Saint-Denis affair is a scheme to maneuver the two colonial governments, French and Spanish, to serve Saint-Denis's personal ends. He doubtless considered the Talon brothers ideally suited for his purposes, for they, like himself, had a foot in both camps. Whether they comprehended the scheme and how they were being used is not known; yet, with their help, Saint-Denis succeeded in bringing the Spaniards and the French face to face on the Red River, where they might carry on the contraband trade of his design and to his benefit. Rather than bolstering the French claim to Texas, as the Spaniards feared, he actually quitclaimed the territory to Spain.

Having fulfilled this historic role, the Talons now fade into obscurity. One source records that Jean-Baptiste remained in Louisiana and that Pierre died in France. Robert is known to have settled at Mobile, where he married Jeanne Prot, or Praux, and fathered children in 1719 and 1721. He was a carpenter by trade, owning, according to a 1721 census, five black slaves, one Indian slave, and two horned cattle. Nothing further is heard of Lucien *fils* after he went to Oléron to work as a servant. Whether or not Marie-Magdelaine was ever reunited with her brothers, she probably returned to her native Canada, where her son was married at Charlesbourg in 1719.[31]

As for the other survivors of the La Salle colony, Eustache Bréman remained in Mexico after the Talons' departure, and nothing more is heard of him. Meunier, L'Archevêque, and Grollet became settlers in New Mexico. As late as 1717, rumors persisted that "there are still some French families among the Indians from La Salle's time whom the sav-

30 Ibid., p. 198.
31 Tanguay, *Dictionnaire généalogique,* VII, 187.

ages have not destroyed."[32] The basis for such a report may have been the Provençal, who had married an Hasinai and whose fate remains unknown.

In view of the somewhat tragic events of their childhood, it is remarkable that the Talons were able to supply, on the eve of Iberville's first sailing for Mississippi, such a comprehensive and comprehensible account of their experiences. Having suffered the early loss of their parents and endured Indian captivity, servitude in an alien land, and separation from their siblings, they embarked at this point on a new phase of their lives: service to France as soldiers, guides, and interpreters in the New World. As they looked back on their previous life, so fraught with bizarre occurrences, they manifested no inclination for bitterness toward the Indians who made them orphans. Although acknowledging the Karankawas' cruelty and barbarity, they speak of these natives with sympathy and understanding, recalling that they themselves were always treated with love and kindness.

Only rarely do the Talons indulge in blame fixing, and that toward La Salle, rather than the Indians. The leader's callous disregard for his followers is suggested as the Talons relate the loss of one of the Duhaut brothers, a likely motivation for his assassination. Duhaut, they say, was not the only one who perished on the same journey, implying that on this and other marches with La Salle, the survival rate was less than half. La Salle, therefore, is charged with responsibility not only for his own death but also for the Fort Saint-Louis massacre; never would there have been war with the natives had he not taken their canoes and refused them even trinkets in exchange. "Nothing, the brothers believed, was easier than winning the Indians' friendship."

The Indians left their mark on the Talons' faces; the tattoos remained with them the rest of their lives, provoking curious stares from Europeans seeing them for the first time. La Salle's mark was of a different sort, less visible, but just as enduring. Of the two, the inner scars surely were the more painful.

32 "Relation par le sieur Derbanne," Isle Dauphine, November 1, 1717, in Margry, *Découvertes,* VI, 209.

Voyage
to the Mississippi
through the
Gulf of Mexico

[Translated by

ANN LINDA BELL

and Annotated by

ROBERT S. WEDDLE]

Brest, the 14th of February, 1698

Memorial on the questions asked of the two Canadians
    who are soldiers in Feuguerolles's Company

[[Questions on the Memorial sent by Monsieg^r. Pontchartrain]]

Answers

These soldiers are two brothers, named Pierre and Jean-Baptiste Talon,
natives of Quebec in Canada, New France, and sons of the late Lucien
Talon, carpenter, and Isabelle [Planteau], who were residents there.[1]

    They left Canada with their father and mother to come to France
when very young. They are unable to tell precisely when, but they say
that it was a short while before the departure of M^r. de la Salle on the
last voyage that he made to Louisiana, because, having disembarked at
La Rochelle and having gone to Paris, they enlisted with the said S^r. de
la Salle, with their father and mother, two younger brothers, and two

---

1 The cover sheet in the Archives Nationales, Outre-Mer (DFC, Louisiane 3)
  contains this caption: "Report of Two Canadian Soldiers who made La
  Salle's Voyage to the Mississippi and have returned thence in 1698." A note in
  a different hand observes, "This piece is very interesting for history. It ends
  with a too-short glossary of some Indian words."

sisters to follow him on the aforementioned voyage, and all returned to La Rochelle to embark with him, having been in France only about two months.

The said S^r. de la Salle had three ships; namely, the *Joly*, with 50 Cannon or thereabouts, on which he embarked; the *Aimable*, with about 20 Cannon, on which the said Talons and the rest of their family embarked; and one other, the name of which they have forgotten [the *Belle*].

1st question: How many men landed with S^r. de la Salle?

About 300, among whom there were three Religious of the Order of St. Francis and two priests, one of whom was the said S^r. de la Salle's brother, and nine women.

They set foot on land at the Baye du St. Esprit [Espíritu Santo Bay] or Ascension in the Gulf of Mexico, because the *Aimable* ran aground there and was lost a cannonshot from shore, by the pilot's fault, according to what they heard tell. Had it not been for this accident, the said S^r. de la Salle intended going farther, to look for the mouth of the Mississipy River. He sent back to France only the ship *Joly*, with her crew. She was commanded by M. [Tanguy Le Gallois] de Beaujeu, who set sail soon after the landing was made. The said S^r. de la Salle kept the other ship, but they took so little care of her that subsequently she also was lost in the Bay.[2]

2nd: The nature of the country where they landed; whether there was a river and, if so, its width and depth at its mouth; whether there were any lakes, and whether the land consisted of prairies or mountains.

The country is flat and has an agreeable aspect—diversified, with woods and prairies or savannas—and appears very fertile. There was flowing into the bay a river whose length or name they did not know. It was a long pistol shot wide and five to six fathoms deep at its mouth. The said

2 La Salle, failing to find the Mississippi at the map location of the Río Escondido, established at Matagorda Bay a base from which to look further. This bay later was mistakenly called Espíritu Santo. The *Aimable* was lost on February 20, 1685; Beaujeu and the *Joly* departed on March 12. The *Belle* was later lost in a squall. A fourth vessel, the *Saint-François,* had been seized by Spanish pirates off Hispaniola.

S^r. de la Salle ascended this river with all his people,[3] using for this purpose some canoes of the savages he found there and some longboats from the ships. About 12 leagues from the mouth, he had built five or six houses of earth and wood to lodge his people, making no other fortification than a battery of eight cannon, which cast terror and fright into the savages' hearts every time they were fired, since the savages had never heard them before.

They lived in this dwelling about a year; that is, until the time of his [La Salle's] death,[4] which will be told later.

During all that time, the said S^r. de la Salle went to explore farther into the country with a detachment of 25 to 30 men, armed with guns, pistols, and sabers or straight swords, each with his own supply of powder and lead. They lived on the abundance of the hunt, for the buffalo [*boeufs sauvages*], deer, roebuck, and other wild animals were plentiful in the whole country, in the woods as well as on the plains. There were also all sorts of game, mainly turkey, partridges, parrots, ducks, plovers,[5] doves, woodcocks, and a prodigious number of little birds of all kinds, which were very good to eat. There are also cranes and swans in large numbers on the rivers and ponds. There are also large numbers of eagles, crows, and other birds of prey and of pillage and also a very particular species that is red all over, a red the color of blood, as also lions, tigers, bears, and wolves.

The hunters of the said S^r. de la Salle discovered the mouth of another beautiful river within this same bay while they were pursuing buffalo along the seashore. It is a musket shot wide and 15 to 20 fathoms deep at its mouth; and, in the nearly 20 leagues that they ascended, it appeared to extend far into the land. It was bordered by woods of very tall trees, but it was full of caimans or crocodiles, as were all the others. The said S^r. de la Salle named it the Rivière aux Cannes [River of Canes], as much because of quantities of beautiful reeds [*Cannes*] or little canes with which the savages made their arrows as because there are many ducks [*Canards*] on the river.[6]

3 This was Garcitas Creek, flowing into Lavaca Bay, an offshoot of Matagorda Bay. The Lavaca River also flows into Lavaca Bay about five miles east of Garcitas Creek.

4 Although the answers recorded for the Talons exaggerate time spans in other instances, this one is reduced. The move to this location occurred in June, 1685, La Salle's death on March 19, 1687. The Fort Saint-Louis massacre is judged to have taken place around Christmas, 1688.

5 *Outardes*, or bustards. The French often applied the name to Canada geese. See Part I, note 33 to translation.

6 Henri Joutel ("Relation de Henri Joutel," in Pierre Margry, ed., *Découvertes et établissements de français dans l'ouest et dans le sud de l'Amérique septentrio-*

There is in all the land a great number of large saltwater as well as freshwater ponds and several small rivers and large streams, most of them abounding in fish. They are also full of crocodiles of which one must be wary. One must no less be on one's guard against the fury of these buffalo. When one had been wounded, it chased the hunters, even lying in wait with determination at the foot of the trees that they were obliged to climb and trying to uproot them with their feet until they had received the fatal shot. Their flesh is very good to eat, but they are quite different from those [cattle] of Europe, being much larger and having a big hump on the neck, their head and their eyes bigger in proportion to their body, and, instead of fur, [they have] a kind of wool, which could be spun. This wool is much longer on the head than elsewhere, so that it gives them the appearance of having a head of hair that almost covers their eyes. Their horns are smaller [than those of European cattle] and very sharp, and they have only a very small tail. All of them, male as well as female, are of a reddish-black color. The Indians dress their hides like those of the chamois, which renders them soft as cloth.

The forests and the woods are of oaks, nuts, pines, and several other kinds of trees, some of which are extremely tall, but they are unable to give the names. There are squirrels in abundance in those trees, especially the pines; and all the rivers are bordered with palms and mulberry trees, which produce much fruit.

3. On advancing inland, what sort of country did they find?

Invariably flat and diversified, as has been said, with forests, woods, and prairies, in fact the most beautiful in the world, traversed by several rivers, of which a number are deep and could carry boats. This whole territory is very temperate. Hardly ever is it too hot or too cold and winter lasts but a short time. This mild climate accounts for the fact that the savages generally live to be very old and nearly always possess perfect health. They also have a marvelous knowledge of the different properties of the medicinal herbs that abound in the whole country and can easily heal themselves of illnesses and wounds that befall them, since there was no professional physician among them. It is usually the old

---

nale [1614–1754], III 261–62) describes the two-fork Rivière aux Cannes in a way that identifies it as the combined Lavaca and Navidad rivers. Concerning the Talons' observations on the flora and fauna, see Del Weniger, "Natural History," in the commentaries that follow.

people who apply their remedies and cure their ailments; and the Talons assure us that, during all the time they stayed among them, they saw no one die of illness.

4. Whether or not they found savages and whether they had communication with them.

The whole country is peopled with savages who are all divided into small nations, each bearing its own name and having a particular language, each different from the other. The aforementioned Talons had communication with two of these nations; specifically, Pierre Talon with the Cenis, which is the most gentle and the most civil of all the nations they have known. This nation lives about one hundred leagues inland. These Cenis Indians have a village and are divided into families in wood houses covered with straw. M^r. de la Salle made friends with them and took the said Pierre Talon there so he could learn their language, which he did perfectly, having stayed five or six consecutive years among them, until the time the Spaniards arrived, as will be said later on. But he has almost forgotten that language because he was for about ten years with the Spaniards in Mexico, where they took him and where he learned their language.[7]

Jean-Baptiste Talon, the younger of these two brothers, his two younger brothers [Lucien and Robert], and one sister [Marie-Magdelaine] also stayed an equal time span and even longer in the nation of the Clamcoehs [Karankawas], a people much more cruel and barbaric than the Cenis or any of the other nations. They inhabit the seashore, without any villages or fixed dwellings, continually roaming, living by hunting and fishing, and camping where night overtakes them in makeshift shelters erected then and there, with two forked branches and one crossbar, which they cover with buffalo skins prepared for this purpose. With rushes they enclose this shelter, which is common with them and the other nomad nations of the country, as well as all those found from the seashore to the Cenis village. The Cenis, however, cultivate the soil and grow maize or corn, beans, and pumpkins of several kinds, with other

---

7 Pierre actually lived about three years among the Cenis, almost seven among the Spaniards in Mexico and while serving in the Armada de Barlovento. Later on, it is said that Pierre and Jean-Baptiste remembered enough of the native languages to make themselves understood. See Schuetz, "Ethnological Data," on the Hasinai (Cenis) and Clamcoëhs (Karankawas), among whom they lived, and on other tribes mentioned.

kinds of vegetables and roots, whose names they do not know. They grow tobacco, but little, and only for their own use. They also raise horses, which they use only to transport their kill, since they are obliged to go very far to hunt the buffalo. [These animals] are very wild and habitually avoid the inhabited places so that they are found no nearer the villages than 15 or 20 leagues. These buffalo have such a sensitive sense of smell that they can scent hunters from far off, when they approach from upwind, and run away. So it is necessary, if one wants to catch them, to approach them from downwind. But once one succeeds in killing one in a herd, either with arrows or with gunshots, all the others surround it and stand looking at it, so that one can easily kill several more of them before they run away. This nation of the Cenis comprises about a thousand persons and is one of the most numerous.

About 12 leagues above the Cenis, going inland, there is another village whose nation is called Ayenny [Hainai], of which Pierre Talon also has knowledge, having communicated with them. They are allies of the Cenis and have the same language and the same manner of living, but they are fewer in number. He heard them say that, farther inland, there are several other villages of diverse small nations. They knew of no other nation more numerous than the Cenis. He heard them say only that there is another nation that is much larger, named Canotino [Kanahotino], which is continually making war on them, but which has no fixed settlements.

All the nations that are along the seashore and up to the village of the Cenis are the most barbaric and cruel, and one can trust them only when they have proved they deserve it and when one is stronger than they are. Those who live farther inland than the Cenis territory are more humane, even helpful, and of easy access; and they extend hospitality to the Europeans who lose their way hunting or under other circumstances.

These different nations often war against each other, as will be said later, and have no other arms than bows and arrows, (which, instead of iron, have at the tip a sort of sharpened piece of stone, fish bones, or fish teeth), and clubs, because they do not know how to forge iron. But their arrows are not poisoned as are those of the Caribs and other savage peoples who are found among the Antilles Islands.

All these nations have the custom of going every morning at daybreak to throw themselves into the nearest river, almost never neglecting to do so, no matter what season, even when the water is frozen. In this case, they often make a hole in the ice and dive into it. They run with all their might, going to the river and also returning, and then they stand in front of the large fire prepared for the purpose. And they stand shaking their arms, their thighs, and their legs for a while until they are thoroughly dry. Then they wrap themselves in buffalo hides rubbed soft like chamois leather, which they use as robes, after which they walk about for some time. They claim that this gives them strength and renders them supple and fleet of foot. The men are very regular in observing this custom, without missing a single day when they are able. The women are not as constant in the practice. They all swim like fish, men as well as women. The Talons were obliged to do like them because they are so desirous that others imitate and resemble them in everything. They often exposed the said Talons and other young Frenchmen to make them become tanned like themselves. They nevertheless did not prevent them from praying to God, but they amused themselves by mumbling and mimicking them, even taking their prayer book when they saw them holding it, or some other book among those that the Clamcoëhs had found in the settlement of the French when they massacred them, as will be told later. They made ugly faces pretending to read, for they are naturally clowns, buffoons, and scoffers. But they are given to drunkenness (because they make liquors that intoxicate almost like wine). They danced and sang, but very rudely, for their only instruments are a certain stick full of notches, which they scrape with another stick, and gourds, which they fill with small pebbles or grains of Indian corn. One of these liquors is made with a sort of red bean, which they chew and soak in water. It is their opinion that its use renders them more supple and fleet of foot. Therefore they drink it to such excess that they vomit several times, drinking and vomiting alternately without pause. They make still another beverage with some leaves, the name of which the said Talons do not remember. These leaves are boiled in water and churned like chocolate, so that it also makes much froth, and they drink it very hot. They drink of it especially after they have walked a great distance.

5. Whether these savages gave them knowledge of whether or not there could be mines.

The savages knew nothing of mines or of minerals; and they do not value pieces of gold or silver money, preferring pins, needles, and pieces of glass or glass beads. Pierre Talon, saw, while he was with the Cenis, that they brought some 50 or 60 gold *louis* that M. de la Salle had on him when he was killed about six leagues or so from their village, as will be told later. The savages set no value on them [the gold pieces] and willingly gave a gold piece or even two for a pin, a needle, a small knife, or some other trifle, so that a man named Pierre Meunier, from Paris, had no trouble appropriating them, and, having taken them to Mexico when he was taken there with the said Talon, he gave them to the viceroy. They did not see any mines, nor did they know whether or not there were any until they went to Mexico, where there is no lack of them, as will be told later, but they all belong to the Spaniards.

6. On the fruits and tender vegetation this land produces.

While describing the nature of the region, mention was made of some of the fruits found there, like nuts, berries, etc., to which one can add red and white grapes, for there are a great many vines in the woods, whose vinestocks are much larger than those in Europe and whose branches climb very high on most trees; but these grapes are sour, since they grow wild and are not cultivated.

Besides the ordinary nuts, there are some extremely large ones. There are also hazelnuts in quantity, and certain fruits that are called figs, but which are not like the figs of Europe. They are very much like the banana. There is also a prodigious quantity of berries with delicious taste that are very good to eat and on which, as well as on the grapes, diverse species of small birds feed; and there are also several other kinds of native fruits of which they know neither the name nor the characteristics. But there is one among the others that is extremely refreshing. It is shaped like an egg and grows on bushes with thorns. The Spaniards eat it and value it very much. They call it "tuna."

The whole country produces maize or corn, potatoes, gourds, pumpkins, and beans of several kinds. The said S^r. de la Salle had some sowed and cultivated at his dwelling and had some grain brought from the Cenis village.

The soil there appears everywhere suitable for producing all sorts of grains and vegetables if one were to sow them there; however, it does not rain very much in that country.

There are many bees in the fields that make their honey in the grass and in trees. But the savages do not cultivate them, contenting themselves with eating the honey wherever they find it.

Tobacco could be grown there because the Cenis cultivate some, though very little, and only for their own use. There is red pepper in quantity, small and strong, but the natives do not use any of it.

The said Talons also speak a great deal about a kind of strong-smelling root, which is common in all the country and which is related to ginger. The natives believe that this root has the virtue of making the hair grow; and in view of this, they rub their heads with it after having chewed it.

They believe also that there is cotton, but they are unable to give any details.

It is believed that there one could gather and process turtles, there being an abundance of turtles of all sorts, large and small, aquatic and land, whose flesh is perfectly good to eat.

The savages have nothing to barter but buffalo and deer skins, which they dress like chamois skins and make soft as cloth, despite the fact that the cattle of this country [buffalo] are much larger than those of Europe, as has been said previously.

There will be presently a quantity of runaway or wild pigs all over the country, the French having released some that had already reproduced prodigiously by the time the Talons left there. The savages do not eat them, saying that they are the dogs of the French, which they imagined because they have not known dogs other than the wolves they capture when very small, tame, and train for the hunt.

The ordinary hens that were in the French settlement before the massacre, which will be spoken of later, and which escaped to the woods, had also multiplied considerably. The savages have not the same aversion for these chickens as for the pigs because they eat them without hesitation and find them good. There would be no lack of milk in this country if one took the trouble to tame the [buffalo] cows that give it in abundance. But the savages do not want to take the trouble, contenting themselves, when they have killed one, to suck at once all the milk she has.

According to the rather vague statements of the Talons, one can infer that there is salt, because they say that the French used to gather a sort of white sand along the seashore and the banks of saltwater ponds, which they boiled in water until it came to the consistency of salt, and with which they seasoned soups and meats. As for the savages, they use almost no salt; and to preserve their meats they simply dry them in the sun, after having cut them into very thin, round slices.

7. Up to what spot did the said S^r. de la Salle take them?

The explorations of the said S^r. de la Salle did not go any farther than the Cenis village, which is about one hundred leagues inland (as mentioned previously). During this second journey, which he undertook in hopes of penetrating farther, he was shot in the head and killed by a Basque named Duhau [Duhaut]; about six leagues before arriving at the village he [Duhaut] did this to avenge the death of his older brother, who, he had been told, had been killed by the said S^r. de la Salle on the first trip he made to the interior to explore, immediately after his landing. The said Duhau the elder and many others who accompanied him did not return. He was not the only one who perished on this trip; most of those who had accompanied the said S^r. de la Salle, both on this journey and on others that he made into the country later, met the same fate. These trips lasted two or three months. Once he was six months without returning to the settlement,[8] to which he brought back only about half of those who had left with him, some getting lost and thus dying from exhaustion in the woods, where they were killed by the savage Clamcoehs, with whom they were at war; others deserting to live with the savages, among whom they were well received.

8. What happened at the death of the said S^r. de la Salle?

The said Duhau the younger, having thus resolved to kill the said Sieur de la Salle, took the time appointed to him as the sixth one to go hunting (they were, as stated previously, six leagues from the Cenis village) to conspire against him; but he found among the five who were with him only one, an Englishman named James,[9] who agreed with his plan, which obliged the two to kill the four others while they slept. Among these four was a savage named Nica, a good hunter, whom the said S^r. de la Salle had brought from Canada, and the S^r. de la Salle's valet named Sagé [Saget]. The others were two Frenchmen whose names have escaped Pierre Talon, who is the one relating this deed, and who was with the said S^r. de la Salle when he arrived, having been brought with the intention of leaving him with the Cenis to try to learn their

---

8 La Salle was absent from the settlement from October, 1685, to March, 1686, when he inspected the Matagorda Bay area "before passing beyond"; from April 22 to late August, 1686, the first journey to the Cenis; and on several shorter journeys in late summer and early fall of 1685 (Margry, *Découvertes*, III, 248, 541).

9 Father Anastase Douay (Isaac Joslin Cox, ed., the *Journeys of Réné Robert Cavelier, Sieur de La Salle*, I, 224) calls him Hiens, "a German from Wittemburg." Joutel ("Relation," p. 336) refers to "Hiems, freebooter whom M. de La Salle had engaged at Petit Goâve as cannoneer." "Hiems" or "Hiens" is a French rendering of James.

language. The said S^r. de la Salle, impatient at not seeing his hunters return, went toward the place he had sent them, which was not far, to try to learn the cause of their delay. [He was] accompanied only by a religious of St. Francis [Anastase Douay]. The said Duhau and James, who had expected him to do this very thing, had placed themselves in ambush in two different places, so that if one missed him, the other would surely not. The said Duhau, having shot first, killed him outright with one shot in the forehead and then returned to join the group with the said James, as if they had done nothing.

Duhau told the brother of the one he had just killed, who was a good priest, and one of his nephews, a young boy of ten or twelve years, what he had just done to avenge (said he) the death of his brother. He told them that they could withdraw and go wherever they wished, for he would not be able from then on to see them without pain. At this the uncle and the nephew, full of sorrow, took off with the same religious who had been present at this murder and two or three other Frenchmen, friends of theirs, whose names he does not remember, by way of the Cenis village, where they left the said Pierre Talon, following the intentions of the late S^r. de la Salle, and undertook to travel through woods and unknown lands to reach Canada. They provided themselves with guns and ammunition for hunting, preferring to expose themselves to all perils that they would have to endure and to place themselves at the mercy of diverse nations of savages that they would have to travel through, rather than submit to the domination of the said\Duhau, who seized command of those of this unfortunate party who remained, numbering only about eighteen or twenty. But he did not enjoy very long the authority that he had acquired for himself by his crime because division crept in among them. James, his accomplice, killed him two or three days later with a pistol shot, and, having seized command, the jealousy of the others procured for him the same fate as had befallen Duhau, for he also was killed several days later by a French sailor named Rutre [Ruter], who was subsequently killed by a surgeon, also French.[10] This surgeon, fearing that someone would do the same to him, fled to the nation of savages named Toho, close neighbors of the Cenis, who received him well, for he had with him his gun and ammunition. Not long afterward, they took him to war against another nation of savages

10 This passage contains several ambiguous statements. Whereas Pierre seems to say Duhaut was slain after the one group departed for Canada, the eighteen or twenty who remained obviously included both groups, which actually totaled fourteen or fifteen.

named Paoüites or Temerlouans.[11] They also took along the said Pierre Talon. This surgeon perished on that occasion. Having stayed behind when the Toho took flight—which those savages always do when they find their enemies on guard and ready to face them, as all these people are extremely fast and fleet of foot—this surgeon was not able to follow the said Toho, and, having fallen or lagged behind, he was slain. The said Talon would have had the same fate had he not mounted a horse that belonged to the aforementioned surgeon, who had given it to him to go into combat, that he might be better able to shoot a gun. The said Pierre Talon returned to the Cenis village, where he always stayed—that is to say, during five or six years[12] until the arrival of the Spaniards who brought him to Mexico, which will be discussed later. He has never since heard tell of the said brother and nephew of the late M[r]. de la Salle, or the others who accompanied him.[13]

9. What were the most remarkable things that happened to them up to this time?

What could be said on this question would be only useless repetition of what has been said already and which can be said later, so we proceed to the next one.

10. The parts played by all the people who were with the said S[r]. de la Salle at the time of his death.

The destiny of several of these who were near M. de la Salle has already been spoken of. Some died, killing one another, as stated, and the others scattered and went away among the savages except those who followed his brother and his nephew.

---

11 The extract of the Interrogations in Margry (*Découvertes,* III, 612) spells the name "Lemerlouans," an obvious misreading of the manuscript. The 1703 Delisle map has it as it is spelled here. See Schuetz, "Ethnological Data," p. 260.

12 Actually about three years.

13 The others were the Sieur de Marle, who drowned in the Red River; La Salle's brother, the Abbé Jean Cavelier; Colin Cavelier, his nephew; the pilot Tessier; Pierre Barthélemy, a young Parisian; Father Anastase Douay, who was to return to the New World with the Louisiana founding expedition of 1699; and Joutel, who spurned the opportunity to do likewise. Weddle, "La Salle's Survivors," p. 415.

One named Pierre Meunier, a young Frenchman, went with the Cenis, where he always lived in company with the said Pierre Talon, and in the same way, until they were freed by the Spaniards, as will be told later.[14]

As for those who stayed at the settlement when the said S[r]. de la Salle undertook the journey on which he was killed, Jean-Baptiste Talon, who was of the number, reports that they were no more than twenty or twenty-five persons, counting the women, one priest, and two Religious of the Order of St. Francis. They were nearly all massacred by the savages named Clamcoehs, who had waged war against them because the said S[r]. de la Salle, on arriving, arbitrarily took their canoes for ascending the river to establish a settlement. Even though they had made peace with them, they had no sooner learned of the S[r]. de la Salle's death and the disunity that had arisen among his people than they came to surprise those who remained at the aforementioned settlement by the worst treachery in the world. As the French were no longer on their guard, believing them [the Clamcoëhs] to be friends, these had little trouble slaughtering them all, except the said Jean-Baptiste Talon; two of his brothers, younger than he, named Robert and Lucien; their older sister, named Marie-Magdeleine; and another young Parisian named Eustache Bréman, who was said to be of the family. They were saved by some savage women who, touched with compassion by their youth, loaded them on their backs and carried them into their cabins while their husbands massacred the rest, after the said Talons had seen their mother fall before their eyes.

As for their father, he had become lost in the woods sometime previously, having gone in a party with the said S[r]. de la Salle, and no one ever knew how he perished. Their other sister [Marie-Elizabeth] had died of illness at the settlement.

The aforementioned savage women also saved in the same way the wife of a French officer [Gabriel Minime, Sieur Barbier] who commanded the settlement in the absence of the said S[r]. de la Salle and who was also slain. They were likewise moved with tenderness at the sight of the three-month-old baby she had at breast, but the savages returned to their cabins after the massacre, killed her first, and then her child, which one of them dashed against a tree while holding it by a foot. But they did not hurt the said Talons or Eustache Bréman, who were reared and loved by these same savage women who had saved them, as if they were

14 See Pierre Meunier, "Declaración," Mexico City, Aug. 19, 1690, UT transcript 69, AGI, Mexico 617.

their own children, for the six or seven years[15] that they stayed among them, living as they did until the Spaniards from Mexico came and freed them, as will be said later.

11. What they did, and their details.

The said Talons have already said something of their particular movements and how they fell into the power of the savages, who first tattooed them on the face, the hands, the arms, and in several other places on their bodies as they do on themselves, with several bizarre black marks, which they make with charcoal of walnut wood, crushed and soaked in water. Then they insert this mixture between the flesh and the skin, making incisions with strong, sharp thorns, which cause them to suffer great pain. Thus, the dissolved carbon mixes with the blood and oozes from these incisions and forms indelible marks and characters on the skin. These marks still show, despite a hundred remedies that the Spaniards applied to try to erase them.[16] They [the Talons] went to hunt and to war with them [the Indians], who taught them how to shoot an arrow and how to run like them. These savages run so swiftly that there is no galloping horse, no matter how fast, that they cannot follow, and even leave behind. They all went naked like them, and every morning at daybreak, in any season, they went to plunge into the nearest river. Like them, they ate meat from the hunt, fresh or cured in the sun, but most often half raw. The only meals that horrified them were those they made of human flesh, as they are all cannibals, but toward their savage enemies only. They never ate a single Frenchman that they had killed because, they said, they do not eat them. And the said Jean-Baptiste Talon vouches that he once went three days without eating, because nothing presented itself during that time except some human flesh of the Ayennis whom they had killed on one of the expeditions, which will be discussed later.

Pierre Talon, the older of these two brothers, having been left with the Cenis as previously stated, remained always with their chief, who appeared to have no authority over the others except in war. Yet this authority is itself so limited that each one quits and returns to the dwelling when he feels like it, without asking permission or authorization from the commander. They wage war without observing a single rule or discipline, but only by surprise and without exposing themselves too

15 Actually two or three years.
16 See Enríquez Barroto's description (diary, April 18) of tattooing by the Atákapas.

much. These peoples never go to attack their enemies except at night or at break of day, when they believe them sound asleep. When they can surprise them and kill a few of them, they pull off their scalp with the hair, which they dry and then fill with hay, each one keeping those he was able to carry off to make trophies, hanging them on sticks on the timbers of the roof of their huts or cabins, or holding them in his hands while exhibiting them or raising them aloft, with much display and ostentation. Upon returning from some war that was favorable to them, they dance to the songs that are for celebrating their victory, as is their custom. The one who has the most scalps is the most esteemed by the others, and it is in this that all their glory consists.

The father of the Cenis chief was still living and he also bore the title of chief. They lived together, but it appeared that all authority resided in the son. The father was already old and had apparently bestowed on him [the son] all the honor of commanding, but they lived in concord and in an admirable union. Moreover, the said Talons affirm that they were always treated by these savage people with the greatest kindness in the world, without ever having been maltreated with blows or otherwise. On the contrary, they loved them tenderly and appeared to be very angry when anyone displeased them in any way and took their part on these occasions, even against their own children.

12. In what way they fell into the hands of the Spaniards.

The Spaniards from Mexico, having been informed of the incursion and of M^r. de la Salle's plan for the French settlement in La Louisiane, resolved to thwart him; and to that end made three expeditions,[17] even though they had to pass through an unknown and faraway land, according to what the said Talons reported having heard them say, where they had never been before. On the first expedition, they were about 500 men on horseback, armed with muskets or small harquebuses, pistols, and swords and all wearing coats of mail or iron wire made like nets of very small links, which protected them from the consequences of the savages' arrows. But, as it was already a long time after the massacre of

17 Reference is to Alonso de León's expeditions of 1689 and 1690 and to that of Domingo Terán de los Ríos in 1691. Diaries of all three are published in Lino Gómez Canedo, ed., *Primeras exploraciones y poblamiento de Texas (1686–1694)*. On León's 1689 expedition there were 85 soldiers and servants to a total of 113 Spaniards, plus an unspecified number of Indians (Massanet letter in Herbert Eugene Bolton, ed., *Spanish Exploration in the Southwest, 1502–1706*, p. 357).

the French when they arrived in the country, they found only two of those who had scattered after the death of the said Sr. de la Salle and who were with the savage nations closer to the borders of Mexico than the ones who have been mentioned previously. One of these Frenchmen was a young man from Bayonne named Larchevesque [L'Archevêque], who appeared to be of noble birth and well educated, and the other a sailor named Groulé [Grollet]. The Spaniards seized them and took them with them to Mexico, where the said Talons saw them, as they will say later on.

On the second trip the Spaniards were no more than 200,[18] having diminished their number because they had learned from the aforementioned L'archevesque and Groulé of the French disaster, and that there remained only a few who had escaped the various perils they had encountered and who were scattered among the savages. Finally, wanting absolutely to have in their power these wretched few who survived, they penetrated farther than they had on the first journey. Pierre Talon and Meunier, having learned from some savages that the Spaniards were looking for them and were drawing closer to them, wanted to evade them, fearing their cruelty. They believed they were fleeing from them, going farther into the territory from nation to nation. But they [the Spaniards] met them on their way and captured them. They made the two Frenchmen take them to the Cenis village, to see if there were any others.[19] Not finding any, they stayed there several days and, finding this nation more docile and, in some ways, more civil than the others, they left with them three Spanish Religious of the Order of St. Francis,[20] with several soldiers as their guard, who built them a house in the village. They left them some clothes, some flour, and other provisions, which they did not lack, having more than 400 horses of which those not used by the horsemen were loaded with baggage and provisions.

18 The second León *entrada* (1690), to found a Franciscan mission among the Cenis, or Tejas, actually was larger than the first. It had 110 soldiers and 4 priests. Alonso de León, "Diario," March 26–July 11, 1690, in Canedo, *Primeras exploraciones,* p. 138.
19 By that time all the others were dead, with the possible exception of the man from Provence (mentioned later), who had become thoroughly Indianized. His ultimate fate is not known.
20 Besides Fray Damián Massanet, who was to return to Mexico to arrange for expansion of the missionary enterprise, the priests were Francisco Casañas de Jesús María, whom Massanet left in charge, and Miguel de Fontcuberta, and Antonio de Bordoy (Massanet letter, to Carlos de Sigüenza y Gongora in Bolton, *Spanish Exploration,* p. 368). They came to establish the Mission San Francisco de los Tejas, on a tributary of the Neches River in present-day Houston County, Texas.

These Religious, while the said Talon and Meunier stayed with them, worked at making a compilation of words for learning the Cenis language. Talon and Meunier served them as interpreters by means of the captain and lieutenant of this Spanish troop, who spoke good French.[21] They heard them say many times that they wanted to live in this country, that it belonged to them and not to the French. They also heard them say this later to the viceroy of Mexico.

As the aforementioned Pierre Talon saw that the Spaniards treated him very humanely, he made known to them that there were still in the country his three brothers and one sister and other Frenchmen, who were with the Clamcoeh nation, that he might have the consolation of seeing them brought with him and among Christians. It came to pass, for the Spaniards went there and brought his sister but only two of his brothers, namely Robert and Lucien. His other brother, Jean-Baptiste, and Eustache Bréman again remained with this savage nation—how this happened he could not say—until about a year later, when a third troop of about 250 Spaniards returned to fetch them and take them to Mexico.[22] Reluctantly, the savages allowed them to go, because they saw very well that the Spaniards were ready to carry them away by force if they refused. On the other hand, the Spaniards did not want to bring on themselves a war with [the natives] because they intended to establish themselves in the country. They agreed to give in exchange one horse for each French head. But when it came to the Talons' sister, who was taller and older, being their eldest, the savages wanted two horses for her. Beyond that, there arose a dispute that made them take recourse to arms, so that there were two or three savages killed with musket shots, which made the others flee because they greatly feared firearms. Finally, they gave up the girl for one horse as they had done for each of the boys. To appease them the Spaniards gave them some smoking tobacco, which they love so much that there is nothing they will not do to get it. On the Spaniards' side, only one horse was wounded by the savages' arrows, which they shot in great numbers. However, these had no

21 Reference is to Captain Gregorio de Salinas Varona, who was on the 1690 León expedition and that of Terán in 1691, and the *alférez* (sublieutenant) Francisco Martínez, who was with León in 1689 and Terán. Both were fluent in French and both served later at Pensacola, where they had frequent encounters with the French colonists of Mobile and Biloxi.

22 This was the Terán expedition, which had fifty soldiers and thirteen religious. An additional fifty men under Salinas Varona were brought by sea aboard the frigate *Santo Cristo de San Román*, of which Juan Enríquez Barroto was captain (Domingo Terán de los Ríos, "Diario," in Canedo, *Primeras exploraciones,* pp. 189, 191, 222).

effect against the Spaniards because of their coats of mail. These idiots feared not only the noise of the firearms, but even that of the drums; for example, the Clamcoëhs, having mobilized for the purpose of destroying the French, because M. de la Salle had arbitrarily taken their canoes, as has been said, were so terrified at the sound of the drum, which [the Spaniards] beat to prepare themselves for defense, that they all fled. Since then they have become somewhat accustomed to these noises of war; and, instead of fleeing immediately in terror, they were content thereafter with throwing themselves on the ground as soon as they heard the shot of cannon or musket, believing thus to put themselves out of reach. They felt so much regret on having to part with the brothers and sister of Jean-Baptiste Talon that the latter (who stayed yet some time with them, as stated previously) affirms that they all wept bitterly when the Spaniards took them; and they mourned them for a month afterward, especially the smaller ones, for whom they had greater attachment and tenderness than for the older ones. They cried no less when they parted from the said Jean-Baptiste Talon and Eustache Bréman and urged the former to desert the Spaniards and return to them as soon as possible, with a number of horses. This he promised them but without intending to keep his word, since he felt more at ease among Christians than with barbarians.

On the second expedition that the Spaniards made—the first time they penetrated as far as the Clamcoeh nation [23]—they brought also an Italian who happened to be among them. They have forgotten his name. He never wanted to acknowledge being of the number of those of M. de la Salle, even though the Talons believed that he was. He said that he had come alone to this region from Canada by land, which can hardly be believed.

13. They were asked what they saw in New Spain and in the countries they passed through to get there, and they gave the greatest detail they could.

The Talons and their comrades, having been captured by the Spaniards, as has been said, crossed with them—before arriving in New Spain—a big country very much like the one they had just left, and which they have previously described, also populated with savages separated into small nations, each one having its own particular name and language.

23 León's 1690 expedition, the first to make contact with the Karankawa group that held the Talon children.

They often made war among themselves, but always by surprise and without previous declaration. That is why it is always necessary for Europeans who would go there and settle to remain on their guard and beware of them, it being naturally as easy for them to break the peace as to make it.

All their dialects are the more difficult to learn because they bear no relationship to the languages of Europe. Moreover, their way of living is rather uniform. Living mostly as nomads, by hunting and fishing, they are concerned only about what is necessary for their subsistence, going naked, possessing nothing as their own, knowing nothing about any sort of bread or biscuits, and living off the flesh of fish and fruit, without any seasoning or preparation of the food for cooking, simply roasting or boiling, which they do only halfway.

After two months and more of travel on horseback, they arrived at the village of savages that is only a quarter of a league from the Spanish dwellings.

Those savages are, in part, Christians and live with the Spaniards on good enough terms. They remember neither the name of the village nor the one of the nation that inhabits it, having only passed through there; but they remember very well that their number did not exceed 300.[24] It was there that they began to see some high mountains, which are like a natural separation of the countries inhabited by the savages from the one inhabited by the Spaniards. Several of these mountains are of a prodigious height, and there are a few that are covered with snow almost all the time, even though none falls on the plains. It is always hot, especially on the other side of the mountains toward the south. This snow will be refreshing to the Spaniards who send to fetch some for a cool drink. Among these mountains, there are also some that belch forth flames continually through their summits.

Leaving there, they entered a Spanish village named Caouil,[25] where there are only about 20 houses. They remained there almost a month. The inhabitants live there like in Europe, cultivating the lands, which produce good wheat and maize, or corn. They also make sugar there.

Having left this village, they arrived after six days of travel, always

24 Reference apparently is to the 1690 journey of Pierre, Marie-Magdelaine, Lucien, and Robert. They left the scene of the encounter on June 22 and reached Monclova on July 15, having crossed the Rio Grande near the later site of San Juan Bautista (Guerrero, Coahuila) (Weddle, *Wilderness Manhunt*, pp. 212–13; León, "Diario," in Canedo, *Primeras exploraciones*, p. 147).
25 San Francisco de Coahuila, now Monclova.

on horseback—during which they passed by several other Spanish villages, separated one from the other by only one or two leagues—at the town of St. Louis de Potosy [San Luis Potosí], which is large and beautiful, about like La Rochelle, and the See of a Bishop but without any fortification or surrounding wall. It is densely populated with Spaniards, who are all wealthy, working in the gold and silver mines not far away. The Talons did not see the mines, having simply passed through the town, where they slept one night only.

From there they continued on their road until they came to the one leading to Mexico, capital of the country, archbishopric, and place where the Spanish viceroy makes his residence. It appeared to them very large and beautiful, and they heard someone tell the Spaniards that it was as large as Madrid. The houses there are well built, all on a very high level and all with terraced roofs, so that one can go over them without difficulty, from one end of the street to the other. There are many coaches.[26]

The viceroy had ten of them for his own use and that of his household. And he is the only one in the city who can have coaches with six horses or six mules, it being permitted to others to have only 4 or 2, unless they are traveling out into the country. He alone can have teams of horses, even though they are numerous in that country. Private individuals and a few noblemen are allowed to have only mules. The town is heavily populated, but the majority are natives of the country; that is, descendants of the Indian peoples or savages, rather than of Spaniards. And it is not permitted to these natives to keep arms, which ensures that they do not know how to use them. Thus, they fight among themselves only by throwing rocks at each other. They [the Spaniards] take this precaution because of their great number and their inclination to revolt, for they endure the Spanish yoke only with difficulty. They revolted in the year 1692; and even though they were armed only with rocks, they put such a great fear into the hearts of the Spaniards that they all fled. Even the viceroy escaped through a window of his palace, with Madame his wife, and they took refuge at the archbishop's residence. On this occasion this prelate went in procession, followed by his clergy, through all the streets, carrying the Holy Sacrament; but the mutineers threw rocks at him and were not appeased. The principal ones among them call themselves by all the titles and dignities that the Spaniards have from the highest to the least. They would have ill-treated the viceroy if they

26 Concerning the coaches of Mexico City in this period, see "Los coches de la ciudad de Mexico durante la época colonial," *Boletín del Archivo General de la Nación,* old series, 25, no 4: 537–87.

had found him. They set fire to his palace, reducing it to ashes, and would have created greater troubles or disorder if the Count of Santiago,[27] who is great lord of the Creoles—that is to say, of those born in the country but of Spanish origin—had not appeased them the next day. And even though he assembled what soldiers he could, he used only persuasion, having great trust in the spirit of these Indians. Afterward, when they were dispersed and those who had come from the fields had returned home, the viceroy had the cavalry dismount and made several examples of the more rebellious, who were flogged and put to death. It is to be noticed that the Creoles have no less an inclination to revolt than the descendants of the Indians because the Spaniards, mistrusting them, deprive them of all the civil and military offices. These descendants of the Indians are always so much inclined to idolatry, even though they have embraced Christianity, that there are still several who secretly adore carved idols that represent different sorts of animals with bizarre and unusual faces. This gives no little work to the Spanish Religious who want to try to abolish these superstitions entirely. It was during their long sojourn in this town that they saw boarded, in quantity and on all sides, gold and silver in ingots and bars, brought there from the aforementioned town of St. Louis de Potosy and the mines around it and Mexico, from which the closest mine is twelve leagues. Much of it comes also from a country the Spaniards call Sonora, which they heard tell is 200 leagues from there [Mexico]. Le Paral [Parral, Chihuahua] is another country inhabited by the Spaniards, which they say is 300 leagues from Mexico; but the said Talons could not tell whether there are mines there. The savages or Indians of the vicinity of Paral continually make war against the Spaniards and steal their horses and mules, which they eat.[28]

Mexico is a very temperate country and very healthful, abounding in everything, producing all sorts of fruits, those that grow in Europe as well as those of the Indies. One sees there also some of nearly all kinds of animals, both land and aquatic, as well as birds. The Spanish inhabitants there are pleasant and courteous, and the savages who live in their vicinity are Christians, civilized, and hardworking. They perform all the

27 The same man who in May, 1683, gathered two thousand men to repel the pirate invasion of Veracruz but arrived after the pirates had withdrawn: Fernando Altamirano de Velasco Legazpi y Castilla: Conde de Santiago to Crown, Mexico, July 26, 1683, AGI, Mexico 91, ramo 3; Weddle, *Spanish Sea*, p. 400.
28 Concerning the continuous warfare in the Chihuahua (Nueva Vizcaya) region in this period, see Jack D. Forbes, *Apache, Navaho, and Spaniard*, p. 209 ff.

work along with the Negroes, mulattoes, *metis* [mestizos], both in the mines and on the land. [[The mulattoes are the children issuing from a Negro and a white woman, or a white man and a Negro woman, and the mestizos are those of a Spaniard and an Indian woman. There is a great number of the one and the other of these breeds in all of Mexico.]] The Spaniards live there in excessive indolence and great idleness and are neither warriors nor well armed.

Neither the said town of Mexico nor that of St. Louis de Potosy is defended by any fort or fortification. It is the same for all the other towns in this land, excepting Vera Cruz, which is 80 leagues from the city of Mexico. It is the seaport at which the fleet arrives from Spain to load the gold, silver, and merchandise from all Mexico. It is fortified and surrounded by eight small forts of four, six, and eight cannon and is defended on the side of the sea by another large fort, which is built in the sea a cannonshot from the town. There are at least one hundred pieces of cannon in the town, most of them made of bronze. Protected by this fort, the fleet and the galleons set forth for Porto Bello [Portobelo] or Cartagenne [Cartagena] to take on the gold, silver, and merchandise that come from Perou [Peru].[29]

The said Talons also went to another town 20 leagues from Mexico City going toward Vera Cruz named La Puebla, which is the See of a Bishop, half as large as that of Mexico, where there is also a large number of carriages. There are also several other towns in the vicinity and in all the surrounding country, but they are smaller; also a number of beautiful villages, whose houses are all covered with red tile.

There are all over this country some very venomous snakes and scorpions; and there is among the serpents one singular species that is called rattlesnake, for they actually have something like rattles on the tail, by means of which they can be heard when they move if ever one comes near. They are the most venomous and always crawl on the ground, never climbing trees, as some others there do.

The said Talons cannot say precisely how far it is from the Cenis village to the city of Mexico, but one can judge by the long time it took them to make this journey that it is far. It is true also that it is necessary to consider that traveling in groups and in unknown country, where there were no cleared roads and where they found rivers that had to be crossed nearly every day, they did not make much progress; but they

29 The fleet itinerary is confused. The Tierra Firme fleet that went to Portobelo via Cartagena sailed after lading directly to Havana, where it met the New Spain fleet from Veracruz (Lucas de Molina, "Quenta que se tomo a Lucas de Molina," February, 1554, AGI, Contaduría 876).

affirm that it is 300 leagues by sea from the bay where M. de la Salle disembarked to Vera Cruz.[30]

L'archevesque and Groulé, who were previously mentioned, having been sent to Madrid with the fleet, were detained there in prison for about six months,[31] after which time they were returned to Mexico, where the said Talons saw them, chains on their feet for being sent back, so said the Spaniards, to a faraway land about 400 or 500 leagues distant, which they wanted to settle and which they called New Mexico; and they did this, so they believed, to get rid of them because they were grown men who were intelligent, especially L'archevesque. They feared that they would bring back to France too much knowledge of this particular country, which they dreaded greatly; and there is nothing they would not do to prevent this.[32] It was apparent that this same distrust led them to imprison the Italian, mentioned previously, in one of the forts of Vera Cruz, where they saw him also and where he subsequently died. They did not have the same mistrust of the Talons because the viceroy took them into his home, four brothers and one sister that they were, still of tender age, and he raised them in their [the Spaniards'] own ways during the nine to ten years[33] that they lived in his palace, with great kindness and all sorts of good treatment, regarding them as his household servants and as naturalized citizens. That is so true that when the said Pierre and Jean-Baptiste Talon and another of their brothers, named Lucien, had come of age to carry arms, the viceroy made all three of them embark from Vera Cruz in one of the five warships that made up the Armada de Barlovento[34] to serve as soldiers. And the viceroy, having been relieved a short time later by another sent from Spain,[35] embarked with the fleet to return to Europe, taking with him their

30 Straight across the Gulf, the distance is about 375 nautical miles, somewhat short of 300 leagues (3.43 miles per Spanish marine league).
31 Actually thirty months. See Weddle, *Wilderness Manhunt*, p. 236. Depositions of L'Archevêque and Grollet and related documents are translated in Walter J. O'Donnell, *La Salle's Occupation of Texas*.
32 The Talons understand the Spaniards' motivation quite well. See Report of Junta de Guerra de Indias, Madrid, May 6, 1692, AGI, Mexico 617, for the Spanish view.
33 Actually six or seven years.
34 This Windward fleet was assigned to guard Spanish interests in the Gulf and Caribbean, protecting shipping and coastal settlements. It was often ineffective but occasionally scored a coup, as in the capture of 120 French pirates fleeing after the sack of Campeche in 1685, among whom were deserters from La Salle's company who revealed his mission.
35 Gaspar de la Cerda Sandoval Silva y Mendoza, Conde de Galve, was succeeded as viceroy of New Spain in February, 1696, by Juan Ortega y Mon-

other brother, named Robert (who was the youngest of the four), and their sister, Marie-Magdelaine, who must be in Spain now, if God preserved them. And to say things as they are, the said Pierre, Jean-Baptiste, and Lucien were so accustomed to the Spaniards that, when they were taken by Mᴿ. Désaugiers, captain of the king's ships who carried off the vessel on which they were soldiers last year, they were very angry, and they relaxed only on returning to Europe, that they might be able to go to Spain to rejoin their other brother and their sister, the separation from whom they still felt severely. When the Sᴿ. de Boissieux obliged the first two to enlist in the naval company of Feugerolles, of which he was lieutenant, he had the other [Lucien] placed as a servant because he was found too young to be a soldier.[36]

14. Their special question: Whether they saw the Mississipy River and what they learned of its course and of the place it empties into the sea.

Mᴿ. de la Salle, having been killed without discovering the mouth of the Mississipy River that he had gone to look for, the said Talons cannot say positively whether it is one of these mouths that they saw after his death, because they were among the savages. But Jean-Baptiste Talon reports that a short time after the murder, and the subsequent massacre of the Frenchmen at the settlement, as he has stated previously, the Clamcoehs with whom he was, having no more French to fight, turned their schemes against the Cenis, their ancient enemies. In preparation for surprising them in their village, they decamped from near the French settlement and embarked in canoes to go, according to their custom, to look for some safe and remote spot that could serve as refuge for their aged, their women, and their children while they were busy with their expedition. Navigating all along the coast of the Gulf of Mexico, they passed the Riviere des Cannes, which has been mentioned elsewhere. Continuing their navigation, they finally stopped and entered a

---

táñez, bishop of Michoacán, who served only until the following December (Herbert Eugene Bolton, *Guide to Materials for the History of the United States in the Principal Archives of Mexico,* p. 469).

36 A letter of the Sieur de Boissieux, dated Morlaix, January 7, 1698, in Margry, *Découvertes,* IV, 43–44, indicates that the brothers had been denied permission to go to Spain. The trip, if made at all, must have been after they were interrogated the following February 14. Boissieux (p. 43) also says that the third brother from the Spanish ship (Lucien) was at Oléron, where he was apparently placed as a servant.

large river, distant from the Riviere des Cannes, toward the south of the Gulf, about as far as from the Riviere des Cannes to the bay where the said S^r. de la Salle made his incursion.[37] Finding this place very convenient for their plans, because of its natural shelter made by the mountains of sand and the woods around the two mouths of this river as by the abundance of fish, buffaloes, turkeys, ducks, and several other kinds of venison and game as well as all sorts of fruits that are found in the surrounding area, they left their aged, their women, and their children with the said Jean-Baptiste Talon; his two little brothers, Lucien and Robert; his sister, Marie-Magdelaine; and Eustache Bréman. They stayed there about six weeks, waiting for the return of their warriors, who came back at the end of that time. Victorious there, not over the Cenis, whom they had gone to look for, but over the Ayennis, neighbors and allies of the Cenis, they brought back about 50 to 60 scalps and 30 or 40 slaves (some of whom they served up as a feast) and several horses. This action is confirmed by Pierre Talon, who was then with the Cenis and who says he remembers very well this raid of the Clamcoehs, news of which was brought to the Cenis by an Ayenny woman who had escaped from among their slaves. And this woman said that the Ayenny (who were not informed of the massacre of their own people) believed that some of the French were among them, because of several gunshots that had been fired at them, of which they had all been terrified. But, having known the contrary, from the chief of the Cenis, as well as from the four Frenchmen who were yet with them—namely, Pierre Talon, Pierre Meunier, the French sailor Rutre, and a man from Provence whose name he has forgotten—knowing without doubt that it was the Clamcoehs themselves who had fired the shots from guns they had found loaded at the French settlement when they had committed the massacre, she returned to disabuse those of her nation, for they had believed that the French had been in the party with the Clamcoehs.

To return to the subject of this river, the said Jean-Baptiste Talon affirms that it is very beautiful, more than two musket shots wide, and very deep, that it empties into the sea by two mouths, that it appears to be of great length and is a mighty river, having ebb and flow. He was unable to say if it is the Mississipy River, not having heard its name; but there is much evidence that it is. There are a great number of palm trees and pines along the banks and in the surrounding area.

37 The passage is misleading. The Talons have said previously that the Rivière des Cannes emptied into the same bay as the river on which the French settlement was situated (question 2), and other accounts (e.g., Joutel, "Rela-

15. To know whether they passed many other rivers on the way to Mexico, their size, and their depth.

The Talons, while going from the country of the savages to Mexico, crossed some rivers nearly every day while they were traveling; but most of them were small and several fordable, or, if it happened that they were deep, as a number of them were found to be, they were so narrow that to cross them all the Spaniards had to do was cut down a few trees on both sides, which fell one on top of the other across the stream and formed a sort of bridge. It is true that among these trees there were some marvelously high and extremely thick ones. As for the horses, they swam across. They are unable to tell more precisely either the width or the depth of all these rivers, among which they found only one that appeared to them so wide that to cross it the Spaniards were obliged to make boats of buffalo hides [*cuires de boeufs*], prepared for that purpose. It was more than one long musket shot wide, very deep, appeared to be very long, and was not very swift. They could tell neither its name nor its exact location but they estimated that it was about midway on the road they traveled between the Cenis village and that of Caouil [Coahuila, or Monclova] and that it seemed to be the same one of which they spoke in answering the preceding question.[38]

16. What sort of Indians did they meet along the way, and did it seem to them that they could trade with them?

This question has been partly answered by the different accounts that have been given in answering the preceding ones. All the different nations of savages in this whole country live in a rather uniform manner and resemble each other so much that it is very difficult, not to say impossible, to distinguish them except with respect to their different dialects and the different geographical regions inhabited by those who have villages. As for those who are from nations that have no fixed

tion," pp. 261–62) indicate that it was the Lavaca River and its tributary, the Navidad. They could not have passed it while traveling by canoe along the Gulf Coast.

38 The river described is the Rio Grande, which was at flood stage when Pierre Talon, with Alonso de León, crossed it in 1690 near present-day Guerrero, Coahuila. Jean-Baptiste's conclusion that it was the one where the Karankawa noncombatants had remained during the raid on the Ayenny (Hainai) is invalid, for the crossing is 250 miles from the mouth of the river.

dwelling place and wander continually, camping wherever they find themselves in the manner that has been reported, they have no place set apart. They move about often without ever coming to dispute the territory among themselves, not knowing what ownership is, or its limits or confrontations. They believe that all that the earth, the sea, and the air produces, being in common, incontestably belongs to the first ones who take possession of it.

As for trade among them, nothing appeared easier, for they communicate voluntarily with the Europeans, whom they call the Sons of the Sun. They consider this celestial body, as well as the moon, to be some sort of divinity, without, however, their rendering them any worship; they do not think that they ever showed veneration for them. M. de la Salle would never have had war with the Clamcoehs if on arriving he had not high-handedly taken their canoes and refused them some little article of use that they asked him in return for them and for other services that they were ready to render to him. Nothing is easier than winning their friendship: a hatchet, a knife, a pair of scissors, a pin, a needle, a necklace or a bracelet or glass, wampum, or some other such trinkets being ordinarily the price, because they love passionately all sorts of knickknacks and baubles that are useful or ornamental. But also, as they give voluntarily of what they have, they do not like to be refused. And, while they are never aggressors, neither do they ever forget the pride of honor in their vengeance. But one need not fear their numbers, no matter how great. They never dare attack from the front Europeans armed with muskets and other firearms. There is nothing to fear from them but surprise attacks. It is for that reason that the Spaniards all have coats of mail when they travel among them. An unfailing means, other than small gifts, that the Europeans still have of winning the friendship of the nations whose alliance could help them the most in their settlements is to take part in the wars that they often wage against others. They believe themselves unconquerable when they unite with Europeans and spread terror and fright everywhere among their enemies by the noise and the effects of firearms, which they have never used and which they always have looked upon as inconceivable marvels. If the French had made more of a mystery to them about firearms, they would have regarded the French themselves as prodigies and invincible men; if they had squandered their lives less, and if they had taken greater precautions to preserve themselves as the Spaniards shrewdly do. For it is established that they never, as a people, had seen Europeans before the arrival in their country of the said S^r. de la Salle.[39]

39 A questionable statement. See Enríquez Barroto diary entry for April 7,

All the savages are of such a great simplicity, so credulous and so sensitive to the friendship that is offered them, that nothing is easier than to impose on them; some examples that the said Talons relate establish that truth.

Here they are.

The savage Clamcoehs had greatly desired to abuse their sister, Marie-Magdelaine, who was already tall, being the eldest, quite pretty, and well built.[40] They came in force and were all unaware of a stratagem to save her honor. Eustache Bréman, who has been mentioned previously, made them believe that, if they did violence to her, this girl's God would make them all die. This ploy succeeded, a fact that indicates this people's disposition to fear God, if someone were to teach them. The Italian, also mentioned previously, having lived a long time with these same Clamcoehs, had learned their language perfectly. But it happened finally that he displeased them in something, so that they determined to kill him. He thwarted this with a trick, which marks the subtlety of his spirit and the credulity of these savages. Here it is. He told these idiots that they were going to kill a man who loved them so much that he carried all of them in his heart; and if they doubted it, he would prove it to them the next day, if they were willing to grant him these terms: he would show them his open heart, and they would all see themselves there. The savages, having spared his life until the next day to put him to the test, did not fail to come around him very early in the morning in great numbers to see the effect of his promise, or to kill him if he did not keep it. The Italian had so well affixed just over his heart a pocket mirror he had that the savages, who had never seen a mirror, did not suspect the trick; and, calling them all, one after the other, he said to each one: "There is my open heart. Look! Do you not see yourself?" And, each one in fact seeing himself in the mirror, they all remained amazed and allowed him to live. Jean-Baptiste heard this deed described by the savage Clamcoehs as a marvel they could not understand; and Pierre Talon confirms it, having heard the Italian himself tell about it when they saw

---

1687, concerning a prior visit to Matagorda Bay by Juan Poule and his pirate ship. Extent of the Karankawas' contact with Europeans before La Salle is not known, but the natives seem to have demonstrated, in pillaging the wrecked *Aimable*'s stores, that they were accustomed to plundering lost ships.

40 Alonso de León, in his letter to the viceroy of July 12, 1690 (in Canedo, *Primeras exploraciones*, p. 157), referred to Marie-Magdelaine as "a little French girl of twelve or fourteen," suggesting that she was small for her age, which was sixteen.

each other in Mexico, as of a stratagem he had conceived to save his life in an extremely pressing danger.

One need have no fear about breaking relations with the savages over their wives and daughters, for they are not at all jealous of them and take no offense concerning their honor, willingly prostituting them and not being angry if they have intercourse with the Europeans. Some of M^r. de la Salle's people had even taken wives among them. The French sailor named Rutre, who was spoken of previously, had changed seven or eight times and left two children by one of these women, following in this, as in all the rest, the custom of the savages, who have in truth only one wife at a time, but who change them whenever they want to, which is to say often.[41]

Several of these women accompany their husbands to war, but their only job is to carry away from the battlefield the enemy corpses to make a feast, all together, upon their return.

People of the same nation live among themselves in a marvelous union, never having scandalous quarrels, and never striking each other, especially the men. The women often have little quarrels among themselves, in which the husbands never take part. This is because one does not know, among the savages, what justice, or punishment, is. They help each other when the need arises; and those whose hunt was productive share it willingly with their unsuccessful neighbors.

It appears, however, that they have not a single principle or smattering of religion: one could only infer that they have some confused impression of the immortality of their souls [[and the resurrection of the dead]] by the ceremonies that they observe in the burial of their dead. After having wrapped the corpse in a well-prepared buffalo hide, the same one that he had used in life to cover himself, they bury him with his club, his bow, and his arrows, a quantity of smoked meat, some corn and vegetables, and two pieces of a certain wood that they use instead of gun flint to make fire [[For this purpose they make a little hole in one of the pieces of wood, which is flat, and which they lean against something; and, having sharpened the other, which is round, they adjust the

---

41 Father Anastase Douay (in Cox, ed., *Journeys,* I, 267) claims that several of the Frenchmen had married Indian women "to multiply the colony" at Fort St.-Louis and (p. 237) that the colony had been joined by some Indian families. The only "marriage" of French men and Indian women mentioned by the Talons and other sources were among the Cenis and certainly not entered into, as Douay says, with the intention of augmenting the colony. Joutel (cited in Cox, *Journeys,* I 237n., and II, 88) denies that any Indians joined the colony.

point of it in the hole and make some fire by rubbing these two pieces of wood, by turning the one that is round between their hands, as fast as they can.]] and all that in order that he may use them (so they say) when he wakes up.

Jean-Baptiste Talon says that the Clamcoehs wear mourning for their dead parents by smearing their body with a black substance made with charcoal of walnut wood soaked in water; and all those in the family weep regularly at a certain hour, evening and morning, for a very long time, without being able to say precisely how long.

Pierre Talon reports that he saw the Cenis practice a ceremony that resembles an act of sacrifice, for when they have killed a buffalo, a deer, or some other beast, they do not eat any of it; neither do they have it cooked, before the eldest—after having mumbled several words very low, which the said Talon was never able to make out—had thrown a piece of it into the fire, after which they put this meat either to boil or to roast, and then they eat it.

One sees among all these peoples only males [that are] well built and well formed, as well as those of the other sex, because, if it happens that a woman gives birth to a deformed child, she buries it alive as soon as it is born. They also practice this inhumanity toward the unborn children they are carrying if their husbands abandon them. Then they take another husband, and that happens frequently. These women give birth just like animals do, in some grassy spot, and in an open field, alone and without help, then go at once to wash themselves and their child in the nearest river or in the sea. And as soon as the child is born, if it is without defect and to their liking, they mark it by cutting its tender skin; and it was said elsewhere they did this to the said Talons and to the French children who stayed with them. If the child cries a great deal during this painful operation, they have a bad opinion of its courage and do not like it as much. This is why they like pins and needles [for tattooing] above all things, even though they have no clothes to fasten and do not know how to sew. They find needles better than pins and use them instead to make these incisions.

All the savages, generally, are strong and robust and made for all sorts of hardship. It has already been said that it was their old men who practiced medicine and dressed the wounds. They do this free and with so much success that never did the curable sick die while in their hands. Besides the perfect knowledge they have of the properties of medicinal herbs, as has been said, they draw blood and practice the sucking of wounds. To draw blood, they have little combs, made with the teeth of a kind of large rat found in that country, with which they scrape and tear the skin, and the very spot where one feels the pain. When they want to

cure a headache, they prick the skin [of the head] in several places, depending on where the pain is; and then they suck the blood, which
spurts out with very great force. These practices are successful.

The Cenis eat the roasted grain of maize, or corn. They also make
flour with it and various kinds of gruel; and, from time to time, all the
aged of the village assemble at their chief's house, where they enter into
conversation with each other and entertain each other in various ways.
Then this chief treats each of them to a large jug of gruel made with
corn, very clear, which they drink, and sometimes he gives them presents of bows and arrows, which come from a nation that lives above the
Cenis. These bows are made of a more beautiful wood than their own,
extremely strong and hard, and are red and yellow in color.[42]

They shoot the bow with admirable accuracy, and they know so
well how to choose the exact place of the joints in the shoulders of a
buffalo that it is rare to see them miss their shot. Also, it is the first exer-
cise taught their children, who practice continually as soon as they have
sufficient strength to shoot at little birds with small bows. These savages
not only kill buffalo, deer, roebucks, and all other kinds of beasts and
birds with the bow and arrow, but they also fish in the sea and in the
rivers, having for that purpose bows and arrows that are larger than
ordinary. They have a thousand other inventions for fishing because, in
addition to nets, which they make of hemp and in the same manner as
ours, they fish also with a line and, even though they have no hook, they
arrange the sharp wood with the bait so skillfully that it serves the same
purpose. They harpoon the larger fish with the harpoon at the end of a
long line, which they release when they have wounded the fish; and at
the end of this line there is a sort of buoy made of a certain floating
wood to enable them to find it. Their other inventions for fishing,
which are numerous, are very clever.

Nearly all these people speak very much from the throat,[43] which
renders their dialects difficult to learn. That of the Cenis is one of the
less harsh, for they speak less from the throat than do the other savages.

---

42 The wood was Osage orange, or bois d'arc (*Maclura pomifera*), the common
name of which means "bow wood" in French. It is found abundantly in the
Caddoan country of northeastern Texas and adjacent areas of Arkansas and
Oklahoma. The tree has a yellow heart wood.

43 Minet (Part II, entry for February 27, 1685) also describes the Karankawas'
speech, saying they clapped the tongue against the palate, making a sound
like one makes when speaking to a horse. The Chevalier Grenier, shipwrecked at Matagorda Bay in 1745, observed that they spoke with teeth together, "making a clucking sound with the end of the tongue as one does
when calling chickens" ("Relation," manuscript copy from Archives de Marine, UT archives).

Also, they are the most gentle and the most polite among them, as has been said elsewhere.

They listened with docility to the Spanish Religious who stayed among them—and who, having learned their language, began to preach to them—and willingly allowed them to baptize their children. This Jean-Baptiste Talon avows, having stayed in the country a long time after his brother Pierre and having gone to the Cenis village with the Spaniards, who brought him [away] on their third expedition, as has also been said. [[There is much [reason] to fear that the Spaniards had prejudiced these savage and credulous peoples against the French, to render them odious.]]

All these savage peoples generally are great gesticulators while talking and have a marvelous talent for understanding one another and communicating their thoughts by signs. And this talent is common to all these different nations, so that when they meet or visit one another, even though their languages are different, they understand one another by signs.

17. Whether they saw the Spaniards' mines, the places where they are situated, and how one would go there.

They saw only the mines of Tescoupe [Texcoco] and Patchouque [Pachuca], the former 12 leagues and the others 20 leagues from the City of Mexico, but they know very well that there are many others. It would be very easy to get there by land, via the road that they made, and which the Spaniards smoothed on their three different expeditions; or by other roads, which one could easily follow for the country is everywhere beautiful and flat. They even say that two Cenis men had accompanied the Spaniards as far as Mexico on their second trip, and then had returned to their village; that these two men might still be alive, or had transmitted to their posterity, as is their custom, the knowledge of this road and the things they had seen during their trip. They also said that there are many horses among the Cenis and other savage nations who habitually live in that land, who also raise horses, and from whom one could easily get some in exchange for hatchets, knives, and other trifles.[44] They have seen them several times exchange a horse for a single hatchet or a single knife. And the way the said Talons spoke, it seems

44 This ready availability of horses in eastern Texas at this early date is noteworthy; the nearest Spanish settlement was hundreds of miles away. It testifies to the spread of European influences far beyond the areas actually pene-

that it would not be too difficult for them to find the means of making this trip if they could find again the same nations with whom they had lived, for they still remembered enough of their languages to make themselves understood and to understand them also. In any case, they affirm that they could make themselves understood not only by the nations with whom they have lived but even by other nations of savages, no matter who they be, by means of signs they learned by practice.[45]

They added that neither the city of Mexico nor that of St. Louis de Potosy nor any of the others in the country have any defense or fortification, as far as the seashore, where lies Vera Cruz, which is the only fortified city, as they explained previously. That fact, combined with the indolence of the Spaniards of that country, who are neither warriors nor well armed, would facilitate access.

Nations with which the said Talons were acquainted in the country of La Louisiane: [46]

The Clamcoehs . . . who are on the seashore and almost never leave it.
The Temerlouans . . . who are a little farther up.

} These two nations are cruel and made war on M. de La Salle because he had taken their canoes to use them.

The Toho . . . Still a little farther up, inland
The Cenis . . . A little farther up.
The Ayenny . . . Still a little farther up.

} The first is a wandering nation like the Clamcoehs and Temerlouans and the other two have villages and cultivate the land.

The Amalcham . . . another roving nation.

The Canotino . . . another roving nation that is always at war against all the others, being the most wicked.

The Caouiles . . . another wandering nation but not so wicked.

Choman . . . another nation. These Choman visit the Cenis and other nations quite often, not having war against anyone. They are neighbors of the Spaniards, but on a different side from the one by which the Talons passed. There are many among them who speak Spanish.

---

trated by Europeans. The animals came through native trade channels from as far as Chihuahua. See Enríquez Barroto diary entry for April 18, 1687.

45 Pierre Talon and his brother Robert evidently did make themselves understood when they served as guides and interpreters for the Saint-Denis expedition across Texas in 1714.

46 See Scheutz, "Ethnological Data," in following commentaries.

There is still a great number of nations of which the whole country is filled but whose names the Talons do not know.

There is, besides, a small collection of some Indian words, which the Talons remembered, and which is included only to give a little idea of their idioms

Clamcoeh Language[47]

The fire . . . Cohoille	A bull . . . Teck
The sun . . . Colonu	A cow . . . Tech-nen
The wood . . . Cohab	A calf . . . Cocho
The water . . . Comcom	A stag or deer } Tecomandoi-sen
The Sea . . . Cocomden, which is to say, saltwater	A knife . . . Bequecomb
A man . . . Techoyou	An eagle . . . Balséhé
The woman . . . Achadu	Another common bird Te cot sen
A boy . . . Colohs	European clothes Alames
A bow . . . Crouin	A sword . . . Techbeillé
An arrow . . . Demo	Good, something good Couist-baha
A cabin . . . Caham	Tall Large Counin
Fire pot . . . Coco	
Tobacco . . . Cahé	

The Spaniards . . . They call them Cahamqueamy, which is to say, people of the land, because they came to them by land.

The French . . . They call them Calbasses, as one might say, people coming from the sea.

A horse . . . Canonaium. And all the savage nations generally call it thus.

A wolf . . . Thus the savages call them who tame them, who use them as dogs: Quez.

A pig . . . Quez Calbasses, which is to say, dogs of the French.

Language of the Cenis and of the Ayenny, much easier than the one of the Clamoehs

Water . . . Coko	Good, something good . . . Conhistanhat
A bull . . . Tenaha	Wicked . . . Abana
A woman . . . Senaty	A European, Spaniard or French, without
Grease . . . Assayo	making any distinction: Yayecha

47 See Rudolph Troike, "Linguistic Data," in the commentaries.

Commentaries
on the Interrogations

Ethnological Data
MARDITH K. SCHUETZ

From the time Lucien and Isabelle Talon and their five children boarded one of La Salle's ships bound for the Gulf of Mexico in July, 1684, the family shared the misfortunes of the colony while experiencing a series of tragedies all its own. During the two-month voyage from La Rochelle to Saint-Domingue (Haiti), Madam Talon gave birth to her sixth child. Within a few months of the misplaced landing at Texas' Matagorda Bay, her husband was listed among the colony's numerous dead. There followed the death of her eldest child, Marie-Elizabeth; separation from her oldest son, Pierre, taken by La Salle to the Cenis, or Hasinai, Indians to learn their language; and, finally, the massacre at Fort Saint-Louis, where the four remaining children, ages three and one-half to fourteen, saw their mother slain by the Karankawa Indians and were themselves adopted into that tribe.

Although Pierre was spared this horror, he experienced at age eleven the turmoil surrounding the death of La Salle and a number of his companions. For the next three years he lived among the Hasinai, adapting to their ways as his siblings did to the Karankawas'. Such is the resilience of youth that the five Talon children were able to rise to the demands placed on them by circumstance. Not only were they able to survive the trauma and adjust to the life, first of their Indian captors, then of their Spanish rescuers, but also to leave a valuable record of their experiences. Our knowledge of both the abortive French settlement and the native peoples with whom the colonists came in contact is enriched thereby.

This record is contained in the transcript of the Interrogations of Pierre and Jean-Baptiste on their return to France in 1698. Although the rambling order of the questions presents problems for the analyst, it is clear that Pierre, having lived three years among the Cenis, is responsible for most of the observations on that tribe. Jean-Baptiste's contact with the Cenis, to whom he was taken by the Spaniards after his ransom from the Karankawas and before his removal to Mexico, was relatively brief. Although both boys were exposed to aspects of the Karankawan culture during the life of the French colony, the younger brother must be considered the primary source for information on the coastal Indians. In addition to these distinct cultural areas, they came in contact with inland Texas tribes, some of which can be identified as Tonkawan, and, en route to Mexico, with Coahuiltecan tribes. In many instances we would be unable to determine which cultural group or geographical area is being described were it not for other sources. For example, we read that the "whole country produces (maize or) corn, potatoes, gourds, pumpkins, and beans of several kinds" and that the area generally abounded in "tunas" and "figs." From other observers it is known that agriculture was practiced only by the Cenis and other Caddoan speakers of northeastern Texas and that the fruits of the prickly pear (tunas) and yucca (figs) were harvested in southern Texas. Some of the brothers' observations concerning Indians pertain to a distinct cultural area rather than relate to all the tribes, as the text indicates. Therefore, to avoid redundancy, it is expedient to discuss the descriptions in terms of cultural traits, rather than cultural area. After the ethnic groups mentioned have been identified, the brothers' comments will be compared with contemporary French and Spanish accounts.

The Talon brothers actually named very few of the tribes with whom they came in contact: Clamcoëhs (variously read as Clamcoëts and Clamcoches), Temerlouans (or Paouites), Tohos, Cenis, Ayennys, Amalchams, Canotinos, Caouiles, and Chomans. The linguistic evidence provided in the document dispels any doubt that the Clamcoëhs were one of several nomadic Karankawan groups inhabiting the mainland and offshore islands between Galveston and Corpus Christi bays.

The Temerlouans are probably the Kannehonans listed by Joutel but cannot be equated with any group identified by the Spaniards. Since the Tohos, a Tonkawan tribe that is well known from Spanish sources, were at war with this nation, it appears likely that they belonged to a distinct linguistic group. Joutel included the Kannehonans among those tribes found west and northwest of the Maligne River (identifiable as the Brazos).[1]

The Toho (Tohaha or Tohaka in Joutel) was but one of many nomadic tribes repeatedly encountered by the Spaniards along the Camino Real between the Guadalupe and Trinity rivers and extending toward the coast. Many tribes in this area shared a distinct language (Tonka-

---

1 Henri Joutel, *Joutel's Journal of La Salle's Last Voyage,* ed. Henry Reed Stiles, p. 90.

wan), although with dialectical differences.[2] By the nineteenth century, tribal distinctions had been lost and they were generically known as Tonkawas. It was from some of these peoples that the Spaniards first learned of the massacre at Fort Saint-Louis and among them that they found the first two French survivors, Jean L'Archevêque and Jacques Grollet.

The Cenis of the French were the Tejas or Hasinai of the Spaniards. These terms are generally used to denote a confederacy of various tribes or villages of the southern Caddoan speakers who intermarried and regarded themselves as kin. Some of the better-known tribes belonging to the confederacy were the Tejas or Hasinai proper, Neches, Nabedaches, Nacogdoches, Nasonis, Nadacos, and Hainai (The Talons' Ayenny).[3] These tribes, located on the upper reaches of the Neches and Angelina rivers, were sedentary horticulturalists who, with their cousins of the Cadohadacho Confederacy living north of them on the great bend of the Red River, represented the most culturally advanced natives of Texas.

The Caouiles were the Coahuiltecans with whom the French survivors came in contact as they passed through southern Texas and northeastern Mexico en route to the capital of New Spain. These were small nomadic nations, each with its own name and language, which lived by hunting, fishing, and gathering. The brothers' notations concerning their bellicosity, nakedness, and paucity of artifacts are amply borne out by contemporary chroniclers.

And, finally, the Chomans were the Jumanos who lived on the Conchos River of eastern Chihuahua, where it joins the Río Grande. The Spaniards were aware that they came every year to the headwaters of the Guadalupe River to hunt buffalo and were frequently found with the central Texas groups such as the Tohos or the Tejas.[4]

In spite of the diversity of tribes, customs, and languages, the Indians were able to communicate by sign language. The brothers noted that "this talent is common to all these different nations, so that when they meet or visit one another, even though their languages are different, they understand one another by signs." The universality of the sign language was noted by every European who came in contact with the natives of northeastern Mexico and Texas.

The Talon children found the natives physically impressive. They

2 Damián Massanet, *Diary of the Missionaries on the Expedition of Don Domingo Terán de los Ríos into Texas, 1691–1692*, trans. Mattie Austin Hatcher, p. 56.
3 Juan Agustín Morfi, *History of Texas, 1673–1779*, I, 82.
4 Massanet, *Diary*, pp. 58–59.

were well formed, normally lived to an old age, and possessed "nearly perfect health," the latter characteristics generally being attributed to the mild climate. Congenital deformity was not seen because, according to the brothers, deformed babies were buried alive. The notation is significant in that it extends the practice, previously reported only for the Coahuiltecans, to other cultural areas of Texas.[5] Although the custom of inducing abortion was widespread among the American Indians, abandonment by a husband as a reason is new information.[6]

Important to the general health of the Indian populations upon initial European contact was the stamina required for their life-style, which was fostered from birth. The same regimen to which the Indians themselves adhered was imposed on the French adoptees: swimming, daily bathing at daybreak regardless of the weather, and running, which was deemed essential for survival among a people engaged in continual warfare. Spanish accounts substantiate the importance of sports and competition as means of staying fit. Coahuiltecans engaged in footraces, mock warfare, wrestling matches, and ball games, which were taken so seriously that they sometimes provoked wars. The Karankawas were such passionate wrestlers that the Tonkawas called them by a name that reflected the trait. Footraces by youths were important features of Hasinai celebrations held the first part of May and at the autumnal equinox. The importance of being fleet in both instances was significantly linked to warfare and survival.[7]

Those who suffered wounds or fell sick had recourse to shamans or medical practitioners who, according to the general observation of the brothers, "have a marvelous knowledge of the different properties of the medicinal herbs that abound in the whole country and can easily heal themselves of illnesses and wounds that befall them." They further practiced bloodletting and sucking out the cause of the malady. Curing techniques and herbal medicine practiced by all American Indians were pretty much the same. Illness was often laid to bewitchment. Fray

5 Vicente de Santa María, "Relación histórica de la Colonia del Nuevo Santandér y Costa del Seno Mexicano," in *Estado general de las fundaciones hechas por Don José de Escandón en la Colonia del Nuevo Santander,* vol. II, 401.
6 For an assessment of the practice of infanticide, see Mardith K. Schuetz, "The Indians of the San Antonio Missions, 1718–1821," Ph.D. diss., pp. 176–79.
7 Santa María, "Relación," p. 409; Frederick Ruecking, Jr., "Social Organization of the Coahuiltecan Indians of Southern Texas and Northeastern Mexico," *Texas Journal of Science* 7 (1955): 382; Albert S. Gatschet, *The Karankawa Indians: The Coast People of Texas,* pp. 44; Isidro Félix de Espinosa, *Crónica de los colegios de propaganda fide de la Nueva España,* pp. 708–10.

Isidro Félix de Espinosa recorded that the Hasinai were convinced that witches from the Bidais, Ays (Eyeish), or Yacdoas caused illness either by coming among them unobserved or by shooting the malady into them with a bow as a "sharp thing like a dart."[8]

The notation in the Talon document that old men were the medical practitioners requires amplification. Medicine men generally were held in high esteem in native societies, and the cultural areas being considered were no exception. Nevertheless, according to Spanish observers, at least one Caddoan tribe (the Nacogdoches) and the Tonkawas sometimes killed a shaman for an unsuccessful ministration.[9] It is also known from contemporary sources that healing was not the prerogative of old men, as the Talons say it was. Espinosa claimed that among the Hasinai young men of "scarcely twenty years" were initiated as new "surgeons." Given the developed institutions of the Caddoans and the prominent roles accorded old men, it is likely that the new initiates underwent a long apprenticeship. Such a conjecture would provide a reasonable explanation of why Pierre thought healing was the province of the elders. The fact that shamans were also called on for measuring houses to be built, blessing them, and blessing warriors and new corn, suggests either specialization within the profession or the delegation of duties according to importance and rank of the practitioner. Cabeza de Vaca observed the privileged status of Karankawan curers, who, alone among the population, were allowed multiple wives and were cremated rather than buried like everyone else. Coahuiltecan shamans of Nuevo León and Tamaulipas might be of either sex, according to Fray Vicente de Santa María.[10]

Jean-Baptiste Talon confirms accounts by contemporaries that the Karankawas, being constantly on the move hunting or fishing, lacked permanent villages and fixed dwellings. However, his description of crude lean-tos covered with buffalo skins differs from those of other members of La Salle's party. Joutel's report of a village of about fifty oven-shaped huts covered with rush mats and skins located on elevated ground substantiates Cabeza de Vaca's observation of huts made of a framework of "four hoops" covered with mats, erected on beds of oyster shell. The circular house form, but covered only with skins, was still in

---

8 Espinosa, *Cronica*, pp. 702–703.
9 Ibid., p. 703; Isidro Félix de Espinosa, *The Espinosa-Olivares-Aguirre Expedition of 1709: Espinosa's Diary*, trans. Gabriel Tous, p. 12.
10 Alvar Núñez Cabeza de Vaca, "The Narrative of Cabeza de Vaca," in Frederick Webb Hodge and Theodore H. Lewis, eds., *Spanish Explorers in the Southern United States, 1528–1543*, pp. 51–52; Santa María, "Relación," p. 41.

use in the nineteenth century.[11] Jean-Baptiste's lean-to may have been a seasonal variation.

Pierre Talon reported that the sedentary, agricultural Cenis, comprising some one thousand persons, lived in villages that were "divided into families" who inhabited "wood houses covered with straw." His brief comments can be elucidated from other sources. His population estimate probably refers to a single tribe of the Hasinai Confederacy, because Father Morfi, writing a century later, after various European-introduced diseases had taken their toll, recorded about 420 warriors in three villages, 300 of them belonging to the Nacogdoches tribe.[12] Both Spanish and other contemporary sources make it clear that each village consisted of a center where the houses of chiefs, council houses, and temples were situated, and the settlement pattern embraced scattered lodges and farms. Joutel describes the beehive-shaped lodges, thatched with straw, which measured as much as sixty feet in diameter and housed fifteen to twenty persons. The interiors were divided into compartments that afforded some privacy to the nuclear families making up what must have been extended families. Raised beds of canes were provided with finely woven mats and skins and a perpetual fire in the center of the lodge was common to all.[13] The clustered lodges with their separate fields probably represented clan divisions and what Pierre meant by villages that were "divided into families."

The Caddoans were the only Indians in Texas who were engaged in intensive agriculture at the time of European contact. Pierre reported that they cultivated corn, beans, pumpkins of several kinds (*cucurbita* family), and tobacco, as well as unidentified "vegetables and roots." Espinosa noted cantaloupes, watermelons, and sunflower seeds, the latter mixed with ground corn to make a flavorful bread.[14] Corn was the staple crop, however, as the same Spanish friar made clear. Fields were prepared for planting in the spring by communal effort, although planting was left to individual families. Two crops were harvested each year.

Other tribes encountered by the French relied on harvesting of natural products, such as fruits, nuts, and tubers, and on fishing and hunting. The Talons' references to specific implements used in the latter

11 Joutel, *Journal,* p. 35; Cabeza de Vaca, "Narrative," pp. 52, 66; Gatschet, *Karankawa Indians,* pp. 10, 17, 62. See Jean Béranger (*Béranger's Discovery of Aransas Pass,* p. 22): "Their huts are of hide that they fold like tents and carry with them."
12 Morfi, *History,* I, 82.
13 Joutel, *Journal,* pp. 108–109. See also, Minet, Part I and note 73, concerning the Natchez's perpetual fire encountered by La Salle in 1682.
14 Espinosa, *Crónica,* p. 689.

pursuits contain new information. The bow and arrow were universally used, but little was known concerning their construction. Arrow points of fish bones or fish teeth described by the brothers were heretofore unknown. The French named a river near the colony the "River of Canes" (the Lavaca-Navidad, according to Joutel's description) because of the "reeds or little canes with which the savages make arrows." The use of cane indicates the manufacture of a compound arrow with a cane shaft and hardwood foreshaft carrying the projectile point. This technique of manufacture is implied in the account of Cabeza de Vaca, who mentions "hard canes to make arrows" among the items he traded between coastal and interior tribes during the sixteenth century. Such arrows were also used by the Coahuiltecans of Nuevo León, according to Alonso de León. Karankawas in the nineteenth century had apparently changed to an arrow of simple construction.[15] The Talons also state that a tribe located north of the Hasinai made bows, which were much sought after, of "beautiful wood," strong, hard, and "red and yellow" in color. These probably were made of bois d'arc by the Cadohadachos, the likely origin of the bows that were a trade specialty in the 1500s. Both the Talon brothers and Joutel mention the use of clubs. The former do not make it clear whether the club was used by all the tribes, but, since Joutel mentions it in connection with the Cenis and it is not reported for other tribes in Texas, we may assume that its use was limited to the Caddoan peoples.[16] It is unfortunate that none of the chroniclers describes the weapon. Curiously, the Talons failed to mention lances, which were reported by other survivors of the La Salle episode, as well as by the Spaniards.

Hunting provided not only meat but also skins used for clothing, bedding, and, among the Karankawas, covering for their huts or lean-tos. Buffalo and deerskins dressed like chamois and made as "soft as cloth" had been an important item of intertribal trade in Cabeza de Vaca's day and were still important in the trade, according to the Talon account and contemporary reports.[17]

The brothers report the use of bows and arrows for fishing, pre-

15 Cabeza de Vaca, "Narrative," p. 56; Alonso de León, Juan Bautista Chapa, and Fernando Sánchez de Zamora, *Historia de Nuevo León, con noticias sobre Coahuila, Tamaulipas, Texas y Nuevo México,* pp. 36–37; Gatschet, *Karankawa Indians,* pp. 12–13.

16 Cabeza de Vaca, "Narrative," p. 56; Joutel, *Journal,* pp. 106–107. Presumably, the reference is to the war club; the use of the rabbit club among the Coahuiltecans is therefore excluded from the discussion.

17 Cabeza de Vaca, "Narrative," p. 56; Espinosa, *Espinosa-Olivares-Aguirre Expedition,* p. 12.

sumably by all the ethnic groups, because they were used both in the "ocean" (bays) and rivers. These bows were longer than those used for hunting. They name as other methods of fishing the use of nets, a line equipped with a baited, sharpened piece of wood in lieu of a hook, and, most important, a harpoon used for larger fish. The other "clever inventions" they mention are not enumerated. Fishing techniques have previously been described only for Karankawas and Coahuiltecans of Nuevo León. In the sixteenth century, says Cabeza de Vaca, the Capoques (a Karankawan tribe) trapped fish in cane weirs—probably one of the Talons' "clever inventions." In the nineteenth century the Karankawas fished with bows and arrows, either from canoes or by wading. The use of both bow and arrow and nets in Nuevo León is reported by Alonso de León.[18] Nothing was known of fishing techniques among the Caddoan or Tonkawan groups heretofore; nor has the use of a harpoon been noted. There is no doubt about the identity of the weapon, because the Talons describe a line equipped with a wooden buoy.

Karankawan canoes figure prominently in this account, since their seizure by the French without payment is said to have provoked the Indians' hostility. These primitive dugouts, unsuitable for deep, open water, were used within the relatively shallow waters between the islands and the mainland. Their size, however, must have been impressive. The chroniclers of the Alarcón expedition tell of an encounter with a canoe in which four men and women and eight children were being transported.[19]

That ancient companion to man, the dog, was first noted among the coastal tribes by Cabeza de Vaca. The Talons' statement that wolves were taken as pups and tamed for the hunt identifies the breed. Solís reported in 1767 that the Hasinai bred a dog called a "jubin," a cross between a wolf and a coyote. He describes it as being very thin with a pointed nose, quick of scent, "easily provoked and just as dishonest" as its master. Other Spaniards reported that the Tonkawans (?) Emet and Cavas used their dogs with the travois. In the nineteenth century the "barkless dogs of a fox-like race" kept by the Karankawas were described.[20]

18 Cabeza de Vaca, "Narrative," p. 50; Gatschet, *Karankawa Indians*, p. 50; León, *Historia*, p. 21.
19 Francicso Céliz, *Diary of the Alarcón Expedition into Texas, 1718–1719*, trans. Fritz Leo Hoffman, p. 66.
20 Cabeza de Vaca, "Narrative," pp. 80–81; José de Solís, *The Solís Diary of 1767*, trans. Peter Forrestal, p. 28; Massanet, "Letter of Fray Damián Massanet to Don Carlos de Sigüenza, 1690," in Herbert Eugene Bolton, ed., *Spanish Ex-*

Among what appear to be observations on the Indians generally, Pierre and Jean-Baptiste relate that a woman gave birth, unassisted, in an open, grassy field, washed herself and the child in the nearest body of water, and promptly returned to the village. This must be understood as pertaining to the Karankawas and other coastal groups, because both the Hasinai and the Tonkawa women delivered in parturition huts.[21] The newborn was tattooed, and excessive crying was considered indicative of a lack of courage, according to the Talons. The practice of tattooing, universal among Texas Indians, has been well documented, but the brothers' information that tattoos were applied shortly after birth— surely as tribal identification marks—provides new insight into the custom. All the French survivors held by the Indian tribes were tattooed as overt proof of their adoption. Pierre's face would have been marked with a straight line running from the top of the forehead and over the nose to the tip of the chin, according to information on the Cenis. Of his and Jean-Baptiste's brothers and sister, we are told that "all were marked with a stripe on the face."[22] The other captives held by the Karankawas were tattooed, and several descriptions indicate possible variations among these coastal people. In the eighteenth century, virgins of an unidentified band or bands were marked, like the Cenis, with a single narrow line extending from the forehead to the chin. In the following century the Cocos (a Karankawan band) of both sexes were identified by small circles over the cheekbones. In the same century the Karankawas proper exhibited a small circle over each cheekbone, a horizontal line from the outer angle of the eye toward the ear, and three parallel lines from the lower lip to the chin. Such tribal identification, although provoking disgust among Europeans, nevertheless assured the safety of the French captives among the various tribes, serving as a passport, so to speak. We know less about markings on other parts of the body, although Joutel specified that the Cenis traced animals, leaves, and

ploration in the Southwest, p. 359; Alonso de León, "Itinerary of the De León Expedition, 1690," in Bolton, *Spanish Exploration,* p. 395; Gatschet, *Karankawa Indians,* p. 44.

21 Solís, *Diary,* pp. 36–37; Andrée Sjoberg, "The Culture of the Tonkawa: A Texas Coastal Tribe," *Texas Journal of Science* 5, no. 3 (1963): 291.

22 Joutel, *Journal,* pp. 110–11; Alonso de León to the viceroy, Rio Grande, June 12, 1690, in Lino Gómez Canedo, ed., *Primeras exploraciones y poblamiento de Texas (1686–1694),* p. 157. See Juan Enríquez Barroto's description of the Atákapan tattoos on the Mexican boy found on the Calcasieu River of Louisiana, in the diary entry of April 18, 1687.

flowers over the shoulders, thighs, and other areas.[23] Such designs may have reflected age, sex, or accomplishments.

The Talons reported that the Indians, though monogamous, changed spouses frequently. Presumably, this description was typical of Caddoan, Tonkawan, and Karankawan tribes. Espinosa confirms that marriage among the Hasinai was casual and readily dissolved. Among the Karankawan bands in the sixteenth century, Cabeza de Vaca says that only the shamans were allowed multiple wives. The Talons relate that the sailor Rutre (or Ruter) had taken seven or eight Cenis wives "in succession." Whether or not any of the Frenchmen took Tonkawan wives is not known, but we can pretty well rule out Karankawan wives, given their general hostility toward Europeans and Joutel's statement that there were no natives in the fort because La Salle had expressly forbidden communication with them. The claim, apparently made by Pierre concerning the Cenis, that wives and daughters willingly gave themselves to La Salle's men without societal censure can be substantiated from contemporary sources. Joutel recounts that they did so readily in return for needles (valued as tattooing instruments), knives, and beads and that they were rarely punished by their husbands. Espinosa wrote that infidelity was not considered a serious offense; although some men might beat their wives, they ordinarily closed their eyes to flirtations, obscene jesting, or alliances.[24]

The French children recognized that the Indians believed in an afterlife from their observation of burials in which the dead person, wrapped in his buffalo robe, was buried with his weapons, food, and fire stick[25] for use when he "woke up." There is no reason to doubt that the custom was universal. Solís relates that the Hasinai buried their dead in a sitting position, and Espinosa reveals that a special funeral was held for those who died in battle or away from home. Cabeza de Vaca noted an exception: Karankawan shamans were cremated rather than buried like ordinary people. Jean-Baptiste observed that dead parents of the Karankawas were mourned by family members, who smeared their bodies with black paint made from the charcoal of walnut wood soaked in water and that family members wept regularly at a given hour, both morning and evening, for a long time. Cabeza de Vaca states that

23 Solís, *Diary,* p. 13; Jean Louis Berlandier, *The Indians of Texas in 1830,* ed. John C. Ewars, plate 16; Gatschet, *Karankawa Indians,* p. 62.

24 Espinosa, *Crónica,* p. 701; Cabeza de Vaca, "Narrative," pp. 51–52; Joutel, *Journal,* pp. 77, 111.

25 The description of fire making is accurate. Such equipment has been recovered from prehistoric sites in dry cave shelters of extreme southwestern Texas and in Coahuila.

mourning lasted a year and relatives and others wailed before dawn, at noon, and again at sunset. On the first anniversary of the death, "they wash and purify themselves from the stain of smoke." This last sentence, the meaning of which has been in doubt, is clarified by Jean-Baptiste: the year's mourning period ended when the charcoal paint was washed off. The Hasinai belief in an afterlife, described by Espinosa, where everyone was happy and there was no hunger, sickness, or other pain, probably was shared by all tribes.[26]

Apart from the belief in a hereafter, the Talons, like most of their European contemporaries, perceived no concept of religion among the Indians. That youngsters brought up in the Catholic church, with its opulent ritual, failed to recognize other forms of worship is understandable in the context of the age. Even the Spaniards, with their longer acquaintance with the Hasinai, perceived but dimly a theology manifested in the rich ceremonialism described by observers such as Espinosa. Pierre noted that the oldest among any assembly of the Cenis, or Hasinai, made an offering of any game taken by uttering a prayer and throwing a piece of meat into the fire. Joutel, in referring to the same tribe, acknowledged the new-corn offering and the blessing of young warriors by an "old man."[27] Spanish sources reveal that the Caddoans lived under a theocracy with a *chenesi*, or high priest (always an old man), holding the highest rank in society, with lesser priests, or medicine men, under him. The "old man" of Joutel's account probably was the *chenesi*. The Spaniards' descriptions of so many details of the Caddoan religious hierarchy, ritual, and ceremonial centers is an ironic contradiction to the claim that no developed religious concept could be detected.[28]

Karankawas and Tonkawas, being less culturally advanced than the Caddoans, apparently manifested their belief in no manner that the Talon children were able to recognize. Joutel, probably referring to the Tonkawas, thought he had discovered some concept of a superior being when the Indians lifted their hands and eyes toward Heaven.[29] Pierre

26 Solís, *Diary*, p. 29; Espinosa, *Crónica*, pp. 697–99; Cabeza de Vaca, "Narrative," pp. 51–52.
27 Joutel, *Journal*, p. 113.
28 On the Hasinai religion, see Espinosa, *Crónica*, pp. 681, 695–98, 708; Solís, *Diary*, pp. 28–29; Massanet, "Letter," pp. 380–81; Morfi, *History*, I, 70; Céliz, *Diary*, p. 78; Juan Antonio de la Peña, "Derrotero seguida por el Marqués de San Miguel de Aguayo en su viage y expedición a la Provincia de Texas (1720–1722)," in *Documentos eclesiásticos y civiles de la provincia de Texas ó Nuevas Philipinas, 1720–1779*, p. 50.
29 Joutel, *Journal*, p. 113.

and Jean-Baptiste observed that the sun and the moon, though not worshiped, were regarded as divinities. From the order of the interrogation, they appear to have been referring to Coahuiltecan groups, but astral deities undoubtedly were recognized universally. An awareness of the heavenly bodies and of the seasonal pattern of their movements was essential to the Indians. They told them when to plant, when certain fruits would ripen, and when fishing would be good. The course of the sun was believed to trace the path of the dead on their travels to a paradisiacal home with the Great Spirit. Small wonder that so many celebrations of all the groups discussed coincided with phases of the moon or the vernal and autumnal equinoxes.[30]

Astral deities could become incarnate. The Europeans, having come out of the east by ship, arrived with the sun, in a manner of speaking, and, as the Talon brothers observed, were hailed as children of the sun.

Affecting the Europeans' blindness to native religions was the fact that the nomadic peoples had no regular places of worship, no religious edifices, no recognizable vested clergy, and professed moral codes that differed sharply from their own. Because the Indians' religion was so completely integrated with all aspects of life, it was lost on the outside observer.

Although the religious factor in Indian ceremonialism was not understood by Europeans, one overt aspect of it was the consumption of intoxicating beverages. The Talon brothers' mention of brews made from a red bean and a certain leaf calls for clarification because both were not, as far as we know, used by all the tribes of Texas. The red bean was the mountain laurel (*Sophora secundaflora*), which is native to south Texas. Its prehistoric use in southern Texas and nothern Mexico, and contemporary use by Coahuiltecans and Tonkawas, is well documented. It was an important article of trade into Caddoan territory at least as early as the sixteenth century, and its eighteenth-century use in that region was also noted. There is no historical evidence that the Karankawas used this particular intoxicant. The second beverage described by the Talons was made from the parched leaves of the yaupon (*Ilex cassine* or *vomitoria*) and was consumed as the "black drink" among Indians throughout the Gulf states. Its use among the Karankawas was first noted in the sixteenth century, and continued use is affirmed throughout the following three centuries. The importance of the drink in

30 Concerning veneration of astral deities, see reference in note 28 above; also Santa María, "Relación," p. 407; Gatschet, *Karankawa Indians*, p. 18; Sjoberg, "Culture," p. 293; John R. Swanton, *Linguistic Material from the Tribes of Southern Texas and Northeastern Mexico*.

Hasinai ceremonialism was recorded by Espinosa in the eighteenth century. Pierre's observation that "they drink of it especially when they have walked a long distance" is puzzling. We might infer that he was describing the convening of Hasinai tribes for a joint celebration, the distance traveled impressing his young mind. There is no historical evidence that Tonkawas and Coahuiltecans shared the "black drink" ceremony with the Caddoans and Karankawas.[31]

The nomadic tribes' government was so unstructured that the young Frenchmen accord it no mention. Pierre lived with a Cenis war chief whose father lived with him and bore the same title. From Spanish sources it would appear that each Hasinai village had both a peace chief and a war chief who were responsible for secular considerations. Pierre's notation that both father and son held the same title (although not simultaneously active, in all probability) is of interest because war chiefs held their positions through popular acceptance and not inheritance. Yet the fact that authority tended to run in certain families has been demonstrated for other Texas tribes of the eighteenth century.[32] Ranked above the village chiefs was a supreme chief, whom the Spaniards referred to as the "governor." He probably headed the confederacy of the several tribes or villages. In addition, there was a council of elders that was deemed essential to the proper functioning of both civil and religious aspects of society. All these officials were, nevertheless, subordinate to the high priest, as stated previously.[33]

Warfare, with its concomitant horrors of scalping and the torture and eating of captives, was a fact of life among Texas Indians. The French brothers stated that war was begun by surprise attack at night or daybreak, when the enemy was asleep and the attackers' risk was minimal. The surprise night raid was described in reference to Coahuiltecan warfare in the sixteenth century.[34] The practice among other tribes is new information. The careful planning that went into a raid was observed by Jean-Baptiste. Only after the Karankawas had removed their women, children, and aged to a safe refuge did they go in search of the Cenis. Failing to find these traditional enemies, they instead attacked the Ayenny (Hainai), returning with horses, fifty to sixty scalps, and

31 For an assessment of the use of intoxicants in Coahuiltecan, Tonkawan, and Karankawan ceremonies, see Schuetz, "Indians," pp. 96–99. The role of these beverages in Hasinai culture is revealed in Espinosa, *Crónica* (see note 28 above).
32 Schuetz, "Indians," pp. 254–67.
33 The Hasinai hierarchy is best described in Espinosa, *Crónica*, pp. 704, 708–10; Massanet, "Letter," p. 381; Joutel, *Journal*, pp. 106–107.
34 Cabeza de Vaca, "Narrative," pp. 84–86.

thirty to forty captives, several of whom were subsequently eaten. This being the sort of spectacle to which a youngster would pay particular attention, Jean-Baptiste probably does not exaggerate the spoils. Furthermore, Joutel reports a victorious raid against an enemy tribe by the Cenis that returned with forty-eight scalps.[35]

Although there is no direct evidence of Tonkawas and Karankawas taking scalps, the practice probably was universal, and the display of such trophies and dancing with or around them was *de rigueur* to celebrate a victory. The Talons probably refer to the Cenis in declaring that the dried scalps were filled with hay, strung on sticks, and suspended from lodge roofs. Entire heads displayed as war trophies were seen on two occasions by Spaniards: the first in a Coahuiltecan camp, the second among the Hasinai.[36] Yet these appear to be isolated occurrences. Since the trait was common to tribes of the Sierra Madre, in the present Mexican states of Durango and Chihuahua, it might be argued that the examples witnessed this far north were due to the presence of Chomanes (Jumanos) among these tribes.

Cannibalism was widespread, if not universal, among Texas Indians. Both brothers testified that only traditional enemies were eaten; not even the cruel Karankawas consumed French flesh. Their assertion is borne out by others. Joutel relates that a party of six men sent by La Salle to scout the coast were massacred by the Karankawas. Their bodies were found scattered and almost devoured by wolves but untouched by the natives.[37] The Frenchmen L'Archevêque and Grollet, who had been living with the Hasinai, claimed to have buried fourteen victims of the Fort Saint-Louis massacre.[38]

Pierre lived with the friendly Cenis three years. His sister and younger brothers witnessed the horror of the massacre at Fort Saint-Louis and the bludgeoning death of their mother at the hands of their Karankawan captors. In spite of the experience, according to this testimony, the "Talons affirm that they were always treated by these savage people with the greatest kindness in the world, without ever having been maltreated with blows or otherwise" during their captivity. Such contradictions render difficult a true assessment of the Karankawan

35 Joutel, *Journal,* pp. 128–30.
36 León, "Itinerary," pp. 389–90; Espinosa, *Crónica,* p. 710.
37 Joutel, *Journal,* p. 59. It is of interest that Joutel reports that firearms taken from the murdered Frenchmen of the various scouting expeditions were first used against the colonists in June, 1686, two and one-half years prior to the massacre at the fort (p. 71). This is the first recorded instance of native use of firearms in Texas.
38 León, "Itinerary," p. 403.

character. All Europeans of the time agree that the coastal tribes were cruel in comparison to the inland natives. French and Spaniards alike may have invited this hostility to a certain extent. Cabeza de Vaca and other survivors of the sixteenth-century Narváez expedition were at first treated with kindness after they were cast away on Karankawan shores, although instances of cruelty occurred later in their sojourn. The Talon brothers claimed that although the Karankawas were never the aggressors, they never forgave an offense. The French youngsters felt that their countrymen had incurred native hostility by refusing to pay for canoes or services and further damaged their image by quarreling among themselves. There can be no doubt that La Salle erred in failing to be more open-handed with the natives. Joutel states that La Salle initially purchasd two canoes with hatchets but later confiscated two more as payment for articles the Indians had fished from the sea when the store-ship *Aimable* broke up. His men compounded the affront by reclaiming some blankets and, without attempting to barter, taking some hides, which the Indians interpreted as an act of war.[39]

The natives, at least the women, exempted the French children from the culpability of the adults and saved them from the general massacre. For the duration of their captivity, the children were treated and loved as their own; tattooed as tribal members, taught to swim, run, and shoot, and taken on hunts and raiding parties. And, when they were reluctantly turned over to the Spaniards (persuaded that a superior Spanish force would take them if they refused the ransom), the Indians wept and mourned, according to the Talons' own account. As for the captive children, they probably adapted to the native life out of survival instincts. Among the countless white captives taken by various Indian groups, both Spanish and American sources tell of scores who adapted to the native culture. In many cases, those who lived among their captors for long periods refused repatriation.

Because the children of Lucien and Isabelle Talon survived to tell their story, the history of La Salle's doomed colony is enriched by their insights into the events they witnessed and the native peoples who surrounded them. Many of their observations corroborate or amplify contemporary notations on customs and artifacts or provide new data. Their account extends the previously known distribution of the custom of burying deformed babies, the use of the compound arrow, and war raids initiated by surprise attack at night or daybreak. Although the custom of tattooing was known to be universal among the tribes, such marking of the new born was not known. The practice of pregnant

39 Joutel, *Journal,* pp. 39–41.

wives inducing abortion because they were abandoned by their husbands has not been otherwise recorded. The mention of the taming of wolf pups for hunting adds to our knowledge of canine domestication. Heretofore, nothing was known of Tonkawan or Caddoan fishing techniques. The widespread employment of nets (except by certain Coahuiltecans), baited lines, and, most important, harpoons, which had not been noted in Texas previously, is of particular interest to the ethnologist. The description of charcoal paint worn by Karankawan mourners for a year clarifies an incomprehensible passage in Cabeza de Vaca's relation.

The Talons' contributions to the ethnology of Texas Indians can now be added to their participation in certain historic events during the years that followed their captivity. Pierre, following the Spanish expedition that secured the release of his siblings, was returned to the Cenis to assist the Franciscan missionaries and Spanish soldiers as an interpreter. The brothers' responses to the interrogations made at Brest in 1698 proved to be of value to the planners of the Mississippi colony. The Talons joined French expeditions in 1700–1702 and 1714–15 that explored the Gulf coastal region from Mobile to the Rio Grande. In 1714, Pierre and his brother Robert served as guides and interpreters to Louis Juchereau de Saint-Denis during his historic trek across Texas to San Juan Bautista (present-day Guerrero, Coahuila), which resulted in the Spanish reoccupation of Texas. Thus, through the children of the failed French colony, La Salle's influence on the region's history was carried forth.

Natural History
DEL WENIGER

The interrogators of the Talon brothers, in their inquest concerning the ill-fated La Salle expedition, asked specific questions about the topography and the flora and fauna of the country entered. The French government was planning a new attempt to colonize where La Salle had failed, and the witnesses were firsthand observers of that mysterious land. The Talons, having spent several years in the American wilderness, first as members of La Salle's group, then as Indian captives, had experienced the country in ways that explorers never could, and their observations were set down in official records.

This testimony from near the beginning of this area's historical period constitutes one of the earliest reports on natural Texas; hence its considerable significance. The Talons' testimony is a new source to help establish a base from which to measure subsequent change. They deposed on four areas of the country: (1) Matagorda Bay, on the middle Texas coast; (2) the country explored by La Salle, from Fort Saint-Louis northeast to the Cenis village, not far from present-day Nacogdoches, and west to the Rio Grande; (3) "the whole country"; and (4) New Spain and "the countries passed in getting there," which is to say, the parts of Texas and northern Mexico crossed between the Nacogdoches area and the City of Mexico.

The Talons' general statements are brief and repetitious. They describe the country around Lavaca Bay as flat, diversified, and made up of woods and prairies—the same terms they apply to the country as a whole. Although such terms clearly do not fit all of Texas, they do provide an apt description of a strip of east central Texas and the state's central and southern coastal regions. "Prairies" in this context means "meadows" or "savannas," not the huge expanses of treeless plains that "prairie" is apt to connote.

The point is that trees were always part of the prairie, or were not far from it. That it was so in south-central Texas is well substantiated. Ferdinand Roemer, one of the most eminent scientific observers of early Texas, wrote in the mid-nineteenth century of "the forests of the prairies." Ida Kappell Kapp's 1850 account of the exact area of La Salle's landing shows what the Talons sought to describe: "It is peculiar how isolated single groups of trees are on the prairie. The little hills are usually covered with six to eight trees. The flat land is prairie, so that one would swear that they had been planted by human hands. . . . There are, of course, larger woods too." [1]

In the Talons' precise descriptions, the region around Lavaca Bay was diversified with "woods and prairies or savannas"; the whole of the country they had seen was "diversified . . . with forests [*forestre*], woods [*bois*], and prairies." The seeming redundancy calls for further clarification. *Bois* designates "an extent of land covered with trees, bushes, etc."; *forestre*, on the other hand, seems always to indicate an area of large trees. The difference is not in numbers of trees but in size. The Talons— lacking that wonderful Spanish word *chaparral*—apparently were trying to convey that in the southern coastal region the groves and thickets interspersed with grassland were made up of comparatively small trees and shrubby plants; they encountered real forests of large trees only farther up into eastern Texas. If so, they are in agreement with later accounts.

1 Ferdinand von Roemer, *Texas, with Particular Reference to German Immigration and the Physical Appearance of the Country,* p. 76; Ida Kappell Kapp, "A Letter Home by Ida Kappell Kapp," p. 95.

They go on to describe the many rivers traversing Texas: mostly narrow and all bordered by timber, making them easy to cross by felling trees on either bank to form foot bridges. Indeed, the primary channels of most Texas streams are not wide; the nearly universally wooded bottoms are a well-known feature, and on relatively few occasions were explorers of Texas held up at stream crossings. The Talons tell of only one river between the Cenis village and central Mexico that was wide enough to require boats for crossing: the Rio Grande.

The reference to saltwater ponds—one distinguishing feature noted for the coastal country—perhaps refers to the brackish bays, but it is amplified by the later statement that the French gathered salt from the banks in useful quantities. This suggests the true salt lakes, much farther south than Lavaca Bay.[2]

The Talons convey the impression that they saw nothing really distinguishing from Texas to central Mexico, saying that they crossed "a big country very much like the one they had just left." No border divided Texas and Mexico. The "natural separation of the countries inhabited by the savages from the one inhabited by the Spaniards" was where "they began to see some high mountains." Here, deep into Mexico, was the actual end of the Texas–northern Mexico natural region and the beginning of mountainous New Spain: real mountains, some active volcanoes, and some with snow on them.

It is necessary to deal with the rivers the Talons describe to reconstruct the places they visited and to establish as nearly as possible where they found the plants and animals mentioned. They tell specifically of three or four: (1) the river on which La Salle established his fort; (2) the River of Canes; (3) a large, unnamed river with two mouths, surrounded by "mountains of sand"; and (4) the largest river crossed en route from the Cenis village to New Spain, which Jean-Baptiste believed to be the same as the third. Can these rivers be identified with certainty?

The Fort Saint-Louis site requires that the first be Garcitas Creek. Its small size is indicated by the Talons' statement that it was only the width of a pistol shot. The River of Canes was a larger stream, but not huge, since it was "a musket shot" wide. With many waterfowl, it is said to have been bordered by tall trees and much cane. La Salle, they say, discovered this river "emptying into this same bay." Whether they meant Lavaca Bay or the larger Matagorda is open to question.

2 Henri Joutel ("Relation de Henri Joutel," in Pierre Margry, ed., *Découvertes et établissements des français dans l'ouest et dans le sud de l'Amérique septentrionale*, III, 168) tells of skimming "a very white salt" left by evaporation in small saltwater basins near the fort and finding it quite useful.

The Colorado, in its primeval state, would qualify for the name, as many canebreaks lay along its lower course and that of nearby Caney Creek. An anonymous traveler in the region in 1831 described the "tracts of land low and often marshy, overgrown with the long reeds which we know in the Northern States as fishing rods," common to many areas of Texas. The largest extended seventy miles along Caney Creek, "with scarcely a tree to be seen in the whole distance."[3] This cane, growing to a height of twenty feet, was *Arundineria*, the American bamboo. Its great size contrasts with the Talons' "beautiful reeds or little canes with which the savages made their arrows." How would one make an arrow shaft out of the knobby, jointed stems of a bamboo fishing rod? The reed they describe was much smaller. The Indians' arrow shafts came not from the bamboo but from the reed grass, *Phragmites*. Hitchcock wrote of this grass "called 'carrizo,' used for lattices in construction of adobe huts and thatching . . . stems were used by the Indians for shafts of arrows." This, an impressive grass growing from five to ten feet tall, was the Talons' "little cane." Samuel C. Reid's 1846 account of the lower Rio Grande relates that "the huts on the banks were made of mud and cane."[4]

Unfortunately, the Talons give neither the distance nor the direction from Lavaca Bay to the River of Canes. But there are clues. While a captive of the Clamcoëhs, Jean-Baptiste was taken with their women and children to a place of safekeeping during their war with the Cenis. He relates that they "decamped from near the French settlement" and traveled in canoes "all along the coast of the Gulf of Mexico." They passed the River of Canes and finally "entered a large river, distant from the River of Canes, toward the south of the Gulf, about as far as from the river of Canes to the bay where the said Sr. de La Salle made his incursion." The voyage down the Gulf and past the River of Canes, entering the Gulf somewhere to the southeast, had to be south from Lavaca Bay, and the third river a similar distance still farther south—the most remote from the Cenis enemies.

The main clues are the features of the third river. It was chosen because it had "natural shelter made by the mountains of sand and woods around the two mouths," as well as abundant game and all sorts of fruits. There were "a great number of palm trees and pines along the banks and in the surrounding area." The river was beautiful and deep,

3 Robert S. Gray, ed., *A Visit to Texas in 1831,* p. 122.
4 A. S. Hitchcock, *Manual of the Grasses of the U.S.,* p. 190; Samuel C. Reid, Jr., *The Scouting Expeditions of McCulloch's Texas Rangers,* p. 29.

had "ebb and flow," appeared to be of great length, and, of all the rivers they say, was the one the Talons thought most likely to be the Mississippi.

If the assumption as to direction is right, this river would have to be either the Nueces or the Rio Grande. There may have been sand dunes near the mouths of both, but the Rio Grande has the edge, not only because of its greater number of dunes but also because it empties into the Gulf from among the dunes. The Nueces, on the other hand, has its mouth miles back, at the upper end of Corpus Christi Bay, its dunes lying in front of the bay. The Talons' river had two mouths, the Nueces only one. The Rio Grande had two clearly defined mouths, often reported by early explorers. Félix Calleja, for example, describes the Rio Grande's two mouths in his 1795 inspection report. Samuel C. Reid, chronicler of McCulloch's Rangers' 1846 scout of the area, describes the two mouths and some of the features that would have made this river a good hideout.[5]

The Talon report also says that the river of refuge had a great number of pines and palm trees along its banks. Unlike the Nueces, the lowest reaches of the Rio Grande were once a subtropical palm forest,[6] a remnant of which survives and is protected as perhaps the last remaining natural palm forest in the United States. The pines are more difficult to explain, but even they point toward the Rio Grande rather than the Nueces, where no native conifers have ever been reported. Several early explorers reported conifers on the lower Rio Grande. Abbé Domenech, near Brownsville in 1851, observed a large resaca "skirted with palm trees, ebony trees, cedars, green oaks, and sycamores."[7] Although there were never actually any cedars or pines on the lower Rio Grande, there must have been conifers of some kind that were mistaken for cedars by Domenech and for pines by Jean-Baptiste Talon.

One 1857 account relates that bald cypresses grew along the Rio Grande to just below Roma, but no farther.[8] Could they have existed farther down the river in earlier times and been cut out before this

---

5 Felix Calleja, "Nuevo Santander in 1795: A Provincial Inspection by Félix Calleja," *Southwestern Historical Quarterly* 75, no. 4 (April, 1972): 470–71; Reid, *Scouting Expeditions*, pp. 13–14.

6 Victor H. Schoffelmayer, "The Magic Valley—Its Marvelous Future," *Texas Geographic Magazine* 3, no. 1 (Spring, 1937): 7.

7 Emmanuel Henri Domenech, trans., *Missionary Adventures in Texas and Mexico*, p. 310.

8 John Torrey, *U.S. Survey*, I, part 2, 33, in William H. Emory, *Report of United States and Mexican Boundary Survey Made under the Direction of the Secretary of the Interior*.

time? Be this as it may, there is another conifer that has existed in this location all along: *Taxodium mucronatum* Ten., the Montezuma cypress. This is a Mexican species that might well have been dubbed a cedar or a pine. Thus, the presence of conifers and palms, as well as the two mouths, indicates the Rio Grande as the Talons' third river.

All clues seem to point to the Rio Grande as the Talons' river of refuge. Although the canoe trip was long, the protection offered by the wilderness of shifting sand and impenetrable thorn thickets could have made it worth the long trip during wartime. No other river in Texas beyond the Red could be mistaken for the Mississippi by anyone who had ever heard a description of that great stream. In fact, James K. Holland, viewing the Rio Grande in 1847, noted an appearance resembling the Mississippi.[9]

The River of Canes, therefore, must have been either the Guadalupe or the Nueces. The few clues given do not reveal which. In some respects the Guadalupe qualifies better. Francis Moore, Jr.'s 1840 description of this stream reads almost like an expansion of Talon's brief statement. The extensive swamp along its banks, he noted, "is covered with dense, impenetrable thickets of cane, flags and creeping plants, and is the retreat of innumerable flocks of wild-fowl."[10] But the Guadalupe is much too close to have been considered halfway between Lavaca Bay and the Rio Grande. In that regard, the Nueces fits better.

There are few early descriptions of the lower Nueces River, but it is known that there was much swamp cane around its bays. Perhaps we should just say that the River of Canes must have been one of these two and regard the features described as typical of this whole midcoastal area. At any rate, it seems the whole orientation of the Talons' three rivers is south, instead of up the Gulf Coast, and these locations are assumed because of the animals and plants mentioned.[11]

In answering various questions about the land, the Talons named specific plants and animals they had seen, describing some of them in

9 James K. Holland, "Diary of a Texas Volunteer in the Mexican War," *Southwestern Historical Quarterly* 30, no. 1 (July, 1926): 13. For other descriptions drawing parallels to the Mississippi, see José Antonio Pichardo, *Pichardo's Treatise on the Limits of Louisiana and Texas,* I, 441–42; and Nelson Lee, *Three Years among the Comanches,* p. 31.
10 Francis Moore, Jr., *Map and Description of Texas,* pp. 132–34.
11 See Joutel, "Relation," pp. 261–62, and Anastase Douay, in Isaac Joslin Cox, ed., *The Journeys of Réné Robert Cavelier, Sieur de La Salle,* I, 239, for references to the River of Canes. Aransas Bay is generally considered to be the Karankawas' boundary, but in this instance they may have gone beyond it.

detail. These reports are looked at in the light of what is known of the organisms from other sources, in order to evaluate them for new information.

In describing "the forests and woods," the Talons named several major kinds of trees and noted the presence of others they could not identify. They listed oaks, the most numerous, but made no distinction between different oak species. They also listed "nut trees," but again ventured few details except to observe that besides the "ordinary nuts, there are some extremely large ones." It hardly seems that these could have been the small native pecans; Texas's largest native nuts are the black walnut and some of the hickories, which must have been conspicuous in early times.

The brothers added that there were also "hazelnuts in quantity"— an interesting statement, though difficult to explain. The French word translated as hazelnuts is *noisettes*. It is a precise word, usually taken to mean hazelnuts and nothing else. According to the Talons, these were present in quantity; but there is only one hazelnut native to the United States, *Corylos americana* Walt., an eastern species of a small tree or shrub with small, edible nuts. There are no modern records of it in Texas, although there are several other early reports of hazelnuts. Those who have tried to rationalize these away have taken the French *noisette* to be the diminutive of *noix* (fruit of the genus *Jugulinacae*) and suggest that the word should be taken to mean any small nut of that group—a pecan or even a small walnut. They point to one pioneer account to justify their thesis: in 1828, Jean Berlandier described *Juglans microcarpa*, the little walnut he found in the Hill Country, saying it "looks like a large hazel-nut."[12] Yet the French word is exact; it seems unlikely that the Talons would use this designation for a specific nut common in Europe for any small, unknown nuts they found in America. Additionally, several of the earliest Spanish explorers reported the hazelnut in Texas. Typical is the account of Fray José de Solís, of April 25, 1767, of "a great number of fruit trees . . . hazelnuts, chestnuts" in the woods adjacent to the Brazos and Little Brazos rivers, and later along the Navasota River.[13] The Spanish word he used is *avellano*, another specific word meaning only hazelnut. Is it possible that this nut was common here in the seventeenth century and present into the eighteenth but died out in the

12 Jean Louis Berlandier, *Journey to Mexico during the Years 1826–1834,* trans. Sheila M. Ohlendorf, Josette M. Begelow, and Mary M. Standefer, II, 360–61.
13 José de Solís, *The Solís Diary of 1767,* trans. Peter P. Forrestal, pp. 25–26.

whole area before the nineteenth-century explorers and settlers came? This seems to be the testimony of the early witnesses.

Last among the forest trees, the Talons listed pines. The French word is *pinot*, a rather ambiguous term indicating anything of the pine genus, as well as other trees such as the firs and the cypress. They must have used the word generically here also, merely making the quite accurate general statement that conifers made up an important part of the forests they saw.

Two other trees are mentioned specifically: palms and mulberries, which are said to have bordered "all the rivers." But the brothers were answering only for the area they had covered: the south central and southern coastal parts of Texas. Mulberries are and, according to every account, were throughout historical times scattered all along the rivers in this area. They were often large trees in the bottoms, but the statement about their bordering the rivers bring to mind especially the Texas mulberry, which forms shrubby thickets on stream banks and even on bars in the stream beds south and west of the Colorado.

Palms along the rivers are harder to picture. The reference to the palm of the river of refuge, presumably the Rio Grande has been noted. But this impressive palm, *Sabal texana*, is apparently closely limited within the United States to the subtropical zone on the lowest extremity of the Rio Grande. What could they mean by palms along all the rivers of coastal and south central Texas? *Sabal palmetto*, the large cabbage palm or tree palmetto, is not a possibility, as it never grows naturally west of Florida. *Sabal minor*, the dwarf palmetto, is a true palm, but one that never grows an aboveground trunk. It produces an underground stem or, at its most vigorous, an inconspicuous base at ground level, with the visible part of the plant consisting of large leaves that often stand six feet high. This palm is widely distributed in low areas all over the southeastern United States and is common in the river bottoms of southeastern Texas. It still grows luxuriantly at places along the Blanco, Guadalupe, and San Antonio rivers, but these may be its most southwestern range. However, with this palm growing along all the rivers to the San Antonio, and with *Sabal texana* on the Rio Grande, we have all the main rivers covered except the Nueces.

There is yet another palm that could have figured in the picture. Near the coast between the Brazos and the Colorado rivers, a few specimens of a really fine palm still survive. Some of these have trunks ten feet tall, and the largest measured, before it was removed, had an eighteen-foot trunk. Also surviving are some trunked palms, which appear to be this same plant, at a spring near the Blanco River in Blanco

County. Many botanists regard all these as merely overly vigorous specimens of the dwarf palmetto, but others have considered them a separate
form and applied the name *Sabal louisiana* or *S. deeringiana*.

The presence of these true palm trees on the upper Texas coast
brings up the question of just how widespread Texas palms may have
actually been at the beginning of the historical period. Because of confusion in the use of the term "palm," it is not possible to provide an
answer. Josiah Gregg, writing in 1846, illustrates the confused termi-
nology: "There are two or three species of palms—in the low wet bottoms we find the fan leaf—in the high lands the *palmilla*, of which the
root is used for *mole* in Northern Mexico—also the date-palm or 'Spanish dagger.'" [14] So to some observers, yuccas were palms.

That the Talons took notice of grapes is not surprising, for Texas
has an abundance of wild grapes. The brothers perceived the basic difference between the grapes of this region and those of Europe in noting
that here the vines grew large and high into the tree (old grape vines
with trunks to ten inches thick and branches lying over the tops of trees
more than twenty feet tall can still be found in Texas) and that the
grapes were sour. American grapes are notoriously acid and low in
sugar. But the mention of "red and white grapes" is puzzling. All the
native species in Texas are normally red to black. The only possible explanation found for their white grapes is that the sweet mountain grape,
Vitis monticola Buckl., common in central Texas, has rare vines with
white fruit.

These Frenchmen were much impressed by the "prodigious quantity of berries with delicious taste," suggesting the wild blackberries
and dewberries. But it was a different berry on which they chose to
elaborate. This "extremely refreshing" berry, "shaped like an egg," growing on "bushes with thorns," and greatly valued by the Spaniards, was
the *tuna*, the fruit of the prickly-pear cactus.

Harder to identity are their "figs," which were not at all like the figs
we know but "very much like the banana." This North American fig has
occasionally been identified as the quite-common persimmon, but it is
hard to see any great similarity between persimmons and bananas.
There is in Texas only one native fruit that really compares with a banana: the pawpaw, sometimes called the custard-banana. The fruit of
this shrub, *Asimina triloba* (L.) Den., is two to seven inches long,
banana-shaped, and somewhat similar to the banana in consistency and
taste. Its range, however, is limited to the northeast corner of Texas,

---

14 Josiah Gregg, *Diary and Letters of Josiah Gregg: Southwestern Enterprises,
1840–1847*, I, 241.

a hundred miles or more from the Cenis village. There is no record of Talon's ever having gone there, but his close associate, Pierre Meunier, did and doubtless brought some of the fruit back to his friend.[15]

The Talons describe the animals they saw more fully than the plants. Most discussed is the buffalo, or bison, the remarkable bovine that impressed all Europeans. This animal, they observed, was "plentiful . . . in the woods, as well as the plains." This idea of buffalo looming over a Gulf beach is foreign to the impression one is apt to have of the animals as denizens of the high plains. Yet Joutel affirms that they were often hunted in the environs of the French fort. Enríquez Barroto tells of a buffalo hunt by members of the Rivas-Iriarte voyage near San Luis Pass in 1687. Alonso de León in 1690 found buffaloes below the Rio Grande, in Coahuila. Near Fort Saint-Louis he found "some plains covered with buffalo." Terán de los Ríos, nearing Matagorda Bay in 1691, encountered a buffalo herd of more than a thousand.[16]

These accounts establish that buffalo were present routinely and sometimes in great numbers on the central Texas coast and beyond the Rio Grande in the seventeenth century. We have occasional reports of them on the coast in the eighteenth century, and a few from the early part of the nineteenth; the last notice of them in the whole coastal region was in 1848. About that time they forsook south Texas permanently. The Talons provide the explanation: buffalo were extremely wild and avoided the "inhabited regions," keeping fifteen or twenty leagues between themselves and even the Indian villages. Incompatible with humans, they retreated as settlers filled the land.

The Talons give a graphic description of the fury of the wounded buffalo, which sometimes chased the hunters into trees, then tried to uproot the trees to get at their adversaries.

The brothers thought milk could be obtained from buffalo cows if they were tamed but found the Indians unwilling to attempt it. No doubt the natives realized the impracticability of taminig buffalo, let alone milking them. But the Indians apparently knew the value of milk and were quick to appropriate it when it was available. The picture of an

15 Pierre Meunier, "Declaración," Mexico, August 19, 1690, UT archives, transcript 69, AGI, Mexico 617.
16 Joutel, "Relation," pp. 214, 245–46; Juan Enríquez Barroto, diary entries for April 12 and 13, 1687 (microcopy in Old Spanish Missions Research Library, Our Lady of the Lake University, San Antonio); Alonso de León, "Itinerary of the De León Expedition of 1690," in Herbert Eugene Bolton, ed., *Spanish Exploration in the Southwest, 1542–1706*, pp. 406–20; Domingo Terán de los Ríos, *Itinerary and Daily Account Kept by General Domingo de Terán, Begun May 16, 1691, Finished April 15, 1692*, p. 23.

Indian sucking the milk from a dead cow at the end of a hunt is one of those surprising raw glimpses of everyday life in those times that comes as a bonus from the Talons.

The young Frenchmen used two words to indicate the deer they saw: *cerfs* and *chevreuils*, suggesting that they saw two kinds of deer in south Texas. Unfortunately, both words are too general to provide clear identification.

Carnivores mentiond are "lions, tigers, bears, and wolves." Again, the Talons are brief and give no details. The lions are, of course, the mountain lions, so often mentioned by early explorers and settlers that we know they were common. The "tigers" of that day would include the jaguar, the ocelot, and perhaps the margay and the jaguarundi—quite a formidable assortment of striped and spotted felines. Many early observers have testified to the region's numerous bears. The same is true of wolves, which the Talons say were often captured by the Indians as pups and tamed for use in hunting.

They also relate that the rivers and ponds, besides abounding in fish, were full of "crocodiles" (alligators), a statement that might raise doubts today, but it is substantiated by other sources. León in 1689 attributed to the alligators his failure to find human remains at the site of La Salle's fort after it was destroyed. Stephen F. Austin, in present-day Victoria County in 1821, mentioned stopping at a pond in the Guadalupe River bottom "with Alligators plenty." Nelson Lee had a narrow escape from a huge alligator in the Aransas River in 1842, and Steinert reported a "great number of alligators" in a pond in the Victoria vicinity in 1849.[17]

The Talons were prophetic in their suggestion for a venture into processing turtles, as such an industry, the harvesting of giant sea turtles, actually came about two hundred years later.

The list of Texas birds the young Frenchmen recited is impressive. They offered no details, yet divided them into logical categories. First were those called game birds, "very good to eat." Foremost was the turkey, mentioned as a staple in the diet of most early explorers. Next is what is translated as partridges. The French word *perdrix*, taken literally, indicates the family *Phasianidae*, of which the only Texas representatives

17 Alonso de León, "Itinerary of the De León Expedition," in Bolton, ed., *Spanish Exploration*, p. 398; Stephen F. Austin, "Journal of Stephen F. Austin on His First Trip to Texas, 1821," *Southwestern Historical Quarterly* 7, no. 4 (April, 1904): 300; Nelson Lee, *Three Years*, pp. 28–29; W. Steinert, "W. Steinert's View of Texas in 1849," trans. Gilbert J. Jordan, *Southwestern Historical Quarterly* 80, no. 1 (July, 1976): 69.

are the quail. Whether the brothers meant it to include prairie chickens, for which there is no separate French word, is not known. The parrot mentioned would have been the ill-fated Carolina parakeet, which once ranged over east and central Texas but was last reported, in the Corpus Christi area, about 1895. Apparently the French learned to eat this exotic bird.

The ducks are all lumped together as important game. Then came *outardes*, translated as plovers, although the specific French word for that bird is *pluvier*. *Outardes* translates literally as bustards, which are members of the family *Otididae*, Old World and Australian game birds not found in the Western Hemisphere. These are long-legged birds related to both the plovers and the cranes, but since the Talons mention the cranes separately, it is assumed that other long-legged wading birds are meant, of which the plovers are examples. The doves, of which there are several species in Texas, probably included the passenger pigeons, another lost species. Then woodcocks are mentioned. The French word is *becassas*, indicating the family *Scolopacidae*, which includes the American woodcock, as well as the snipes, curlews, and sandpipers.

The Talons finished the list of game birds with "a prodigious quantity of little birds," described as being good to eat—indicating that they ate songbirds. A "particular species which is red all over . . . the color of blood," may have been the cardinal.

The second category of birds were "birds of prey and of pillage": eagles, of which there were "a large number." Since no hawks are mentioned, it appears that they did not distinguish between hawks and eagles. Surprisingly, they also listed *corbeaux*, literally ravens, but including any of the passerine birds related to the crows. Ravens and crows are northern and eastern birds never common in central and south Texas, although some of them venture into the area at times. The vultures are conspicuous for their absence, perhaps obscured among the "other birds of prey and of pillage."

Two groups are appended in the final category, both said to have been seen in large numbers on the rivers and ponds. They are the cranes and the swans. Other accounts reveal that various cranes and two species of swan were once numerous in the coastal region. One of the swan species has not been recorded here in recent times, and the other is now a rare visitor. Most of the cranes in Texas now are in desperate straits.

The Talons devoted little comment to the invertebrates, but with significant exceptions. There were, they say, "many bees in the fields that make their honey in the grass and in trees." Yet the natives did not cultivate them, "contenting themselves with eating the honey wherever they find it." The implication that bees making honey in usable quantities were found in Texas in the seventeenth century is at odds with previous conclusions.

Most authorities do not concede any honeybees as native to this continent, explaining the great numbers of them present in Texas in the nineteenth century as the result of rapid migration of the domesticated European bees from the eastern colonies. (The fact that the earliest Spaniards in Yucatan, in 1517, found the Mayas engaging in bee culture and serving up honey "by the gourdful" has not been adequately addressed.) [18]

Doubts arise from reading accounts like that of W. B. DeWees, who wrote of the Robertson County area in 1822, "There are a vast quantity of bee trees about here, so that we have no want of honey." An anonymous visitor in 1837 to Gonzales County wrote of hunting for bee trees, "which are very abundant in every part of Texas." Another, in Brazoria County in 1831, wrote that he had seen a bee tree. Wild honey was abundant, "obtained at the expense of only a little care and labor, from the hollow trees in which it is deposited." [19] A score of such accounts from that time could be quoted. Could all of these be explained by the European bees just invading Texas? This would have meant a major change in a whole microhabitat.

The history of the European honeybee in the United States is well summarized by Oertel. [20] He cites as the earliest mention of bees being shipped to the English colonies a letter of the Virginia Company dated December 5, 1621. Whether any of the bees arrived alive is not known. There is mention of domesticated hives in Virginia between 1650 and 1670. Yet the Talons, in their recollection of the years 1684–92, relate that Texas Indians were routinely eating honey found in the trees and the grass. If this was honey from European honeybees, the migration from the east coast to Texas was made in record time for any introduced species, and the Indians adapted to a new food source with amazing swiftness.

18 Bartolomé de las Casas, in Henry R. Wagner, ed., *The Discovery of Yucatán by Francisco Hernández de Córdoba*, p. 50. Las Casas says these early Spaniards found wooden beehives and much fine honey. There are numerous mentions in colonial records of the abundance of honey in Yucatán and of the Mayas' paying tribute in honey.

19 W. B. DeWees, *Letters from an Early Settler of Texas*, ed. Cara Cardelle, p. 25; Andrew Forest Muir, ed., *Texas in 1837: An Anonymous, Contemporary Narrative*, p. 92; Gray, *Visit to Texas*, p. 32.

20 Everett Oertel, "Bicentennial Bees—Early Records of Honey Bees in the Eastern U.S.," *American Bee Journal* 116, nos. 2, 3, 4 (February, March, April, 1976): 70–71, 114, 128, 156–57.

There is a reference earlier than the Talons' that does not jibe with the accepted history. Members of Hernando de Soto's expedition reported finding in an Indian village in 1540 a cache of honey in a tree. This find, in what is now Georgia, has never been explained satisfactorily, nor does it seem that it can be while holding to the claim that all American honeybees were the later-introduced European type. Additionally, Oertel has amassed evidence that there were so many bees in Georgia, Florida, and Alabama in the eighteenth century that the Indians traded honey and beeswax to Europeans.[21] This, taken with reports from both the Soto and the La Salle expeditions, indicates that a better explanation is needed than that given and that there is indeed support for a different conclusion.

Steyermark's suggestion that the honeybee entered North America by way of the Bering Strait pointed the way for a search for other honeybees from the west,[22] and they were found in a guidebook to the Big Bend area by Ross A. Maxwell. Maxwell tells of a native honeybee found in southwestern Texas and of its fate. This black bee customarily stored its honey in small caves, as the Big Bend has few hollow trees. As Anglo-American settlers introduced other types, some of these escaped, and "now most of the bee caves are occupied by once domesticated varieties that have gone wild; one seldom sees colonies of the small black wild bees that were native to the area."[23]

Thus we have what seems to be the only plausible explanation of the Talons' statement concerning bees in Texas before any of the eastern varieties could have come in. Many questions remain unanswered, but one wonders whether these native honeybees might not have once lived all across the South, only to be replaced before they were even identified.

It was in speaking of Mexico that the Talons remarked on the venomous snakes and scorpions "all over this country." It is not clear whether or not the statement was meant to include Texas. Their familiarity with at least some of them, however, is apparent from their accurate description of the rattlesnake's rattle and habits, as well as from the fact that one of La Salle's colonists died from a rattlesnake bite.[24]

Considered as a whole, the Talons' testimony about the flora and fauna of the new land is excellent. They pictured the topography, plants, and animals they encountered with deft strokes that even today evoke

---

21 Ibid., p. 156.
22 Julian A. Steyermark, *Vegetational History of the Ozark Forest*, p. 35.
23 Ross A. Maxwell, *The Big Bend of the Rio Grande*, p. 109.
24 Joutel, "Relation," pp. 167–68.

scenes of seventeenth-century Texas. They cataloged the important living things in logical and remarkably complete lists confirmed by many later reports, and here and there gave significant new details of the natural community at that early date. When allowance is made for inexactness of language, we find no examples of demonstrable error. Seldom did any European government get from a commissioned explorer any better picture of the natural history of the New World than the French government got from these men who grew up in the land, were hauled over it by the agents of three cultures, and almost miraculously lived to return and report on the whole experience.

Karankawa Linguistic Data
RUDOLPH C. TROIKE

More than two hundred different Indian languages—some as distinct from one another as English and Chinese—were spoken in North America prior to the coming of the Europeans. Today fewer than one hundred remain alive and most of these are marked for extinction within the next generation. Our knowledge of the various Indian languages originally spoken in the present-day state of Texas is, for the most part, regrettably meager, since missionaries and colonists were more interested in converting the Indians or driving them off their land then in preserving information about them. Two native Texas languages, Tonkawa and Caddo (which contributed the name of the state), still survive among a handful of speakers in Oklahoma, but the others have completely died out, as far as we know.

With the exception of Caddo and Tonkawa, which have been studied by linguists, and Coahuilteco, preserved in a confessor's manual used in the San Antonio missions, the only extant information on the Indian languages of Texas consists of a few words reported by explorers and officials, or word lists collected by linguists in the nineteenth century from among the final speakers of the languages. In a number of instances, it is known only that a particular group existed, but nothing is known of the language they spoke.

For this reason, even the two or three dozen words from an Indian language preserved in the Talon Interrogations inadequately recorded as they may have been, are of great interest. The information is of even greater interest and significance because it is earlier than that from any other source and because it can be tied to ethnographic data on a group living in a specific locality.

Linguistic data are of great historical value for a number of reasons. They can make possible the positive identification of groups, the determination of relationships among languages, and sometimes the reconstruction of historical movements of peoples. Thus we can say with confidence, as will be demonstrated below, that the "Clamcoëhs" group among whom La Salle and the Talon family lived at Matagorda Bay were definitely Karankawa.[1] The ethnohistorical information on the ill-fated colony leaves little room for doubt on this point, and the linguistic data serve to reinforce the identification.

The shorter list of seven words from "the language of the Cenis and the Ayenny" (the Hasinai and the Hainai) given by the Talons confirms also that these groups were Caddo, though this fact is already well known from other sources.[2] The brothers' conclusion that the language was "much easier than that of the Clamcoëhs" is difficult to evaluate for want of more information on Karankawa. However, enough is known to affirm that Caddo and Karankawa are not demonstrably related to each other and that, whereas Caddo is related to Pawnee and Wichita, Karankawa has no known relatives.

In view of the lack of relationship between Caddo and Karankawa, the close similarity in their words for water—"*koko*" and "*komkom*," both using reduplicated syllables—poses an interesting puzzle, since the resemblance is too close to be ascribed to chance. The most likely explanation appears to be that this functionally important term was diffused across linguistic boundaries from another source and borrowed into Karankawa and Caddo independently. As has been suggested elsewhere,

---

1 The name given by Jean-Baptiste Talon to the Karankawa group with whom he and his younger brothers and sister lived has a long history of different renderings by those who have had access to the original manuscript, and still further deformations by others who have not, complicating an already confusing picture of variant names for Indian groups in south Texas. The first in the line of interpreters of the manuscript was, apparently, Pierre Le Moyne, Sieur d'Iberville, who in 1704 sent an extract of the Talon Interrogations to the Abbé Cavelier, La Salle's brother. The extract is published with Iberville's letter to Cavelier in Pierre Margry, ed., *Découvertes et établissements des français dans l'ouest et dans le sud de l'Amérique septentrionale*, III, 610–21; the letter is on p. 622. The Indian name appears throughout the Margry version as "Clamcoët." The same form, but without the diaeresis, was used by Pierre François Xavier Charlevoix in his *Histoire et description générale de la Nouvelle France*, first published in 1744, as quoted in Thomas Falconer, *On the Discovery of the Mississippi, and on the South-western, Oregon, and North-western Boundary of the United States*, 22a. The full text of Charlevoix's discussion indicates, from the information given, that his source was the original, not the extract. As discussed in note 8, other writers have read the name as Clamcoches or Clamcochs, but a new reading, Clamcoëhs, is argued for here.

2 John R. Swanton, *Source Material on the History and Ethnology of the Caddo Indians*, p. 8.

the probable source was Atákapa, another coastal language spoken from Galveston Bay to southwestern Louisiana, adjacent to both the Karankawa and Caddo areas.[3]

It is curious that much of our information on Karankawa, like the present data, has come to us secondhand. Nearly a third of the known material was obtained by Albert S. Gatschet in 1888 from a woman in Massachusetts, Mrs. Alice Oliver, who had grown up on the Texas coast. As a child she had known members of the last Karankawa band and learned some words from them, which she later wrote down from memory. A few additional words were secured by Gatschet from two members of the Tonkawa tribe (formerly of central Texas) who had learned some Karankawa.[4] The only actual firsthand data are contained in two word lists, the first of 106 words recorded in 1720 by Jean Béranger, a French ship captain sent to explore the Gulf Coast from the Mississippi River to Matagorda Bay, who overshot his intended terminus and entered Aransas Pass;[5] and the second of 158 words (which will not be considered here) collected by Jean Louis Berlandier on the Mexican border in 1828.[6] Béranger's list remained unknown in the French archives for nearly two hundred years until it was discovered and published in 1919 by Villiers du Terrage and Rivet, who later also published the Talon vocabulary.[7] The Talon linguistic data, though not firsthand, hold the distinction of being the earliest known to date, having been written

3 Rudolph C. Troike, "The Caddo Word for 'Water,'" *International Journal of American Linguistics* 30, no. 1, (January, 1964): 96–98.
4 Albert S. Gatschet, *The Karankawa Indians.*
5 Jean Béranger, "Mémoire sur la Louisiane," typescript, UT archives. The manuscript, preserved in AN, Colonies, C13, C.4:72–100, has been published (1983) as *Béranger's Discovery of Aransas Pass*. Béranger (p. 20) tells of passing St. Bernard, or Matagorda, Bay and landing another thirty leagues southwest. The map prepared by Devin, a member of the expedition (facsimile inserted in the translation) indicates that he anchored off Live Oak Point in Aransas Bay, above present-day Rockport, Texas. The following year Béranger accompanied Jean-Baptiste Bénard de la Harpe and Simars de Bellisle on a voyage to Galveston Bay, where he compiled an Atákapa word list (pp. 31–39).
6 Published in Herbert Landar, "The Karankawa Invasion of Texas," *International Journal of American Linguistics* 34, no. 4 (October, 1968): 242–58. The Cariban relationship proposed for Karankawa by Landar has received no support from other linguists.
7 Marc de Villiers du Terrage and Paul Rivet, "Les Indiens du Texas et les expéditions françaises de 1720 et 1721 a la 'Baie Saint-Bernard,'" *Journal de la Société des Américanistes de Paris* 11, part 2 (1919): 403–42; and idem, "Deux vocabulaires inédits recueillis au Texas vers 1688," *Journal de la Société des Américanistes de Paris* 21, part 2 (1929): 307–11.

down in 1698 but reflecting the brothers' experience some years earlier. The two relevant pages from the original manuscript are reproduced in plates 11 and 12.

As noted, the Clamcoëh (Karankawa) vocabulary obtained from Jean-Baptiste Talon has been published previously and was included by John R. Swanton in his 1940 compilation of linguistic material from the area. However, a careful examination of a photocopy of the original manuscript has made it possible to correct some of the errors in Swanton's transcription. The Talon list is given in table 1, together with comparative data recorded in other sources.[8]

In trying to reconstruct the probable original Karankawa pronunciations from a manuscript such as this, several steps are necessary. First of all, it is important to consider the task faced by the writers of the

8 John R. Swanton, *Linguistic Material from the Tribes of Southern Texas*, p. 124–33. One major difference between the present reading of the manuscript and that by Villiers and Rivet ("Deux vocabulaires") is in the name of the Indian group itself, given by them (followed by Swanton) as "Clamcoches" and here as "Clamcoëhs." See note 1 above for another reading, "Clamcoëts," which is also followed in the earlier Villiers and Rivet article (Les Indiens"). To resolve the discrepant readings, I undertook an intensive examination of the handwriting in the entire manuscript. On the basis of this analysis, I determined that (1) the final two letters of the word must definitely be regarded as *hs,* and (2) there is such nearly complete overlap in the writing of *c* and *e* that they generally cannot be distinguished without reference to context; the use of a diaeresis over the letter in two occurrences of the tribal name, however, constitutes decisive evidence that the letter must be taken as *e,* pronounced as a separate syllable. Significantly, this new reading is much closer to the modern pronunciation of *Karankawa,* a fact that further supports the interpretation.

A partly contradictory spelling of the name, which may not have its origin in the manuscript of the Talon Interrogations, is *Quelamelouech* in a 1703 map by Claude Delisle (*Carte du Mexique et de la Floride*), and an apparently distorted derivative *Quelamoueche(s?)* in a 1718 map by his son Guillaume (*Carte de la Louisiane et du cours du Mississipi*). Both of these maps are reproduced in Historic New Orleans Collection, *Degrees of Discovery.* Jean Delanglez ("The Source of the Delisle Map") indicates that Delisle had discussions with the Abbé d'Esmanville, who returned from the La Salle enterprise with Captain Beaujeu on the *Joly* (Weddle, personal communication). If this represents an independent oral transmission of the name, it would seem to support both the *e* and the *c* reading at the same time. Doubt as to the accuracy of the Delisle form is raised by the additional *l* it contains, but if it was transmitted orally and written down from memory, it is possible that the somewhat anomalous *h* in *Clamocoëhs,* particularly if it represented a fricative sound (though normally *h* in written French is silent), could have been reinterpreted with a *ch*. More information is needed before the credibility of the Delisle form can be given much weight.

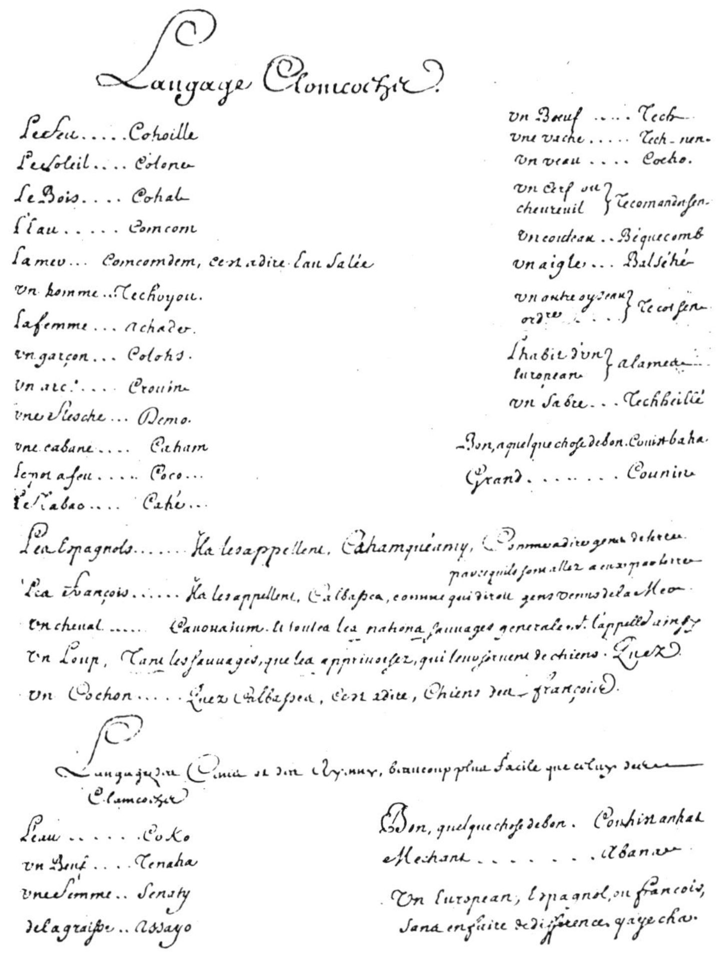

Langage Cloucouchie

Le feu..... Cohoille
Le foleil.... Colona
Le Bois.... Cohal
l'Eau..... Comcom
L'ameu... Comcomdem, c'est à dire l'eau falée
Un homme..Techoyou.
La femme... Achada.
un garçon... Colohs.
Un arc.'.... Crouin
une flesche ... Demo.
une cabane.... Ceham
Le mot a feu..... Coco...
Le Tabac..... Cehe..

Un Boeuf ..... Tech
Une vache ..... Tech-nen
Un veau .... Cocko.
Un cerf ou chevreuil } Tecomandafen.
Un cordeau ..Biquecomb
Un aigle... Balsehe
un autre oyseau ordre.... } Tecorfen
L'habit d'un European } alamea
Un Sabre... Techbeilie
Bon, a quelque chose de bon.Comirbaha
Grand........ Counin

Les Espagnols...... Ils les appellent. Cahamquéanny, comme à dire gens de terre, parce qu'ils font aller à eux pour boire

Les François...... Ils les appellent, Calbapea, comme qui diroit gens venus de la Mer

Un cheval ..... Canoualium. Il toutes les nations sauvages generalement l'appelle ainsy

Un Loup, Tant les sauvages, que les apprivoisez, qui leur servent de chiens. Quex

Un Cochon..... Quex Calbapea, c'est à dire, Chiens des François.

Langage des Cenis et des Cyanur, beaucoup plus facile que celuy des Clamcoehie

Le feu ...... Coko
un Boeuf .... Tenaha
Une femme.. Sensty
de la graisse.. Assayo

Bon, quelque chose de bon. Conhin anhal
Mechant .... Abana
Un European, Espaanol, ou françois,
Sans enfuire de difference, qaye cha.

PLATE II. The Talons' Indian vocabularies.
(Courtesy of the Archives Nationales, Outre-Mer, Paris)

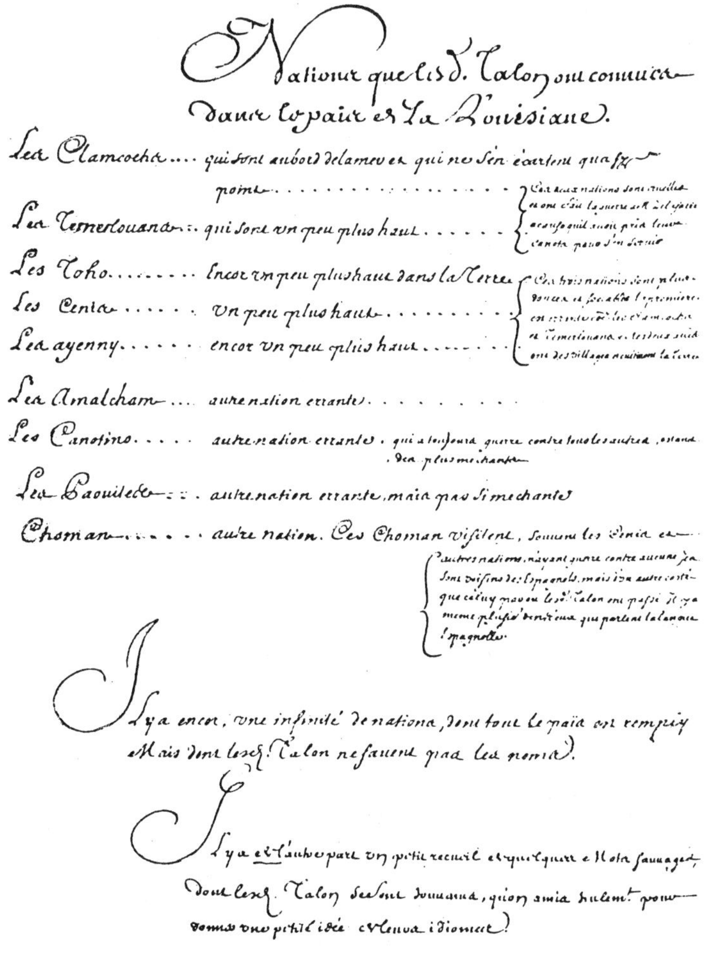

Nations que les d. Talon ont connuë
dans le païs de La Louïsiane.

Les Clamcoëha .... qui sont auboïd delameu et qui ne s'en écartent quasy
point . . . .

Les Tirmerlouana ... qui sont un peu plus haut . . . . . .

Les Toho . . . . Encor un peu plushaut dans la terre

Les Cenia . . . . . . Un peu plus haut . . . .

Les ayenny . . . . . . encor un peu plus haut . . . .

Les Amalcham ____ autre nation errantes . . . .

Les Canotino . . . . . autre nation errantes . qui a toujours guerre contre toutes les autres . estant . des plus méchantes

Les Caouïcke ___ ... autre nation errante, mais pas si méchantes

Choman ____ . . . . autre nation. Ces Choman visitent, souvent les Cenia et

J y a encor, une infinité de nations, dont tout le païs est rempliy
Mais dont le sd. Talon ne savent pas les noms.

J y a et l'autre part un petit recueil et quelques mots sauvages,
dont le sd. Talon se sont souuenus, qu'on a mis seulem.t pour
donner une petite idée de leur idiome.

PLATE 12. The Talons' list of Indian tribes.
(Courtesy of the Archives Nationales, Outre-Mer, Paris)

Table 1

Karankawa (Clamcoëh) vocabulary in the Talon manuscript, with forms from other sources.

Arrow   *Demo* /demo/; /dĕmóa/ (O).

Big, Large   *Counin* /kunin/.

Bird   Tecotsen /tekotsen/ 'a common type'; *coutsen* /kutsen/ 'lark' (B); cf. /kutn, kodn/ 'bird' (O).

Bow   *Crouin* /kruyn, kruin/.

Boy   *Colohs* /kolohs, kolo's/; /gló'ĕsn/ (O).

Buffalo   See Bull.

Bull   *Tech* /tesh/ 'male buffalo'; /tets'oa/ 'beef, cow, cattle' (O); perhaps cf. *tequedolan* /tekedolan/ 'cow-horn' (B); perhaps also cf. Man; see also Calf, Cow.

Calf   *Cocho* /kosho/ 'young buffalo'.

Clothing   *Alames* /alames/ (Sw. alamea), 'European clothing'; *alams* /alams/ 'clothing of all kinds' (B).

Cow   *Tech-nen* /teshnen/ 'female buffalo'; cf. Bull: -/nen/ perhaps means 'female'.

Deer   *Tecomandotsen* /tekomandotsen/; /dōtn, do'atn/ 'deer' (O); perhaps cf. *tequedolan* /tekedolan/ 'cow-horn' (B).

Dog   See Wolf.

Eagle   *Balséhé* /balséhé/.

Female   *-nen* /nen/; see Cow.

Fire   *Cohoille* /kohoylye/ (Sw. /kohoi/); *quoylesem* /kwoylesem/ (B).

French   *Calbasses* /kalbases/ "i.e., people coming from the sea"; cf. Spaniards.

Good   *Couistbaha* /kwistbaha/, also 'something good'; cf. *baa* 'expression of satisfaction' (B).

Horse   *Cauouaium* /kawwayum/ 'and all the savage nations generally call it thus' (Sw. *canouaium* /kanueüm/); /kuwáyi, kuwáy/ (O); < Spanish *caballo* /kabayo/.

House   *Cahum* /kaham/ (French translation is *cabane*: 'cabin, hut').

Karankawa   *Clamcoëhs* /klamkoehs, klamko'ehs/.

Knife	*Béquecomb* /békekomb/; cf. *beseceba* 'pin' (B).
Man	*Techoyou* /teshoyu/; cf. Bull (?), Sword(?).
Pig, Hog	*Quez Calbasses* /kez kalbases/ 'i.e., dogs of the French' (Sw. kez kalbassez); *queche* /keshe/ 'dog, pig' (B).
Pot	*Coko* /koko/ 'fire-pot' (pot-a-feu); *coq* /kok/ 'bowl, pail' (B).
Sea/Ocean	*Comcomdem* /komkomdem/ 'i.e., salt water'; /komkom/ 'water' + /dem/ 'salt' (?).
Spaniards	*Cahamquéamy* /kahamkéami/ 'i.e., people of the land, because they came to them by land'; cf. French.
Sun	*Colone* /kolone/; *clos* /klos/ (B).
Sword	*Techheillé* /teshheylyé/ (Sw. *tehheillé* /teheyel/); perhaps /tesh/ 'male' + /heylyé/ (=?).
Tobacco	*Cahé* /kahé/ (Sw. *Caké*); /kahé/ (S).
Water	*Comcom* /komkom/; /gle'i/ (O); cf. Sea/Ocean.
Wolf, Dog	*Quez* /kez/ 'the wild ones as well as the tame ones, which they use as dogs'; *queche* /keshe/ 'dog' (B); /kiss/ 'dog' (O).
Woman	*Achade* /ashade/.
Wood	*Cohal* /kohal/; *quesoul* /kesul/ (B).

NOTE: The Talon forms are taken directly from the manuscript. Forms recorded in other sources are taken from Swanton, as indicated by abbreviations: (B) for Béranger, (O) for Oliver, and (S) for Old Simon, one of the Tonkawa interviewed by Gatschet. Where Swanton's transcription of Talon differs from mine, his is also given in parentheses, preceded by Sw.
Here and elsewhere in the discussion orthographic forms are italicized and inferred pronunciations or linguistic transcriptions are given between slanted lines. The following consonant symbols deserve comment: /sh/ is used for an alveopalatal fricative similar to the English "sh-sound" (represented in French by ch); /ch/ for an alveopalatal affricate like the English "ch-sound"; /ts/ for the dental affricate similar to the English ts in *cats;* /ly/ for a palatal lateral similar to the lli in *million.* Vowels generally have the same phonetic value they do in French or Spanish: /i/ as in *keep,* /e/ as in *break,* /a/ as in ah, /o/ as in *coat,* /u/ as in *rude,* /ay/ as in *by,* /aw/ as in *cow.* /'/ represents a brief stoppage in the vocal cords (the "glottal stop"). Stress (accent) is marked as in the manuscript. A doubled vowel, e.g., /aa/, indicates a lengthened vowel sound.

manuscript, who were attempting to use French spelling patterns of the time to represent sounds and combinations of sounds that were in some instances quite foreign to them. Thus in some cases they might make quite novel uses of letters for sounds not found in French. Next, it is necessary to take into consideration French orthographic practices of the period and the probable pronunciation of sounds in French at that time. On these bases, hypotheses can be developed as to what sounds the spellings might have represented, and corroboration or refutation of the hypotheses may be sought wherever possible. The whole process is not unlike solving a mystery.[9]

The process can perhaps best be illustrated by comparing one of Swanton's transcriptions of a word in the manuscript, and the pronunciation he assumed for it, with the phonetic value given here. The first step is to analyze the paleography of the manuscript, which dates from the time before the present letters *u* and *v* were regularly distinguished in writing. Thus, for example, the French word today spelled *sauvage* was written *sauuage* (see plate 12). Although on the basis of the manuscript alone one could only guess whether *uu* represented /wv/ or /vu/, our knowledge of the present form of the language shows that /wv/ is the correct choice. In the case of an Indian language, however, where there are no more recent data available, inferences must be based on the French. Additionally, the written differenes in the manuscript between *u* and *n* are often minimal, providing a further potential source of confusion. Finally, one must judge whether a *u* or *ou* is being used syllabically as a vowel /u/, or nonsyllabically as a consonant/glide /w/.

All of these problems come together in *cauouaium*, "horse," which Swanton transcribed as *canouaium*, having misread the first *u* as *n*.[10] If the first *u* is taken to represent the glide /w/ (/v/ is unlikely because of its rarity in Karankawa), and the following *ou* is regarded as representing the nonsyllabic /w/ rather than /u/, our reading of the word becomes / kawwayum/. This is quite close to the Spanish *caballo* /kabayo/, from

9 The extent to which the Talon children were literate is not known, although there is mention of Jean-Baptiste's having had a prayer book while with the Karankawas. Their answers to the interrogations were given orally and recorded by someone else, a procedure that may also have contributed to the distortion of word forms. Since we know nothing about the scribe who actually wrote the document, we cannot ascertain what effect his linguistic background may have had on the spellings used.

10 For the most part Swanton (*Linguistic Material*) appears merely to have followed the transcription of Villiers and Rivet ("Deux vocabulaires"), so any reading of the orthography must be regarded as theirs rather than his. However, Swanton made his own interpretation of the probable pronunciation.

which in fact the word was originally borrowed (the Spanish /b/, when used between vowels, is usually pronounced as a bilabial fricative intermediate between /v/ and /w/). Mrs. Oliver's later pronunciation of /kuway/, recorded by Gatschet, strongly supports the interpretation proposed here, rather than Swanton's /kanueüm/.

A second example reflects an issue created by a sound change in French, namely, the pronunciation of the ending *-ille*, which today is pronounced as -/y/ after a vowel, but earlier represented -/ylye/. Swanton, perhaps overlooking the change in French pronunciation, interpreted this as -/y/ or -/i/, as in /kohoi/ for *cohoille*, "fire." However, we find an indication in the corresponding Béranger form *quoylesem* that the spelling *ille* was indeed intended to represent the older French pronunciation.

The similarity of forms in Talon and in Béranger and Oliver is at the crux of the evidence attesting to the identification of the Talon data as definitely Karankawa (since Béranger does not actually name the group from which his data were derived, the Oliver list is crucial for both). The similarities among the three are summarized in table 2.

Table 2

Shared forms in Talon, Béranger, and Oliver.

	Talon	*Béranger*	*Oliver*
Arrow	demo	—	děmó'a
Bird	(te)kotsen	kutsen	kutn
Boy	kolohs	—	gló'sn
Bull	tesh	(teke-)??	tets'oa
Clothing	alames	alams	—
Deer	tekomandotsen	—	dōt'n
Fire	kohoylye	kwoylesem	—
Horse	kawwáyum	—	kuwáyi
Pot	koko	kok	—
Sun	kolone	klos	—
Tobacco	kahé	—	káhe (S)
Wolf, Dog	kez	kesh	kiss
Wood	kohal	kesul	—

The seven or eight forms that the Talon list has in common with the other two lists provide evidence that the language involved in all three cases was the same. Indeed, the degree of similarity adds considerable support to the credibility of the materials themselves, despite their having been recorded under such uncertain circumstances.

Having confirmed that all three lists represent the same language, we must also account for the differences among them. Several explanations are possible. First, since the lists come from different periods, with the earliest and latest being 150 years apart (recognizing that the time of collection did not reflect the time of learning), the normal tendency of languages to change over time could be a factor. Second, at least some of the differences could reflect errors or misunderstandings on the part of the original recorders. None of the material was recorded from native speakers by trained linguists, and incorrect interpretations of intended meanings, misperceptions of pronunciations, and lapses of memory could easily account for some of the variation.

A third and very likely possibility is that the lists come from different Karankawa groups and reflect regional diversity in the language. (From what we know of not only Karankawa but also other languages in the area, this diversity may have been the rule rather than the exception, so much so that it has been suggested that the Indian sign language first developed in this region.) There is a limited amount of internal information that gives support to this explanation. The words for *bird* and *deer* contain a /ts/ in the Talon list (and in one instance in the Béranger list) but a /t/ in the Oliver list. This comparison indicates a possible *regular sound correspondence,* the type of evidence linguists utilize in defining regional varieties of a language. The evidence suggests that a sound change occurred in one part of the Karankawa area, presumably in the east, and that a line (isogloss) could be drawn separating Eastern Karankawa (with /ts/) from Western Karankawa (with /t/). Since it is more common among languages for /t/ to change to /ts/ than vice versa, the /t/ may be presumed to be the original sound.

An examination of similarities and differences in vocabulary items does not support a simple Eastern-Western split, however. As seen in table 3, the distribution of similarities places Béranger's list between Talon's and Oliver's, since it shares forms with both, whereas Talon and Oliver agree on only one form that is not shared with Béranger (excluding the similarities in table 2, where no comparable form is given by Béranger).

The comparison of vocabulary would suggest a possible division into *Eastern, Central,* and *Western* varieties of Karankawa, corresponding to the lists of Talon, Béranger, and Oliver, with the Eastern and

Table 3

Evidence for relative placement of the Talon,
Béranger, and Oliver data sources.

	Talon	Béranger	Oliver
Bow	kruin	—	gái
Bull	*tesh*	didót (bison)	*tets'*oa (beef, cattle)
Fire	*kohoylye*	*kwoyle*sum	kwachi humhe (S)
Fish	—	kiles	am
Good	(kwist)*baha*	*baa*	pla
House	kaham	—	ba'ak
Knife	békekomb	ku*sila*	*sile*káyi
Man	teshoyu	ahaks	yámawe
Sun	*kol*one	k*los*	dó'owal
Water	komkom	*klay*	*gle'i*

Central sharing the sound change of /t/ to /ts/. This conclusion is strengthened by the fact that the form *komkom,* for "water," which resembles the terms in Atákapa and Akokisa (spoken east of the Karankawa area), is found only in the Talon list. It should be noted that my analysis disagrees with those of Villiers and Rivet and Swanton, who saw closer resemblances between the Talon and Oliver lists than between Béranger and Oliver. It also poses an apparent problem in that the Béranger data were collected farther west than the others, near Aransas Bay (see note 5). However, by the nineteenth century the Karankawa had been severely dislocated and largely decimated, so that the group Mrs. Oliver knew in her youth on the north shore of Matagorda Bay could easily have originated farther west or south. The data suggest that they did.

It is regrettable that more Caddo words were not recorded from Pierre Talon, particularly since these would have reflected the Hasinai-Hainai (Southern Caddo) usage and could have yielded valuable information on regional differences in the language. From a methodological point of view, it must be remarked that La Salle's strategy of sending the young boy to live with the Caddo (Hasinai) to learn their language, a step designed to take advantage of the child's natural rapid language learning ability, was an astute move that later French colonizers of Louisiana were to emulate.[11]

Most of the words given in the brief list have counterparts in other sources. Table 4 provides a comparison (forms from Talon are given in

Table 4

Caddo (Cenis and Ayenny) words in the Talon manuscript compared with other sources.

	Talon	*Other Sources*
Bull/Buffalo	*tenaha*	tanaha
Good (Thing)	*couhistanhat*	hanhat
Grease	*Assayo*	'asaayu
Water	*coko*	koko
White Man	*Yeyecha*	inkinis
Woman	*senaty*	nati

the orthography of the manuscript). As can be seen, only the term for "white man" fails to correspond at least in part to later usage, which is based primarily on the Northern Caddo (Kadohadacho) variety. Indeed, it might have been expected that the differences would have been greater. Evidently, internal differentiation within Caddo was much less than within Karankawa and other languages of South Texas.

This discussion has endeavored to illustrate the value of linguistic data, even as scanty as those preserved in the Talon Interrogations, for

11 Sauvole, left in charge of Fort Maurepas (Ocean Springs, Mississippi), in 1700, sent two boys with the Bayogoula chief, one to learn his language, the other destined for the Houma for the same purpose (Margry, *Découvertes*, IV, 448). See also Minister of Marine to Iberville, July 20, 1701, in *Découvertes*, IV, 488, in which the minister relays the king's approval for Iberville's having sent six boys for language study among the Indians; also Minister of Marine, Comte de Maurepas, to Bienville and Salmon, September 2, 1732, granting approval of a plan to place French boys with Indian groups to learn their language and study the natural history of Louisiana (University of Southwestern Louisiana, Lafayette, LC microfilm, reel 15, AC., B 57:814; Weddle, personal communication).

reconstructing the ethnohistorical situation among Indian groups at the time of first European contact. From the few data that we have on Karankawa and other languages of the area, it appears that South Texas, including the Gulf Coast, was one of the most linguistically complex areas in the world. In view of this, it is to be regretted that more people did not have the time and interest to preserve information on these languages before they, and the invaluable evidence on the history of the area they could have provided, irretrievably disappeared.

Bibliography

Manuscript Sources

Archives

Archives Nationales, Paris (AN)
    Colonies, Series C13A, 13B
    Marine: Dépot des Cartes et Plans, vol. 67, no. 15
    Outre-Mer, DFC, Louisiane 3
    Service Hydrographique: group 115, Delisle papers, maps.

Archivo General de Indias, Seville (AGI)
    Audiencia de Mexico, legajos 91, 560, 616, 617
    Audiencia de Santo Domingo, legajo 839
    Contaduría, legajos 58, 876
    Mapas y Planos

Archivo General de la Nación (AGN) Mexico
    Historia

Bancroft Library, Bolton Collection, University of California, Berkeley
    (typescript from Archivo de Santa Cruz de Querétaro)

Biblioteca del Real Palacio, Madrid
    Manuscript 2667

Bibliothèque Nationale, Paris (BN)
    Clairambault Manuscript 1016

John Carter Brown Library, Brown University, Providence, R.I.
    (manuscript collection)

Old Spanish Missions Research Library, Our Lady of the Lake University, San Antonio, Tex. (microfilm from Spanish and French archives)

Public Archives of Canada, Manuscript Division, Ottawa (microfilm reel H-1022)

University of Texas Archives, Austin (transcripts from AGI; AGN, Historia; and Archives Nationales)

Dissertation

Schuetz, Mardith K. "The Indians of the San Antonio Missions, 1718–1821." Ph.D. dissertation, University of Texas at Austin, 1975.

Published Sources

Arnold, J. Barto, III, and Robert S. Weddle. *The Nautical Archeology of Padre Island: The Spanish Shipwrecks of 1554*. New York: Academic Press, 1978.

Austin, Stephen F. "Journal of Stephen F. Austin on His First Trip to Texas, 1821." *Southwestern Historical Quarterly* 7, no. 4 (April, 1904): 286–307.

Bancroft, Hubert Howe. *History of the North Mexican States and Texas*. 2 vols. San Francisco: A. L. Bancroft, 1889.

Benavides, Alonso de. *Benavides' Memorial of 1630*. Translated by Peter B. Forrestal. Washington, D.C.: Academy of American Franciscan History, 1954.

Béranger, Jean. *Béranger's Discovery of Aransas Pass*. Translated by William M. Carroll and edited by Frank Wagner. Corpus Christi, Tex.: Friends of the Corpus Christi Museum, 1983.

Berlandier, Jean Louis. *The Indians of Texas in 1830*. Edited by John C. Ewers. Washington, D.C.: Smithsonian Institution Press, 1969.

———. *Journey to Mexico during the Years 1826 to 1834*. Translated by Sheila M. Ohlendorf, Josette M. Bigelow, and Mary M. Standefer. 2 vols. Austin: Texas State Historical Association, 1980.

Blakeslee, Donald J. "Origin and Spread of the Calumet Ceremony." *American Antiquity* 46 (1981): 759–68.

Bolton, Herbert Eugene. *Guide to Materials for the History of the United States in the Principal Archives of Mexico*. Reprint. New York: Kraus, 1965.

———. "The Location of La Salle's Colony on the Gulf of Mexico." *Southwestern Historical Quarterly* 27, no. 3 (January, 1924): 171–89.

———, ed. *Spanish Exploration in the Southwest: 1542–1706*. Reprint. New York: Barnes and Noble, 1963.

Brain, Jeffrey P. "The Archaeology of the Tunica: Trial on the Yazoo." National Geographic Society Research Reports. Washington, D.C.: National Geographic Society, 1975.

———. "Late Prehistoric Settlement Patterning in the Yazoo Basin and Natchez Bluffs Regions of the Lower Mississippi Valley." In Bruce D. Smith, ed., *Mississippian Settlement Patterns*, pp. 331–68. New York: Academic Press, 1978.

———. "La Salle at the Natchez." In Patricia Galloway, ed., *La Salle and His Legacy: Frenchmen and Indians in the Lower Mississippi Valley,* pp. 49–59.

Branda, Eldon Stephen, ed. *The Handbook of Texas,* III. Austin: Texas State Historical Association, 1976.

Brannon, Peter. *The Southern Indian Trade.* Montgomery, Ala.: Paragon Press, 1935.

Brasseaux, Carl A. trans. and ed. *A Comparative View of French Louisiana, 1699 and 1762: The Journals of Pierre Le Moyne d'Iberville and Jean-Jacques-Blaise d'Abbadie.* Lafayette: Center for Louisiana Studies, University of Southwestern Louisiana, 1979.

Brazill, W. N. "Gored by a Wounded Buffalo." *Frontier Times* 7 (April, 1924): 15.

Bushnell, David. "Drawings of A. De Batz in Louisiana, 1732–1735." *Smithsonian Miscellaneous Collections* 80, no. 5.

Cabeza de Vaca. *The Journey of Alvar Nuñez Cabeza de Vaca and His Companions from Florida to the Pacific, 1528–1536.* Translated by Fanny Bandelier. Reprint. Chicago: Rio Grande Press, 1964.

———. "The Narrative of Cabeza de Vaca." In Frederick Webb Hodge and Theodore H. Lewis, *Spanish Explorers in the Southern United States, 1528–1543.*

Calleja, Félix. "Nuevo Santander in 1795: A Provincial Inspection by Félix Calleja." Translated and edited by David M. Vigness. *Southwestern Historical Quarterly* 75, no. 4 (April, 1972): 461–506.

Canedo, Lino Gómez [*sic*], ed. *Primeras exploraciones y poblamiento de Texas (1686–1694).* Monterrey: Instituto Technológico y de Estudios Superiores de Monterrey, 1968.

Céliz, Francisco. *Diary of the Alarcón Expedition into Texas, 1718–1719.* Translated by Fritz Leo Hoffman. Reprint. New York: Arno Press, 1967.

Chabot, Victorin. "Journal inédit relatant les expeditions de Cavelier de La Salle." *The Archivist* 8 (1981): 8–9.

Chesnel, Paul. *History of Cavelier de La Salle, 1643–1687.* Translated by Andrée Chesnel Meany. New York: Putnam, 1932.

Clark, W. P. *The Indian Sign Language.* Reprint. Lincoln: University of Nebraska Press, 1982.

"Los coches de la ciudad de Mexico durante la época colonial." *Boletin del Archivo General de la Nación,* old series, 15, no. 4: 538–87.

Colección de diarios y relaciones para la historia de los viajes y descubrimientos, IV. Madrid: Instituto Histórico de Marina, 1944.

Cox, Isaac Joslin, ed. *The Journeys of Réné Robert Cavelier, Sieur de La Salle.* 2 vols. Reprint. Austin: Pemberton Press, 1968.

Cumming, W. P., R. A. Skelton, and D. B. Quinn. *The Discovery of North America*. New York: American Heritage Press, 1972.

Dampier, William. *Dampier's Voyages: Consisting of a New Voyage Round the World, Two Voyages to Campeachey, a Discourse on Winds, a Voyage to New Holland, and a Vindication in Answer to the Commercial Relation of William Funnell*. Edited by John Masefield. 2 vols. London: E. Grant Richards, 1906.

Delanglez, Jean. *The Journal of Jean Cavelier: The Account of a Survivor of La Salle's Texas Expedition*. Chicago: Institute of Jesuit History, 1938.

———. "La Salle's Expedition of 1682." *Mid-America* 22 (1940): 3–37.

———. *Some La Salle Journeys*. Chicago: Institute of Jesuit History, 1938.

———. "The Sources of the Delisle Map of America, 1703." *Mid-America* 25, no. 4 (October, 1943): 275–98.

DeWees, W. B. *Letters from an Early Settler of Texas*. Edited by Cara Cardelle. Waco, Tex.: Texian Press, 1968.

Documentos eclesiásticos y civiles de la provincia de Texas ó Nuevas Philipinas, 1720–1779. Madrid: José Porrúa Turanzas, 1961.

Domenech, Emmanuel Henri, trans. *Missionary Adventures in Texas and Mexico*. London: Longman, Brown, Green, Longman & Roberts, 1858.

Duaine, Carl L., trans. *Caverns of Oblivion*. Corpus Christi, Tex.: privately printed, 1971.

Dunn, William Edward. *Spanish and French Rivalry in the Gulf Region of the United States, 1678–1702: The Beginnings of Texas and Pensacola*. Bulletin 1705, Studies in History 1. Austin: University of Texas, 1917.

Eccles, W. J. *France in America*. New York: Harper and Row, 1972.

d'Esmanville, Abbé. "Journal de l'Abbé d'Esmanville." In Pierre Margry, ed., *Découvertes et établissements des français dans l'ouest et dans le sud de l'Amérique septentrionale (1614–1754)*, II, 510–17.

Espinosa, Isidro Félix. *Crónica de los colegios de propaganda fide de la Nueva España*. New edition with notes and introduction by Lino Gómez Canedo. Washington, D.C.: Academy of American Franciscan History, 1964.

———. *The Espinosa-Olivares-Aguirre Expedition of 1709: Espinosa's Diary*. Translated by Gabriel Tous. Preliminary Studies 1, no. 3. Austin: Texas Catholic Historical Society, 1930.

Esquemeling, John. *The Buccaneers of America*. Reprint. New York: Dover, 1967.

Falconer, Thomas. *On the Discovery of the Mississippi, and on the South-western, Oregon, and North-western Boundary of the United States.* Reprint. Austin, Tex.: Shoal Creek, 1975.

Forbes, Jack, D. *Apache, Navaho, and Spaniard.* Norman: University of Oklahoma Press, 1960.

Fundaburk, Emma Lila, and Mary Douglas Fundaburk Foreman. *Sun Circles and Human Hands.* Luverne, Ala.: E. L. Fundaburk, 1957.

Galloway, Patricia K., ed. *La Salle and His Legacy: Frenchmen and Indians in the Lower Mississippi Valley.* Jackson: University Press of Mississippi, 1982.

———. "Sources for the La Salle Expedition of 1682." In Patricia Galloway, ed., *La Salle and His Legacy: Frenchmen and Indians in the Lower Mississippi Valley,* pp. 3–10.

Gatschet, Albert S. *The Karankawa Indians: The Coast People of Texas.* Archeological and Ethnological Papers of the Peabody Museum 1, no. 2. Cambridge, Mass.: Harvard University, 1891.

Gravier, Jacques. "Journal." In *The Jesuit Relations and Allied Documents: Travels and Explorations of the Jesuit Missionaries in New France, 1610–1791,* LXV. Edited by Reuben Gold Thwaites. Cleveland, Ohio: Burrows Brothers, 1900.

Gray, Robert S., ed. *A Visit to Texas in 1831.* 3rd ed. Houston: Cordovan Press, 1975.

Green, Thomas Jefferson. *Journal of the Texian Expedition against Mier.* Reprint. Austin, Tex.: Steck, 1935.

Gregg, Josiah. *Diary and Letters of Josiah Gregg: Southwestern Enterprises, 1840–1847.* Edited by Maurice Garland Fulton. Norman: University of Oklahoma Press, 1941.

Habig, Marion A. *The Franciscan Pére Marquette: A Critical Biography of Father Zénobe Membré, O.F.M. La Salle's Chaplain and Missionary Companion.* New York: Joseph Wagner, 1934.

Hackett, Charles Wilson, ed. *Historical Documents Relating to New Mexico, Nueva Vizcaya, and Approaches Thereto, to 1773.* 2 vols. Washington, D.C.: Carnegie Institution, 1923, 1926.

Haring, Clarence Henry. *The Buccaneers of the West Indies in the XVII Century.* Reprint. Hamden, Conn.: Archon Books, 1966.

———. *Trade and Navigation between Spain and the Indies to the Time of the Hapsburgs.* Reprint. Gloucester, Mass.: Peter Smith, 1964.

Higginbotham, Jay. *Old Mobile: Fort Louis de la Louisiane, 1702–1711.* Mobile, Ala.: Museum of the City of Mobile, 1977.

Historic New Orleans Collection. *Degrees of Discovery: From New World to New Orleans.* Exhibition catalog. New Orleans, 1977.

Hitchcock, A. S. *Manual of the Grasses of the U.S.* 2nd ed. Miscellaneous Publications no. 200. Washington, D.C.: U.S. Department of Agriculture, 1950.

Hodge, Frederick Webb. *Handbook of American Indians North of Mexico.* 2 vols. Bureau of American Ethnology Bulletin 30. Washington, D.C.: Smithsonian Institution, 1907, 1910.

Hodge, Frederick Webb, and Theodore H. Lewis. *Spanish Explorers in the Southern United States, 1528–1543.* Reprint. New York: Barnes and Noble, 1971.

Hoese, H. Dickson. "On the Correct Landfall of La Salle in Texas, 1685." *Louisiana History* 19, no. 1 (Winter, 1978): 5–32.

Holland, James K. "Diary of a Texas Volunteer in the Mexican War." *Southwestern Historical Quarterly* 30, no. 1 (July, 1926): 1–33.

Holmes, Jack D. L. "Andrés de Pez and Spanish Reaction to French Expansion into the Gulf of Mexico." In Patricia K. Galloway, ed., *La Salle and His Legacy: Frenchmen and Indians in the Lower Mississippi Valley,* pp. 106–28.

Hudson, Charles. *The Southeastern Indians.* Knoxville: University of Tennessee Press, 1976.

Huntington, R. T., trans. "The Interrogation of the Talon Brothers, 1698." Afterword by Wayne Franklin. *Iowa Review* 15, no. 2 (Spring–Summer, 1985): 99–131.

Jaenen, Cornelius. *Friend and Foe.* New York: Columbia University Press, 1976.

Joutel, Henri. *Joutel's Journal of La Salle's Last Voyage.* Edited and with an introduction by Henry Reed Stiles. Reprint. New York: Corinth, 1962.

———. "Relation de Henri Joutel." In Pierre Margry, ed., *Découvertes et établissements des français dans l'ouest et dans le sud de l'Amérique septentrionale (1614–1754),* vol. 3.

Kapp, Ida Kappell. "A Letter Home by Ida Kappell Kapp." Translated by Oscar Haas. In Crystal Sasse Ragsdale, ed., *The Golden Free Land,* pp. 89–111. Austin, Tex.: Landmark Press, 1976.

Landar, Herbert. "The Karankawa Invasion of Texas." *International Journal of American Linguistics* 34, no. 4 (October, 1968): 242–58.

Le Clercq, Chrétien. *Premier éstablissement de la foi dans la Nouvelle France.* 2 vols. Paris: Amable Auroy, 1691.

Lee, Douglas. "Mississippi Delta: The Land of the River." *National Geographic* 164, no. 2 (August, 1982): 226–52.

Lee, Nelson. *Three Years among the Comanches.* Norman: University of Oklahoma Press, 1957.

León, Alonso de. "Itinerary of the De León Expedition of 1689." In

Herbert Eugene Bolton, ed., *Spanish Exploration in the Southwest, 1402–1706*, pp. 388–404.

———. "Itinerary of the De León Expedition of 1690." In Herbert Eugene Bolton, ed., *Spanish Exploration in the Southwest, 1402–1706*, pp. 405–23.

León, Alonso de, Juan Bautista Chapa, and Fernando Sánchez de Zamora. *Historia de Nuevo León, con noticias sobre Coahuila, Tamaulipas, Texas y Nuevo México*. Monterrey: Centro de Estudios Humanísticas de la Universidad de Nuevo León, 1961.

Leonard, Irving A., ed. *Documentos inéditos de Don Carlos de Sigüenza y Góngora*. Mexico City: Bibliotheca Mexicana, 1963.

———, trans. *Spanish Approach to Pensacola, 1689–1693*. Reprint. New York: Arno Press, 1967.

———, trans. and ed. "The Spanish Re-exploration of the Gulf Coast in 1686." *Mississippi Valley Historical Review* 22, no. 4 (March, 1936): 547–57.

Le Page du Pratz, Antoine Simon. *Histoire de la Louisiane française*. 4 vols. Paris: De Bure, 1758.

López de Velasco, Juan. *Geografía y descripción universal de las Indias* (1574). Biblioteca de Autores Españoles, vol. 248. New ed. Madrid: Ediciones Atlas, 1971.

Louant, Armand. *Le cas de père Louis Hennepin, récollet*. Ath, Belgium: Cercle Royal d'Histoire et d'Archéologie d'Ath et de la Région et Musées Athois, 1980.

McClintock, William A. "Journal of a Trip Through Texas and Northern Mexico in 1846–47." *Southwestern Historical Quarterly* 34, no. 3 (January, 1931): 231–38.

McDermott, John Francis, ed. *Frenchmen and French Ways in the Mississippi Valley*. Urbana: University of Illinois Press, 1969.

McHugh, Tom. *The Time of the Buffalo*. New York: Knopf, 1972.

McWilliams, Richbourg Gaillard. "Iberville at the Birdfoot Subdelta: Final Discovery of the Mississippi River." In John Francis McDermott, ed., *Frenchmen and French Ways in the Mississippi Valley*. Urbana: University of Illinois Press, 1969.

Margry, Pierre, ed. *Découvertes et établissements des français dans l'ouest et dans le sud de l'Amérique septentrionale (1614–1754)*. 6 vols. Paris: Maisonneuve, 1876–86.

Martin, Robert Sidney, and James C. Martin. *Contours of Discovery: Printed Maps Delineating the Texas and Southwestern Chapters in the Cartographic History of North America, 1513–1930—A User's Guide*. Austin: Texas State Historical Association, 1982.

Massenet, Damián. *Diary of the Missionaries on the Expedition of Don*

Domingo Terán de los Ríos into Texas, 1691–1692. Translated by Mattie Austin Hatcher. Preliminary Studies 2, no. 1. Austin: Texas Catholic Historical Society, 1932.

——. "Letter of Fray Damián Massanet to Don Carlos de Sigüenza, 1690." In Herbert Eugene Bolton, ed., *Spanish Exploration in the Southwest, 1542–1706,* pp. 353–87.

Maxwell, Ross A. *The Big Bend of the Rio Grande.* Austin, Tex.: Bureau of Economic Geology, 1971.

Moore, Francis, Jr. *Map and Description of Texas.* Reprint. Waco, Tex.: Texian Press, 1965.

Morfi, Juan Agustín. *History of Texas, 1673–1779.* Translated and edited by Carlos E. Castañeda. 2 vols. Reprint. New York: Arno Press, 1967.

Muir, Andrew Forest, ed. *Texas in 1837: An Anonymous, Contemporary Narrative.* Austin: University of Texas Press, 1958.

O'Crouley, Pedro Alonso. *A Description of the Kingdom of New Spain, 1774.* Translated and edited by Seán Galvin. [San Francisco]: John Howell Books, 1972.

O'Donnell, Walter J., trans. *La Salle's Occupation of Texas.* Preliminary Studies 3, no. 2. Austin: Texas Catholic Historical Society, 1936.

Oertel, Everett. "Bicentennial Bees—Early Records of Honey Bees in the Eastern U.S." *American Bee Journal* 116, nos. 2, 3, and 4 (February, March, April, 1976): 70–71, 114, 128, 156–57.

Ogg, Frederic Austin. *The Opening of the Mississippi: A Struggle for Supremacy in the American Interior.* Reprint. New York: Cooper Square, 1968.

Parkman, Francis. *La Salle and the Discovery of the Great West.* Reprint. New York: New American Library, 1963.

Parry, J. H. *The Age of Reconnaissance.* New York: New American Library, 1964.

Peña, Antonio de la. "Derrotero Seguida por el Marqués de San Miguel de Aguayo en su viage y expedición a la Provincia de Texas (1720–1722)." In *Documentos eclesiásticos y civiles de la provincia de Texas ó Nuevas Philipinas, 1720–1779,* pp. 1–86.

Phillips, Paul Crisler. *The Fur Trade.* 2 vols. Norman: University of Oklahoma Press, 1961.

Phillips, Philip, James A. Ford, and James B. Griffin. *Archaeological Survey in the Lower Mississippi Alluvial Valley, 1940–1947.* Peabody Museum of Archaeology and Ethnology Papers 25. Cambridge, Mass.: Harvard University Press, 1951.

Pichardo, José Antonio. *Pichardo's Treatise on the Limits of Louisiana and Texas.* 4 vols. Translated by Charles Wilson Hackett,

Charmion Clair Shelby, and Mary Ruth Splawn. Edited by
  Charles Wilson Hackett. Austin: University of Texas Press,
  1931–34.
Quimby, George I. *The Bayou Goula Site, Iberville Parish, Louisiana.*
  Fieldiana: Anthropology 7. Chicago: Field Museum of Natural
  History, 1957.
———. "The Natchezan Culture Type." *American Antiquity* 7 (1942):
  255–75.
Reid, Samuel C., Jr. *The Scouting Expeditions of McCulloch's Texas Rangers.* Reprint. Austin, Tex.: Steck, 1935.
Roemer, Ferdinand von. *Texas, with Particular Reference to German Immigration and the Physical Appearance of the Country.* Translated by
  Oswald Mueller. San Antonio: Standard Printing Company, 1935.
Rowland, Dunbar, Albert Godfrey Sanders, and Patricia Galloway,
  eds. and trans. *Mississippi Provincial Archives: French Dominion,*
  vols. 4 and 5. Baton Rouge: Louisiana State University Press, 1984.
Rudloe, Jack, and Ann Rudloe. "Louisiana's Atchafalaya: Trouble in
  Bayou Country." *National Geographic* 156, no. 3 (September, 1979):
  377–96.
Ruecking, Frederick Jr. "Ceremonies of the Coahuiltecan Indians of
  Southern Texas and Northeastern Mexico." *Texas Journal of Science*
  6, no. 3 (1954): 330–39.
———. "Social Organization of the Coahuiltecan Indians of Southern
  Texas and Northeastern Mexico." *Texas Journal of Science* 7 (1955):
  357–88.
Rule, John C. "Jérôme Phélypeaux, Comte de Ponchartrain, and the
  Establishment of Louisiana, 1696–1715." In John Francis McDermott, ed., *Frenchmen and French Ways in the Mississippi Valley.*
Santa María, Vicente de. "Relación histórica de la Colonia de Nuevo
  Santander y Costa del Seno Mexicano." In *Estado general de las
  fundaciones heches por Don José de Escandón en la Colonia del Nuevo
  Santander,* vol. 11. Mexico City: Talleres Gráficas de la Nación, 1930.
Schoffelmayer, Victor H. "The Magic Valley—Its Marvelous Future."
  Texas Geographic Magazine 3, no. 1 (Spring, 1939): 7.
Shea, John Gilmary, ed. *Discovery and Exploration of the Mississippi Valley.* New York: Redfield, 1852.
Sjoberg, Andrée. "The Culture of the Tonkawa: A Texas Coastal
  Tribe." *Texas Journal of Science* 5, no. 3 (1963): 280–304.
Solís, José de. *The Solís Diary of 1767.* Translated by Peter P. Forrestal.
  Preliminary Studies 1, no. 6, Austin: Texas Catholic Historical
  Society, 1931.
Steinert, W. "W. Steinert's View of Texas in 1849." Translated and

edited by Gilbert J. Jordan. *Southwestern Historical Quarterly* 80, no. 1 (July, 1976): 57–78.

Steyermark, Julian A. *Vegetational History of the Ozark Forest.* Columbia: University of Missouri Studies, 1959.

Stubbs, John. "The Chickasaw Contact with the La Salle Expedition in 1682." In Patricia Galloway, ed., *La Salle and His Legacy: Frenchmen and Indians in the Lower Mississippi Valley.*

Swanton, John R. *Indians of the Southeastern United States.* Bureau of American Ethnology Bulletin 137. Washington, D.C.: Smithsonian Institution, 1946.

———. *The Indian Tribes of North America.* Bureau of American Ethnology Bulletin 145. Washington, D.C.: Smithsonian Institution, 1952.

———. *Linguistic Material from the Tribes of Southern Texas and Northeastern Mexico.* Bureau of American Ethnology Bulletin 127. Washington, D.C.: Smithsonian Institution, 1940.

———. *Source Material on the History and Ethnology of the Caddo Indians.* Bureau of American Ethnology Bulletin 132. Washington, D.C.: Smithsonian Institution, 1942.

Tanguay, Cyprian. *Dictionnaire généalogique des familles canadiennes depuis la fondation de la colonie jusqu'a nos jours.* 7 vols. Quebec (I) and Montreal (II–VII): E. Senecal & Fils, 1871–80.

Temple, Waynce C. *Indian Villages of the Illinois Country.* Illinois State Museum Scientific Papers 2, part 2. Springfield, Ill., 1977.

Terán de los Ríos, Domingo. *Itinerary and Daily Account Kept by General Domingo de Terán, Begun May 16, 1691, Finished April 15, 1692.* Translated by Mattie Austin Hatcher. Preliminary Studies 2, no. 1. Austin: Texas Catholic Historical Society, 1932.

Torrey, John. *U.S. Survey,* I, part 2. In William H. Emory, *Report on the United States and Mexican Boundary Survey Made under the Direction of the Secretary of the Interior.* 34th Cong., 1st sess., Sen. Exec. Doc. 108. 2 vols. Washington, D.C.: Government Printing Office, 1857, 1859.

Troike, Rudolph C. "The Caddo Word for 'Water.'" *International Journal of American Linguistics* 30, no. 1 (1964): 96–98.

———. "The Origins of Plains Mescalism." *American Anthropologist* 64, no. 5 (1962): 949–50.

Tucker, Sarah Jones. *Indian Villages of the Illinois Country.* Atlas, including supplement by Wayne C. Temple. Illinois State Museum Scientific Papers 1, part 1. Springfield, Ill., 1975.

Vásquez de Espinosa, Antonio. *Description of the Indies (c. 1620).* Trans-

lated by Charles Upson Clark. Washington, D.C.: Smithsonian
Institution, 1968.

Villiers du Terrage, Marc de. *Les dernières années de la Louisiane française*. Paris: Maisonneuve, 1903.

———. *L'Expédition de Cavelier de La Salle dans le Golfe du Mexique
(1684–1687)*. Librairie d'Amérique et d'Orient. Paris: Adrien-Mai-
sonneuve, 1934.

Villiers du Terrage, Marc de, and Paul Rivet. "Deux vocabulaires inédits
recueillis au Texas vers 1688." *Journal de la Société des Américanistes
de Paris* 21, no. 2 (1929): 307–11.

———. "Les Indiens du Texas et les expéditions françaises de 1720 et
1721 a la 'Baie Saint-Bernard.'" *Journal de la Société des Américanistes
de Paris* 11, no. 2 (1919): 403–42.

Wagner, Henry R., ed. *The Discovery of Yucatán by Francisco Hernández
de Córdoba*. Berkeley, Calif.: Cortés Society, 1941.

Ward, Fred. "Inside Cuba Today." *National Geographic* 151, no. 1 (January, 1977): 32–69.

Weddle, Robert S. "La Salle's Survivors." *Southwestern Historical Quarterly* 75, no. 4 (April, 1972): 414–33.

———. *Spanish Sea: The Gulf of Mexico in North American Discovery,
1500–1685*. College Station: Texas A & M University Press, 1985.

———. *Wilderness Manhunt: The Spanish Search for La Salle*. Austin:
University of Texas Press, 1973.

Williams, Stephen. "On the Location of the Historic Taensa Villages."
Fifth Conference on Historic Site Archaeology Papers, 1965–1966 1:2–
13. Columbia, S.C., 1967.

Winsor, Justin. *Cartier to Frontenac*. Reprint. New York: Cooper
Square, 1970.

Wood, Peter H. "La Salle: Discovery of a Lost Explorer." *American
Historical Review* 89, no. 2 (April, 1984): 294–323.

Maps

Alvarez de Pineda, Alonso. Map sketch of the Gulf of Mexico, 1519.
AGI, Mapas y Planos.

Coronelli, Marco Vincenzo. "Partie occidentale du Canada ou de la
Nouvelle France," 1688. Published in supplement to Sarah Jones
Tucker, *Indian Villages of the Illinois Country*. Original in Winsor
Memorial Map Collection, Harvard College Library.

Hutchins, Thomas. "A New Map of the Western Parts of Virginia,
Pennsylvania, Maryland, and North Carolina." Printed copy, 1778,
in Library of Congress.

Jesuit Map of 1671. Paris, Bibliothèque National, Ge DD 2987-8695.

Marquette, Jacques. Map of 1673. Montreal, Sainte-Marie Archives.

Minet. "Carte de la Louisiane." Paris, AN, Service Hydrographique.

"Parkman No. 4." Cambridge, Mass., Winsor Memorial Map Collection, Harvard College Library.

Randin, Hugues. "Carte de l'Amérique septentrionale depuis l'embouchure de la Rivière St. Laurens jusques au Sein Mexique, 1674–1681." Providence, R.I., John Carter Brown Library, Brown University.

Contributors

ANN LINDA BELL, CDP, is chairman of the Foreign Language Department of Our Lady of the Lake University, San Antonio, Texas, and has taught in both elementary and secondary schools. Her M.A. in French is from the Université Laval, Quebec City, Canada.

PATRICIA GALLOWAY is special projects officer with the Mississippi Department of Archives and History, Jackson. She holds the Ph.D. in comparative literature, was translator and editor of vols. 4 and 5 of the *Mississippi Provincial Archives: The French Dominion,* and is editor of *La Salle and His Legacy: Frenchmen and Indians in the Lower Mississippi Valley.*

MARY CHRISTINE MORKOVSKY, CDP, Ph.D., is head of the Department of Philosophy of Wadhams Hall Seminary-College, Ogdensburg, New York, having served previously as professor of philosophy and director of the Humanities Division at Our Lady of the Lake University, San Antonio. She has also taught in both elementary and high schools. Having done extensive historical research in both French and Spanish archives, she has lectured widely and published numerous articles in professional journals.

MARDITH K. SCHUETZ, Ph.D., who has taught anthropology, sociology, and history, currently is an independent contractor in the fields of archaeology and historical research. Her specialties include Spanish site archaeology, history, and ethnology of New Spain's northern borderlands and Spanish colonial architecture. Her numerous publications include *San Antonio in the Eighteenth Century* and *The Practice of Architecture in Mexico City.*

RUDOLPH C. TROIKE, a professor at the University of Illinois at Urbana-Champaign, holds the Ph.D. in linguistics from the University of Texas at Austin. His special research fields are American Indian linguistics and the languages and ethnohistory of northeastern Mexico and southern Texas. He has researched extensively in Mexican archives. His publications include *An Introduction to Spoken Bolivian Quechua* and *Coahuilteco: An Indian Language of Texas.*

ROBERT S. WEDDLE has been recognized with various awards for his achievements as both journalist and author of historical works. He is author and coauthor of eight books, including *Wilderness Manhunt: The Spanish Search for La Salle* and *Spanish Sea: The Gulf of Mexico in North American Discovery, 1500–1685,* as well as numerous articles. His special interest is the Spanish borderlands and exploration of the Gulf region. A graduate of Texas Tech University, he lives and writes on his ranch near Bonham, Texas.

DEL WENIGER is chairman of the Biology Department of Our Lady of the Lake University, San Antonio. He has done extensive research in Texas's biohistory, resulting in his book *The Explorers' Texas.* He is also the author of *Cacti of the Southwest* and *Cacti of Texas and the Neighboring States.*

Index

Accau, Michel, 34n
Acosta, Gerónimo de, 133, 138, 189
Aigron, —— (captain of *Aimable*), 102, 108, 111, 122
Aimable, the (flute): accident of, 92; captain and crew of, 5, 108, 113; chartering of, 84; described, 23, 226, 273; develops list, 102; Galveston Bay sighted from, 106n. 47; at Isle of Pines, 91; Joutel, La Salle sail on, 72, 89; navigational quality of, 90; ordered into bay, 106, 108; separates from *Joly*, 93, 95; and Talons, 226; wreck of, 73, 79, 109, 110, 111, 136, 169, 169n, 226, 267
Alarcón expedition, 266
Aldama, Francisco, 174, 186
Allouez, Father Claude, 31n.4, 39n.19
Alvarado (Veracruz), 130
Alvarez de Pineda, Alonso: map sketch of, 93n.9, 129n.2; and Mississippi Delta, 135; and Río del Espíritu Santo, 5, 7, 129n.2
Angel, Antoine (*dit* Picard du Gay), 34n.11
animals, domesticated: dogs, 58, 62, 256, 266; pigs, 91, 233, 258
—horses: captured by Clamcoëhs, 249; as food, 245; French children ransomed with, 241; raised by Indians, 256; as pack animals, 230; reports of, by Atákapas, 179, 186–87; of viceroy, 244; in warfare, 236
animals, wild: alligators, 54, 57, 284; bears, 44, 59, 284; flying squirrels, 121; jaguar, 284; margay, 284; mountain lions, 284; muskrats, 91; ocelot, 284; wolves, 233, 266, 274, 284; squirrels, 256
—buffalo: described, 228, 283; Enríquez on, 105, 175, 176, 186; as food, 227; hunted, 43, 63, 230, 255; range of, 105, 175, 176, 186, 249, 283; sacrificed, 254; uses of hides of, 47, 58, 228, 233, 250, 263, 265
—deer: eaten by colonists, 227; hunted,

43, 44, 45, 49, 52, 59, 63, 173, 255; kinds of, 284; sacrificed, 254; word for, 258
Apalache, province of, 195, 200; Corso seeks, 131; on Enríquez map, 205; garrison of, 139; Indian guide from, 174; missions of, 182n
Apalache Bay, 131
Apalachicola River, 141
Aramburu, Joseph de, 145
Aranda y Avellaneda, Pedro, 139, 196, 196n.61
Aransas Bay, 279, 290n.5, 299
Armada de Barlovento (Windward Fleet), 175; captures La Salle defectors, 90n.12; Enríquez Barroto and, 129, 130, 132, 146; and search for La Salle, 129, 130, 132; Pez and, 146; ships lost from, 146; Talons serve, 218; and Tampico pirates, 179n.37
Arnoul, —— (intendant): and Minet, 84, 122, 126
Assiniboile River, 65
Astina, Admiral Antonio, 150
Astina, Pedro de, 133, 180
Atchafalaya River, 26, 134, 138, 189, 190n.52
Austin, Stephen F., 284

Bahama Channel: Armada de Barlovento in, 146; and Gulf Stream, 115n.59, 200n; *Joly* in, 116, 117n.63
Bahía de Carlos, 198
Bahía de Guadiana, 115, 115n.60
Bahía del Espíritu Santo. *See* Espíritu Santo (river and bay)
Bahía de Mobila. *See* Mobile Bay
Bahía de San Panzacola. *See* Pensacola Bay
Bahía de San Bernardo, 140, 142, 145. *See also* Matagorda Bay
Bancroft, Hubert Howe, 10
Barataria Bay, 95n.23
Barbier, Gabriel Minime, Sieur: aids Minet, 21, 85; career of, 20; child of, 237; as Minet's informant, 12, 17, 20–22, 29;

named lieutenant, 84; and Nicolas de La Salle, 21; and 1682 expedition, 25, 29, 45, 55, 64, 65; wife of, 211, 216
Barbier, Madame, 237
Barrier Islands (of Texas), 135
Barroa, Miguel de, 174
Barroto, Juan Enríquez. *See* Enríquez Barroto, Juan
Barthelemy, Pierre, 236n.13
Baudrand, Abbé, 111
Baugis, M. de, 64
Baye du Saint-Esprit: 94, 95, 96, 113n.56, 226; bays mistaken for, 97–98, 106n.47; concept of 99; ignorance of, 114; as rendezvous, 99; report on, 89. *See also* Espíritu Santo (river and bay)
Beaujeu, Tanguy Le Gallois de: and Aigron, 108, 140; aided by English, 117; and *Aimable*, 103, 108–109, 110, 111; commands *Joly*, 84, 226; concerns of, 79; illness of, 88; at Jamestown, 119; and La Salle, 4, 71, 72, 73, 77, 79, 80, 84–113 *passim*, 123, 124, 126; and Minet, 1, 77, 78, 79, 80, 103, 106, 108, 113n.54, 116; as navigator, 92, 100; pays ransom, 116; and pirate captain, 157n.9; provisions ship, 89; returns to France, 5, 79, 226, 291; sounds Texas coast, 104, 105; suspicions of, 93, 98, 99
Bégon, Michel de, 78, 87, 88, 89, 219
Belle, the (frigate), 84, 91, 92, 105; enters Matagorda Bay, 106, 108; land sighted from, 94; loss of, 5, 80, 226n; separation of, from *Joly*, 96; wreckage of, 136, 172
Bellisle, François Simars de, 290n.5
Benavides, Alonso de, 5, 129n.2
Béranger, Jean, 164, 290, 290n.5, 297–99
Bering Strait, 287
Berlandier, Jean Louis, 280, 290
Bibliothèque Nationale, 73
Big Bend (of the Rio Grande), 287
Big Constance Bayou, 188
Biloxi Bay, 220
Biñales, Pedro, 159, 201
Blanco County (Texas), 281–82
Blanco River, 281
Blind Bay, 56
Boca Chica, 175
Bois d'Ardenne (La Salle's secretary), 35
Boisrondel, Sieur de, 39
Boissieux, Sieur de: and Talons, 218, 219, 248
Bon (French warship), 218
Brazoria County (Texas), 286
Brazos River, 176n.30, 260, 280

Bréman, Eustache, 216, 223, 237, 241, 242, 249
Brest (France), 219
Bréton Sound, 142
Brigaut, Nicolás, 196n.61
Brownsville (Texas), 278
Cabañas (Cuba), 200, 201, 202
Cabeza de Vaca, Alvar Núñez, 2, 274; and buffalo, 105; on cannibalism, 137; on dogs, 266; on Indian way of life, 263, 265, 266, 268
Cabo de Lodo (Mud Cape), 132, 143, 193, 195, 205
Cabo Rojo, 154, 156, 157, 160n
Cabo San Antonio (Saint-Antoine), 91, 114, 115
Calcasieu River, 134, 137, 178n.34, 179n.38, 181. *See also* Río del Mexicano
Calleja, Félix, 278
Campeche: *cenotes* of, 190; pirate raid on, 78, 90n.12, 129, 130, 196n.61; Rivas-Iriarte at, 203; salines of, 203
Canada, 3, 137n.21
Caney Creek, 175n, 277
cannibalism: by French, 54; by Indians, 38, 51, 238, 249, 253, 271–72; by Spanish castaways, 137, 181
Cap Enragé (Mad Cape), 39
Cape Escondido, 94. *See also* Río Escondido
Cape San Blas, 141, 142, 195n.60
Cárdenas y Magaña, Manuel José, 142–45
Caribbean current, 114, 134, 202n. *See also* ocean currents
Caribbean Sea, 4, 6, 130, 131
Carlos II (of Spain), 140
Carolina, 120, 145, 146
Cartigny, ——, 111
Carvajal y de la Cueva, Luis de, 161
Castro, Diego de, 136, 152
Castro, Pedro de, 179, 181, 182, 187, 195
Cavelier, Abbé Jean (La Salle's brother), 33, 41, 226, 235; inquiry by, 209; journal of, 71, 74, 76; and La Salle, 33n.9, 41; and La Salle's survivors, 236n.13
Cavelier, Colin (La Salle's nephew), 235, 236n.13
Cayo de Huesos (Key West), 198, 199
Cedar Bayou: location of, 100, 104n, 169n.21; on Minet map, 76n.23, 100n.36; named, 168; ship remnants found at, 136. *See also* Río de Flores
Cedar Lake, 176n.30
Cerralvo (Nuevo León), 161n

Champetón (Campeche), 203
Chandeleur Islands, 138
Chandeleur Sound, 131, 142, 143
Charles I (of England), 121, 121n.67
Charles II (of England), 116n.62, 121, 121n.68, 122n
Charlevoix, Pierre François Xavier: and Talon document, 209–10, 289n.1
Charlotte Harbor, 198
Chesapeake Bay, 118, 119
Chicacha River (Wolf or Margot River), 46, 46n.37
China: passage to, 3, 29
Choucagoua River, 68. *See also* Ohio River
Chubusna (Yucatán), 203
Chucagoa fragment, 7, 8
Coahuila, 142, 145, 243
Coatzacoalcos (Veracruz), 204
Colbert, Jean-Baptiste (French minister), 7, 29, 31
Colbert River (Rivière Colbert), 8, 63, 65, 100, 106, 114n.56, 126. *See also* Mississippi River
Colorado River (of Texas), 277
Cordillera de los Organos, 115n.59
Corpus Christi (Texas), 164n
Corpus Christi Bay, 8, 136, 166n, 260
Corso, Juan: and castaways, 130, 136, 137, 138, 156n, 162n; death of, 181; and Espíritu Santo Bay, 130, 131; and French colony, 130; galley of, 130, 131; in maritime war, 130–31; survivors of, 140
Cortés, Hernando, 5, 152
Cromwell, Oliver, 116n.62, 121nn.67,68
Crystal River, 197n.64
Cuba, 90, 200–202
Cussy, Tarin de, 78, 87, 88n.9

D'Aire, Chevalier, 99, 109, 120
Dauphin Island, 104n
D'Autray, Jean Bourbon, Sieur, 58, 67, 84n
Delanglez, Jean, 19, 71, 74, 77
Delgado, Marcos, 196nn.61,62
Delisle, Claude, 22, 135, 142, 166n, 189n.49, 291n
Delisle, Guillaume: 135, 166n, 175n, 179n.38
Desaugiers, squadron of, 218, 248
Desclouzeaux (intendant), 219
De Soto, Hernando. *See* Soto, Hernando de
"De Soto" map, 99–100n.35
DeWees, W. B., 286
Dollier-Gallinée expedition, 31n.3
Domenech, Abbé Emmanuel Henri, 278

Douay, Anastase (Father), 10, 211, 220, 235, 236n.13
Du Chesne (pirate captain), 89n.10, 157n.9
Du Hamel, Ensign, 106–108, 112, 113
Duhaut, Dominique, 212, 234
Duhaut, Pierre (the elder), 106–108, 212, 234, 235
Duke of York, 122
Du Lhut, Daniel Greysolon, 34, 34n.11
Durango, 83
Dutch, 4. *See also* pirates and privateers
Du Val (king's scribe), 106

East Matagorda Bay, 175n
Echagaray, Martín de, 6n, 130n.2
England: affairs of, 121nn.67,68, 122n; allied with France, 116n.62; in colonial rivalry, 4; kings of, 121, 122; menace of, 145; ships of, 131; and Spanish ambassador, 140
Enríquez Barroto, Juan: as adviser, 132; on Atákapas, 137–38; on buffalo, 105n.45, 283; on cannibalism, 137; contribution of, 146–47; and Corso's men, 131, 137; diaries critiqued by, 141, 142; diary of, 1, 2, 12, 131, 134, 141, 142, 149–205; ferries supplies, 145; on Florida bays, 198n; on French ships, 172n.23, 175; on Indian tattoos, 267; on Juan Poule, 172, 173, 199n.67; on Karankawas, 136; lost at sea, 145–46; mapmakers borrow from, 142, 179n.38; maps and charts of, 132, 140–41, 173, 205; misjudgment of, 135, 163n; at Mobile Bay, 139; navigational skills of, 134–35, 138, 140, 154n.6; and Pensacola Bay, 131, 146; and Pez, 146; as pilot, 133, 149; qualities of, 130, 146; report of, 140; and search for La Salle, 1, 129, 131, 141–42; and Sigüenza, 146; and Terán, 142–45; as witness, 142
d'Esmanville, Abbé: account of, 71; on Gulf landfall, 94n.21; quits enterprise, 113n.54; returns to France, 291n; on sea voyage, 73, 92n.16; on ship reunion, 99n.35, 100n.36; as source, 74; and Spanish pirates, 116
Espinosa, Fray Isidro Félix de, 268, 269, 270–71
Espíritu Santo (river and bay), 223; bays confused with, 113–14n.56, 139, 141, 142; Corso seeks, 131, 132; described, 89; on early maps, 93n.19, 129; features of, 56n.63, 96n, 98, 135; and Mississippi, 129; La Salle's concept of, 7, 56n.63, 93;

naming of, 5; plan to reconnoiter, 113n.56; proposals on, 5–6; reconnaissance of, 141; as rendezvous, 93, 124; sought by Spaniards, 133–34, 135, 149; and Talons, 226
Espíritu Santo Bay (Florida), 198, 198n

Fer, Nicolas de, 142, 166n, 179n.38
Feugerolles's company, 219, 225, 248
flooding: of Mississippi River, 52, 53, 54, 56, 57, 58, 59
Florida: bays of, 198n; castaways in, 152n.3; English menace to, 145; governors of, 196, 199; keys of, 198–200; missions of, 182n
Fort Crèvecoeur (Pimiteouy), 35n.14, 42, 63
Fort Frontenac, 26, 31, 32, 34, 35
Fort Maurepas, 220, 300n
Fort Niagara, 32–33, 34
Fort Saint-Louis (of the Illinois), 5, 38
Fort Saint-Louis (of Texas), 1, 11, 12, 276, 283; massacre at, 2, 5, 110n.51, 237–38, 259; ruins of, 142; ship found near, 137
Fouquet, Louise, 121
Fouquet, Nicolas, 121n.69
France, 4–7; Beaujeu returns to, 140; colonial policy of, 7; and England, 116n.62; La Salle in, 3
Franciscans, 226, 237, 240–41
Franquenet (governor of Saint-Domingue), 87
French West Indies Company, 87n.7

Gabaret, ——, 105, 108
Galve, Conde de (Gaspar de la Cerda Sandoval Silva y Mendoza, viceroy), 146, 216, 217, 218
Galveston Bay, 177n.32, 178nn.35,36; Beranger at, 290n.5; Cabeza de Vaca near, 137; exploration of, 134, 138; first designation for, 142; French ships at, 97, 106n.47; 113–14n.56; Indian tribes of, 136–37, 138
Galveston Island, 176n.30
Garcitas Creek, 226; French settlement on, 11, 110n.51, 227, 276
Gasparilla Island, 198n
Gatschet, Albert S., 290, 295
Golfo de Guanahacabibes, 202n.71
Gómez Raposo, Luis, 141
Gónzales County (Texas), 286
Graff, Laurens de (Lorencillo), 78
Grammont, Michel de, 78, 88, 196n.61
Grand Goâve (Haiti), 87, 90
Grand Gosier Islands, 193n

Gravier, Father Jacques, 220
Great Lakes, 25; map showing, 143
Grenier, Chevalier: on Karankawan speech, 255n.43
Grijalva, Juan de, 140, 190n.50
Grollet, Jacques: as deserter, 137n.21; and Fort Saint-Louis massacre, 214, 272; and Indians, 214, 240, 261; on La Salle's murder, 215; as New Mexico settler, 223, 247; as Spanish captive, 142, 215, 217, 240, 247n.31
Guadalupe River, 281, 284; described, 279; Indians on, 260, 261; and Magdelaine River, 100n.35
Gulf of California, 3
Gulf of Gonâve, 87
Gulf of Mexico, 3, 153n; circumnavigation of, 1, 134, 139, 140, 147, 149; corrections on, 200; current in, 114n.58, 202, 203; on early maps, 7, 8; exploration in, 6, 12; foreigners in, 139; Iberville and, 210, 219; and Jolliet-Marquette expedition, 31n.4; La Salle and, 1, 4, 56, 64n.84, 65; on La Salle's map, 83; maritime war in, 130; and Mississippi, 93n.18; new expedition to, 126n; and pirates, 78, 89; Spain, 129, 146; and Talons, 218, 226; threat to, 132. *See also* Seno Mexicano
Gulf Stream, 115n.59, 200n. *See also* ocean currents
Guzmán, Joseph, 203

Havana (Cuba), 152, 195, 198, 199, 200; Enríquez voyages from, 130, 131; capture of Talons at, 218
Hennepin, Father Louis, 34
Hernández de Córdoba, Francisco, 190n.50
Hidalgo, Fray Francisco, 221–22
Hiems. *See* James
Higginbotham, Jay, 18
Hispaniola: 4–5, 86, 87n.7, 88n.9. *See also* Saint Domingue; Santo Domingo
Hita Salazar, Pablo de, 6n
Hutchins, Thomas: map by, 42n.28

Ibarra, Antonio de, 133
Iberville, Pierre Le Moyne, Sieur d': first voyage of, 126; and Indian language study, 300n; and Talons, 209, 210, 219–21, 289n.1
Iberville River, 59n
Ile de Gonâve, 86
Ile de Tortue (Tortuga), 78, 86, 87
Indian languages: Atákapa, 290; Bayogoula, 300n; Caddo, 260, 288, 289,

300; Chickasaw, 45n.36; Coahuiltecan, 288; Hasinai, 234, 241, 259; Houma, 300n; Karankawa, 258, 289, 290–91, 294–95, 298–99; Pawnee, 289; Tonkawa, 260–61, 288; Wichita, 289
Indians, 273–74; abortion among, 262, 274; and aged, 263, 271; alliances of, 59n.71, 251; arms of, 110, 253, arrows of, 57, 230, 265, 273; bathing customs of, 230, 238, 254, 262, 267; beds of, 264; beverages of, 231, 270, 271; burial customs of, 253, 262, 268; and calumet, 26, 46–47, 49, 51, 57, 63; ceremonies of, 46, 61, 251, 270; and childbirth, 254, 267; crops of, 41, 46, 52, 60, 229, 232, 233, 260, 264; dances of, 57, 231, 239, 272; and deity, 269–70; and dogs, 58, 266, 274; and fire worship, 60, 61; fishing techniques of, 51, 53, 255, 265, 274; games of, 262; and infanticide, 254, 262; marriage customs of, 268; mourning customs of, 253, 254, 268–69, 273, 274; musical instruments of, 231; and prostitution, 253, 268; and scalping, 57, 58, 239, 249, 273; and slavery, 38, 249; and sun worship, 61, 251, 270; and tobacco, 109, 230, 232, 241, 258, 264; war cry of (*saçacoie*), 35, 46, 51, 58, 60. *See also* Indian tribes; medicine men
Indian tribes: Abnaki, 42n.29; Acolapissa, 61n.76; Algonkin, 58n.69; Amalcham, 257, 260; Apache, 119; Apalachino, 131, 133, 137, 162n, 179; Bayogoula, 11, 50n.46, 300n; Cadohadacho, 220, 261, 265; Cahokia, 33n.8; Chakchiuma, 53n.53; Chickasaw (Chicacha), 20, 25, 45nn.35,36, 47; Chinook, 10; Chippewa (Sauteur), 33; Chiquilousa, 57; Chisca, 182; Chitimacha, 178n.36; Choctaw, 45n.36, 110n.52; Cíbolo, 11; Coahuiltecan (Caouiles), 109n, 114n.57, 161n, 167n, 257, 260, 261, 262; Flathead, 52, 119; Houma (Ouma), 53, 57, 59; Huron, 33; Illinois, 33, 34, 62; Kanahotino (Canotino), 230, 257, 260; Kaskaskia, 33n.8; Kickapoo, 38n.17; Mahican, 42n.27; Malaguita, 136, 167n; Mascoutin, 63, 64, 82; Maya, 190n.50, 286; Miami, 33, 34, 40n.23, 63; Michigamea, 33n.8; Missouri (Chiwere Sioux), 40n.21; Moingwena, 33n.8; Mosopelea, 47, 62; Nabedache, 261; Nacogdoches, 261, 263, 264; Nadacos, 261; Nasoni, 261; Natchez (Natché), 51n.49, 52, 58n.69, 60, 60n.73, 264n.13; Neches, 261; Nipissing (Nipisingue), 41; Olive, 157; Ottawa

(Ataouais), 32, 33, 41; Pawnee (Pana, Panismaha), 40, 64, 119; Panzacola, 131; Pelon, 136, 161; Peoria (Pimiteouy), 33, 35; Potowatomi (Poutouatami), 33, 39, 40; Quapaw (Accansea, Accansa: Arkansas), 47, 49, 62, 68; Quinipissa (Kenipisa, Tenipisa: Mugulasha), 25, 57, 53n.55, 58, 59, 71; Salish, 110n.52; Shawnee (Chaouanon), 81; Tamaholipa, 160, 162; Tamaroa, 33n.8, 43; Tangipahoa, 54n.56, 57n.65; Temerlouans (Paouites), 213, 236, 257, 260; Toho (Tohaha, Tohaka), 213, 235, 236, 257, 260; Tonkawa, 260, 263, 270; Tunica, 49, 178; Waxhaw, 110n.52; Wichita (Panis), 119n.66; Yuchi, 182n
—Atákapa: 136–37, 162n; backwardness of, 137; castaways among, 178–81; and Rivas-Iriarte expedition, 178–86; tattoos of, 137, 180; vocabulary of, 290n.5
—Coroa: allies of, 59; ambush of, 60; confused with Natchez, 51; culture of, 52; and La Salle, 59; move of, 51n.49
—Hainai (Ayenny): and Cenis, 230, 238, 261; and Clamcoëhs, 249; location of, 230, 257; and Talons, 260
—Hasinai (Cenis, Tejas): agriculture of, 229, 232, 257, 261, 264; celebrations of, 262, 271; and childbirth, 267; confederacy of, 263; culture of, 263, 264, described, 229; and French deserters, 186n.43; and La Salle, 211; linguistic data on, 2; location of, 229, 233, 257, 261; and marriage, 268; and Saint-Denis, 220–21; and Talons, 234, 259, 260, 272, 274; tattoos of, 137, 267, 268; war trophies of, 272; weapons of, 265
—Iroquois: and Accansae, 68; and Chaouanons, 64; dog feast of, 58n.69; at Fort Frontenac, 34; and Illinois, 35, 38; and La Salle, 31, 41; Minet on, 119; and Tamaroa, 62
—Karankawa (Clamcoëh): and Atákapas, 138; and Ayenny (Hainai), 271; and Cenis, 234, 271; cruelty of, 229, 257; customs of, 229; described, 229, 257; dwellings of, 229; fears of, 234; and French children, 229, 237–38; kill French infant, 216; language of, 288–301; and La Salle, 109n, 110–111n.52; location of, 136–37, 176, 229, 257, 260; and massacre at Fort Saint-Louis, 215, 231, 237, 259; prey on colonists, 234; and Rivas-Iriarte expedition, 169, 169n.20, 174, 174n; Talons as source on, 2, 260; vocabulary of, 258, 292

—Jumano (Chouman): and Cenis, 257; hunting ground of, 261; influence of, 272; location of, 261; and Spaniards, 214, 257–58; and Talons, 260
—Loup (Mahican), 42, 45, 62, 63
—Taensa: allied with Accancea, 50; ceremony of, 61; culture of, 52; location of, 60; and La Salle's settlement plan, 85; and Mosopelea, 47n.42; related to Natchez, 50n.46; relocations of, 50n.46; temple of, 61
—Tonkawa: fishing techniques of, 274; and La Salle's survivors, 260, 261; language of, 288; location of, 260; and medicine men, 263; Spaniards informed by, 260; use of intoxicants by, 270
Iriarte, Pedro de: 131, 198, 205; commands *piragua*, 133, 149; debriefed, 140; Diego de Castro embarks with, 136, 152; examines Gómez diary, 141; finds French ship, 141, 171–72; illness of, 154, 200; and Indians, 162, 167, 169, 174, 182, 183; seeks lost ship, 185; sounds coast, 164, 165. *See also* Rivas-Iriarte voyage
Isla Blanca, 154
Isla de la Juventud. *See* Isle of Pines
Isla de Lobos, 153–56
Isle of Pines, 90, 90n.13, 91
Isles Dernieres, 95n.23
Italian, the: imprisonment and death of, 247; mystery of, 216–17; rescued, 242; trick of, 252, 253

Jamaica, 4
James (Hiems: Englishman with La Salle), 212, 234
James II (of England), 122
Jamestown (Virginia), 79, 120–21
Jarry, Jean, 114n.57
Jefferys, Thomas, 142, 166n, 169n.21, 175n, 179n.38
Jesuits: 31, 39, 42; and La Salle, 3, 123–24; missions of, 33; and Tonti, 40
Jol, Cornelius Corneliszoon (Peg Leg), 153
Jolliet, Louis, 31
Jolliet-Marquette expedition, 3, 31n.4
Joly, the (ship): accident of, 84–85; captain of, 84; and d'Esmanville, 73; and La Salle, 78, 89; and Minet, 1, 23; officers of, 106, 109; record of, 72, 73; reprovisioned, 88; returns to France, 5, 79, 226; on Texas coast, 79, 80; voyage of, 84–99, 114–22
Jordán de la Reina, Juan, 132n.7, 193n
Joutel, Henri: 265, 273, 276, 287; on *Aimable's* voyage, 94n.21; on buffalo hunt,

283; credibility of, 213; on deserters, 137n.21; on Galveston Bay, 106n.47; on Gulf landfall, 94n.21, 95n.23; on Indians, 263–64, 268, 269, 272; on La Salle's murder, 212–13; latitude and longitude estimates of, 92–93nn.16-17; on Minet, 100n.36, 113n.54; as officer, 78; relation of, 2, 11, 71, 72, 73, 78, 80, 89n.11, 214, 219; on River of Canes, 279

Kaap, Ida Kappell, 275
Keller Bay, 173n.26
Kinney County (Texas), 114n.57

La Chine rapids, 3
Lacosta Island, 198
La Esperanza. *See* L'Espérance
La Forest, Major, 32, 33
Lafourche Bayou, 26, 65n.87
La Galette (Canada), 32
Laguna, Marqués de. *See* Paredes, Conde de
Laguna de Mobila. *See* Mobile Bay
Laguna de Pez, 142; map showing, 143
Laguna de Pueblo Viejo, 160
Laguna de Tamiahua, 154, 160
Laguna de Términos, 130, 139, 203–204n.74
Laguna de Ysmuth, 162, 163
Laguna Madre, 163n
La Harpe, Jean-Baptiste Bénard de, 290n
Lake Erie, 32, 33
Lake Huron, 41n.26
Lake Ontario, 26, 29
Lake Pimiteouy, 35
Lake Taronteau (Lake Simcoe), 41
La Motte, ——, 31
Langtry (Texas), 11
L'Archevêque, Jean: and Fort Saint-Louis massacre, 214, 272; and Indians, 214, 215, 240, 261; interrogation of, 142; and La Salle's murder, 212, 215; as New Mexico settler, 223, 247; and Spaniards, 146, 214, 217, 240, 247
La Mothe, Antoine, Sieur de Cadillac, 222
La Ribourde, Father Gabriel de, 35, 38
La Rochelle (France): La Salle at, 65; Minet imprisoned at, 122; as port, 1, 4, 84, 31, 225–26, 259
La Salle, Nicolas de: account of, 11, 17, 19, 23, 29; career of, 18n.4; identity of, 77; and La Salle, 18, 21, 31, 55, 63; and Minet, 12, 17, 22, 25, 72
La Salle, René-Robert Cavelier, Sieur de: 47, 50, 78, 136, 140, 142, 201; and Abbé

Cavelier, 33n.9, 41; and Aigron, 108, 109, 110, 111, 122; and Beaujeu, 4, 71, 73, 84–113 *passim;* and Bégon, 88, 89; betrayal of, 129; borrowing by, 84; character of, 10; contradictions of, 17; death of, 1, 5, 11, 212-14, 234, 235; deserters from, 129, 137; and d'Esmanville, 73–74; destination of, 93; early exploration of, 1, 29–42 *passim;* examines Texas coast, 100, 102, 104; failure of, 8; and French policy, 7; geographical concepts of, 7–8, 93, 94, 99, 100, 103, 104, 113–14n.56; illnesses of, 62, 73, 86, 87, 90, 124; and Indians, 47, 62, 63, 64, 109, 110, 112, 224, 273; irrational behavior of, 80, 103; and Jesuits, 34, 42; journeys of, to Cenis, 233–34; latitudes of, 43, 56, 93; and L'Espérance, 64, 129n.1; letters of, 7, 80; and loss of *Aimable*, 106–11; and Minet, 1, 23, 72, 77, 78, 84, 85, 102, 103, 106, 122–26; patent of, 31; and Peñalosa, 4; and pirates, 78–79, 88, 89, 139; plans trading posts, 23; and Río Escondido, 7–8, 93nn.18,19; and Seignelay, 83, 86; and separation of ships, 93, 95, 98, 99; sketch of, 3; Spanish reaction to, 129, 132, 139, 147; and Talons, 234, 274, 299; territorial claim of, 55, 56; voyage of, to Gulf, 1, 4–5, 71–81 *passim*
Las Minas de Carvajal, 161, 16ın
Lavaca Bay, 173n.26
Lavazares (Las Bazares), Guido, 8, 171
Lee, Nelson, 284
Léogâne (Haiti), 87
León, Alonso de: on alligators, 184; on buffalo, 283; expeditions of, 215, 239–42; and Fort Saint-Louis massacre, 110n.51; and French captives, 215; and French ruins, 142; on Karankawas, 136; misnames Matagorda Bay, 142; route of, mapped, 142
León, Alonso de (the elder), 265, 266
Le Page, ——, 31
Lerma (Campeche), 203
Le Sage (pirate captain), 89
L'Espérance (La Esperanza), 64, 129
Library of Congress, 76
Liotot (surgeon), 212
Little Brazos River, 280
Little Cayman, 90
Llanos, Francisco de, 142–45
López de Gamarra, Francisco, 138, 140, 141, 146
López-Pez voyage, 141
Louisiana, 26, 83, 220, 257
Louisiana Purchase, 8

Louis XIV (of France), 56; gift of, 172n.23; and Ile de Tortue, 87n.7; influence of, 116–17n.62, 121n.68; James II and, 122n; policy of, 4
Louisville (Kentucky), 31n.3
lunar eclipse, 92

Magdelaine River (Madelaine, Madelena, Magdalena), 99, 100nn.35,36; 223
maps: of Alvarez de Pineda, 93n.19, 129n.2; of Cabo de Lodo, 143, 145; Cap Enragé on, 39n.20; by Cárdenas y Magaña, 142–45; of Chandeleur Sound, 143; by Delisle (Claude and Guillaume), 22n.17, 32n.7, 135, 142, 166n, 175n, 179n.38, 189, 291n; by Enríquez Barroto, 132, 140–41, 142, 173, 205; of Espíritu Santo Bay (or river), 56n.63, 93n.19, 129; by Fer, 142, 166n, 179n.38; by Franquelin, 75; of Gulf of Mexico, 7, 8, 141, 201; by Hutchins, 42n.28; by Jefferys, 142, 166n, 175n, 179n.38; Jesuit, of 1671, 33n.10; La Salle's, 83; of La Salle's voyage, 73n.8; of León's route, 142; Magdalaine River on, 100n.35; by Marquette, 47n.42; of Matagorda Bay, 76, 142, 145; by Minet, 36, 47n.42, 66, 75–76, 79, 87, 101, 105, 107, 122n, 140, 173n.27; of Mississippi Delta, 26; of Mississippi River, 66, 129, 143; Parkman No. 4, 41n.26; of Petit Goâve, 75-76, 87; Randin's, 32n.6; Río Escondido on, 56n.63, 93n.19, 100n.35; and Río de Flores, 145, 169n.21; Río del Mexicano on, 179; Río de San Joseph on, 166n; by Santa Cruz, 99–100n.35; by Sigüenza y Góngora, 142
Margot River. *See* Chicacha River
Margry, Pierre, 18, 19, 73, 74, 75, 76, 77
Marien (Cuba), 200, 201
Marle, Sieur de, 236n.13
Mar Pequeño, 96
Marquette, Father Jacques, 31. *See also* Jolliet-Marquette expedition
Márquez Cabrera, Juan (Florida governor), 196, 199
Martínez, Francisco, 241
Maryland, 120–21
Massanet, Fray Damián, 215
Matagorda Bay, 133; anonymous map of, *144;* and Béranger, 290n.5; and French ships, 104, 169n.20; and Karankawas, 136–37; and La Salle, 7, 8, 11, 79, 289; mapped, 142–45; Minet's drawings of, 76, 98n.30, 101, 107; and River of Canes, 276

Matagorda Island, 110, 171n
Matagorda Peninsula, 97, 171n
Matas de Salvador, 96
Mateos, Antonio, 196
Maupate, province of, 161
Maurepas, Comte de, 300n. *See also*
    Pontchartrain, Jérôme Phélypeaux,
    Comte de; Pontchartrain, Louis Phé-
    lypeaux, Comte de
Maxwell, Ross A., 287
Médanos de Magdalena, 100n.35
Médanos de Pacara, 195
medicine men, 254, 262, 263, 268
Membré, Zénobe (Father): account of, 11,
    29; and Cenis mission, 211; as chaplain,
    21; contradictions of, 17; with Illinois,
    35; letters of, 17, 22; on Mississippi jour-
    ney, 29, 54n.57, 55
Menguad, Zacharie, 102n.38
Mercado, Fray Juan, 131
Mermentau River, 188n.46
Mesquite Bay, 98n.32, 169n.21
Meunier, Pierre: deposition of, 216; as in-
    terpreter, 216, 241; and Pierre Talon,
    232, 237, 240, 249, 283; rescued, 215; as
    settler, 223
Mexico: 158, 160, 196; castaway from, 179,
    180; and French captives, 232; La Salle's
    designs on, 3, 4, 6n, 7; missions of, 167n
Mexico City: debriefing at, 140; riot in,
    217; roads to, 256; Talons on, 217, 244,
    257
Michelimaquina: La Salle at, 39, 40, 64;
    location of, 38; Tonti at, 38
Miller County (Arkansas), 145
mines and minerals: Indians' disinterest
    in, 231; location of, 83, 244, 245; river
    access to, 83; Talons on, 218, 232, 256;
    wealth from, 245
Minet, ——, 4; and Barbier, 21; and Beau-
    jeu, 72, 80; on buccaneering, 88, 89;
    cites La Salle's letters, 7; on English
    colonies, 119–21; on Gulf navigation,
    89; imprisonment of, 23, 122, 126; on In-
    dians, 109, 110, 110–11n.52, 112–13, 119;
    on Jamestown, 120–21; journal of, 1, 11,
    12, 13, 71–81, 83–126; and Joutel, 72–73,
    95n.24; and La Salle, 10, 23, 72, 77, 78,
    83–126 *passim;* latitudes of, 98n.31; on
    L'Espérance, 129; on loss of ships, 87,
    109; on lunar eclipse, 92; maps of,
    75–76, 76n.23, 79, 87, 107, 122n, 140,
    173n.27, on Membré, 17; and Nicolas de
    La Salle, 19, 25; on pirate encounter, 116;
    questions of, 122–26; relation of, 17–27,

29–68 *passim;* returns to France, 5, 122;
    on Saint-Dominique, 87; on separation
    of ships, 95–99; sources of, 20–27; on
    Texas landfall, 99–100; voyage of, 1,
    83–122
Mississippi Delta: Alvarez de Pineda and,
    135; changes in, 138; Corso at, 131; delin-
    eation of, 134; early sketch of, 143; ex-
    ploration of, 6, 138, 145; map of, 26
Mississippi River, 93nn.18,19, 196; and As-
    censión Bay, 189n.49; branches of, 55;
    changes in, 192; discharge of, 138; dis-
    covery of, 3; distributary network of,
    190n.52; Enríquez-Romero at, 132; ex-
    plored, 1; flooding on, 43–44, 52–54;
    and La Salle, 7, 129; La Salle's concept
    of, 93, 93nn.18,19; on maps, 66, 129, 143;
    misidentifications of, 7–8, 129; name of,
    5, 29, 43, 44; passes of, described, 134;
    as search target, 134; Spain's neglect of,
    145; strategic importance of, 7; supp-
    posed features of, 96n; Talons on,
    248–50, 278–79. *See also* Río de la
    Palizada
Mississippi Sound, 131
Mississippi Valley, 7
Missouri River, 40, 43, 63
Mobile Bay, 13, 131, 139, 141
Mobile River, 50n.46
Monclova, Conde de: becomes viceroy,
    132; captains report to, 152; diary deliv-
    ered to, 204–205; Enríquez and
    Romero advise, 132; orders of, 149, 201;
    provisions voyage, 51
Monclova (Coahuila), 243n.25
Monte Cristi (Haiti), 86
Montreal (Quebec), 3, 32
Moore, Francis, Jr., 279
Moranger, Crevel de, 84n, 112, 212
Morel, ——, 84
Morfi, Fray Juan Agustín, 264

Narváez, Pánfilo de, 13, 136, 273
Navarro, Admiral Francisco, 150, 202
Navasota River, 280
navigation: compass correction for, 155;
    currents' effects on, 94, 114n.58, 115n.59,
    200, 202, 203; Enríquez's accuracy in,
    135; instruments of, 92, 135; longitude
    computations for, 92–93n.17; and lunar
    eclipse, 92; sounding lead in, 134; tech-
    niques of, 92
Navío Quebrado, 172, 174
New France, 139
New Mexico, 83, 223

New Spain, 4, 132, 149
Niagara, 32–33
Nica (La Salle's Indian hunter), 212, 213, 234
Nueces River, 7–8, 56n.63, 228, 278, 279
Nuestra Señora de la Esperanza (piragua): armament of, 133; Diego de Castro boards, 136; makes port, 140; officers of, 133, 149; voyage of, 149–205
Nuestra Señora de la Soledad (ship), 130
Nuestra Señora del Rosario (piragua): armament of, 133; interpreter for, 160; makes port, 140; officers of, 133, 149; runs aground, 139; voyage of, 149–205
Nueva Vizcaya, 65n.86, 83

ocean currents: in Bahama Channel, 115n.59; at Cabo Rojo, 156; on Cuban coast, 200; Enríquez observes, 134; in Gulf of Mexico, 114n.58, 203; on Louisiana coast, 94; pirates warn of, 94n.22; in Straits of Florida, 200n; in Yucatán Channel, 114n.58, 134, 202
Ocean Springs (Mississippi), 300
Oertel, Everett, 287
Ohio River: discovered by La Salle, 3, 30–31; La Salle at mouth of, 44; and Minet map, 47n.42
Oklahoma, 288
Oliver, Alice: on Karankawa language, 297–99
Olmos, Fray Andrés de, 157n.10
Ortiz Parrilia, Diego, 136
Ouabache (Houabache) River. *See* Ohio River
Our Lady of the Lake University, 2

Pachuca (Hidalgo), mines of, 256
Padre Island, 136
Padre Island National Seashore, 164n
Palacios, Admiral Gaspar de, 129, 132
Pánuco (Veracruz), 159
Paredes, Conde de (viceroy), 132
Paris, 65
Parkman, Francis, 10, 209–10
Parral (Chihuahua), 245
Patoulet, Captain, 218
Payta, Antonio (interpreter), 160, 174
Pedro the Apalachino: 137, 140, 179, 182, 183
Penigault, André, 222
Peñalosa, Diego de, 4
Pensacola Bay: occupation of, 6, 145, 147; and Pez memorial, 146, 215; rediscovery of, 131, 146

Petit Goâve (Haiti): 72, 73, 78, 79; defections at, 90, 129; La Salle at, 23, 86, 90, 124; mapped by Minet, 75–76, 87; Valigny left at, 90
Petit Trou de Nippes (Haiti), 87, 90
Pez, Andrés de: career of, 146; conducts French prisoners, 215; and Enríquez, 141; exploration by, 138, 140, 141, 142; on León's diary, 142; and Pensacola project, 145; and Pez memorial, 146, 215
pirates and privateers (buccaneers, *flibustiers*): advise La Salle, 78, 89; attack Campeche, 78–79, 90n.12; Beaujeu encounters, 79, 116; defections to, 90; disclose La Salle's mission, 6, 79, 90n.12, 129; as diversion, 78–79; Dutch, on Gulf of Mexico, 89, 153n; and Gulf currents, 94n.22; Juan Poule and, 133; in maritime war, 130; origin of, 86n; at Puerto Real, 203–204n.74; at St. Augustine, 196; and Santo Domingo, 78, 88; ship seized by, 5; ships of, 132; Spanish concern over, 139; Tampico raided by, 89n.10, 133, 179n.37
Planteau, Isabelle. *See* Talon, Isabelle Planteau
Point au Fer Island, 95
Point Muspa, 198
Pontchartrain, Jérôme Phélypeaux, Comte de, 126n, 221
Pontchartrain, Louis Phélypeaux, Comte de, 126n, 218, 219, 225
Port de Paix (Haiti), 87
Port Mansfield (Texas), 166n
Portugal, 209
Poule, Juan: captured as pirate, 133, 162n, 172; in Florida Keys, 199n.67; as hostage, 162; as interpreter, 141–42; knowledge of, 133; at Matagorda Bay, 172, 173, 174
Prot (Praux), Jeanne (wife of Robert Talon), 223
Provençal, the: takes Indian wives, 137, 224; remains with Cenis, 214, 249
Prudhomme, Pierre, 45
Public Archives of Canada, 1, 17, 74–75, 76, 77
Puebla, 246
Puerto Real (Campeche), 203, 203–204n.74
Punta de Culebras, 171, 172, 173, 174, 175
Punta de San Francisco, 145, 171

Quebec, 31–32, 64, 210, 225
Quiahuitzlan (archaeological site), 152n.4

Quinté (Canada), 32
Quiroga y Losada, Diego de, 142

Ramírez, Alonso, 160, 161
Ramón, Diego, 222
Randin, Hugues, map of, 32n.6
Rasquita, Juan de, 201
Récollets (Recollects), 34. *See also*
　Franciscans
Red River, 53, 223
Reid, Samuel C., 277
Renaudot, Abbé Eusèbe, 23, 65n.86
Richaud, Elie: pilot of *Belle,* 105, 105n.42
Río Bajo, 177, 178, 185. *See also* Galveston
　Bay
Río Bravo, 162, 164. *See also* Rio Grande
Río de Alvarado, 203
Río de Canas, 204
Río de Cazones, 150
Río de Flores, 169n.21, 173; on maps, 145;
　named, 168; ship remnants found at,
　168–69, 172
Río de Grijalva, 204n.74
Río de la Aguada, 138, 192
Río de la Ascensión, 189, 189n.49, 190
Río de la Mobila (Mobile River), 139, 194
Río de la Palizada, 190, 192; on Enríquez's
　map, 205; mouths of, 193; named, 132;
　North Pass identified as, 138; and Terán,
　145. *See also* Mississippi River
Río de las Palmas, 161, 161n. *See also* Río
　Soto la Marina
Río del Espíritu Santo. *See* Espíritu Santo
　(river and bay)
Río del Mexicano, 170, 183, 184, 187, 188.
　See also Calcasieu River
Río de Maupate, 161, 162, 173, 178. *See also*
　Río Soto la Marina
Río de Mora, 190
Río de Puercos, 202
Río de San Bernardo, 171, 189. *See also*
　Bahía de San Bernardo; Matagorda Bay
Río de San Joseph, 166, 166n, 168, 174
Río de Santa Suzana, 176, 176n.30
Río de Tecolutla, 150
Río de Tocail, 188
Río de Tuxpán (Tuzpa), 154
Río de Zívoras (Cíbolas), 135, 175, 176n.30
Río Dulce, 177, 181, 183, 185, 186n.42, 187.
　See also Sabine River
Río Escondido, 93n.18,19, 94n.22; on early
　maps, 100n.35; Mississippi confused
　with, 7, 8, 56n.63, 63; near Magdelaine
　River, 100n.35
Rio Grande: described, 278–79; Indians

on, 261; La Salle at, 11; mouth of, 136;
　and Talons, 276. *See also* Río Bravo
Río Lagartos (Yucatán), 203
Río Pánuco, 13
Río Soto la marina, 135, 157n.10, 161,
　178n.35. *See also* Río de Maupate
Rivas, Martín de, 131, 165; captain of *pira-
　gua,* 149; commands voyage, 133; finds
　French wreckage, 141; illness of, 140, 155,
　199, 200–201; and Indians, 167, 168, 174,
　184; and Pez, 140–41. *See also* Rivas-
　Iriarte voyage
Rivas-Iriarte voyage, 138, 140, 141; and As-
　censión Bay, 189n.49; and buffalo hunt,
　283; conclusions of, 142; diary of,
　149–205; and French ships, 215; ships
　of, 145. *See also* Iriarte, Pedro de; Rivas,
　Martín de
River of Canes (Rivière aux Cannes), 227,
　248–49, 265, 276, 279
Rivet, Paul, 290
Rivière Colbert. *See* Colbert River
Rivière des Risques, 59
Robertson County (Texas), 286
Rochefort (France), 4, 65n, 122
Roemer, Ferdinand von, 275
Rojas, Josepha de, 180
Roma (Texas), 278
romero, Antonio: debriefed, 140; and En-
　ríquez Barroto, 129, 131, 132, 135, 139; on
　Gomez diary, 141; on voyage of *pi-
　raguas,* 133, 149, 176, 205
Ronquillo, Pedro de, 122n, 140
Rouen (France), 3, 65n.85
Rutre (Ruter): deserts La Salle, 137n.21,
　212; and Indians, 137n.21, 249; marriages
　of, 212, 253, 268; and murders, 213, 235

Sabine Pass, 134, 138
Sabine River, 177, 178
Sablonnière, Marquis de, 84
Saget (La Salle's servant), 212, 213, 234
St. Augustine (Florida), 130, 131, 196
Saint-Denis, Louis Juchereau de, 220,
　221–22, 223
Saint-Domingue (Haiti), 84, 85; de-
　scribed, 87–88; La Salle at, 4, 86–89;
　Minet surveys, 75; pirates of, 88, 94n.22,
　157n.9
Saint-François (ketch), 84, 87, 226n
Saint-Honoré (ship), 31, 65
Saint-Ignace (Jesuit mission), 33n
St. Ignace (Michigan), 33n
Saint-Laurent (island governor), 78, 87, 88
St. Lawrence River, 32

St. Louis, 43n.32
Saint-Michel, Lieutenant, 32
Saint-Nicolas Tower (prison), 122
Salinas Varona, Gregorio de, 145, 241
San Antonio Bay, 98n.32
San Antonio missions, 288
San Bernard River, 176n.30
Sand Island, 194n
Sandoval Silva y Mendoza, Gaspar de la
   Cerda. See Galve, Conde de
San Jose Island, 166n
San Joseph (ship), 145
San Juan de Ulúa, 133, 140, 153, 181n, 204
San Luis de Apalache, 179
San Luis de Tampico Mission, 157
San Luis Potosí, 217, 244, 245, 257
San Marcos de Apalache (St. Mark's, Flor-
   ida), 129, 131, 133, 138, 140
Santa Barbara (Nueva Vizcaya), mines of,
   83
Santa Cruz, Alonso de, 99n.35
Santa Cruz de Sabacola Mission, 131
Santa María, Vicente de, 263
Santiago, Count of (Fernando Altamirano
   de Velasco Legazpi y Castilla), 245
Santo Cristo (flagship of Armada de Barlo-
   vento), 218
Santo Cristo de San Román (ship), 141, 145,
   146
Santo Domingo (Hispaniola), 78, 88
Santo Tomás (ship), 146
Seignelay, Jean-Baptiste, Marquis de: and
   Beaujeu, 73; and d'Esmanville, 74; and
   La Salle, 65, 83, 86; and Minet, 23, 78,
   85, 103, 123; and pirates, 88
Seignelay River, 59, 83, 84. See also Red
   River
Seno Mexicano, 141, 149, 200, 201, 204.
   See also Gulf of Mexico
Shea, John Gilmary, 10, 31n.4
Sierra del Fraile, 161
Sierra del Maupate, 161
Sierra de San Juan, 151, 152, 154
Sierras de Jaruco, 200
Sierras de San Martín, 204n.75
Sigüenza y Góngora, Carlos, 130, 142, 145,
   146
Simon, Pierre (husband of Marie-Mag-
   delaine Talon), 221
Solís, Fray José de, 280
Sonora, mines of, 245
Soto, Hernando de, 13, 51n.48, 129, 198n;
   exploration by, 19; and Mississippi
   River, 5; and native bees, 287; and
   Tunicas, 49n

Spain, 4–7, 122n, 140, 146, 147, 205
Starved Rock, 38n.16, 63n.80, 64n.81
Steyermark, Julian A., 287
Straits of Florida, 114n.58, 117n.63, 200n
Sulpicians, 32, 33
Swanton, John R., 291, 295, 299

Talon, Isabelle Planteau: and Barbier, 211;
   children of, 210, 211, 225–26, 273; death
   of, 216; and La Salle, 225
Talon, Jean Baptiste: and Cenis, 256; family of, 210, 225–26, 248; on Fort Saint-
   Louis massacre, 216, 237, 259; in French
   service, 219; and Iberville, 220–21; interrogation of, 219, 259; on Karankawas,
   174n, 242, 248–49, 252, 254, 259, 260,
   263–64, 273, 277; in Louisiana, 223; provides vocabulary, 291; reared as Indian,
   229, 237; repatriated, 218, 248; rescue of,
   216, 256; and Saint-Denis, 210, 220; in
   Spanish service, 218–47
Talon, Lucien (junior): and Armada de
   Barlovento, 218, 247; family of, 210, 225,
   248; and Karankawas, 237, 249, 259; repatriated, 218, 248; rescued, 215; as servant, 219, 223, 248
Talon, Lucien (senior), 211, 225, 237, 259
Talon, Marie-Elizabeth, 211, 237, 259
Talon, Marie-Magdelaine: adopted by Karankawas, 237, 259; in Indian refuge,
   249; marriage of, 221; rescued by Spaniards, 215, 241; son of, 221, 223; in Spain,
   218, 221, 248; witnesses massacre, 259,
   272
Talon, Pierre: in Armada de Barlovento,
   218, 247; and Cenis, 229, 234, 235–38,
   249, 254, 259, 260, 272, 273; as Cenis interpreter, 2, 241, 274; family of, 210,
   225–26, 248; in French service, 219, 220;
   and Iberville, 220–21; interrogated, 259;
   and the Italian, 252–53; journeys with
   La Salle, 211; on La Salle's murder,
   212–14, 216; in Mexico, 229; in Portugal, 221; records Caddo words, 299;
   repatriated, 218, 247–48; rescued by
   León, 215, 222, 236, 256; and Saint-
   Denis, 220, 221, 222, 274
Talon, Robert: adopted by Karankawas,
   237, 249, 259; born at sea, 211; rescued
   by León, 215, 222, 241; and Saint-Denis,
   221, 222, 274; settles at Mobile, 223;
   taken to Spain, 218, 248; witnesses Fort
   Saint-Louis massacre, 237, 259, 272
Talon brothers: adventures of, 2; ethnological data of, 259–74; interrogation

of, 102, 137n.21, 219, 225–58, 259; linguistic data of, 288–301; natural history
data of, 274–88
Tamaholipa, salines of, 160
Tamaulipas, 136, 161n, 163n
Tamiaha (Veracruz), 152, 153
Tampa Bay, 198
Tampico (Tamaulipas): 154, 155, 160, 161,
162; anchorage at, 156, 157; guides and
interpreters from, 134, 151, 160; Juan
Poule and, 162n, 172; landmarks of, 157;
latitude of, 158; and pirates, 89n.10, 133,
157n.9, 162n, 179; provisioning at, 133,
151; salines of, 160; voyages from 136,
140
Tampico Alto (Veracruz), 160n
Tanguiso (Veracruz), 153
Tarpon Springs (Florida), 93n.18, 197n.65
tattooing: by Atákapas, 137, 180; durability
of, 221, 224; of French children, 215, 238;
by Hasinai, 215, 267; method of, 238; of
newborns, 254, 267, 273; patterns of,
267; significance of, 273; by Texas
coastal Indians, 136
Terán de los Ríos, Domingo: and buffalo,
283; and Enríquez, 145; expedition of,
216, 239n, 241–44; and Mississippi, 145
Tessler (pilot), 236n.13
Texas: claims to, 6, 8; Indians of, 137;
León's route across, 142; missions of,
145, 167
Texcoco (Mexico), mines of, 256
Thomas, Denis: betrays La Salle, 90n.12,
196n.61; and L'Espérance, 64n.84
Timbalier, ——, 31
Timbalier Island, 95n.23
Toledo, Doña Elvira de (viceroy's wife),
217, 218
Tonalá (Tabasco), 204
Tonti, Henri de, 84, account of, 11, 17, 22,
35; and Illinois fort, 34, 63; and Iro-
quois, 35; letters of, 17, 22; memoir of,
17, 25; and Mississippi exploration, 45,
51, 55, 56, 68; and 1678 expedition, 31
Torrey, John, 278

Toulon (France), 19
treaties: Ratisbon, 4; Trequa, 116
Trinidad Bar, 160
Trinity River, 260
Tropic of Cancer, 85
Tuxpán (Veracruz), 133, 136, 151, 154, 158

Valigny, Lieutenant, 84, 90, 123
Vargas, Nicolás de, 179, 180
Vauban, Sébastien Le Prestre, Marquis de,
23, 78, 126, 126n
Veracruz, 158, 159, 160, 164, 165; *piraguas*
built at, 149; and pirates, 196n.61, 204;
sites of, 181n.40; Talons on, 246, 257;
and Villa Rica, 152n.4; voyages from,
130, 132, 138, 139, 140, 145, 149, 201, 205
Veracruz Antigua, 181n.40
Veracruz Nueva, 181
Victoria County (Texas), 11, 284
Villa Rica de la Vera Cruz, 152, 152n.4
Ville d'Emden (ship), 219
Villermont, Cabart de, 73, 77
Villiers du Terrage, Marc de, 20n.12; and
Cavelier journal, 71, 74; challenged, 299;
Karankawa word lists of, 290, 291n,
296n.10; and Minet journal, 72, 75, 76,
78
Virginia, 79, 117, 118–21, 286
Virginia Company, 286
Vital, ——, 64

Wilkinson, Ralph, 141, 142
William and Mary (of England), 122n
Windward Fleet. *See* Armado de
Barlovento
Windward Islands, 111
Wolf River. *See* Chicacha River
Wood, Peter H., 7

Yazoo River, 49–50nn.44,45; 51n.49
Ysmuth, province of, 160
Yucatán, 89, 190, 286
Yucatán Channel, 114n.58, 134

Zacatecas, mines of, 83

La Salle, the Mississippi, and the Gulf was composed into type on a Linotron 202 phototypesetter in ten point Galliard with two points of spacing between the lines. Galliard was also selected for display. The book was designed by Cameron Poulter, composed by G&S Typesetters, Inc., printed offset by Thomson-Shore, Inc., and bound by John H. Dekker & Sons. The paper on which this book is printed bears acid-free characteristics for an effective life of at least three hundred years.

TEXAS A&M UNIVERSITY PRESS
COLLEGE STATION